MAD GIRL'S LOVE SONG

Also by Andrew Wilson

Shadow of the Titanic:
The Extraordinary Stories of Those Who Survived

Harold Robbins:
The Man Who Invented Sex

Beautiful Shadow:
A Life of Patricia Highsmith

The Lying Tongue

MAD GIRL'S LOVE SONG

Sylvia Plath and Life Before Ted

Andrew Wilson

SIMON &
SCHUSTER

London · New York · Sydney · Toronto · New Delhi

A CBS COMPANY

First published in Great Britain by Simon & Schuster UK Ltd, 2013
This paperback edition published by Simon & Schuster UK Ltd, 2014
A CBS COMPANY

1 3 5 7 9 10 8 6 4 2

Simon & Schuster UK Ltd
1st Floor
222 Gray's Inn Road
London WC1X 8HB

www.simonandschuster.co.uk

Simon & Schuster Australia,
Sydney

Simon & Schuster India,
New Delhi

A CIP catalogue record for this book is available from the British Library

ISBN: 978-0-85720-589-6
eBook ISBN: 978-0-85720-590-2

Typeset in the UK by Hewer Text
Printed in the UK by CPI Group (UK) Ltd, Croydon, CR0 4YY

CONTENTS

INTRODUCTION

On 25 February 1956, twenty-three-year-old Sylvia Plath stepped into a roomful of people and immediately spotted what she later described in her diary as a 'big, dark, hunky boy'. She asked her companions if anyone knew the name of this young man, but she received no answer. The party was in full swing and the freeform rhythms of the jazz – the 'syncopated strut' of the piano, the seductive siren call of the trumpet – made conversation difficult.[1] Sylvia, in Cambridge studying on a Fulbright fellowship, had been drinking all night: a lethal line of 'red-gold' Whisky Macs at a pub in town with her date for that night, Hamish Stewart. The potent combination of Scotch and ginger wine had left her feeling like she could almost walk through the air.[2] In fact the alcohol had had the opposite effect; as she had been walking to the party she had found herself so inebriated that she had kept banging into trees.

On arrival at the Women's Union – the venue in Falcon Yard chosen to celebrate the first issue of the slim literary journal the *St Botolph's Review* – Sylvia saw that the room was packed with young men in turtleneck sweaters and women in elegant black dresses. Counterpointing the jazz, the sound of poetry was in the air: great chunks of it being quoted back and forth like rallies in a game of literary dominance and seduction.

Sylvia was in a bullish mood that night. One of the contributors to *St Botolph's Review*, Daniel Huws, had sneered at two of her poems that had appeared in another Cambridge literary magazine, *Chequer*, dismissing her work as too polished and well made. 'Quaint and electric artfulness,' he had written in *Broadsheet*. 'My better half tells me "Fraud, fraud," but I will not say so; who am I to know how beautiful she may be.'[3] Plath felt justifiably angry; after all, she had been writing for publication since the age of eight and she had already earned sizeable sums for poems and short stories from *Harper's Magazine*, the *Atlantic Monthly*, *Mademoiselle* and *Seventeen*. She walked up to Huws, a pale, freckle-faced undergraduate at Peterhouse, and said in a tone of 'friendly aggression',[4] 'Is this the better or worse half?'[5] Huws, who later regarded the words as a 'fair retaliation' for his 'facetious and wounding' remarks, did not know quite how to respond.[6] From her point of view, Huws looked too boyish and immature to have an adult opinion. Plath was equally as dismissive of the rest of the *Saint Botolph's* set, describing Lucas Myers, who was studying at Downing College, as inebriated and wearing a 'satanic smile', and Than Minton, reading natural sciences at Trinity as so small-framed you would have to sit down if you wanted to talk to him (in Plath's world a short man was about as useful and attractive as a homosexual).[7]

By this point Sylvia had knocked back another drink, emptying its contents into her mouth, down her hands and on to the floor. She then tried to dance the twist with Myers and, while her movements may well have been less than smooth, her memory was razor-sharp. As she danced, she proceeded to recite the whole of Myers' poem 'Fools Encountered', a piece she had read for the first time earlier that day in *Saint Botolph's Review*.[8] When the music came to a temporary halt, she saw out of the corner of her eye somebody approaching. It was the same 'hunky boy', the one she had seen earlier 'hunching' around over women.[9] He introduced himself as Ted Hughes. She recalled the three poems he had published in *Saint Botolph's Review* and, in an effort to dazzle him with her vivacity, she immediately began reciting segments of them to him. In retrospect, it's ironic that one of the poems she declaimed, 'Law in the Country of the Cats', addresses the theme of the violent, irrational sense of enmity and rivalry that can often exist between individuals, even strangers.[10] On first meeting, the attraction between Hughes – who had graduated from Cambridge in 1954 and had a job in London as a reader for the film company J. Arthur Rank – and Plath was instant. But Sylvia sensed something else too. 'There is a panther stalks me down:/One day I'll have my death of him,' she wrote in 'Pursuit', a poem that she composed two days later.[11]

Plath recorded this encounter – now one of the most famous in all literary history – in her journal the next day. Suffering from a terrible hangover – she joked she thought she might be suffering from the DTs – she described the sexual tension that had flared up between them. After she had quoted some lines of his poem 'The Casualty', Hughes had shouted back over the music at her, in a voice that made her think he might be Polish, 'You like?' Did she want brandy, he had asked. 'Yes,' she yelled back, at which point he led her into another room. Hughes slammed the door and started pouring her glassfuls of brandy, which Plath tried to drink, but she didn't manage to find her mouth.[12] Almost immediately, they started discussing Huws' critique of her poetry. Hughes joked that his friend knew Plath was beautiful, that she could take such criticism, and that he would never have attacked her had she been a 'cripple'. He told her he had 'obligations' in the next room – in effect, another Cambridge student named Shirley – and that he was working in London and earning ten pounds a week. Then, suddenly, Hughes leant towards her and kissed her 'bang smash on the mouth'. As he did so he ripped the red hairband from her head and ravished her with such force that her silver earrings came unclipped from her ears. He moved down to kiss her neck, and Plath bit him 'long and hard' on the cheek. As Plath bit deep into his skin, she thought about the battle to the death that Hughes had described in his poem 'Law in the Country of the Cats' and the perpetrator's admission of the crime: 'I did it, I.'[13] When the couple emerged from the room, blood was pouring down Hughes' face.[14] He carried the 'swelling ring-moat of tooth marks' for the next month or so, and admitted that both the encounter and the woman remained branded on his self 'for good'.[15]

Hughes left his mark on Plath and her reputation too. After her suicide, in February 1963, as her estranged but not divorced husband, he became Plath's literary executor, the guardian of her writings, and, in effect, responsible for how she was perceived. A great deal has been written about the way in which Plath's posthumous journals were edited; and, since they were first published in abridged form in 1982, questions have been raised about Hughes' influence and motivation. At what point did editorialising (the understandable deletion of information because of repetition or legal problems) mutate into the altogether more sinister act of censorship? What part did he take in excising certain sensitive parts of the diaries? Why did he destroy one of the later journals? (He said, in his defence, that he did so because he didn't want his children from his marriage with Plath, Frieda and Nicholas, to read them: 'in those days', he claimed, he 'regarded forgetfulness as an essential part of survival'.[16])

Sylvia viewed Ted as something of a colossus, and to this day his enormous shadow obscures many aspects of Plath's life and work. The sensational aspects of the Plath-Hughes relationship (from that intense first meeting, through to their marriage only four months later, to the birth of their children, followed by Ted's infidelity, their separation, and then Sylvia's death at the age of thirty) have dominated the cultural landscape to such an extent that their story has taken on the resonance of a modern myth. In addition, Hughes' determination to market *Ariel* – a volume of poetry that was published in 1965, three years after Plath's death – as the crowning glory of her poetical career has meant that her other work has been marginalised. In Hughes' view, the poetry she wrote towards the end of her life was the most important; anything that came before was mere dress rehearsal. Stories, letters, journal entries, poems – hundreds of them – were nothing more than 'impurities', 'by-products' of a process of transformation.[17] Hughes cited the backstory of Shakespeare's *The Tempest* to draw an analogy between Plath's long-imprisoned creative talent and its sudden liberation during the writing of the *Ariel* collection. Her poetry, he said, was the 'biology' of Ariel, the back story of the airy spirit who was once trapped in the pine until she was set free by Prospero.[18]

The implication is clear. Plath, as a poet (perhaps even as a woman) did not exist – so the argument goes – before she created these late poems. During the process of crafting them, she finally became, in the words of Robert Lowell, who wrote the introduction to the American edition of *Ariel* (published in 1966), 'herself'.

Lowell's essay set the tone for Plath studies for the rest of the twentieth century. In writing *Ariel*, Plath 'becomes something imaginary, newly, wildly and subtly created – hardly a person at all, or a woman, certainly not another "poetess", but one of those super-real, hypnotic, great classical heroines [. . .] The voice is now coolly amused, witty, now sour, now fanciful, girlish, charming, now sinking to the strident rasp of the vampire – a Dido, Phaedra, or Medea.' The work is distinct because of its 'controlled hallucination, the autobiography of a fever. She burns to be on the move, a walk, a ride, a journey, the flight of the queen bee. She is driven forward by the pounding pistons of her heart [. . .] She herself is a little like a racehorse [the collection's title is a reference to the name of a horse Plath used to ride], galloping relentlessly with risked, outstretched neck, death hurdle after death hurdle topped [. . .] Suicide, father-hatred, self-loathing – nothing is too much for the macabre gaiety of her control. Yet it is too much; her art's immortality is life's disintegration.'[19]

It is one thing for Hughes to argue that the writing that came before *Ariel* was a product of Plath's 'lesser and artificial selves'[20] and quite another to believe that her 'mature' work only began in 1956. Yet, in his introduction to Plath's *Collected Poems*, this is the date that Hughes gives as the year in which Plath started to move away from the 'juvenilia' he associates with her early years. It also happens to be the year in which the couple met.

Hughes, in his role of editor, chose to confine a selection of fifty poems written before 1956 to a small section at the end of the volume, a gesture that almost feels like an apology or an afterthought. Defending his decision, Hughes said that Plath, had she lived, would have rejected these poems. Yet, in the same paragraph, he added a number of reasons why he decided to include fifty of them in the *Collected Poems*. At their best he said, they possessed a lyrical quality that rivalled the poems she wrote later in life. They also showed, he added, traces of the 'super-charged system of inner symbols and images', that made up her creative universe.[21] In the end, Hughes, like all editors, had to make a value judgement and selected what he thought were Plath's 'best' early poems. Yet, for those 'specialists' who really wanted to investigate the links between her late and early work, he said he would accompany the 'juvenilia' with a list, arranged alphabetically, of all the poems that she wrote before 1956.[22]

There is only one problem: the list is far from complete. One of the missing poems is her 1953 villanelle 'Mad Girl's Love Song', which Plath described as one of her favourites.[23] The poem is written from the perspective of a young woman who is waiting for her date to turn up. When she closes her eyes the 'world drops dead' and she is forced to question whether her lover is real or just a projected fantasy. Has she really just made him up inside her head? she asks herself. The form of the villanelle – the repetition of the first and third lines of the first stanza – lends itself to the peculiar intensity of the poem's emotional content. The refrains echo throughout the poem like obsessional thoughts that refuse to be dispersed by the reality of the world around her. The mad girl of the title suffers from a double solipsism, imprisoned within both the boundaries of herself (when she shuts her eyes the world simply disappears; when she opens them again external reality is restored) and the confines of her feelings for her absent lover. In her journal, she recalled how she had been inspired to write the poem, after a boyfriend, 'Mike', didn't turn up for a date.[24]

The Mike she refers to is Myron Lotz, one of a myriad of Plath's early boyfriends who, over the years, have been obscured by the 'dark, hunky' presence of Ted Hughes. Yet these men – figures who have not been explored in any depth in any previous biography – influenced and shaped both Plath's life and her work in a way that has not been fully appreciated. Although Hughes was 'her husband' (as he once described himself in the third person)[25] he was not the only man in her life: before she met him she had gone out with literally hundreds of men – some who were innocent dates, others who were more serious. As she said herself in an early poem, 'Adolescence', she knew she would never be able to confine her love to just one man.[26] These men inspired both her poetry – for instance, Gordon Lameyer, who was unofficially engaged to Plath in August 1954, was the source of 'Sonnet for a Green-Eyed Sailor' – and her prose: she regurgitated her toxic feelings for boyfriend Dick Norton by penning a vicious portrait of him as the unimaginative Buddy Willard in her autobiographical novel *The Bell Jar*.

Dick Norton (whom Plath dated between 1951 and 1953) became a symbol of everything Plath hated about the American hypocritical attitude towards sex. In an unpublished letter she wrote to her friend Ann Davidow in January 1952, Plath talks of her anger at learning that Dick was not a virgin (after he had pretended to be one). In this letter she outlined how she did not object from a moral point of view, but because she wished she could have enjoyed the same pleasures herself.[27] Plath was an addict of experience and she could not bear the fact that young women like her were denied something so life-enhancing. In the same letter she went on to write of her deep envy of males, anger she described as 'insidious, malignant, latent'.[28]

Sex – or rather the constraints and repressions surrounding it – played a central role in Plath's creative and psychological development. She realised, as she wrote in her journal in the autumn of 1950, she was too well brought up to disregard tradition, yet she hated boys who could express themselves sexually, while she had no choice but to 'drag' herself from one date to the next in 'soggy desire'. The system, she added, disgusted her.[29]

If too much has been made of the symptoms of Plath's mental illness, so too little attention has been paid to its possible causes. Sylvia Plath was an angry young woman born in a country and at a time that only exacerbated and intensified her fury. Not only did she feel maddened that she could not express herself sexually, but she also was furious that she had not been born into a family of greater means. Her letters and journals are full of references to feeling inferior and self-consciously lowly of status. As a scholarship girl at Smith College – one of America's top universities for women – she was surrounded by the daughters of the country's great and the good. She peeled potatoes, chopped vegetables and waited on tables as a way of reducing her course fees. In order to try to take the burden off her mother – who worked at Boston University's College of Practical Arts and Letters to pay the shortfall between her daughter's fees and her scholarship – Sylvia volunteered for extra jobs at the college and, in whatever spare time she had, wrote poems and stories for money. If she took boys home to her family's two-bedroom house in Wellesley, Massachusetts – where she was forced to share a room with her mother – she worried that they would see the marks and rips in the wallpaper; on occasions like these, the lights would have to be kept low so as to try to disguise the blemishes.[30] In her first semester at Smith, in the autumn of 1950, she wrote in her journal of the arduous transition period between childhood and young adulthood. To help her make sense of this new, troubling reality she made a list of certain aspects of life that she found difficult, an inventory of notes addressed to herself that she could use to boost her confidence when it was low. One of the sections focuses on her economic position in society. She noted how she knew she would have to compete with other girls who had been born into wealthier families. The Plaths, she realised, were not only of modest means, but they didn't come from a line of well-connected intellectuals. She observed how boys from richer families would often remark, in a casual fashion, of her "side of town", and although they didn't mean to be cruel, she felt the comments keenly.[31]

Plath's struggle to come to terms with her self in all its many facets – a battle that, ultimately, she did not win – generated the peculiar set of psychological circumstances that inspired her greatest poetry. There is no doubt that writing was her outlet for venting the host of negative feelings that crowded within her. Although it is easy to interpret the *Ariel* poems as, in the words of one of her lovers, Peter Davison, a sign that she was at last finding 'her real identity, for the first time, and the horror was like blood and afterbirth',[32] the reality is much more complex, and perhaps even more disturbing.

In truth, Sylvia did not have one coherent identity; rather, her self was constructed of a number of different personalities, some quite at odds with the others. 'Most of us who knew Sylvia knew a different Sylvia,' wrote her friend Clarissa Roche. 'This is partly because she was secretive and devious and selective, but I think too it was because aspects of her character were dispersed. In a curious way she seemed uncompleted. Like fragments of mercury racing and quivering toward a center to settle in a self-contained mass, the myriad ramifications of her personality sought a focal point.'[33] At times, Plath thought of herself as a figure approaching near-mythical status. 'She herself had the imagination to view herself in many mythic guises, such as Eve or Alice in Wonderland, metamorphosing into other roles but always engaged in some type of ritual of initiation,' writes boyfriend Gordon Lameyer in an unpublished memoir. 'I liked to see her as [a] combination of opposites: a Nasikaa who wanted to be a Calypso, a Dido who verged on being a Circe, an Artemis who was not far from becoming an Aphrodite.'[34] In the same autobiography, Lameyer recalls the words of a friend of his who had attended Cambridge and who had heard that Plath had been described like 'a time bomb that seemed always about to explode'.[35]

Plath had a compulsion to use herself as a kind of Anatomical Venus, opening up her psyche up for all 'the peanut-crunching crowd' to see.[36] In 1951 she accompanied Dick Norton, then a student at Harvard Medical School, to a dissection room where she witnessed at close quarters the dismemberment of a number of corpses. In *The Bell Jar* she described the bodies as smelling like old pickle jars,[37] and in her poem 'Two Views of a Cadaver Room', she compares the black cadavers to 'burnt turkey'.[38]

While on a visit to the university Plath also saw a couple of dead, malformed babies floating in formaldehyde, a detail she incorporated into *The Bell Jar*.[39] Like one of the cadavers on the slab or the dead babies in their bottles, Plath presented herself to the world as a specimen, an experimental subject that opened itself up to be investigated, probed and dissected. She once said that she would die if she could not write about anything apart from herself,[40] yet ultimately she had to filter everything – even extremes such as the Holocaust – through herself.

'Sylvia Plath is an example of the egotistical sublime: her subject is herself, her predicament, her violent Romantic emotions,' stated Craig Raine in the *Times Literary Supplement*.[41] This is true only up to a certain point. I would argue that she is more abject than sublime, more modern than romantic: her self is the site of all the horrors in the world. She carried around within herself a kind of black hole that sucked many into its path. Being near the periphery of her creative vacuum was a dangerous prospect, as many of those close to her witnessed. Ted Hughes wrote to Aurelia, Sylvia's mother, in March 1963 about how her daughter often punished the people she loved most.[42] Even worse was the fact that Plath viewed those near her as subjects that she could transpose – often in fairly undisguised ways – directly into her work. It's not surprising then that the figure of the vampire fascinated Plath – it manifests itself in her poetry ('Daddy') and in her journals (where she casts her mother in the role of the parasitic un-dead). One of Plath's many 'unwritten' stories (those for which only an outline exists) – 'The Fringe-Dweller', inspired by Henry James' 'The Altar of the Dead' – centres on a girl who, like a vampire, constructs her identity from scraps and fragments of second-hand experience around her: films, books, overheard conversations, strangers. She feels she is at the point of becoming an authentic self yet she never quite realises it and, finally, at the end of the story she awakens and discovers that she is inside a coffin. In effect, she has constructed her own grave.[43]

Another classic myth that has resonances within Plath's life is that of Frankenstein's monster. After an unsuccessful suicide attempt in the summer of 1953, Plath felt that she had been reborn, a living lady Lazarus. This, together with a botched ECT treatment – when she felt like she was being electrified – transformed her into both the creator of the monster and the horrific creature itself, one of the perfect doubles with which she was so obsessed. It is this experience – more than any of the betrayals or marital infidelities that came later – that was central to the development of her poetic vision. Her disturbing, horrific, transgressive voice started to find expression in her work many years before *Ariel* and late poems such as 'Edge'.

In her journal in 1950 she wrote of how she was living on the 'edge'. She was not alone, she added, as all of us were standing on the edge of a precipice looking down into darkness, peering into an unnerving pit below.[44]

This book will show what compelled Plath to peek over the edge and stare into the abyss of the human psyche. *Mad Girl's*

Love Song will trace the sources of her mental instabilities and will examine how a range of personal, economic and societal factors – the real disquieting muses – conspired against her. Although a great deal has been written about Plath, this is the first book that concentrates exclusively on her life before she met Ted Hughes, a period that has been given scant attention in other biographies. In addition, I have had access to a number of previously unavailable archives (some in private hands) and I have interviewed a wide range of friends and lovers who have never spoken openly about Plath before. As Ted Hughes admitted the public tended to regard Sylvia's story as a kind of 'mysterious dream', a tabula rasa on which they could project their own fantasies and desires.[45] With this in mind, I have tried to avoid relying on secondary sources, such as other Plath biographies, drawing instead on primary materials (such as letters, diaries, memoirs) and interviews with those who knew Plath.

In 1948, sixteen-year-old Sylvia wrote a poem (still unpublished) called 'Neither Moonlight nor Starlight'. In it, she tries to address the reasons why she feels compelled to write (even at this young age she was prolific). Finally, she states that there was a voice that raged inside of her that would never be 'still'.[46] While this book cannot answer that question completely – the source of creation is still very much a mystery – I hope to examine some of the origins of Plath's unsettled and unsettling voice, a voice that, fifty years after her death, still has the power to haunt and disturb.

One

THIS HAUNTING NAMELESS PAIN

When Sylvia Plath was a child, her mother would sit down at the family piano and play the 'plaintive' nineteenth-century German song 'The Legend of the Lorelei'. The ballad – originally written by Clemens von Brentano in 1801 – tells the story of a beautiful sorceress, the Lore Lei, whose gaze prompts men to fall immediately in love with her. A bishop sends for the woman to be judged, but even he cannot resist her and the Lore Lei pleads with him to end her life. Instead of condemning her to death he pledges three knights to accompany the young woman to a nunnery, but on the way to the convent the group passes a steep rock on the east bank of the Rhine and the woman asks the knights if they would grant her permission to climb up to the viewpoint so as to see the majestic river for the last time. Once at the top of the precipice, the Lore Lei throws herself to her death.

The story proved so popular that it was rewritten by various authors during the nineteenth century, with the Lore Lei variously represented as a witch, a mermaid that lures sailors to their deaths, and a virgin with golden hair. The version that Plath heard as a child was Heinrich Heine's 1823 poem 'Die Lorelei', which was set to music by Friedrich Silcher, and later translated by Mark Twain. It's significant that Plath associated the legend with her early years; in July 1958, as she was composing her poem

'Lorelei', she outlined in her journal the appeal of the story: not only had it originated in Germany but it illustrated perfectly one of Plath's recurring themes, that of the 'death wish'.[1] She described how the Rhine sirens were her 'Own Kin'[2] and indeed she came to see herself as a modern-day Lorelei, a sorceress who had the power to attract men with a flash of her intense eyes, a tortured soul whose only destiny was death by her own hand.

The song that echoed through the Plath household can also be used to interpret Sylvia's childhood and the various problems it presents to a biographer:

> I cannot divine what it meaneth,
> This haunting nameless pain:
> A tale of the bygone ages
> Keeps brooding through my brain.[3]

By virtue of her mother's obsessive curatorial zeal, we know a great deal about the facts of Plath's early years – for instance Aurelia went so far as to document her daughter's weight (noting it down at birth, two weeks, one month, six months, eight months, nine months, one year, eighteen months, two years, twenty-six and a half months, two years nine months and three years). Yet, despite this excess of information, there is an absence, a 'haunting nameless pain' that even Plath herself acknowledged. Reading the poet's journals one gets the sense that she spent much of her adult life trying to make sense of what she described as 'the complex mosaic of my childhood';[4] no matter how hard she looked, or how much she wrote, she was destined to fail. Determined to try to chronicle her experience in an attempt to impose some kind of order on the chaos that raged inside her, Sylvia often looked back on her childhood in the hope of finding the answer to her problems. But, as she writes in her poem 'The Ghost's Leavetaking', she encountered nothing but a mass of unreadable hieroglyphs, unknowable beings that spoke in a lost language.[5]

Sylvia Plath was born at the Robinson Memorial Hospital, Boston, Massachusetts, at 2:10 p.m. on 27 October 1932, the first child of Otto Emil Plath and Aurelia Frances Schober. The couple had married on 4 January 1932 – he was forty-six, a professor of biology at Boston University, and she was a twenty-five-year-old former student of his whom he had met in 1929. In an unpublished letter, Aurelia – who had studied for a master's degree in English and German at Boston University's College of Practical Arts and Letters – described the encounter. 'I wanted to read the great German poem on which Wagner based his operas (some of them) called "Das Nibelungen Lied" . . .' she wrote. 'Well, I went to the head of the German department and asked if anyone taught this and was advised to take the course in Middle-High German which was taught, strangely enough, by a professor of biology [. . .] I was his [Otto Plath's] prize student, but he very properly did not ask me out socially until the day when I handed in my final examination to him, because in those days socializing between professors and students was forbidden. He was tall, rosy-cheeked, with the bluest eyes I have ever seen. I thought he was an awful poke, because every time he called on me to recite, he looked down at his shoes – never directly at me!'[6]

Otto Plath – whom his daughter would later immortalise in her poem 'Daddy' – was born on 13 April 1885 in Grabow, Germany, a place to which Plath would refer in *The Bell Jar* as a 'manic-depressive hamlet in the black heart of Prussia'.[7] He was the eldest of six, the son of Ernestine Kottke and Theodore Platt, who had emigrated to America in 1901. 'He and his family lived in the countryside, grew all their own fruit and vegetables,' Aurelia wrote to her grandson Nicholas Hughes. 'His father was a blacksmith and a very skilled mechanic – so skilled that when he came to the United States, he invented an improvement for the famous McCormick reaper, which was a harvesting machine.'[8]

In August 1900, Otto's grandfather, John – who had immigrated to Watertown, Wisconsin in 1885 – paid for passage for his grandson on the *Auguste Victoria*, which sailed from Hamburg to New York. Records show that the fifteen-year-old boy described himself as a 'bootmaker' and that he arrived in New York on 8 September. John had heard of Otto's brilliant academic record and had offered to pay his way through Northwestern College, Wisconsin, on the condition that his grandson enter the Lutheran ministry. 'The opportunity appeared dazzling,' said Aurelia. 'Not only would he have the higher education which in Germany would be unobtainable for a boy in his circumstances, but he would escape military service, the thought of which he dreaded, for he was already a confirmed pacifist.'[9] In Manhattan, Otto lived for a year with an uncle who ran a liquor and food store. So determined was he to master English that he gained permission to audit classes in grade school – he could attend lessons but not take them for credit – and would sit at the back of the classroom, taking a large quantity of notes, making sure he practised his conversational skills with pupils and teachers alike. As soon as he felt comfortable with a level, he promoted himself to the next class; during the course of a year he managed to work his way through all eight grades and could speak English with no trace of a foreign accent. By 1903 Otto was living in Watertown, Wisconsin, where he had enrolled at the Northwestern Preparatory School, and after graduation in June 1906 he entered Northwestern

College, where he studied classical languages and where he stayed until 1910. 'The college was really a classic German Gymnasium,' recalls Max Gaebler, whose father, Hans, was a fellow student and close friend of Otto's. 'It was called a preparatory school and college, but the eight classes went by the old Latin names: sexta, quinta, quarta, tertia, unter und ober secunda, unter und ober prima. All instruction was in the German language.'[10]

Otto built up a glittering academic record – something that pleased his grandparents – but in his spare time became fascinated by the writings of Charles Darwin. 'Darwin had become his hero and when Otto entered the Lutheran seminary [. . .] he was shocked to find all Darwin's writings among the proscribed books.'[11] Otto tried his best to conform, but after a number of 'miserable months of agonizing doubt and self-evaluation' he made the decision to leave the seminary and abandon all plans to enter the ministry.[12] When he told his grandparents of his change of career – he now planned to become a teacher – he was informed, in no uncertain terms, that this was something he would have to do without their support. 'If he adhered to this infamous decision, he would no longer be a part of the family,' said Aurelia, 'his name would be stricken from the family Bible. And so it was done. He was on his own for the rest of his life.'[13] Plath would rework this family history into her novel *The Bell Jar*, whose heroine, Esther, describes her father being a Lutheran living in Wisconsin before ending up a cynical atheist.[14]

Otto moved first to Seattle, where, in February 1911, he enrolled at the University of Washington; in June of the following year he received a Master of Arts degree. On 7 August 1912, in Spokane, Washington State, he married Lydia Clara Bartz, the twenty-three-year-old sister of his friend Rupert

Bartz, from Eau Claire, Wisconsin. Yet the marriage proved to be a disaster from the very beginning. As Aurelia wrote to her granddaughter Frieda:

> In those days when literature was more circumspect and less realistic and there was no radio or television, it was possible (and, hard as it is for young people today to believe) for people to get married without knowing very much about marriage itself [. . .] Well, Lydia had been what was then termed 'delicately raised' and educated along very idealistic lines. She was not prepared for the physical side of marriage at all. So when she and Otto were married, the two found they had decidedly different attitudes (too bad they didn't discuss all this before!) and the upshot was that Lydia left Otto after three weeks and returned to her family. The two people never saw each other again – ever![15]

For the rest of her life, Lydia, who worked as a nurse, never remarried and she died, apparently without having said a word about either Otto or his famous daughter, in Eau Claire on 22 February 1988.

Otto carried his own secret with him to the grave. In October 1918, while living in Berkeley, California, Plath had been investigated by the FBI for suspected 'pro-German' leanings. The allegations had their root in Plath's status as a registered 'alien enemy', the fact that he had not bought Liberty Bonds to help the war effort and his supposed antipathy towards America 'on account [. . .] he lost a position teaching school in the State of Washington, and another position at the University of California.' Although the recently released FBI files show that Plath was eventually cleared of any pro-German sympathies, the records reveal that the investigator regarded him as 'a man who makes no friends and with whom no one is really well acquainted' and someone possessed of a 'nervous and morbid disposition'.

Otto explained himself as best he could – he didn't buy Liberty Bonds because, at the time, he was $1,400 in debt, 'on which he was paying 5 and 6% interest, and that he was attempting to earn a living and do work at the University at the same time and did not feel that he could afford to do so.' He told the agent that his grandparents had emigrated to America 'because of the better conditions here and that some things are rotten in Germany, but not all; that the German people and their character is not altogether rotten, but that they are misled.' The investigator also interviewed Plath's supervisor at Berkeley, who explained that Otto had not been given an assistantship at the university 'because he has not the personality that is required of an instructor [. . .] being very nervous and not able to interest students; second, because the Regents of the University have made a rule prohibiting the hiring of Germans on the faculty.' According to the source, 'whatever indiscreet remarks [the] subject has made at times is probably due to this brooding over the bad luck he is having making a living on account of his nationality.' In addition to his studies at the university, Otto was forced to work at the Lincoln market for several hours each day, and, in the evenings, he operated an elevator; his pay for both jobs was twenty cents an hour.[15a]

Otto's work ethic was unremitting. After Berkeley, he attended the Massachusetts Institute of Technology (as an instructor in modern languages from 1915 to 1918). Between 1921 and 1925 he studied zoology at Harvard, which also employed him as an assistant in entomology, and in 1928 the university awarded him a doctorate in applied biology. By the time that he met Aurelia Schober in 1929, he had been an assistant professor of biology at Boston University for a year. The university also engaged him to teach a course in

Middle-High German – and on the last day of class, while nervously playing with a pen on his desk, he asked his favourite student whether she would like to join him as his guest at the country home of another professor and his wife. That weekend Otto told Aurelia about his brief marriage and informed her that were he 'to form a serious relationship with a young woman now, of course he would obtain a divorce.'[16] He also told her of his love of bees, a passion that had its roots in his boyhood in Grabow. 'Having repeatedly observed the activities of a neighboring bee-keeper, I thought it might be possible to transfer bumblebee colonies to artificial domiciles, and thus have honey available at all times,' Otto wrote. 'The method employed in "transplanting" these colonies was rather crude, and so it happened that I was sometimes severely punished by the more vindictive species.'[17]

Otto's interest in bees grew into a scientific obsession, and by the time he had met Aurelia he had collected a mass of data gathered from years of study. As soon as the couple married – in Carson City, Nevada, on 4 January 1932, the same day that Plath divorced his first wife, Lydia – their lives were taken over by Otto's work on his book *Bumblebees and Their Ways*, which was based on his doctoral thesis. 'During the first year of our married life all had to be given up for THE BOOK,' Aurelia wrote years later.[18] Although Otto acknowledged the help of his new wife – writing in the preface of 'the service of my wife, Aurelia S. Plath, who has aided me greatly in editing the manuscript and proofreading' – from reading certain sections of the resulting 1934 book it looks as though Aurelia's influence extended beyond the secretarial. The first chapter opens with the words: 'If one takes a walk on a clear, sunny day in middle April, when the first willows are in bloom, one may often see young bumblebee queens eagerly sipping nectar from the catkins. It is a delightful thing to pause and watch these queens, clad in their costumes of rich velvet, their wings not yet torn by the long foraging flights which they will be obliged to take later.'[19]

Aurelia had, after all, always wanted to be writer, but, as she told one interviewer, 'I didn't feel that I could expose my children to the uncertainty of a writer's success or failure.'[20] Aurelia was born into a hardworking, immigrant family – her father, Franz Schober, was an Austrian who grew up in Bad Aussee, near Salzburg, and who sailed from Bremen on the *Kronprinz Wilhelm*, arriving in America in March 1903, while her Vienna-born mother, Aurelia Grunwald (later Greenwood), arrived in the United States a year later. The couple married in Boston in July 1905 and on 26 April of the following year their daughter, whom they named Aurelia Frances, was born.

Sylvia's mother grew up by the ocean, at 892 Shirley Street, Point Shirley, in a household that spoke German: although Frank (as he now called himself) had spent two years in England, where he had worked as a waiter, the family communicated using their mother tongue. Aurelia often felt isolated at school, as she later related in the introduction to *Letters Home*: 'The two words I heard most frequently were "Shut up!", so when I went home at the end of the school day and met my father, I answered his greeting proudly and loudly with "Shut up!" I still remember how his face reddened.' Frank took his daughter across his knee and spanked her, only for her to plead, '*Aber was bedeutet das, Papa*?' ('What does that mean, Papa?') When Frank realised that Aurelia did not understand the words that she had used he hugged her and asked her to forgive him; 'from that time on we always spoke English,' she said.[21] Years later Plath would write that her grandparents always spoke with a heavy accent, saying 'cholly' for 'jolly' and 'ven' instead of 'when'.[22] Growing up in the Italian-Irish neighbourhood of Winthrop, Aurelia often suffered prejudice, especially during the years of the First World War. She was often called 'spy-face' and one day she was pushed off the steps of the school bus by another child while the driver kept his eyes straight ahead and drove away.

As a child, Aurelia – like her daughter after her – found her escape in reading, working her way through Louisa May Alcott, Horatio Alger, Harold Bell Wright, Gene Stratton-Porter and every romantic historical novel she found in her local library, before moving on, at high school, to the novels of Scott, Thackeray, Dickens, George Eliot, Jane Austen, the Brontës, Hardy, Hawthorne, Melville and Henry James and the poetry of Emily Dickinson. 'I lived in a dream world,' said Aurelia, 'a book tucked under every mattress of the beds it was my chore to make up daily; a book in the bathroom hamper, and the family's stock answer to "What's RiRi [my nickname] doing?" was "Oh, she's reading *again*."'[23] In the summer after graduating from high school, she took a full-time job with an insurance company, typing letters for eight hours a day, which she later described as a 'grim experience', something that she vowed 'no child of mine would ever have to endure'.[24] She had always dreamed of going to Wellesley College, but such an expensive education was out of her reach 'as my parents could not afford to send me there and as I knew nothing about scholarships then – which perhaps I could have won, for I was second in my graduating class'.[25] Instead, in 1924 Aurelia enrolled on the two-year course at Boston University's College of Practical Arts and Letters, helping with expenses by taking a series of part-time jobs. After this, she took another two-year course that would enable her to qualify as a high-school teacher of English and German.

In 1925, when she was nineteen, Aurelia fell in love – not with Otto, but another, unnamed man, an engineer and artist, whom she met in her junior year. 'I recall the thrill, the excitement and wonder of becoming the most important person in another's life,' she wrote to her granddaughter Frieda in 1978.

> For the first time, I felt transfigured, beautiful; all was possible. Indeed [. . .] for a time, it was almost impossible for me to concentrate on anything else – that beloved face appeared between me and anything I was trying to read or study. I felt I spilled joy from every pore; the whole world and everyone in it were beautiful. We shared it all then – for a little over two years – the music, the arts, books, our ideas on every possible subject, the earth, the sky, the sea; our hopes and dreams for ourselves and each other.

Then, in 1927, her lover was sent on a work project to Brazil and from there to Russia – 'and we never met again,' wrote Aurelia. '(I don't want to recall the hurt that remained in lessening degrees until your mother was born.) However, the memory of that exhilarating joy is still precious to recall; it changed my thinking, therefore, my life in many ways.'[26]

It was in this rather dejected state that Aurelia met Otto, a man whom she admired for his brilliant mind rather than the warmth of his personality. From the autumn of 1930 onwards the couple spent an increasing amount of time together, hiking in the Blue Hills and walking through the Arnold Arboretum and the Fells Reservation. Together they mapped out their future together: a family of at least two children and a book that they could work on together, which they provisionally entitled *The Evolution of Parental Care in the Animal Kingdom*. While waiting for Otto's divorce to come through, Aurelia took a job teaching English and German at Brookline High School but, after their marriage in January 1932, she yielded to her husband's wish that she retire from work to take on the role of housewife. By all accounts, Otto was something of a tyrant in the home. When he was writing a chapter on insect societies for the 1935 book *A Handbook of Social Psychology* he worked in the dining room of their apartment at 24 Prince Street, Jamaica Plain. The table served as his desk while the sideboard became a depository for the seventy reference books that he regularly needed to consult and he forbade Aurelia from moving a single paper or book. 'I drew a plan of the arrangement and managed to have friends in occasionally for dinner the one evening a week that my husband gave a course at Harvard night school, always replacing every item correctly before his return,' she said.[27]

A stickler for order and a lover of logic, Otto rather admired the regimented nature of insect societies; human nature was rather messy in comparison. He did his best to rule his household according to his strict requirements, edicts that Aurelia found difficult to live with. At the end of their first year of marriage she realised that if she wanted her children to grow up in a peaceful home she would have to become more 'submissive', although this was against her nature. As a result, Otto took on the role of '*der Herr des Hauses*' ('head of the house') and Aurelia often had to remain silent.[28] Aurelia – who was intelligent and imaginative, but obviously intellectually and creatively repressed – needed a project, something that could contain and channel her energies. The birth of her daughter Sylvia in October 1932 presented her with the perfect opportunity: the chance to document and shape the growth of another human being. The budding writer now came into her own.

'Most theories of development assume that *mothers don't write, they are written*,' observes academic Anita Helle, Sylvia's cousin. 'Yet in Aurelia Plath we have quite the opposite case, a mother whose energies so readily transformed themselves into verbal expression that *she writes her daughter*, frames her rites of passage with verbal rituals, colonizes her world with words. One only has to recall that at the family dinner table, Aurelia and Sylvia Plath buried messages to each other under the table napkins, in order to understand how female attachment appeared quite literally as subrosal, subtextual language within the family system.'[29]

Trained by Otto in the methodology of scientific classification, Aurelia began to record, in minute detail, the key moments of her daughter's life in a baby book. 'The record of Sylvia Plath by her "mummy",' reads the inscription in Aurelia's neat handwriting on the inside of the book. At birth, Sylvia measured 22 inches; at six months, 28 inches; at eight months, 29 inches; at sixteen months she was 32.5 inches and at two years she stood 36.5 inches. Aurelia regularly snipped off locks of Sylvia's hair and kept them preserved: in the archive at the Lilly Library, Indiana, one can see not only the lock taken on Plath's first birthday, but also samples from 1938 and 1941, a tress from 1942 and a couple of light-brown braids that today are wrapped in white muslin, together with an accompanying note from Aurelia that reads, 'At the age of 12 yrs 10 m S's braids were cut.'[30] At six weeks, Sylvia imitated vowel sounds; at eight weeks she could say 'ga' and 'goo'; at six months she would utter 'gully gully' whenever Aurelia offered her a bottle – an echo of the words 'goody goody', which she would say to her daughter when giving her milk. At eight months, Sylvia could say the words 'mama', 'dada' and 'bye bye' and, Aurelia noted, the little girl took delight in the world around her, particularly birds, squirrels, chipmunks, automobiles and other babies. 'She wants to touch other babies and stretches out her arms to them, shouting with excitement,' her mother said. In September 1933, Aurelia observed that one day when the rag man passed down the street her daughter shouted out 'ags', an imitation of the word 'rags'; on 1 November, the one-year-old girl said the phrases 'I tee' ('I see'), 'haw' (for 'hot') and 'ba' (her shorthand for 'bath'); while on 19 December Sylvia shouted out the word, 'Daddy', which Aurelia commented was 'said specially when someone shakes the furnace.'[31] At the end of the baby book, Aurelia listed Sylvia's 'sayings and antics', observing that on 3 February 1934, 'When placed on the pottie, she immediately calls out – "Aw-done! Aw-done!" (She fibs already!).'[32]

It's obvious from reading Aurelia's notes that Sylvia was a child bathed in love. For her first birthday, her parents presented her with a cake; and after the little makeshift party Aurelia noted in the baby book that 'her daddy and I agree that the whole world doesn't hold another one-year-old as wonderful and so sweet – at least it doesn't for us!'[33] One gets the impression that Otto was also able to gain pleasure from his daughter's development from a scientific perspective: when Sylvia was six months old he held her against a rope that was attached to a bamboo shade and, as Aurelia writes, 'he was delighted by the fact that her feet grasped the rope in the same manner as her hands – to him proof of man's evolutionary process as well as the gradual loss of flexibility when man started to wear shoes and used his feet only for walking.'[34]

In the winter of 1934 to 1935, when Aurelia was pregnant with her second child, she told Sylvia that soon she would have a brother or sister, a Warren or an Evelyn, and that she would need to call on her daughter to help prepare for the new arrival. One day, when Sylvia leant her head against Aurelia's stomach, she heard the baby moving. 'I can *hear* him!' she cried out. 'He is saying, "Hó da! Hó da!" That means "I *love* you! I *love* you!"'[35] The week before the birth Aurelia took her daughter to stay at her parents' house, not leaving until 27 April, the day of the delivery. Apparently, when Sylvia was informed that she now had a baby brother, she pulled a face and said, pointedly,

'I wanted an Evelyn, *not* a Warren.'[36] In her autobiographical essay 'Ocean 1212-W' – named after her grandparents' telephone number – Plath writes that Warren's appearance resulted in a kind of existential crisis: before his birth, Sylvia had believed that she had enjoyed a 'beautiful fusion' with the world; now she felt separated, no longer special.[37] Yet, from Aurelia's perspective, Sylvia's childhood was overwhelmingly 'laughter-shared';[38] indeed, the girl's original sense of humour was evident at a young age. One day in October 1935, after a doctor had treated Aurelia for an abscess on her breast, Sylvia said, 'You're a good Mummy, you are! You know what I'm going to give you? Two new breasts – without holes in them!'[39]

Aurelia found nursing her new baby difficult because whenever she brought Warren towards her breast Sylvia wanted to crawl up into her mother's lap. 'Fortunately, around this time she discovered the alphabet from the capital letters on packaged goods on the pantry shelves,' said Aurelia.[40] From the beginning of her development, Sylvia – or Sivvy, as her family called her – came to associate words as a substitute for love. Each time when Aurelia took up Warren to nurse him, Sylvia would grab a newspaper, sit on the floor in front of her mother and proceed to pick out the capital letters. 'I read and sang to them [her children] for hours and hours,' said Aurelia, 'and I encouraged them from their very first steps to be aware of all things about them – shades of color, shadows, colors within shadows – to have a painter's eye as well as a writer's eye.'[41] Plath identified with the physicality of words to such an extent that she often wished, as she says in *The Bell Jar*, that she could return to the womblike space of the printed page.[42] Later, Plath would recall the memory of her mother reading to her Matthew Arnold's poem 'The Forsaken Merman': 'Sand-strewn caverns, cool and deep,/Where the winds are all asleep . . .' and seeing the gooseflesh rise on her skin. 'I did not know what made it,' she wrote. 'I was not cold. Had a ghost passed over me? No, it was the poetry [. . .] I had fallen into a new way of being happy.'[43] When Sylvia was eight and a half years old she wrote a letter to the *Boston Sunday Herald*, enclosing a poem about her impressions of a warm summer night. The editor was so impressed by her four-line stanza that the newspaper published it.[44]

Aurelia remembered one occasion – Sylvia was about eight years old – when she took the two children down to the beach to watch the spectacle of the new moon. 'I carried my son and she stood by my side,' she said. 'And she more or less drew away, stood apart and gazed at the moon. And then quietly I heard her start to say very slowly,

> The moon is a lock of witch's hair
> Tawny and golden and red.
> And the night winds pause and stare at the
> Strand from a witch's head.[45]

In 1936, a year after Warren was born, Otto began to suffer from ill health. He started to lose weight, was wracked by an awful cough, plagued by sinusitis – an ailment that would affect Sylvia throughout her life – and seemed constantly irritable and short-tempered. During that hot summer, Aurelia took herself and her two children to live with her parents at their home in Point Shirley, and in the autumn the family made the decision to move from their cramped apartment to a more spacious seven-room house at 92 Johnson Avenue, Winthrop, situated three miles from the Schobers. 'My husband was failing in health and that was the real main reason [for the move] and I wanted to be near my parents,' Aurelia said later. 'We loved the shore, we loved the house and I hoped, of course, that he'd recover.'[46]

Otto had had a friend who had died from lung cancer and he feared that he too was suffering from the disease. 'He told me that he had diagnosed his own case and that he would never submit to surgery,' said Aurelia.[47] Although Aurelia tried to persuade her husband to seek medical attention, whenever the subject was mentioned he became consumed by 'explosive outbursts of anger'.[48] Aurelia did all she could to protect Sylvia and Warren, keeping the children upstairs away from the wrath of Otto, who spent the majority of his time in his large study. Otto also suffered from spasms in his legs, which would cause him to moan in pain, and when he returned from work he was invariably exhausted and on edge. Later Plath would write in her journal of how Otto became ill the second he married Aurelia and the extent to which her mother loathed her husband.[49]

At the time, however, Sylvia enjoyed what she described as an idyllic childhood. In the spring of 1937 she became fast friends with four-year-old Ruth Freeman, who had moved to nearby Somerset Terrace, Winthrop, with her parents, William and Marion, and her elder brother, David.

'One day, our mothers were out walking to the beach with their children when they met and from that moment onwards we spent hundreds and hundreds of hours together,' says Ruth. 'Sylvia's house was on the water and I was half a block from it. Her home was a typical New England house, and I lived there for several months because my mother became seriously ill with what then was called a nervous breakdown; now, I know that my mother suffered from bipolar disorder, but nobody defined it in those terms back then. Sylvia and I would go down to the ocean early in the morning with a picnic lunch and when the tide went out we would play on the mudflats, where we would dig for clams. I remember that Otto would go to the beach each day too – he was not a terribly pleasant man. He used to sunbathe and would always say that he was storing up his health for the winter. I remember that if I ever went back to Sylvia's house I would have to be extremely quiet – there was an atmosphere, it was all very controlled – and I realized that the household was run on very Germanic lines. Both of us went to the nearby Sunshine School, a private nursery school, and although our parents had to pay for it I'm sure it was very reasonable as nobody really had any money in those days. It was a nice, cheery place, like its name suggests. When people ask whether Sylvia was depressed as a child I can only say that she wasn't: from what I saw Sylvia was a bright, fun person.'[50]

Aurelia converted the largest bedroom into a playroom for the children. Each night Sylvia and Warren would have their supper sitting at a small maple table by a large window, after which they would amuse themselves while Aurelia and Otto had dinner. For half an hour before bed the children would be allowed downstairs, during which time Sylvia might dance for her father – who was usually lying prostate on the living-room couch – or Warren might show his father the drawings he had done during the day. Sylvia lived, she later said, in a fantastical world populated by fairies, imps and spirits,[51] and her imagination was so vivid that she dreamt fully-formed narratives in Technicolor.[52] Her mother read to her poems by Eugene Field, A. A. Milne and Robert Louis Stevenson, practically everything from the children's anthology *Sung Under the Silver Umbrella*, Dr Seuss' *Horton Hatches an Egg* and Tolkien's *The Hobbit*, and she also invented a number of stories that featured Warren's favourite teddy bear, Mixie Blackshort, a character that makes an appearance in Plath's poem 'The Disquieting Muses'.

Sylvia and Warren enjoyed a close but at times competitive relationship. Aurelia recalled that her daughter would 'monopolize' the lunch-table conversation after school and would often try to dazzle and outsmart her younger brother with her ever-expanding vocabulary.[53] Warren tried to emulate Sylvia's already heightened sense of creativity: when he was only two and a half he dreamed up a series of stories called 'The Other Side of the Moon', the first tale of which began: 'On the other side of the moon, where I was *nine* years old and lived before I met you, Mother.'[54]

Later in life, Plath would write in her journal of a memory from her childhood involving 'the feast, the beast, and the jelly-bean.'[55] According to Warren's daughter, Susan Plath Winston, when 'he and Sylvia were quite young and still living in Winthrop, they would get a little spooked – or at least pretend to be spooked – when it was time for them to walk up the darkened staircase to their rooms to get ready for bed. On one such occasion, when Sylvia asked Warren what he thought they would find at the top of the stairs, my father [Warren] replied, "A feast. . . and a beast. . . and a jellybean!" A fit of giggles reportedly ensued, and the saying became family lore.'[56] Occasionally Sylvia bullied Warren – she fought with him, threw tin soldiers at his head and once she accidentally cut his neck with a flick of the blade on her ice skate. She grew up resentful of the fact that Warren, by the mere fact of his maleness, could shape a life for himself without all the constrictions and conventionalities that circumscribed a young woman's independence and growth. In her journal, Plath would write of the sibling rivalry that existed between her and Warren and how this was symbolic of the larger battle she had to fight with men for independence and recognition.[57] When Plath was an adult she became fascinated by Freud, and in her own copy of the Modern Library edition of *The Basic Writings of Sigmund Freud* she underlined the section dealing with the relationship between brothers and sisters: 'I do not know why we presuppose that it must be a loving one, since examples of enmity among adult brothers and sisters are frequent [. . .] Children at this time of life are capable of jealousy that is perfectly evident and extremely intense.'[58]

As a child, Sylvia developed an irrational fear of bobby pins and buttons to such an extent that one day when she heard a woman, bending over a baby carriage, comment on the infant's button nose, the girl ran away screaming.[59] When Sylvia was in high school she wrote an essay entitled 'Childhood Fears', in which she described the fright she felt when her mother produced the vacuum cleaner, and the sense of delicious terror shared between her and her friend Ruth Freeman when the other girl stayed overnight in her bed. One night, unable to sleep, Ruth told Sylvia that she was sure she could see a gorilla standing in front of the closet door; in the morning, the 'gorilla' was revealed to be nothing more than an old coat flung over the door, but the image stayed with Plath and later, in an unpublished poem, 'The Desperate Hours', she wrote of the memory. In 'Childhood Fears' Sylvia also described her terror of subways – the feeling that she might stand too close to the edge of the platform and either fall or get pushed into the path of an oncoming train – as well as the thought that a burglar might have stolen into her room and be hiding in a closet or cupboard.

Plath, as a child, as a woman and as a poet, was constantly in search of an overarching metaphor that would perfectly capture her strange complexity. In her journal she wrote of the 'potently rich sea of my subconscious', and often associated its murky origins with the dark ocean floor of her childhood, a place that she felt she needed to return to if she ever wanted to find success as a writer. It's intriguing that Plath came to associate her father with the sea, casting and recasting him in her poetry as a Neptune-like character who served as a 'father-sea-god muse'.[60] Her poem 'Full Fathom Five' – a reference to Ariel's song in

Shakespeare's *The Tempest* – describes her ambiguous relationship with this powerful man-turned-myth, a white-haired figure who surfaces from deep within Plath's subconscious to haunt her. The poem ends with Sylvia's recollection of her father's 'shelled' bed and a suggestion that she would rather drown than share his 'murderous' air.[61]

Plath was fascinated by Hawthorne's short story 'Rappaccini's Daughter', a tale of a young scholar, Giovanni Guasconti, who, while in Padua, is entranced by the sight of a beautiful young woman, Beatrice Rappaccini, who tends a garden full of exotic plants. During the course of the story, Guasconti learns that Beatrice, with whom he falls in love, is the subject of a scientific experiment overseen by her father. She has the power, in the words of Signor Rappaccini, 'to be as terrible as thou art beautiful,': having been brought up on poisons her presence is so deadly it can kill. The image is an apt metaphor for Plath's view of her relationship with her own father: she too felt as though she had been poisoned by Otto, or at least left contaminated by a fantasy version of him. Otto haunts Plath's work like a corpse that refuses to sink, making ghostly appearances in poems such as 'Lament', 'On the Decline of Oracles', 'Electra on Azalea Path', 'The Beekeeper's Daughter', 'The Colossus', 'Little Fugue', 'Berck-Plage', 'Daddy' and 'Lady Lazarus'.

In the short story 'Among the Bumblebees' – which had the original title of 'The Two Gods of Alice Denway' – Plath wrote that Otto was a 'giant of a man', a personification of the glories and power of nature itself.[62] In the story, Alice – a barely fictionalised Sylvia – is her father's favourite, his 'pet'. Ever since she was small she could remember people telling her how much she resembled her daddy; Warren, who was often sickly, took after their mother's side of the family. 'Alice's father feared nothing,' Plath wrote. One day, in August 1937, when Winthrop was hit by a dramatic summer storm, Otto taught his daughter to sing the 'Thunder Song', the lyrics of which are preserved in the Smith College archive:

> Thor is angry
> Thor is angry
> Boom boom boom
> We don't care
> We don't' care
> Boom boom boom.[63]

Plath took the incident straight from life and used the lyrics of the song first in the story – she wrote of how her father's voice drowned out the thunder[64] – and again in her 1957 poem 'The Disquieting Muses'. In the story, Plath also relates Otto's talent for handling bees: as a little girl she remembered being amazed that her father could hold a bee in his hand, close his fist and not be stung. One summer, however, her father fell ill and he could no longer take his daughter outside to play with the bees. Plath describes a poignant last scene between father and daughter: although the girl repeatedly says 'father, father' the ill man does not respond to her calls and she turns from him feeling lost and betrayed. The story ends with a comment about the girl's future, how there would never be another man to compare to her father, a man who had walked with her, 'proud and arrogant among the bumblebees.'[65]

One morning in mid-August 1940 Otto stubbed his little toe against the base of his bureau while rushing out of his study on the way to summer school. Later that day he returned home limping, and when Aurelia asked him to take off his shoes and socks it was obvious that his problem was serious: 'the toes were black and red streaks ran up his ankle.'[66] Aurelia called the doctor who, after taking blood and urine samples, diagnosed that he had diabetes mellitus. 'From that day on life was an alternation of hope and fear; crises were interspersed with amazing recoveries only to give way to crises again,' said Aurelia.[67] Otto developed pneumonia and had to be admitted to Winthrop Hospital, where he stayed for two weeks. On his return to Johnson Avenue, Aurelia arranged for Warren to go and stay with his grandparents; Sylvia remained at home, where the nurse who attended Otto tried to involve the girl in her father's care – an old uniform was used to fashion a nurse's outfit for Sylvia and she was given duties such as bringing her father fruit or cool drinks. On the nurse's first day off, Otto suggested to his wife that she take Sylvia out for an hour; after all, he had everything he needed on the table by his bed. After an hour at the beach, Aurelia dropped by the Freemans' house, where Sylvia stayed for supper, but on her return to Johnson Avenue she discovered Otto lying prostrate on the staircase. 'He had left his bed to go downstairs into the garden to look at his flowers,' recalled Aurelia.[68] She dragged him back to his bed, and repeatedly tried calling the doctor who could not be reached. That night Otto developed a fever, and at one point, as Aurelia was sponging his face, he took hold of her hands and said to her, 'God knows, why have I been so cussed!' In her head, Aurelia said to herself, 'All this needn't have happened; it needn't have happened.'[69]

The next day, the doctor arrived with a specialist, Dr Harvey Loder, from the New England Deaconess Hospital, who informed Aurelia that in order to save Otto's life he would have to amputate the leg. As Aurelia handed the doctor his hat he turned to her and said, 'How could such a brilliant man be so stupid?' The operation was carried out on 12 October, and the couple started to make plans for the future. The president of Boston University, where Otto worked, wrote him a note that read, 'We'd rather have you back at your desk with one leg than any other man with two.'[70] Aurelia also took it upon herself to break the news of the operation to her two children: while Warren seemed to accept the news quietly, Sylvia said, 'When he buys shoes, will he have to buy a *pair*, Mummy?'[71] After the amputation, however, Otto fell into a depression; the operation had, to some extent, already sucked the life out of him and on 5 November 1940, while asleep in the hospital, he suffered an embolism and died. He was fifty-five years old.

Aurelia decided to wait until the morning to tell the children of their father's death. She went first to Warren, who was still sleeping in his room, gently woke him and told him that Daddy's sufferings were at an end and that he was now at rest. 'Oh, Mummy, I'm so glad *you* are young and healthy!' he said. The reaction from Sylvia, who was awake and reading, was rather different. After hearing the news, the girl, who had just turned eight, turned to her mother and said, 'I'll never speak to God again!'[72] According to Aurelia, Sylvia 'had been praying every night that her father would be well and would come home. She loved his praise – at that time she was beginning piano lessons and she would play for him and he would tap her on the head and praise her.'[73]

The next day, Sylvia returned from school and handed her mother a piece of paper that read, 'I PROMISE NEVER TO MARRY AGAIN.' Ruth Freeman remembers what had happened that day at school. 'The kids had been mean to her and told her that she was going to have a stepfather,' she says. 'Sylvia stopped by at my house on the way home, she was crying, and my mother assured her that would not happen. Later, at Sylvia's home, she handed her mother that note, and forced her to sign it while we were sitting at the dining-room table. From that point on, Sylvia kept that note folded up in the back of her diary. I'm sure Sylvia thought that she had resolved her issues by making her mother sign that bit of paper, but of course it didn't resolve anything. The Otto she wrote about later was not a daddy she ever really knew – that figure was very much a fantasy.'[74]

Later, after time spent in therapy, Plath would write in her journal about this traumatic time, blaming her mother for what she saw as the 'murder' of her father. She outlined how she hated Aurelia because of her lack of tenderness for Otto. Of course, he was something of a tyrant, she added, but she did not miss him any the less. Why had Aurelia married a relatively old man? "Damn her eyes," she wrote.[75] From her point of view, Aurelia did everything in her power to love and protect her two young children. She decided not to let them attend Otto's funeral – something Plath would use later to rail against her mother – and tried not to let her children see her cry, which was interpreted by Sylvia as indifference. After her husband's death, Aurelia became the family's sole breadwinner because Otto, like Aurelia's father before him, had lost a great deal of money on the stockmarket.[76]

In January 1941 Aurelia secured a job as a teaching substitute at Braintree High School, earning $25 a week for teaching three classes of German and two of Spanish a day. She left home at 5:30 each morning, and left the care of Sylvia and Warren to her parents. At the end of that spring term she managed to get another job, at the junior high school in Winthrop, which would start in September, but she soon found the heavy workload too much. The combination of full-time teaching, plus the extra responsibility of looking after the school's finances, left her exhausted and suffering from the first symptoms of a duodenal ulcer, a condition that would flare up at particularly stressful moments for the rest of her life. Sylvia would later feel resentful of what she saw as her mother's attitude of noble martyrdom, writing in her journal of how her mother had to work around the clock and how she had to scrimp and save. While Aurelia had to make do with the same old clothes, she was proud to be able to buy new outfits for Sylvia and Warren. It was Aurelia's mission, wrote her daughter, to give her children the things that she had never been able to enjoy herself.[77]

Later in life, Plath would become fascinated by the work of Carl Jung, particularly his book *The Development of Personality*. 'In every adult there lurks a child – an eternal child, something that is always becoming, is never completed, and calls for unceasing care, attention and education,' she wrote, transcribing from the book. 'There is no human horror or fairground freak that has not lain in the womb of a loving mother,' she continued. As she read the section on parental expectations and self-sacrifice, Plath must have felt an uncanny sense that the Swiss psychiatrist was writing about her own family. It was, stated Jung, wrong for parents to try to shape a child's personality; the worst thing they could do, he said, was to try to 'do their best' for their offspring, 'living only for them'. This ideal 'effectively prevents the parents from doing anything about their own development and allows them to thrust their "best" down their children's throats. This so-called "best" turns out to be the very things the parents have most badly neglected in themselves. In this way the children are goaded on to achieve their parents' most dismal failures, and are loaded with ambitions that are never fulfilled. Such methods and ideals only engender educational monstrosities.'[78]

Two

MY THOUGHTS TO SHINING FAME ASPIRE

In the summer of 1942, Aurelia was offered the chance to change her life. The dean of Boston University's College of Practical Arts and Letters had asked if she would be willing to develop a course for medical secretaries. 'I looked upon the appointment as providential,' she said later, 'for it would enable us to leave Winthrop and move as far west of Boston as was possible for a person who had to commute to the city daily.'[1]

On 26 October, the day before Sylvia's tenth birthday, her mother sold the family home in Winthrop and, with the help of her parents, bought a small, six-room, white-frame house at 26 Elmwood Road, Wellesley. The town – which, according to one writer, once bore the name 'Contentment'[2] – was well known for its 'fine old trees', the 'handsome buildings [that] have been erected for the public schools', the 'railroad stations' that were 'objects of beauty' and its imposing private residences. 'A vast tract of woodland furnishes paths for long, lonely strolls,' continued the local historian. 'Wellesley, a residential village with no manufacturing, has long been noted for its pure water and invigorating air.'[3]

The move to this more affluent suburb of Boston signalled a new start for the family. The children had been plagued by frequent illnesses – Sylvia with sinusitis, Warren with bronchitis – which, Aurelia believed, had been exacerbated by living so close to the sea. Grammy (Aurelia's mother) had started to suffer from arthritis, which she thought was being made worse by the damp climate, while Grampy (Aurelia's father, who suffered from macular degeneration) had taken a position as maître d' of a local country club after losing his job as a cost accountant with the Dorothy Muriel Company. 'Sylvia felt a little apologetic about her grandfather, Mr Schober, whom she dearly loved, but who had to work as a maître d',' recalled Gordon Lameyer, one of the Plath's boyfriends.[4]

Aurelia – whose ethos of self-improvement ran through her marrow – had her sights set on her daughter's future. She knew that Wellesley had an excellent school system and that the town's women-only liberal-arts college offered a limited number of scholarships to 'outstanding students'. Yet on her income of only $1,800 – the average teacher's salary, according to data from the 1945 census, was $3,600 – she knew it was inconceivable that she could pay for her children to go to college. After the move to Wellesley, the family, in Aurelia's words, was forced to operate within an extremely 'tight margin' and it was necessary for her to 'plan very carefully'.[5] In the words of school friend Betsy Wallingford, then Powley: 'She moved to Wellesley because of the advantages and she wanted Sylvia to go to Wellesley College. Aurelia had to work so hard to support the family – she really didn't have two nickels to rub together.'[6]

Aurelia was confident that she had made the right decision, no doubt subscribing to one former resident's description of Wellesley as a 'fine village [that] is absolutely free from all evil influences which tend to corrupt youth'.[7] However, Sylvia's problems were not external ones; even at this early age, she seemed to have suffered from some sort of mental disturbance. According to her Wellesley friend Philip McCurdy, Sylvia 'tried to cut her throat when she was ten'.[8] He defines this as a 'suicidal gesture',[9] a sign that she wanted to put an end to her life even as it was just beginning. 'I think I was happy up until the age of about nine, very carefree [. . .]' she said later. 'At nine I was rather disillusioned [. . .]'[10]

For the most part she managed to keep the darkness – the feeling of hollowness that occasionally threatened to swallow her – to the periphery of her being. Certainly, those close to her had no idea that she was experiencing psychological troubles of any kind. After all, she was personable, respectable, highly enthusiastic and obviously intelligent. When Aurelia first moved from Winthrop – where Sylvia had been moved up to the sixth grade – she assumed she would place her daughter in the same class in Wellesley until she discovered that all the other children were almost two years older than her daughter. As a result, Aurelia decided it would be best to place Sylvia in the fifth grade at the Marshall Livingston Perrin Elementary School. 'It is the first time in my teaching experience that a mother has requested an all-A pupil be put *back* a grade,' said the principal on hearing Aurelia's request.[11]

'She was such a happy child,' says Betsy, who met her in 1942. 'I remember the day she came into school – as soon as she walked into the classroom there was an instant connection between us. As the day went on, I thought to myself, "We could be friends." From the beginning it was obvious that she was highly creative. There was always a drawing of hers, usually a pencil drawing, on the walls of the school. I can remember one that was of a ship, with lots of sails.'[12]

At this age, Sylvia's journals are full of fragments of poems and snatches of stories that articulate her desire to escape to another, altogether more exotic world. When one looks at the physical realities of Plath's home it's not hard to see why: the two-bedroom house on Elmwood Road was cramped and, at times, living there must have been claustrophobic for its five occupants. A plan sketched by Aurelia shows that on the ground floor there was a living room, dining room, kitchen, a toilet and Warren's room, while upstairs there was a bathroom and two bedrooms, one for Grammy and Grampy, the other for Aurelia and Sylvia. The basement housed a laundry room and a playroom that the children used for study. 'I believed in magic which influenced me a good bit,' Plath said later. Although she maintained that by this age she had 'stopped believing in elves and Santa Claus and all these little beneficent powers and became realistic and depressed', the otherworldly was the central metaphor through which she could express herself.[13] One of her early poems speaks of her special talent to see, hear and converse with the fairy creatures of a private, intimate world she had created for herself. In a note to Aurelia, written in 1942, she says she would like to give her mother all these supernatural qualities – fairy ears, fairy eyes and fairy wings so that she could have access to her secret universe – but, as she realised that this would be impossible, she would try to be a good girl instead.

In the same letter, Sylvia also writes about her love for the book *A Fairy to Stay*, by Margaret Beatrice Lodge, written in 1929. This tells the story of a motherless girl, Pamela, who is sent to live with two aunts who disapprove of children and who dismiss her love of fairy books as silly nonsense. After being sent to bed, the girl – filled with revengeful thoughts – grabs hold of her aunts' scissors and cuts off the braid of her own hair. As punishment, the young girl is forced to keep her uneven hairstyle – long on one side, short on another. But one day, in the garden, she sees a fairy. After the magical being transforms Pamela's hair and wipes away her tears, the fairy takes it upon herself to discipline the mean-spirited aunts.

It would be easy to interpret Sylvia's enthusiasm for the book as a symbol of the anger she felt towards a mother whom she blamed, albeit unconsciously, for the loss of her beloved father; after all, one would only have to substitute Sylvia for Pamela and Aurelia for the wicked aunts. Yet to do so would be to miss the point entirely. Rather, she saw Aurelia as another Pamela. During her childhood – and for much of her early adult life – Sylvia viewed her mother as being an extension of herself, rather than a seperate person. Her writing was done to delight not only herself but also her mother; words fused into some kind of pleasing order became a tool through which she could guarantee her mother's love. In fact, most of Plath's early writing can be seen as one long Valentine card to Aurelia. 'When she was just a little girl, she used to slip a poem or a drawing (she drew and painted beautifully) under my dinner plate as a surprise for me when I came home from work,' said Aurelia. 'She always painted her own birthday cards for us and composed the verses – her humor on these occasions was delightful.'[14]

The habit began in earnest in February 1943 when her mother was rushed into hospital with a gastric haemorrhage. Aurelia stayed in hospital for three weeks, and then spent a week's convalescence at her sister's house in nearby Weston. Each day without fail Sylvia wrote a letter to her mother, often enclosing poems that she hoped would lift her spirits. In one letter, which she wrote just before going to bed, she told her mother that she had spent forty-five minutes practising the piano and that, during a lesson, she had kept reminding herself of the fingering technique her mother had taught her. As a result, the session was a success. She also reported that she and Warren had been very good in her absence – she had made an effort not to tease him – and that at school she had defended him against some bullies. She spent her time writing and drawing pictures, sketches that she also sent over to her mother. Aurelia recalled that, after Sylvia returned with her grandmother and Warren from a trip to see Walt Disney's *Fantasia*, her daughter drew a picture of the 'Dance of the Mushrooms', which she found enchanting. 'Each mushroom had a little face – each different!' recalled Aurelia years later.[15]

In July 1943, when Aurelia suffered another haemorrhage, Sylvia was sent away from home to spend a month at Camp Weetamoe, situated on Lake Ossipee, New Hampshire. She wrote how, after taking the train from Boston to Mountain View, she arrived at camp in the rain; instead of taking a ride on a hay wagon, as was the custom, the girls had to be ferried to the site by car. The postcards that Sylvia wrote to her mother documented her routine: she woke up to the sound of the bugle, breakfasted, swam in the morning and the afternoon, went hiking, harvested blueberries, enjoyed boating on the lake, attended arts and craft classes (where she made a purse for her grandmother), and at night the girls listened to one of the camp leaders reading *The House At Pooh Corner*. She knew she had to be careful with the few dollars Aurelia had given her and she worried whether she should spend the thirty-five cents it cost for six photographs of herself. In the end, she decided it was worth it, but she noted the cost down in one of the letters home to her mother, together with the money she had spent on laundry (seventy-five cents), fruit (twenty cents), two paper-dolls books (Rita Hayworth and Hedy Lamarr, twenty cents) and other necessities (fifty cents). She adored the camp, and at the end of her stay there she wrote outlining how nice it would be if her mother came to bed at the same time as she did – mother and daughter shared a room in the small house on Elmwood Road – so she could tell her all about it.

She had picked up her obsession for the recording of everyday life from Aurelia, who, as we have seen, had a habit of documenting the quotidian details of her daughter's life. Aurelia encouraged her to use all her senses to observe the world and write down what she had experienced. Among the presents Sylvia received during that Christmas of 1943 – some chocolate creams, a Spanish-grammar book, some mittens, a pair of skates, two hair ribbons, an apron and some nail polish – the one gift she treasured most was the pocket diary Aurelia had slipped into her stocking. One suspects that Aurelia must have, at times, rued the day she gave her daughter the tool through which she could note down the details of her day-to-day existence and record the intimate lives of those close to her; after all, the culmination of this compulsion for chronicalisation was Plath's novel *The Bell Jar*, a book that Aurelia found 'a very embarrassing publication' to say the least.[16]

The first entry Sylvia made in her new diary was a resolution to be more pleasant to people; she wanted to show the world that she wasn't a snob. She knew she had a tendency to look down on those who weren't as intelligent or well mannered as she was; in her letters home to her mother in the summer of 1943 she had made several cutting remarks about some fellow campers whom she noticed peppered their talk with common colloquialisms. But in 1944 she was going to try harder to appear like a 'normal' girl. In private, however, she could write whatever she wanted – no matter how rude – and it was to her diary that she confided thoughts or desires that would have been considered impolite or inappropriate. One can sense the joy with which she noted down, in a section entitled 'peculiarities',[17] certain mocking and sarcastic remarks about friends and acquaintances.[18]

In her notebook – a 6-inch-by-3.5 inch volume with the name 'O.E. Plath' embossed on its cover – Sylvia started to jot down ideas for stories. A number of her tales feature a young girl called Nancy – at this time Sylvia loved the Nancy Drew mysteries – who is transported out of her boring, everyday existence by Star, a supernatural creature who appears first as a snowflake. Star transports Nancy into the sky by means of a staircase of snowflakes and she travels to the upper echelons of the planet, where she sees a dazzling white ice palace populated by ice fairies busy making snowflakes and finally secures a session with the Frost Queen. Another story is told from the point of view of a penny from its 'birth' – inside the confines of a black metal box – through its youth, when he meets a number of his fellow coins and is passed from owner to owner, dropped on to the sidewalk and is picked up by a newsboy who hammers a nail into him and wears him around his neck. After being swapped for a peppermint stick he meets a nickel, called Rosie, with whom he falls in love, but their relationship seems doomed when the penny is dropped down a drain. Lonely and depressed the penny contemplates a grim future underground, until finally another coin drops down next to him, which turns out to be Rosie.

Plath, even at this early stage of her life, had a fascination with the dark and the uncanny. In the same notebook, she scribbled down the outline for a story set in a black, claustrophobic, undefined space. Strange, unseen creatures crawl out of sight, beasts that take on hideous characteristics through the power of the narrator's imagination. A woman's head appears – a figure that possesses a monstrous beauty: she has holes for eyes, sockets from which emanate snake-like flames of fire. The narrator is paralysed by fear until the blackness folds itself around her, smothering her, swallowing her. This entry – written when Sylvia was eleven or twelve years old – shares a number of similarities with some of her late journal entries, when Plath would write of being incarcerated in the ground with a grave full of rotting, zombie-like corpses. The one difference is that the young girl in the earlier story still has the capacity to wake up from her nightmare and make a joke about it: at the end of the sketch she blames a half-eaten cheese and sardine sandwich for her bad dream.[19]

The dead fascinated her. In January 1944 she noted in her diary that at Girl Scouts one day Betsy Powley brought along a friend, Gail, whose sister had perished in a car accident. That April she recorded how one Wellesley boy, Bruce Bullard, had died; she couldn't fathom how his existence could be snuffed out in an instant. Although she had been told that Bruce had died in a car accident, the truth was even more difficult to comprehend. 'Bruce and his older brother Bobby, a contemporary of my brother who is one year my senior, were playing a sort of hide-and-seek game with me and my brother, Mark,' says Betsy. 'Bruce hid in a window well of the house next door and when it was time to run and tag the goal (the game was called "Relievo"), Bruce jumped up out of the window well (which was on the front of the house) and hit his head on a window box which fell from its bracket on to his head. Bruce suffered a severe, fatal blow. My dad saw the dreadful event as he sat on our front steps watching our game. I can still picture Bruce's mother, Betty, rushing out of her front door toward her son as he lay on the ground, her hands trembling as she tried to fasten her skirt.'[20]

Sylvia's interior world may have been a skewed one, but she became expert at pretending, fashioning a mask of normality that she could wear when it suited. Perhaps the only clue to the true nature of her personality was her competitive drive, an instinct that, even at this early age, can be described as approaching the pathological. In January 1944, she wrote in her diary that she had been given a mark of 97 in a history test – all the other girls in her class scored less than 90. At the end of April, she boasted in her diary of being the only girl in the school who would start junior high with an average mark of straight A.

One day in the 1944/1945 school year, Dorothy H. Humphrey, then a senior at Boston University's School of Education enrolled on a course in ability testing – particularly the Revised Stanford-Binet tests of Intelligence – returned to her home town of Wellesley to conduct some research. One of her subjects was the eleven-year-old Sylvia Plath. 'She turned out to be a very unusual and exciting "testee",' recalled Humphrey. 'She was keenly interested in the test and seemed to enjoy the whole lengthy procedure. It was lengthy because she continued to answer items correctly at levels far above average for her age. When I scored Sylvia's test I was excited to find that the results indicated an IQ of about 160 [. . .] this is, of course, well into the "genius" classification [. . .] a brilliant and unusual girl.'[21]

Achievement was central to her world, as essential to her as the other great love of her life: books. The two came together in early 1944 when she decided she wanted to add a couple more tokens of accomplishment to her steadily growing collection of Girl Scout badges. The previous year, at summer camp, she had sewn Foot Traveler, Campcraft, Boating and Weaving on to the sleeve of her uniform. By January 1944 she was finally nearing completion of her Reader's badge, which had involved making a reading plan for a period of six months. 'Add to your list as you work on this badge,' said the organisation's bible, the *Girl Scout Handbook*. Other pointers included: 'Select several magazines that you read regularly and compare the kinds of writing in them. Tell what you like about each magazine'; 'Make your own anthology of poems and quotations on a favorite subject'; 'Read a number of poems by different poets in a good anthology or elsewhere, and select several to read aloud or to use as a choral reading at a troop meeting or campfire'; and 'Select a good place in your own home where you can read in comfort and some privacy. Arrange it so that there is a proper reading light and a safe place to keep your books.'[22]

Plath read the advice and, as was her style, not only followed it but exceeded it. During 1944 she produced little illustrated volumes of her own poetry and read a wide range of books – including *Jane Eyre*, *Gone with the Wind* (which she finished in the space of a week), Marjorie Kinnan Rawlings' *The Yearling* (a Christmas present from Ralph and Max Gaebler, the two sons of Otto's friend Hans), a blank-verse retelling of *The Ring of the Nibelung* (a gift from her mother), and *The Little Prince.* At the beginning of the year she was already top of the class in book reports and by April she boasted that she had amassed a collection of 100 titles. A great deal of her reading was done either in bed (a fact that she concealed from her mother) or sitting in the apple tree in the garden of Elmwood Road. It was in this very special place, she said in an essay she wrote two years later, that she found it easy for her imagination to take flight. The dull earth looked further away, the heavens a little nearer. Writing, she said, was not only her favourite hobby, it was also a way in which she could escape into another world – the world of fantasy.[23]

By May 1944 she had won her Writer's badge from the Girl Scouts, after keeping a notebook in which she recorded daily descriptions, ideas for stories or fragments of verse (which she had been doing regularly for two years). 'Develop three ideas, thoughts or feelings,' said the organisation's handbook, a suggestion Sylvia must have sneered at: after all, she had hundreds – thousands! – of ideas, thoughts and feelings; looking back, perhaps she had too many. In the spring, Sylvia, together with her friend Marcia Egan, submitted her work to the local newspaper, the *Townsman*, and she recorded the sensation of exhilaration she felt when she saw her story in print. Seeing her own name gave her a more solid sense of existence and the sight would prove to be addictive; Sylvia would spend the rest of her life pursuing the elusive thrill of the by-line.

Despite her considerable drive and fierce ambition to succeed at everything, Sylvia still managed to set aside time for play. 'At the back of our house we had a yard, the land sloped down into the woods, and there was a stream running through it,' says Betsy. 'Sylvia and I would cut down the ferns, build a frame with branches and weave the ferns to make a little house. We'd get an old blanket, pile ferns on top of this and haul it back to the fern hut. I remember Sylvia calling this "tug-boating Annie". Then we'd sit inside the hut – it was our secret place to hide. We had another game we played which involved hanging from this rope attached to a tree and then jumping down to a circle of stumps on the ground, a game we called, not surprisingly, "stumps". It was huge fun.'[24]

At the beginning of July, Sylvia returned to Center Ossipee in New Hampshire for nearly three weeks of summer camp. This year, in addition to writing her letters home, she also kept a diary, and, for the first time, the young girl began to confide things in her journal that contradicted the missives she would send back to her mother. For instance, in a letter she wrote to Aurelia on 17 July, she told her mother how much she was looking forward to coming home. However, in her diary she confessed that the thought of leaving camp and returning to Wellesley made her feel blue. Later, this gap between the feelings and experiences she thought might make acceptable reading for her mother and the emotions she felt able to express in the privacy of the pages of her diary would widen to such an extent that, in many respects, the two resulting volumes – *Letters Home*, the book edited by Aurelia, and Plath's *Journals* – read like books written by two different women.

For the most part, however, at this age Sylvia still felt especially close to her mother. On her return from camp, she came down with an ear infection – she suffered from a sore throat and earache, and noted in her diary how pus oozed from her ears – and her mother tried to nurse her better. On 25 July she described spending the day making her own paper doll and fashioning clothes for it, and then playing cards with Aurelia, before mother and daughter retired to bed together at a quarter to ten. In the days following, she recorded that her mother gave her *Ladies' Home Journal* to read, that she regularly took her medicine, and that her mother blew sulphur down her throat to treat her infection.

In mid-August, her friend from Winthrop, Ruth Freeman, came to stay for a few days. 'I remember there were only two big rooms upstairs in that Wellesley house,' says Ruth. 'Sylvia and her mother shared one, while Grammy and Grampy had the other one [Warren slept downstairs].'[25] Ruth describes Sylvia as 'not a morbid child – it was all fun and laughter', she says. 'We even had fun when competing. Her talent showed up early and we were always entering drawing or poetry contests in the newspaper. Of course, she would always win and I might get an honorary mention because she had touched up one of my drawings.'[26]

Sylvia started at the Alice L. Phillips Junior High School on 7 September 1944. She got up at 6:30 a.m. and took the bus to school, where she enrolled in seventh grade determined to succeed. Within a matter of weeks, she started to suffer sleepless nights because of the pressure of writing ten book reports in order to win a certificate. In her diary she complained that one morning she felt so tired that she didn't have the energy to walk to the bus stop; yet she pushed herself on, cramming as many activities into each day – lessons, orchestra practice, writing poetry, household chores – adamant that she would do each task to the best of her abilities. She was rewarded by a line of As in her school report, the only criticism being that in English she sometimes rushed her work. Sylvia's passion and enthusiasm for the written word occasionally resulted in work that was a little jumbled. Yet the school teacher recognised that she had a special talent worth developing.[27]

The day after Thanksgiving she started dancing lessons, learning the steps for a range of styles including the Virginia Reel, the polka, the Lindy Hop and the waltz. Later, Aurelia would mount a defence against the portrayal of herself in her daughter's poem 'The Disquieting Muses', in which Plath writes of a mother who pushes her daughter into ballet and piano lessons. The poet writes of a performance when fellow schoolgirls danced, 'Blinking flashlights like fireflies', but she felt her step was wooden and clumsy.[28] On a copy of the typescript of the poem, Aurelia scribbled next to this stanza the words, 'Fusion and violation of actual circumstance'.[29] In a talk she gave to the Wellesley College Club in March 1976, Aurelia expanded on this point. 'She constantly merged incidents in our two lives,' she said of her daughter. 'Sylvia never took ballet lessons. I did, and I had told her of my part as a nine-year-old in a ballet program. I also told her how I loved every minute of it and pretended I was the "prima ballerina", for my proud parents were sitting out front waiting for the moment when I, with a dozen others, would appear on the stage. Her retelling of this incident undergoes great change in her poem.'[30] Plath may have, in Aurelia's terms, fused and violated certain experiences, but that did not mean the poem lacked emotional truth. In the debate over the authenticity of Plath's work – to what extent did her poetic world mirror the real one? – the two women stand at opposite poles, Aurelia trusting in the concrete and the factual, her daughter opting for the dominion of feelings.

Despite their differences, mother and daughter both believed in the transformative power of ambition and hard work. 'Aurelia expected a great deal of her, but Sylvia was just as motivated by herself,' says her friend Louise Giesey White, who knew her through junior high, high school and Smith College. 'We were what you then called "grinds" – we took our studies very seriously. She, like me, would have died if she'd been given a B in one of her classes. Yet I think Sylvia was very angry that she didn't have the same resources as other families in Wellesley. She lived in Wellesley Fells, to the west of the town, while the rest of us lived in Wellesley Hills. In all the time I knew her, she never once invited me to her home; I don't think many of us were. I think Aurelia protected Sylvia, and she didn't want any of her friends going around to the house. Aurelia wanted to keep her home life private.'[31]

When Aurelia went away – as she did in early January 1945, when she visited her friend Marion Freeman in Winthrop for a few days – Sylvia missed her terribly. Their bond was an exceptionally close one: when, on 6 January, twelve-year-old Sylvia came home from school feeling frozen to the bone, her mother warmed her up by taking her into her bed. For Aurelia's birthday that year Sylvia wrote her a poem, accompanied by a little drawing of a figure walking down some tracks, each one signifying another year, into the distant future. In the poem, she tries to cheer up her mother by telling her that, at thirty-nine, she really wasn't that old. She could reminisce about her 'silver years', but she should always keep in mind that her future would be golden.[32]

In January 1945 Aurelia told her children that if they read *The Tempest* and could tell her the story of the play she would buy tickets for them all to see a production in Boston. She gave Sylvia Shakespeare's complete works, and Warren a copy of Charles and Mary Lamb's illustrated version. Warren, then nine and a half, was 'indignant and read the play in the original' too. On 20 January, the family – Aurelia, the two children and Grammy – took the bus to Boston where they saw Margaret Webster's production of the play, which, over the years, would provide a central metaphor for Plath's later work. The experience – the first play the children had ever seen – was magical, and for Sylvia at least something of a turning point in her young life. On the original playbill, Aurelia scribbled that the children were 'completely transported to the magic island of Prospero [. . .] Everything conspired to make this a celestial occasion – even the snowstorm that had been predicted to strike blizzard-force this year, withheld itself. The sun shone instead on the piles of snow already heaped everywhere; the children were well, and our spirits ready to receive "such stuff as dreams are made of . . ." They were spellbound by its magic.'[33] In her diary, Sylvia described the event as the biggest day of her life and described how she had been transported into another world, one that was superior to the one she inhabited. She also recorded an experience in her journal that her mother was not privy to: on the way home from Boston the train had been so crowded the family had had to sit separately and she found herself next to a handsome young man from the navy. She spent the entire journey talking to the blond, blue-eyed sailor about Shakespeare, the world and life in general.

At this point in her life, Sylvia's attitude towards boys was ambivalent. She felt attracted to them – projecting on to them a range of romantic fantasies – but fearful of rejection. One day, in February 1945, she was on her way to school when the bus passed the home of her current obsession, Frank Irish. She plucked up the courage to send him an invitation to the Scout dance later in the month, and confessed to her diary her amazement at his acceptance; after all, she was sure he would turn her down. Yet, only a few days later, after the postponement of the dance due to heavy snow, she wrote in her journal of her dislike for him. 'We were never sweethearts, we were more friends,' says Frank, who knew her from the age of twelve until she was seventeen. 'I was interested in her, but for some reason it never really jelled. My memory of her is of her being incredibly intense, even as a girl. She was sort of wound up, and always determined to do things right. I remember once we went ice skating and she impressed me with her desire to do it properly. She was gritting her teeth, saying to herself, "I'm going to do this right, I'm going to do this right." She was competitive, but not in an obtrusive manner, she wasn't competing to make others feel bad. But everything she did had to be not just good, but perfect.'[34]

After her brief dalliance with Frank she transferred her attentions to Bob Stockbridge, who flirted with her at the Scout dance. After losing in a game of Truth or Consequences – she refused to write her name in the ground using her toes – she was forced to kiss him. She did like him, she wrote in her diary, but she did not want to get into trouble and become a teenage delinquent. She had her reputation to think about – and if one wanted to get on in life, she told herself, one couldn't risk going off the rails. As a result, Bob's name did not grace the pages of her diary again.

Repeatedly, Sylvia had to test herself and place herself in situations that challenged her. One day in the spring of 1945 she was asked if she would do the responsive reading at Sunday school. Her mother had introduced her to the First Unitarian Society of Wellesley Hills and, although Sylvia felt anxious at the thought – so nervous that the colour drained from her face – she went ahead. As she stood at the pulpit she watched the congregation – including the parents of one girl, Barbara Leach, whom she knew looked down at her – as she gave her reading, which went without a glitch. Another day, in her English class at school, the teacher asked if anyone would care to read the poem 'Rules for the Road' by Edwin Markham. Sylvia knew she wouldn't be able to recite it without making a mistake, and so decided against it, but then, all of a sudden, she saw her hand rise in the air. Soon she could hear herself saying, 'Stand straight:/Step firmly, throw your weight:/The heaven is high above your head,/The good gray road is faithful to your tread [. . .]' Despite her fears, the reading was flawless. She was also congratulated in class for her recital of Longfellow's 'The Courtship of Miles Standish' and Emily Dickinson's 'Sunset and Sunrise'. At this point she was writing a poem a day at school. The inspiration for one, 'Enchantment', about the ability of books to transport oneself to another time, another place, came to her in the middle of a class – and her two poems 'March' and 'Spring Parade' published in the spring issue of *The Phillipian* prompted the editor of the paper to comment on the 'excellence and abundance of Sylvia Plath's poems'.[35] She found subjects everywhere – in nature, friends, seemingly insignificant incidents, even a bird that she discovered close to death. On 11 May, she was walking home from school when she saw a blue jay pecking at a little sparrow that had fallen out of its nest. Without a moment's hesitation, she took the creature home, where she fed it segments of worms on a toothpick. She called the bird 'Dickie' and made a nest for it in the garden fashioned out of an old strawberry box and a piece of flannel; she was careful to secure it by a piece of screening so as to protect the bird from the family's cat, Mowgli. On 19 May, the bird wanted to feed itself, and four days later she decided that the creature was in such good health she should return it to the 'wild'. The resulting poem centres on her duties looking after the bird, her urge to mother it, but also a sense of regret that, as she goes about feeding it worms and fussing over it, so much of life is slipping away from her.

On 20 June, she attended the special assembly at school for the presentation of awards. When she didn't hear her name called out for the second prize her heart sank, but then a moment later she heard the words 'Sylvia Plath'. She had won the Wellesley award for the seventh grade. She walked to the front of the hall, climbed the stairs on to the stage and beamed with pride as she received a copy of the Lambs' *Tales from Shakespeare* and a certificate stating that she had won first prize for excellence in English expression. The following day her English teacher, Miss Raguse, presented her with two commendation cards: one for 'outstanding quality of oral and written work' and the other for 'unusual creative work in English'; she also won another commendation card for the excellent work she had undertaken in helping to look after War Stamp sales.[36] At the end of the year she had achieved seven As on her final report card; the only B was for music.

Her reward for all her hard work was two weeks at Camp Helen Storrow on Buzzards Bay, Massachusetts. She travelled to the camp with her friend Betsy Powley, with whom she shared a cabin. Each day she wrote home, letters that describe the camp's various personalities (leaders nicknamed Dash, Flash and Splash – the latter's job was to look after the activities in the water); the wide range of activities for the girls, including swimming in the bay, hiking, folk-dancing, baseball games, arts and crafts, boating and participating in masquerades and variety shows in the evenings (Sylvia loved to rub charcoal into her face and dress up, in her words, as a little 'pickaninny' girl). While she was at camp, she compiled a ninety-page book dedicated to Betsy, a document featuring a colour drawing of a young, blue-eyed girl clutching a few chicks. Inside, we learn a little more about Betsy – that her favourite word was 'fuzzbuttons', her favourite book was *New Worlds for Josie* by Kathryn Worth, and her favourite actresses were Shirley Temple, Judy Garland, Ingrid Bergman, Margaret O'Brien and Elizabeth Taylor – but a great deal more about the twelve-year-old Plath. The first thing one notices when turning the pages of the homemade book is its neatness; there is not a single mistake or correction. Although it is handwritten – in Plath's super-tidy, super-legible handwriting, a style that did not change much throughout her life – it is so ordered that it displays tendencies that can only be called obsessional. Its contents do nothing to dispel the impression. Each day she wrote down her schedule at camp, a list of times and activities that stretches over four pages. Next comes a list of food she ate at camp, a long litany, broken down into quantities and meal times, of cornflakes, prunes, shredded wheat, orange juice, toast, oatmeal, potato salad, vegetable soup, fish chowder, cabbage salad, Ritz crackers, creamed chicken, goulash, baked potatoes, Jell-O, cookies, sandwiches (grape jelly, peanut butter and marshmallow, cream cheese, egg and lettuce), doughnuts, muffins, and many cups of milk. Indeed, her appetite seems to have been so enormous – at any one meal she could consume enough food for three or four girls – that she got a reputation as something of a glutton. Yet the girl, who was tall for her age, never seemed to gain any excess weight.

Just as she documented each plateful of food, so she recorded the number of paces (5,580) it took her to walk one mile across a dirt track to Fisherman's Cove. She also wrote down the number of nails that she had managed to pick up in a contest to see who could collect the most tacks left on the ground after a barn had been dismantled (420 herself; her unit collected 4,652). Earlier in her journal, Sylvia – who, at the age of twelve, said she kept a diary because it helped steady her mind – had also made a note of the number of peanuts (154) she had hidden in the garden for her brother's birthday party. She also counted the letters she received from her mother during summer camp and boasted that she was the envy of all the other girls because of their quantity and length. As each letter was a token of love she surmised that surely she was loved more than any other girl.

Aurelia had brought up her children with the knowledge that there was a correlation between good behaviour and love. On Sylvia's return from summer camp, Aurelia took her daughter and Warren into Boston. First they went to the dentist, where Sylvia had three fillings, and then, as a treat, to the H. E. Harris & Co. stamp company. There she bought the children – both keen stamp collectors – a pack of 100 Danish stamps, which she made it clear would be given out (at the rate of no more than one a day) if they behaved well. On the day of Sylvia's thirteenth birthday, Aurelia made a card for her daughter with a specially composed verse:

Oh, dear, my head's awhirl
Today, my darling,
You're my teen-age girl!

Your life's been happy?
You wish no change?
Why, my sweetheart
That isn't strange.[37]

As Sylvia started the eighth grade she appeared, to the outside world at least, as a normal, young teenage girl. She went to dancing lessons with her friend Perry Norton; attended Sunday school regularly; enjoyed playing the viola in the school orchestra (in November she played at a concert at Tremont Temple, the Baptist church in Boston); and continued achieving high marks at school (100 per cent in spelling tests, a string of As on her report card). At the beginning of the academic year, in assembly, Principal James Thistle outlined the formula for success at school, which he described as plenty of hard work plus a wide range of stimulating abilities together with what he called the 'X-factor'. Plath had the latter in abundance, but at this early stage of her life it was still undefined. Her teachers, even in junior high, recognised that she had enormous potential and in early 1946 her English teacher, Mrs Warren, told her that she had an extraordinary talent for the subject, that her essays were equal with those a professor might expect of a college student and that she should definitely consider applying to study English on a scholarship.

In February she started to keep a dream book, noting down her night-time visions of escape (a sledge that travelled around the globe; being inside a rocket that shot up from Earth and journeyed to Mars). More often than not she suffered from grotesque nightmares: the bad dreams continued all year – visions of dead bodies, of murder, of unspeakable atrocities. In May, with her new friend Margot, she started to write a three-page murder mystery called 'The Mummy's Tomb' about a young girl who is fascinated by ancient Egypt and who one day goes to a museum to do a spot of research. There, she notices the stench of decomposing flesh coming from one of the mummy cases and sees a suspicious-looking janitor. On her return the next day, she witnesses the white-haired janitor preparing to remove the eyes from one of his female victims. The killer spots her and comes towards her, declaiming the unspeakable tortures that he will inflict upon her, but the girl strikes him with her umbrella, ties him up, frees the woman he was about to kill and, at the end, learns she will receive a reward for the rescue.

Gothic stories such as 'The Mummy's Tomb' gave the young Plath an outlet through which she could express some of the toxic feelings that, at times, astonished and frightened her. She used the poem 'Riddle' to explore the enigma of her identity;[38] she realised she was, as she said, an 'ugly introvert'[39] and, plagued by the onset of acne, she felt increasingly self-consciousness and unattractive. At times, she thought her spots were so bad that she confined herself to her house rather than risk the embarrassment of meeting friends and acquaintances. During the summer of 1946, again at Camp Helen Storrow, Sylvia placed a bandage over a spot on her nose that looked like it was mutating into a growth. One day, her friend Gayle pulled off the sticking plaster with such force that she ripped off the top layer of Sylvia's skin. She clasped a handkerchief to her nose, but it soon turned red. She repeated the process; that handkerchief too filled with blood before she could stop the flow. One girl shrieked out that she should run to the nurse: if the injury wasn't dealt with immediately she would get cancer. Sylvia's reaction was unusual: while most girls of her age would have cried out in pain or astonishment, she started laughing. But her laughter was of the hysterical kind – she admitted that she was frightened – and soon her body was racked by sobs. Some of the girls thought she had turned insane. She was taken to the nurse, and the physical wound healed, yet the psychological symptoms that underlay her reaction were not so easily remedied. The incident can be read as a symbol of the state of Sylvia's emotional template: intense, dramatic and contradictory.

At the age of fourteen, according to her close friend Philip McCurdy, Sylvia once again tried to harm herself, this time by cutting her face. The two did not discuss the incident in great detail, but McCurdy believes that Sylvia would have used 'a single-edged razor blade, [which was] the choice for several troubled teenagers I worked with later in my life.'[40] Sylvia's 'teenage cutting'[41] was a manifestation of aspects of her self – memories, half-memories, fantasies, desires, hatreds, hopes – that she had tried to keep hidden. But what was the source of her problem, she asked herself. The fact that she was unable to come up with a clear interpretation for her own strange behaviour frustrated and angered her even more.

Later, Plath would repeatedly draw on incidents and recollections from this time of her life. However, not all her memories can be relied upon. In her autobiographical essay 'Ocean 1212-W' she recalls walking down to the sea outside her Winthrop home and finding a monkey carved from wood. Plath invests the statue with a near-mythical quality, describing it as a 'simian Thinker'. She outlined the fact that, at some point, she lost this 'Sacred Baboon', one of the many possessions from her childhood that she had mislaid.[42]

There is a reason why Plath no longer possessed the wooden monkey: she wasn't its owner in the first place. In the same essay, she also states that she came across the figure on the day her mother brought her baby brother home from the hospital in 1935. Yet, as her unpublished diary reveals, it was actually discovered by David, the elder brother of her friend Ruth

Freeman, ten years later. On a visit to the Freemans' home, in December 1945, the young Plath writes of David's magical find and how the three children sat around after supper to draw the monkey, which they called Simba. In February 1946, she painted the figure during one of her art classes at school. 'Sylvia wrote about finding this African monkey, which I still have, but actually David and I found it on the beach, when it had been washed up during the war,' says Ruth. 'All kinds of things would be swept up on the shore. I remember once when I was down by the ocean with Sylvia that all these things that looked like balloons were brought up on to the beach by the sea. We ran inside, all excited, carrying them, saying, "Look at all the balloons we found!" but we got a talking to. They were not balloons at all, but condoms.'[43]

At this age, Sylvia was still terribly naïve, sensitive and vulnerable. At the end of April 1946, she plunged into a depression after learning that her fountain pen had been stolen. In her diary, she wrote that the loss transformed her spirits, how the theft had left her feeling full of bitterness and how all the colour had been leached from her world. It wasn't only the disappearance of the pen that upset her: the pen had cost ten dollars, and she knew her mother could not buy a replacement at short notice. Everything Aurelia bought she had to work and save for, and she brought up her two children to be careful with money. Whenever the young Sylvia encountered families that were richer than her own she noted down the details in her diary. In the summer of 1945, she had been invited to the home of Nancy Wiggins, which she described as being the grandest and most gorgeous house she had ever seen, where she enjoyed a mouth-watering lunch served by a maid. In fact, Plath's early diaries are full of economic transactions, recordings of how she spent her fifty-cent weekly allowance. A viola lesson cost fifty cents, a piano lesson a dollar. At the back of her 1945 diary,

Sylvia constructed a table of figures – a grid of incredible neatness and precision – detailing her spending. In December of the previous year, she had saved twelve dollars, a sum that increased to fifty-seven dollars at the end of 1945. For Christmas that year she spent $13.56 on presents for seventeen people, including an embroidered towel for her mother, costing fifty-nine cents, and a bookmark for her grandmother, the most expensive gift at $2.50. When she went away to Camp Helen Storrow, during the summer of 1946, she noted down everything she spent: $1.20 on materials for arts and crafts, ten cents on postcards, ninety-three cents for stamps, twenty-five cents for a sketchpad.

'Sylvia did worry about money,' recalls her friend Perry Norton. 'She was a thrifty sort of person and I know her family had to be very frugal. Their house was small, but adequate, and looking back it was obvious there was a difference between our families. We were secure because my father, who was a professor of history at Boston University, had the kind of position he would not lose in an economic downturn. Although there was a mantra in our family that we were not well off, this was my mother's way of teaching her children to downplay the fact that we were actually very well off indeed.'[44]

In order to supplement her allowance, Sylvia earned twenty-five cents an hour for babysitting. She drew on her experiences for a school essay entitled 'From the Memoirs of a Baby Sitter'. In the four-page composition – which received an A-minus – Plath wrote how, each Sunday, she had to look after three children: two boys, Donnie and Cookie, and a baby. In her view, children were far from the little angels of popular perception; rather they were nothing but an inconvenience. The only saving grace was that, while babysitting, she was allowed to listen to one of her favourite radio serials, *The Shadow*, which featured a crime fighter with psychic powers. Plath would remember, years later, the words of actor Frank Readick Jr, who introduced the programme with, 'Who knows what evil lurks in the hearts of men? The Shadow knows!'[45]

In the days before the start of ninth grade, Sylvia occupied herself by learning how to type; reading (Dickens' *A Tale of Two Cities*, which she adored, and Emily Bronte's *Wuthering Heights*, which she found too depressing); writing poetry (which she did in bed, with a temperature of more than 100°); and, together with her family, travelling to Westford to see friends Max and Carolyn Gaebler. Max would later write fondly of Sylvia and Warren, stating that 'they were delightful children [. . .] they were bright and sunny and eager, a wonderful audience for any story a visitor chose to read them and spirited companions for a walk on the beach or a visit to the playground.'[46] Yet, in her diary, Sylvia wrote a barbed attack on Max, accusing him and Carolyn of stuffing down the contents of the family's picnic, lampooning him for what she read as arrogance and pomposity, and attacking him for boasting about his stamp collection (which numbered 30,000). Next to the entry is a drawing of a turkey, the creature she thought he most resembled.

Later, after her daughter's death, Aurelia would maintain that the spiteful caricatures that peppered *The Bell Jar* were symptomatic of a warped mind influenced by depression or a twisted personality brought on by a botched session of electroconvulsive therapy (ECT). Yet this description of Max shows that Sylvia already had a tendency to write cruel comments about those close to her. Her diary also illustrates a highly sexualised nature, a trait that makes itself visible only for it to be suppressed. A week before her fourteenth birthday, Sylvia sketched a portrait of a blousy redhead girl with swollen breasts and heavy make-up. One can almost feel the yearning ooze off the page. Yet next to this entry, Sylvia wrote of her regret at soiling her diary with such vulgar material, maintaining that she would make an effort to control the impure side of her personality.

Friends and family saw only her polite, respectable, caring side – the girl who could write a tender poem about the death of junior-high-school teacher Catherine Cox, published in *The Phillipian* in November 1946, which also carried two of her poems, 'The Promise' and 'October'. At this time, Plath was still obsessed by the American poet Sara Teasdale – who committed suicide by taking an overdose of sleeping pills in 1933 at the age of forty-nine – and she aspired to be able to write like her. She had first copied one of Teasdale's poems, 'The Falling Star', into a notebook in 1945. In retrospect, the verse could be applied to Plath's own life.

> I saw a star slide down the sky,
> Blinding the north as it went by,
> Too burning and too quick to hold,
> Too lovely to be bought or sold,
> Good only to make wishes on
> And then forever to be gone.[47]

In February 1947, Plath said she was in the mood to write 'thundery' poetry.[48] The only problem was that she felt she had not had enough life experience to pull it off. She did not lack aspiration, however. The same month, in her poem 'Fireside Reveries', which was published in *The Phillipian* (but not included in the *Collected Poems*), she wrote, 'My thoughts to shining fame aspire', a line that could be used to sum up her ambitions at this time.[49] Her drive was phenomenal, her ego extreme, her vision quite clear. At the beginning of the year, she bought a scrapbook, measuring fourteen inches by twelve inches, into which she started to paste photographs of herself, accompanied by a mini-autobiography. There was something about herself that fascinated her. In her diary, still addressing herself, she said that one day she would be the world's greatest author and artist. Sylvia also recorded in her diary, in February 1947, that she wanted to achieve something that had never been accomplished before – the award of a sixth letter at the end of junior high. By June, she had amassed enough credits to qualify for the award, and she was bold enough to walk into the principal's office and tell James Thistle of the fact. He was, as she detailed in her diary, so shocked that he nearly fell over.

On June 6, in her yellow taffeta dress, she attended the senior graduation, where she played in the orchestra; then, five days later, at the special assembly, she enjoyed her own moment – or rather moments – of glory. As soon as she sat down, after receiving one award, she had to climb the stairs on to the stage to receive another. The list was extraordinary: a Wellesley Club award for 'excellence in English expression', for which she was given a copy of Cleanth Brooks' and Robert Penn Warren's *Understanding Poetry: An Anthology for College Students* (a book which she subsequently devoured); awards for fifth and sixth letters (relating to her high credit score at school); commendation cards for excellence in art, her record of As and Bs over the last three years, and punctuality; an honourable mention in a national poetry competition; and a prize for her art work from a contest organised by the Carnegie Foundation. After the ceremony, she found herself clutching a thick raft of coloured certificates all emblazoned with golden seals. Dizzy with achievement, Sylvia attended the school dance in the afternoon; after returning home at 6:15, she settled down to do her homework.

'I think you're either born with that kind of drive or you're not,' says her school friend Betsy Wallingford. 'She had a great deal of energy, positive energy. She wanted to experiment with everything in life – and whatever she experimented with, she excelled at.'[50]

Sylvia noted in her diary that, while one friend planned to celebrate her graduation from high school by attending the International Music Festival in Denmark in 1950, she would try to focus on fulfilling her dream: to win acclaim in the world of journalism, book illustration, or fashion design. Once she established herself then she could enjoy the rewards that came with travel.

Some of her ambitions, however – particularly those that related to popularity – did not come to fruition. She went to great efforts, for instance, to win the post of school secretary, constructing a makeshift boat (emblazoned with the words, 'Sylvia for secretary'), that she planned to sail across the stage. If the school voted for Sylvia, she said, they could expect her to sail straight and true through choppy waters. However, when the boat got stuck in the door (it was being pulled by two lackeys) the hall full of children roared with laughter. Whether this was the reason for the vote of no confidence it was difficult to tell, but the position went to another girl. It seems as though the plan to use the election to boost her profile backfired, as she became less popular, not more, and she became the victim of a series of mean-spirited slurs. She also lost out on top place in the spelling bee, held at the beginning of the year, when she misspelled the word 'apparel'. In retrospect, as she confided to her diary, it was more seemly that she had lost to a boy, Bill. It was, she said, always better to have a boy win such a contest.[51]

Sylvia's identification with her work was total. One day at the end of May 1947, in her private art lesson, she finished a still life using the pastel set that she had received for Christmas. It was a rare thing: a representation (a Chinese jug with a bunch of grapes, an orange and some cherries) of which she was proud. She duly took the artwork home, where her mother, Grammy and Warren were admiring it when the doorbell rang. Just as Sylvia's grandmother went to answer it she tossed her apron on to the table and Sylvia stared in horror as the apron brushed against the pastel. Although she said to Grammy, 'Don't worry, I can patch it up,' privately in her diary she confessed her feelings of anger and devastation. Later that night, she wrote a poem – in Aurelia's words, the 'first [. . .] containing tragic undertones'[52] – expressed in a voice that she herself recognised as fresh and original. The poem, 'I Thought That I Could Not Be Hurt', articulates the extremes of emotion that she experienced before, during and after the incident: the intensity of joy at being alive, soon followed by the blackness of despair. The young Plath – still only fourteen – used the seemingly trivial accident to symbolise the fragility of the human heart.[53]

It was at this time, during the summer of 1947, that Sylvia started to record in detail her thoughts about boys, in diary entries that reflect the fervour yet transience of her feelings. On 18 June she took the bus into Boston, where she went to the dentist for a filling, and then bought a copy of *Seventeen* magazine and an evening dress with a white brocaded bodice and puffed sleeves in a sale for five dollars. On the journey into the city, Sylvia documented her exchange with Tommy Duggin, whom she noted would make the perfect boyfriend. He was tall (always an imperative for her), chatty (without being pompous), attractive and well built. On another trip into Boston, in July (after nearly two weeks spent at a sailing camp in Martha's Vineyard), she went to the movies to see *Cynthia*, starring Elizabeth Taylor. Sylvia identified closely with the film, which tells the story of a frail, sheltered young girl who rebels against her overprotective parents, secures a boyfriend and experiences her first kiss at the school prom. In her diary, Sylvia noted that watching the movie helped her address a number of her own emotional issues – particularly, one suspects, her feelings surrounding her developing sexuality and her relationship with her mother, who could at times be possessive. On the return trip, as the bus stopped, a group of boys spotted Sylvia on board and started calling out, 'Blondie'; one boy even went so far as to push his hand through one of the open windows and pull her hair. People on the bus turned around to look at the commotion, and Sylvia blushed at the attention. She didn't mind the boys' behaviour; indeed, she found the whole incident a boost to her self-esteem.

On 15 July, three days later after the hair-pulling incident, Sylvia travelled back into Boston with her mother to see Aurelia's friend, Madeline, and her son Redmond, who was nearly seventeen. At that first meeting, at Steuben's restaurant, the attraction between the young couple was instant. Redmond thought that she was nearly sixteen (she was actually three months shy of fifteen), and Sylvia didn't think it necessary to correct him. After talking in the restaurant, they all walked across Boston Common where the women sat down on some chairs. Out of sight of the adults, the teenagers sat together and Redmond proceeded to place his hand on top of hers as the couple watched the lights from an airship overhead. Later that night, Sylvia confessed to her diary of her passionate thoughts for Redmond and the strange way he had made her feel. For the next few days she went around – to the conservatory in Boston, where she was having piano lessons, to the movies and to Wellesley College to see a production of *The First Mrs Fraser* – in a kind of daze. At the theatre and in the cinema, she pretended that Redmond was sitting next to her and she repeatedly dreamt about him (in Technicolor). She had so much energy and joy that it seemed to overflow, she said. When she went to see *Gone with the Wind* she identified with Scarlett O'Hara, who in one of the early scenes is surrounded by a flock of young men. One day in August, Redmond's mother, Madeline, telephoned the house, and the call was enough to trigger in Sylvia a cluster of feelings that reduced her to tears, a reaction that surprised her. In preparation for a date with Redmond she went to the hairdresser's – she regarded her long hair, with its lowlights of blonde and burnished copper, as one of her best features – but the stylist cut too much off and she was left, once again, close to tears. Betsy Powley's mother cheered her up by restyling it and, after a session using curlers and a hot fan, her confidence was restored.

On 30 August she spent the whole morning getting ready – she wore a blue dress with a white polka-dot pattern, and a white gardenia in her hair – before she travelled into Boston, together with her mother and Warren, for the date. Despite the fact that they enjoyed a boat trip on the Charles River, during which Redmond put his arm around her, the engagement did not live up to expectations; Sylvia found him boring and uncommunicative. In her diary, she questioned whether Redmond himself had changed or whether she had simply adjusted her view of him. Redmond did not make another appearance in her diary; the dream was over. The incident illustrates, even at this early stage, Plath's tendency to project on to those around her, desires, fantasies and motivations that often had no bearing on reality. The disparity between her imagination – or what could be called the spirit of Ariel – and the world of the real would only grow more extensive over time.

Three

THE GHOST OF SOMEBODY ELSE

At the beginning of September 1947, Sylvia enrolled at Gamaliel Bradford High School. From the moment she met her new English teacher, Wilbury Crockett, she declared him to be an inspiration. 'Bespectacled and slightly stooped, with a crew cut revealing a receding hairline even in his mid-30's, Mr. Crockett rarely raised his voice,' remembers one contemporary. 'When he strode into class from the teachers' lounge, a few cigarette ashes flaked on what seemed to be his one sport coat, he was simply silent until we were. His green-gray eyes, the same color as his sport coat, swept around the classroom – where there were about 20 of us, seated at tables formed seminar-style into a u-shape – and when his eyes stopped, they penetrated.'[1]

In one of Sylvia's first classes, he played to his new students recordings of Edna St Vincent-Millay's 'The Ballad of the Harp-Weaver' and 'Renascence', read by the poet, a performance that Plath thought was so tender that she was almost moved to tears. That day, she returned home and wrote what she considered two of her best poems to date, 'Alone and Alone in the Woods Was I' and 'City Streets'. She noted in her diary that the experience had helped purge her spirit and that now, feeling cleansed, she would be fresh and perceptive enough to be able to create more poems.

Whereas almost half the original pupils dropped out of the class within a matter of days because they considered it too demanding, Sylvia flourished. 'Mr Crockett's classroom was a kind of new-world Academy,' recalls one former student, 'without the olive trees, and like Plato's famous school it was conducted largely by dialogue. There was little instruction in grammar, no lectures on literary history or Elizabethan England or biographies of authors, no list of literary terms to memorize, few in-class exercises or quizzes or examinations, no prepping for the SAT exams (even though Mr Crockett was a reader for many years for the College Board at Princeton). The only quiz I remember was one hastily composed on the spot to embarrass us for not having completed some assignment, and it was not graded. The one examination that I can recall was at the end of sophomore year. There was a single question, based on an assigned reading: "Write an essay on the following quotation from Alfred North Whitehead: What is known is nothing, philosophically speaking."'[2]

Crockett recognised Sylvia's talents early. In one of the first classes, in September 1947, each student had to analyse a Matthew Arnold paragraph and then deliver a paper about it. Whereas, as she wrote to her mother (who had to go into hospital to have uterine polyps removed), most students received only a polite nod from Crockett or a simple 'thank you', when Sylvia had finished the teacher turned to her and declared, 'Very well said.'[3] As she heard the words Sylvia glowed with pride. In her diary she confessed to adoring Crockett, the man they nicknamed 'Davy'; she felt stimulated by his teaching and laughed at his jokes, such as the one about a pupil who, in an exam, wrote out the title of Wordsworth's poem 'Intimations of Immortality' as 'Imitations of Immorality'. Crockett 'led his students on a search for understanding and for moral conduct, a search that was governed by his concern with language, and with the ideas and values that language expresses. His conviction that human beings, even young ones, could act intelligently and honorably had the effect of turning on a switch deep inside his students.'[4]

Each year, Crockett gave his pupils, still in high school, a reading list of between forty and forty-five books – everything from Greek drama and philosophy through Shakespeare and classic American authors such as Hawthorne, Thoreau, Emerson, Dickinson, Crane and Melville to modern writers such as Tolstoy, Flaubert, Dostoevsky, Woolf, Lawrence and Joyce. Each work – which they had to either find in the town's library or buy – had to be not only read but also analysed, discussed, debated and absorbed. It was not a case of working on a select number of set texts or through an established canon; Crockett wanted his students to think and respond to literature. 'He believed that literature was itself a discussion, an experiencing, of the world's great events, ideas, and truths, and he flung us headlong into that discussion as if we were mature enough to handle it,' remembers a former student. 'He also believed that there was a difference between what we read and what we knew, that information was converted to knowledge by being digested and reformulated in careful speech and precise writing. Intellectually, it was sink or swim, and we struggled daily to stay afloat by trying to express ourselves coherently in class and on paper.'[5]

It was clear that Sylvia did more than just stay afloat: she positively sped ahead, energised and transported by the intellectual rigour of the class. On 10 September she gave a few of her poems to Crockett, who proceeded to read four of them to the class. According to her diary entry, the teacher said 'Alone and Alone in the Woods Was I' and 'I Thought That I Could Not Be Hurt' were her best and proclaimed that she had 'a lyric gift beyond the ordinary'.[6] Yet, in the same entry, she doubted whether her skill at composing poetry would do anything to boost her popularity at the school. The next day, she confessed in her diary that she had been so animated by Crockett and his nonconformist methods of teaching that she was being forced to question certain truths, regarding religion and human nature, that she had always taken for granted.

Her perspectives were broadened further when, on 14 December, she travelled into Boston with her Sunday-school group and Minister Bill Rice to visit the Charles Street jail. On the journey into the city the pastor, who also served as minister of the prison, related the background of some of the inmates – a black prostitute who repeatedly found herself in jail for her crimes; a man who had made a series of broadcasts for German radio during the Second World War; plus a smattering of murderers, gunmen and thieves. Sylvia recorded the visit in precise detail in her diary, relishing the unsettling atmosphere of the jail. She recalled how she had walked up to the wooden door in the brick wall and remembered how her minister opened the lock with an enormous key. Inside, an attendant unlocked a set of inner doors and she stepped into a large room the height of three storeys. As she strained her head to look upwards, she saw a sea of faces gazing down at her. She climbed the stairs and made her way along an extremely narrow walkway; at one point the passage became so tight that she was fearful that one of the inmates might push her over and she would fall to her death. On her way to the small Protestant chapel a handsome boy who had committed an armed robbery stopped to stare at her, and inside the place of worship she encountered more eccentric characters: an old women wearing a dress made from what looked like rags; a black prostitute who had a fabulous figure; a woman with bleached blonde hair and wearing a pink satin blouse; a man who played the piano in the chapel who found himself in prison after 'borrowing' money from the bank where he worked to pay for his wife's operation; and a group of giggling women, one of whom asked Sylvia if she had never seen a prisoner before. During the service, which was attended by both sexes, the women repeatedly used foul language but the men, on the whole, remained quiet. After the service the tour continued on to the padded cells and solitary units, where the warden incarcerated them for a few minutes; apparently this was his idea of 'fun'. The highlight of the visit for Sylvia was her talk with a young man who had constructed a church out of matchsticks.

Sylvia admired this kind of achievement: artistic herself, she respected others who could shape something concrete out of next to nothing. Driven by aspiration and ambition, she wanted to fashion something akin to a matchstick church for herself: a self that she could build from the fragments and scraps of her personality. At this time, she worried about the ease with which she could see points of view other than her own. Perhaps this was due, she said, to a feeling of inferiority that haunted her – indeed, in 1948 she wrote a poem in which she stated that her identity was about as sturdy as a soap bubble – and she maintained that she would try to construct a personality that was more robust and resilient. This new identity, however, would only ever be a façade, a veneer that was highly porous and unstable. It's not surprising then to learn of Sylvia's empathy and identification with Virginia Cunningham (played by Olivia de Havilland), the central character in the 1948 film *The Snake Pit*, who wakes up in a mental asylum with no memory of how she arrived there. In a review that Plath wrote while still in high school, she outlined why she believed that the character of Virginia was a symbol of all patients who suffered from mental illness and how madness, in her opinion, was often measured and defined by its social and cultural context. She said that, like the majority of viewers of the film, she felt a sense of "oneness" with Virginia. The director showed the audience that patients in psychiatric hospitals were the responsibility of society and should be treated with respect, kindness and compassion.[7]

Influenced by Crockett, and while still in high school, Plath started to make a reading list of her own, a list of books that every good home should own. It included reference guides (*Roget's Thesaurus*, *Webster's New International Dictionary*), the complete works of Shakespeare, Emerson's essays, William James' *Varieties of Religious Experience*, Thoreau's *Walden*, novels by Fielding, Austen, Dickens, George Eliot, Hardy, Lewis Carroll, Cervantes, Dostoevsky, Henry Miller, Willa Cather, Thomas Wolfe, Mann and Rolland's *Jean-Christophe*, the last of which Crockett expected his pupils to read (all 1576 pages of it) in the space of a week. 'Sylvia was what was called a "Crocketteer", one of Crockett's intellectuals,' says Philip McCurdy, who himself belonged to the same elite group, albeit a couple of years after Plath. 'Crockett would stand at a lectern, at the open end of the classroom, inside of which all the chairs would be arranged like a U. Sylvia and I both bonded over the fact that we loved learning, and we responded particularly well to Crockett's classes. We weren't from the wealthiest families in town, but we knew that if we wanted to go to good colleges we would have to establish academic records that were impeccable. There was a lot of pressure, but there's no question that we enjoyed it.'[8]

Sylvia first met Philip on 16 September when she came home from school to find him enjoying a plate of milk and cookies with her mother and brother. Philip, who was new to the area, had been travelling home on the bus when he had needed to use the bathroom. He got talking to a boy close to his age, Warren Plath, who offered the use of his house. At Elmwood Road, Aurelia made him comfortable until Sylvia returned. The two started chatting and discovered they had a lot in common (learning, books, a love of biology) and, over time, they became good friends. 'I loved the enthusiasm of her,' he says. 'Her nickname for me was "Baby", and she would say things like, "Oh, look at this beetle I found, Baby." We played tennis together on the beaten-up courts in the old school and I would go on nature walks. A couple of times I'd sneak out of my house at night and go and meet her in the park and we would lie down and look at the constellations. As I got to know her, I realized she was a rabid intellectual, she loved school and she was curious to an extraordinary degree.'[9]

Sylvia was particularly intrigued to learn of Philip's complicated family life. 'When I was eleven a teacher, at my school in Brookline, Massachusetts, asked me to go to the office and collect some student records,' he says. 'When I was there, I picked up this stack of sheets, and of course I looked through the records until I found mine. There, I read that the woman whom I thought was my mother was not my mother. In fact, my real mother was none other than my sister, Elizabeth. When I came home from school, my "mother" asked me what I had learnt in school that day. I replied, "That you're not my real mother," and turned to my sister and added, "but Betty is." It did not make for a terribly happy meal. When I told Sylvia this she was fascinated. She was transfixed by the fact that I had never known my father and she would say to me, "With me, baby, you're going to find you are one of the lost princes of Spain." My story helped her, in some ways, with the loss of her own father. She knew that it was not necessary for Otto to die and she still missed him.'[10]

In 1947, Sylvia composed a poem called 'Bereft', which can be read as an early companion piece to later father-centric works such as 'Full Fathom Five', 'Electra on Azalea Path', 'The Colossus', 'Little Fugue' and 'Daddy'. The poem, still unpublished, takes the form of a lament to an unnamed figure who leads the poet down to the sea and says goodbye forever; as Plath herself said, she associated her dead father with the ocean and later would imagine him as a kind of sea god, a submarine Prospero. In the poem, she watches the tide come in and wash away the person's footprints – yet her reaction is much more complicated than one of straightforward mourning. While she notes the deep pain the leave-taking has caused, she also relates her pleasure that the figure has disappeared from her life, since she recognised that he represented an aspect of her character that troubled her. The ambivalence of emotion – the fusion of yearning and exultation, longing and liberation, agony and ecstasy – that informs her later poetry is foreshadowed in 'Bereft'. In fact, many of the poems she wrote around this time, with titles such as 'Obsession', 'Recognition', 'Reflection', 'Earthbound' and 'Tulips at Dawn' (all composed in 1948) articulate classic Plathian themes, such as the mysterious nature of identity, the fear of self-knowledge and the sinister nature of seemingly normal everyday existence.

Her encounters with boys also provided a steady source of inspiration for her poetry. In 'Have You Forgotten' (1948), she writes of the winter walks she took with a companion, under the starlit sky, but questions whether the boy still remembers her. Underneath the title she added the initials P. N., a clue to the identity of the boy: Perry Norton, her former dance partner. In the autumn of 1947, Sylvia and Perry had become particularly close. The relationship, once purely platonic, sparked into a romance in October, when Sylvia, now almost fifteen, went to the sophomore icebreaker. She had resigned herself to dancing with her friend Priscilla, but then Perry asked her if he could accompany her to the school gym, which had been decorated with strings of coloured lights. After the dance – during which they hardly spent a minute apart – Perry walked her home and told her how sweet her hair smelt and how charming she was compared to other girls. As the two teenagers were walking through the Wellesley streets, a pair of kittens started gambolling next to them, at times so close that they nearly tripped over them. As they were crossing a road, a speeding car came out of nowhere and, although they were unharmed, one of the kittens was killed. Perry picked up the dead but unbloodied creature while Sylvia took the other one home, where she released it. The incident, however, did not spoil an otherwise enjoyable evening; her diary entries suggest that she was determined to remain enveloped by a romantic reverie.

Whereas previously she had always regarded herself as something of a clever but not overtly popular girl, now she was determined to channel her intelligence and drive into constructing herself as a classic all-rounder. To go to a dance with a boy was a trophy worth winning for the competitive Sylvia; the absence of an invitation meant social death. While at high school she would also endure the humiliating process of initiation into the sororities that went by the names 'Subdeb' and 'Sugar 'n' Spice', something she would later write about in her autobiographical essay 'America! America!' At the beginning of each new academic year, a series of cards would be sent out from members of the select group to certain girls, those who were beautiful or popular.[11] She remembered how, during her initiation week, she was forbidden from washing, wearing make-up, combing her hair, changing her clothes or speaking to boys. She had to make her 'Big Sister's' bed, carry the older girl's books, walk behind her to school, and follow every order she barked at her – whether it was to hang from a tree, ask passers-by a range of ridiculous questions or walk into shops and ask for perished grapes or rancid rice. At the end of a typical day she felt exhausted, shaped as she had been into 'an Okay Image.'[12] She later wrote about the process in the short story 'Heather-Birds' Eyebrows'. The title came from a conversation that occurred while Sylvia, 'carrying out orders during high school sorority hazing, asked people on the bus what they ate for breakfast,' recalled Aurelia. 'When she told me of the delightfully imaginative reply given by an elderly gentleman, I exclaimed, "There! You have a story!"'[13] The story – which was published as 'Initiation' – expresses Plath's ambiguity towards the power of the group. Flattered to be chosen to be part of the elect sorority – surely a marker of her increased popularity – the central character reflects on how awful it would be if she were destined forever to be the 'plain, shy Millicent' of her early adolescence.[14]

Plath writes tenderly of the sense of wanting to belong, comparing the desire to that of a person sitting outside a dance hall, looking through the windows at the happy scene of the couples inside.[15] Yet, ultimately, Millicent – like Sylvia – after completing all the tasks and being accepted into the group, decides not to join. What was the point of it all, she asked in 'America! America!'. All the sorority girls did was gossip and eat a large quantity of cake. There was something sinister about popularity, something that leached a girl of her individuality.[16]

In November 1947, Sylvia confessed to her diary her fears of not being asked to the football dance; and finally, after no offers, she confided to a friend that she would not be attending. But then, on arriving home after school, the phone rang. It was Perry asking if she would accompany him. Not only was she ecstatic, but her mother was too: when she told her of Perry's invitation Aurelia was in raptures. The evening of the football dance, 21 November, was perfection itself.

Perry remembers Sylvia with fondness. 'One of my first memories of her is playing some sort of board game with her and a few other kids,' he says. 'I made a comment about my strategy, I forget the exact details, but it was along the lines of, "I'm trying to win by doing such and such," and Sylvia was so congratulatory and appreciative, so enthusiastic. She always made me feel very special. She was intellectually ambitious

– she wanted to be the best and she was. She was considered to be the top student in class. One thing that particularly stands out about her is that she was always so incredibly meticulous. She kept a diary back then and she showed me some of her writing. I remember being impressed by the beauty of her script, that there were no corrections, no mistakes at all.'[17]

From her poems, it was obvious that Sylvia thought herself in love. Yet Perry had a rather different perspective. 'We started dating, but it was all incredibly innocent. Our dating comprised of just getting together and talking or bicycle riding. From my point of view, I never thought of us as boyfriend and girlfriend. I viewed her as a tremendously appealing person, but I never recall ever being romantically attracted to her, which puzzled me because she was so pretty.'[18]

Perhaps one of the reasons was Sylvia's emotional inconsistency. Whereas she assumed a boy would remain fixed in his feelings for her – she expected them to remain in awe of her and never waver – she felt able to flit from one heartthrob to another. One could interpret this as the typical behaviour of a teenage girl; but what is interesting is that she did not grow out of this capriciousness. She was forever in a state of emotional flux, yet assumed that those around her to be fixed and blinkered, their gaze directed towards her alone.

The very next night after the football dance she attended with Perry, she went to another dance – where she attracted the attentions of Bruce Palmer, Dick Smith, Tommy Duggin and John Pollard, who pointed her out to his parents in an admiring manner at the Thanksgiving service at Sunday school. On 8 December, John Pollard telephoned her home and asked her on a double date to the Totem Pole – 'which we affectionately called the scrotum pole,' says Philip McCurdy[19] – the following Saturday night. She had high hopes for the evening – and indeed, she luxuriated in the setting of the dance hall, with its tiers of banquettes ranged around the room and an orchestra in a recess – yet John disappointed her. Although he was rich and blond and tall – six feet three, nine inches shorter than the seven-foot-high ceilings of her home – there was something about him that repelled her and she was relieved when he dropped her back at her house without going 'parking' (heavy petting in the back of the car). After another date with him, she confessed in her diary how worried she was that he would tell everyone that she was priggish and straitlaced; one only has to read her journals to realise how far from the truth this was. Indeed, one friend at the time noted that she was boy crazy.

In the first few weeks of 1948 Sylvia directed her attentions towards Tommy Duggin and, after taking a late bus home with him one night, she became infatuated. Two weeks later, still captivated by him, she was sitting in the shadow of a bus shelter when she saw a boy and a girl kissing across the street. She strained her eyes to identify the couple and was horrified to discover Tommy kissing her best friend, Betsy Powley. Fuelled by anger, Sylvia walked across the street and noted Betsy's acute embarrassment; and, although she felt possessed by a murderous fury, she maintained a stream of polite conversation with Betsy all the way home. Yet the moment she was left alone she was reduced to tears.

Tommy, whom she confessed to drooling over, had the power to transport her to the heights of happiness or plunge her into misery. After one get-together, at the end of February, she felt so elated that she had danced with Tommy cheek to cheek – something Betsy could never do since she was a good deal shorter than both of them – that she took out her coloured pencils and drew a rainbow in the margin of that day's entry in her diary. Buoyed by this newfound confidence, on Valentine's Day she asked Tommy whether he would walk her home one day as she had a question of great importance she wanted to ask him. Tommy turned up in his car with a bunch of friends, all of whom had heard of Sylvia's proposal. What was the question she wanted to put to him, Tommy asked as she got into the front seat. Nothing, Sylvia replied, blushing with shame, conscious that the friends in the back were laughing at her. As she got out of the car, and thanked him for giving her a ride home, she noticed that her voice sounded high-pitched and artificial. In her diary she wrote of her complex feelings for him, of the intertwined feelings of love and hate.[20]

These social anxieties were expressed in a 1948 story, 'In This Field We Wander Through'. The tale centres on the fears and preoccupations of Joyce (the Sylvia figure), who prefers the certainties of school life to the chaotic unpredictability of friends and boys. Joyce, like Sylvia, presents herself to the world wearing a mask-like smile, yet behind the polished exterior lurks a hinterland of dark, unseemly thoughts. She bumps into her friend Tracy – whom Sylvia modelled on her school friend Prissy – and tells her that she has a date with Tommy Grayson. The exchange between the two girls – in which Joyce's polite comments to Tracy are counterpointed by a series of sarcastic observations enclosed in parentheses – articulates the double nature of Sylvia's personality. The sheen of surface politeness, accompanied by the private expression of occasional catty comments, was a persona encouraged by her mother. In many ways, Aurelia – who, when the unfortunate John Pollard was out of earshot, called the boy 'Polly' – was a fellow conspirator in an on-going game of mild mockery, a pastime so adored by mother and daughter. If Sylvia noted anything amusing or spotted anyone whom she believed deserved a spot of gentle taunting she went straight to her mother, a figure who rewarded her sharp observations with the gift of laughter. Sylvia functioned as a kind of life spy, reporting back to Aurelia, often via the written word, on the absurdities and eccentricities of those she encountered.

Typical is the card she sent her mother in July 1948, while Sylvia was at the Oaks Bluffs sailing camp in Martha's Vineyard, which tells of an overheard conversation between the camp's nurse and the assistant cook. She couldn't wait to tell her mother the news.[21] Sylvia had stopped by the infirmary to ask for some nose drops – she was plagued, yet again, by one of her sinus headaches – and she was lying on the bed letting the medication take effect when the cook entered the adjoining room. It was obvious that the cook was in a manic state – her voice, Sylvia noted, sound odd and unbalanced – and she told the nurse that the meals she was serving the girls contained nothing but recycled leftovers that had been rescued from the rubbish bin. At the end of the card Sylvia says: 'I hope no one knows I've written this letter.[22] And, although Sylvia had problems with her appearance – most notably attacks of acne which she tried to cure by drinking gallons of water – this did not stop her from sneering at others who suffered a similar fate. While still at summer camp, she wrote to her mother of a visit of a group from Vineyard Haven. Although most of the girls were clean, nice-looking specimens, there was one poor soul who stood out, a girl who was overweight, covered in spots and wore thick glasses. Sylvia pronounced the visitor a freak, something to be pitied, and if this wasn't enough to convince her mother of the full horror of her appearance she accompanied the description with a pen sketch of the girl. She wasn't, as she told her mother, that much of a nice girl after all.[23]

Sylvia was conscious of her psychological vulnerability, acutely aware of the instability of what she termed her 'emotional thermometer'. At camp she suffered from lack of sleep – her friends Ruth Freeman and Betsy Powley chatted into the early hours, prompting Sylvia to comment that if they continued she would hit the voluble Betsy over the head with her suitcase. The exhaustion combined with an infected eye (caused, she thought, by a dirty facecloth), and an attack of jealousy (brought on by being left out of the sailing race around the harbour) was enough to significantly lower her spirits. On 20 July she wrote home to her mother of sitting alone in her tent, feeling on the verge of tears. She felt better, however, after she purged herself by writing of her delicate frame of mind to Aurelia, an act that was proving to be increasingly compulsive. Whenever she felt tension build within her she found that the best way to dissipate and release this psychological pressure was through the form of a written confession to her mother. For Sylvia, writing home would become both an addiction and a curse.

Aurelia was not the only correspondent on whom she depended to bolster her self-confidence during the difficult years of her adolescence. In April 1947 she started to write to a pen pal, Hans Joachim Neupert from Grebenhain, Germany. In her first letter, she outlined the basic facts of her life: she was quite tall, had brown hair and eyes, and liked drawing, writing and playing the piano (she would later tell him that she adored the music of Beethoven, Debussy and Chopin and could even bash out a little boogie-woogie). She played basketball in the winter, went sailing in the summer, and enjoyed studying English, Latin, Art and French; she had not yet started to study German, but told Hans that her mother was fluent. She described her routine – rising at 6:30 each morning, school between 8:30 and 2:30, homework in the evenings and retiring to bed around ten – and told him a little about America. Although it would be easy to assume that most Americans were rich and that young people were superficial and hedonistic, it was not always the case: she, for one, was quite serious, hard-working and far from rich (she enclosed a photograph of her house with an arrow pointing to the window of the room where she liked to write). She feared and loathed the idea of war – in her diary at this time she writes of sitting outside and hearing a fire engine wailing down the street, a noise which she imagines as a harbinger of global conflict – and wrote to Hans that while she had not experienced the terror of being bombed she had read and heard of many horrific stories. She thought that it was strange that she could correspond with Hans, a young person in a foreign country, while other nations sacrificed their young men in the name of war.[24] She told Hans that when she was grown up she would like to be a newspaper reporter, foreign correspondent, artist or author; the profession of poet did not present itself as a serious possibility. The letter was mostly frank and honest, but there was one aspect of herself that she preferred to keep hidden from Hans: her age. She told him that she was nearly sixteen; the truth of the matter was that she was only fourteen years old.

She also used her correspondence with Hans as a way of honing her writing skills. On 24 September 1948, she hurried home from school in the hope that there might be a letter from Hans waiting for her; letters became a form of sustenance for Sylvia, who viewed them as concrete markers of love and affection. Almost immediately she sat down and composed a lengthy letter back to him, a document that illustrates the relationship between her everyday life and the heightened reality as seen through the lens of her writerly eye. The incident was ordinary enough: a night spent on the seashore in Martha's Vineyard with a group of girls from summer camp, but, through the precise use of language, Sylvia managed to transform the experience into something magical and strange. She told him how the ocean occupied a "special" place in her heart. She loved the way the water changed mood according to the weather and the colour of the sky. Her letter manages to capture the beauty of the moment and the sound of the wind in the grass and the crash of the waves on the shore.[25]

Loneliness was one of the central themes of her writing at this time. In the poem 'Lonely Song', which she wrote under the name Sandra Peters in 1949, she calls for the rain that beats down on the roof to keep her company. Feeling desolate and tortured, she yearns to forget something unnamed and unnameable. In 'Passing', also written in 1949 under the same pseudonym, she describes the things that give her comfort: the cold rain falling in a garden, the wet branches of an apple tree, the opaque grey fog of the early morning, the shrill cry of the east wind. In 'I Put My Fingers In My Ears' – an auditory counterpart to 'Mad Girl's Love Song' – she describes the action of the poem's title and its effect on her. As she places her fingers in her ears she can hear the faint noise of wheels turning, which she likens to the sound of thunder in the distance; the noise is that of her life moving forwards. 'Humoresque' describes her sitting alone in her room listening to the garbled, trivial talk from relatives below, a noise she compares unfavourably to the various sounds of nature she has experienced. The embarrassment she feels at the vulgarity of her relatives is something she would go on to explore in the 1951 poem 'Family Reunion', in which describes herself listening to the arrival of her 'nearest and dearest' as she stands at the top of the stairs. She compares herself to a solitary diver looking down into the abyss below. As she frees herself of her personality she prepares to face self-annihilation.[26]

The short stories she wrote in high school are similarly bleak. 'East Wind', written in 1949, features a spinster called Miss Minton, who, one day while out shopping, sees a young boy with hands blue from the cold. The woman feels compassion for the child, but he runs away laughing. The next time she sees him she is reminded of the depressing circumstances of her life – her miserable apartment, her wretched existence, her utter loneliness. In the grip of a depression, a gust of the east wind blows off her hat. Miss Minton, standing on a bridge, overlooking the dark river, contemplates taking her own life; surely, she thinks, the breeze would bear her and her troubles away, but then the direction of the wind changes and her hat lands at her feet. Although she does not commit suicide, she returns home alone to her sad, lonely flat where she tries to forget the emptiness of her life, and is left haunted by the figure of the strange boy and the sound of his sobbing that she can hear in the distance. This wasn't the first time Sylvia had used the name Minton, nor would it be the last. Two years previously, in February 1947, she had thought up the idea for a story she called 'The Miraculous End of Miss Minton', about a woman who gets carried away by the spring breeze and disappears. In 1952, Plath would write 'Sunday at the Mintons', published that August in *Mademoiselle* magazine, at the end of which features a similar scenario to the previous two stories. Elizabeth Minton, the scatterbrained sister of the matter-of-fact and sensible Henry, fantasises that her brother slips to his death in the sea, after which she is borne away by the wind.[27]

Plath's desire for escape – so intense it was almost tangible – found release and expression in her writing. In 'Among the Shadow Throngs', which she wrote in 1949, she is Terry Lane, a young girl who is desperate to transport herself away from the shoddy circumstances of her life. In September 1949, Warren won a four-year scholarship to the elite Phillips Exeter Academy in New Hampshire, an award that must have left Sylvia seething with jealousy. In the story, Plath describes the heroine's bedroom as rather grimy, with an iron bedstead that had paint peeling from its frame, a rather tattered blue rug on the floor and a bed that featured a brightly coloured quilt concealing an uncomfortable mattress beneath. Terry, like her friend Louise, is obsessed with the idea of being published in a magazine, but she has nothing but rejection slips to show for her efforts. Plath also placed her own thoughts in the mouth of Louise, who tells Terry that she has a range of wild, unsettling thoughts and fantasies, ideas so out of kilter with conventional society that if she were to voice them people would no doubt think she was unhinged. Louise also wants to experience everything intensely – even what it is like to be disabled, what it is like to be just about to die – so she could return back to her 'normal' self and then write about it. The idea of being imprisoned in one personality abhorred her. At times she felt no more substantial than an echo, or 'the ghost of somebody else'.[28] When Louise has a poem accepted by a magazine, Terry feels so possessed by rage and jealousy that she first of all writes a poem, 'Portrait', and then, after telephoning Terry to congratulate her on her success, she sits at her typewriter and contemplates the old adage: write what you know. The first lines are the same as the story we have just read, 'Among the Shadow Throngs'.

Plath endlessly recycled experience; nothing was wasted or thrown away and, like Terry, by 1949 Sylvia was beginning to amass an ever-increasing pile of rejection slips. Although she was paid two dollars for a contribution to the lead article 'When I'm a Parent' in the November issue of *Seventeen* magazine, by this point she had already sent thirty-one poems – including 'Bereft', 'Have You Forgotten' and 'Persecuted' – to the same magazine, all of which had been rejected. To *Ladies' Home Journal* she had posted off (and received back) poems including 'The Stranger', 'The Farewell', 'The Stoic' and 'Sorrow'; *Atlantic Monthly* had turned down the poem 'The Invalid'; and *Mademoiselle* had said no to the short story 'East Wind'. The repeated rejections left Sylvia even more determined. 'The [section] editor [of *Seventeen*] made the comment that although Sylvia's writing held promise and present merit, she still had to learn to "slant" her subject matter and treatment toward the requirements of the particular publication from which she hoped acceptance,' said Aurelia. 'She advised Sylvia to go to the library and read every *Seventeen* issue she could find and discover the "trend".'[29]

Sylvia would go one step further: she invested in the annual purchase of the *Writer's Year Book*, a fifty-cent-an-issue guide that was full of specialist advice about particular markets, individual success stories and profiles of bestselling novelists, playwrights and screenwriters. 'This very popular magazine is for young girls under twenty,' the guide said of *Seventeen*. 'Fiction is the one really open market here [. . .] Stories should concern themselves with the "growing up" years and appeal to the audience age-group on realistic terms, affording the reader insight into her own problems and adjustments [. . .] Treatments should be fresh and probing; the "juvenile" approach is unsuitable. Humor is welcome, if it is neither condescending nor caricature.'[30]

In May 1949, just as Sylvia was contemplating possible subjects for fictional exploration (and exploitation) in *Seventeen*, a profile of the magazine appeared in *Time*. Under the helm of former executive editor Alice Thompson – who, in 1939, had first created *Glamour* for Condé Nast and who at the beginning of May had been made publisher of *Seventeen* – and editor-in-chief Helen Valentine, the magazine had built up a circulation of one million and had 'grown in five years from a gangling kid to something of an Amazon'. The magazine was such a hit with teenage girls because the fifty-strong staff gave them exactly what they wanted, 'low-priced fashions, fiction, sensible articles such as "how to get along with parents" and frank discussions of teenage problems which other magazines shy away from.'[31]

Plath, like many other girls of her generation, found herself vexed by the intricacies and contradictions of dating, an issue she explored in 'And Summer Will Not Come Again', a story that she would subsequently sell to *Seventeen* magazine. The story, which takes its title from a line in the Sara Teasdale poem 'An End' is based on Sylvia's own experience with John Hodges. Told from the perspective of Celia, a sixteen-year-old high-school girl, who is trying to forget she ever had a crush on a nineteen-year-old sophomore, Bruce, who is tall with 'knife-blue eyes'.[32] It traces the relationship from uncertainty and insecurity through infatuation to betrayal and disappointment. Like Celia, Plath had met Hodges (who was tall, handsome and blond) at the tennis courts when, on 9 June, he had strolled over and asked if she would like a game. The next day, Sylvia went down to the tennis courts and, in her diary, she confessed to feeling a mix of pleasure and anxiety when she set eyes on a boy wearing a familiar pair of blue shorts. In the story, Plath writes of how Celia feels a similar emotion as she approaches the tennis courts.[33] Right from the beginning of the brief romance, Sylvia seemed to have a premonition that the relationship was doomed. On 10 June, the day after she met John Hodges, she wrote 'To Ariadne (deserted by Theseus)'. The poem – which marks what Aurelia would say was the first appearance of her daughter's 'tragic muse' – describes the rage of a rejected woman.[34]

On 1 August, after her return from Star Island, New Hampshire, where she had attended a National Unitarian youth conference, John rang to ask her out. That night the couple went canoeing, a date Sylvia transposed straight into the story.[35] However, the next day Sylvia saw John with a blonde girl, yet he didn't seem at all embarrassed by the fact he had been spotted dating. The story follows reality, as Celia sees Bruce with a blonde girl coming out of the ice-cream parlour.[36] On their next encounter, Celia spits out a stream of sarcastic words and Bruce, like John, brings the relationship to an end. The story ends with Celia at home, in tears, listening to the fall of rain on the roof of her home and a quote from Teasdale's poem 'An End': 'With my own will I turned the summer from me/And summer will not come to me again.' She found inspiration, as she wrote in her journal, from the sound of the August rain, as she sat on her porch on Elmwood Road, realising that another summer was over.[37] The passions of Plath's summer, however, had not been extinguished; in fact, its fires (both figurative and literal) were only beginning to stir.

Even before her relationship with John Hodges had reached its peak, she was swooning over boys she had met on Star Island, where she arrived on 26 June. She found herself particularly drawn to Dick Gilbert, a boy from Kentucky, whom she met during the aftermath of a fire at the Oceanic Hotel where she was staying for the duration of the Unitarian youth conference. Plath was in full competition mode – not an especially attractive sight – as there were 100 girls in the group and only 60 boys. On 29 June, Sylvia and Dick, together with her roommate Judy and her date, ventured out across the bay. Whereas her three companions seemed to be able to negotiate the slippery, seaweed-covered rocks with ease, Sylvia found it difficult to balance and constantly chafed and cut her knees on the sharp edges. By the end of the day, Dick became sick and tired of her constant moaning, and she in turn was angry with the way he treated her. The next day, as a result, she ignored him, only for him to be immediately monopolised by another girl straight away. Then it dawned on her that she would have no date for the final-night banquet, a horrific thought that prompted her to attract the attentions of one boy, Eddie Mason, whose girl had retired to bed early. Yet Sylvia soon became bored with Eddie, whom she thought too jovial, and so swapped him for the more handsome Hank Glover. The dance, as described in her diary, reads like a detailed description of a battle, with Sylvia playing the role of general and the boys as her troops whom she could manipulate at will. During the dance, Eddie tried to manoeuvre her away from Hank, but she stood firm – she compares herself to the Rock of Gibraltar under fire – until finally she won out. The couple then danced to 'A You're Adorable' and enjoyed a polka, before retiring to the veranda where Hank kissed her three times. The next morning she had to rise at five, and Hank wanted to share breakfast with her, but by then the romantic fantasy had all but disappeared.

Returning home to Wellesley, she continued to date other boys besides John Hodges. One day in July she wrote in her diary that she was going to take a twenty-four-hour break from boys – she had not had a single day to herself since returning from Star Island. In fact, her dating schedule was so dizzying that she was forced to make a list in her diary of the boys' names, ages and details of how she had met them. Another list, which she compiled in August 1949, outlines the twenty-one boys she had gone out with since the autumn of 1948, an inventory that she annotated with a system of stars: one star next to a name symbolised that the date was memorable, two stars signified that the boy was unforgettable. One such boy, with two stars next to his name, was Bruce Elwell, whom she had met at the Wellesley tennis courts in July. Bruce, a six-feet-tall, brown-haired, blue-eyed eighteen-year-old, came from a family with substantially more resources than Plath's – they had a grand house in Cambridge, Massachusetts, and a mansion that sat on top of a hill that they used during the summer months. It was not only his social standing that appealed to Sylvia; she also liked his crazy sense of humour and his love of danger. On 22 July, Bruce took Sylvia to the stock-car races, where she immediately responded to the heady mix of the smell of the exhaust fumes, the scream of the brakes and the noise of the engines. Just as she joked that she was disappointed that there hadn't yet been a crash, one of the cars span out of control and smashed into the crowd. After seven people were carried away on stretchers, the race continued. In her diary, Sylvia confessed that she could not feel much sympathy for the victims; she just wanted to be borne along by the intoxicating spirit of the event. Indeed, after the race she felt so aroused that she wanted to go 'parking', and the fact that she had to pretend to be all sweet and virginal infuriated her.

In her journal she wrote with passion about her loathing of a system she regarded as hypocritical. She didn't want Bruce to think she was "fast" because then she knew she would start to attract the wrong type of boy. But what was so bad about showing love and affection? Why were people so embarrassed about expressing their desires? Perhaps, she said, if everyone talked openly about these issues then certain problems surrounding sex would be easier to solve. Her own issue was this: how far could she go with a boy without losing his respect?[38]

The double standard that wormed its way through society particularly angered her: the fact that if a girl said she was going steady with a boy they could do almost anything, whereas if a girl dated lots of guys she was considered loose and cheap. The whole system was just so stupid, she said. Perhaps one day, when she was ready, she would create the perfect boyfriend from the depths of her imagination and he would appear as if by magic.[39]

By mid-August, Sylvia had forgotten both John Hodges and Bruce Elwell: now her sights were set on eighteen-year-old John Hall, a freshman at Williams College. Although she had known him for two years – she and Betsy used to drool over him while he was playing basketball – on 15 August the tall, athletic boy (who merited three stars on her list of boys) introduced himself to her at the tennis courts. By the end of the month, they took a trip down to the Cape in his car. Sylvia and John set out early and arrived in West Falmouth at 9 a.m., where they met up with some of his friends. That day, after enjoying a swim, the couple were sitting on a raft in the ocean when she brushed her leg against his. The action prompted him to confess that he had a deformity on one of his feet: according to Sylvia it seemed as though the sole lay on top instead of underneath the foot, and his toes appeared twisted and doubled over. The disability only made her feel more affectionate towards him and, after another swim, Sylvia felt so happy that she later wrote in her journal of the importance of enjoying a life-enhancing experience with another soul, someone who had the power not only to validate her existence but also fuse her with the very essence of the universe too. She wrote of how she felt a wave of ecstasy wash over her and John, connecting both of them to the sky and the sea. This was not merely a momentary flash of insight, rather something deeper and more profound. The result, she said, was transformative.[40]

Back in Wellesley, the couple continued to spend time together; he taught her the basics of golf and basketball, and they often enjoyed tennis games in the afternoon. She also liked the fact that they could communicate honestly with one another. John told her of two friends he knew who had sex each week 'like a couple of dogs', and not surprisingly the girl worried about pregnancy; later that afternoon, Sylvia opened the local paper to see a notice announcing that the couple had married. And to think, noted Sylvia in her diary, the girl had been in her art class the year before. Full intercourse was out of the question for Sylvia: she was too fearful of pregnancy and frightened of losing her reputation. Her feelings for John went beyond a mere physical attraction, she said, and he told her that he adored every single thing about her. Yet, the relationship did not last and by the end of November she had decided that she did not like him enough to continue 'going steady' with him. She broke the news to him when he came over on 24 November for a Thanksgiving dinner; after saying goodbye to him,

Sylvia opened the door a little to see him sobbing his heart out in his car.

In fact, by this time Sylvia had already started dating Bob Riedeman, whom she had met at the tennis courts that summer. Bob, a nineteen-year-old, blond-haired sophomore at the University of New Hampshire, had also attended Wellesley High School, where Sylvia remembered being particularly impressed by a reading he had given when she was just fifteen. On 13 November, Bob took her dancing to the Totem Pole, after which he drove her down to an isolated spot and parked the car. Sylvia protested – after all, this was only their second date – but Bob insisted on kissing her. Although she loved the sensation – she said she could kiss him forever – she had to pretend not to enjoy it. She had to obey the damned artificial rules, she said.[41]

More and more, Sylvia began to notice the disparity between the patina of superficial appearances and the realities of one's inner world. On 27 November she attended a party in Belmont, Massachusetts, with another date, Rod. As she stepped into the room she noticed that a lot of the group were quite drunk, and although she was in high spirits herself – especially when one young man approached her and asked her if he could kiss her – she soon began to notice that the event was not quite as jolly as it at first seemed. She compared it to a Christmas decoration – bright and polished on the surface, but completely empty inside. She observed that a number of the young men and women there who had been going steady on Star Island had changed their partners; she likened this fickleness to the act of shuffling through a deck of cards to form an infinite number of different possibilities. She realised that she was merely playing a part too – Rod didn't mean anything to her – and she was anxious that she might accept an artificial way of communicating as the norm. She would rather live an honest life, even one that would prove to be more disturbing and distressing, she said. In her diary she wrote how sometimes she felt like screaming. If she closed her eyes and let her mind wander she could hear the sound of dissonant voices, a sound that she likened to that of a flock of chattering birds. The chaos of it all frightened her and she felt imprisoned and powerless. How could she express herself, she wondered. How could she forge some kind of meaning out of this disorder?[42]

Sylvia continued to see Bob Riedeman through the autumn of 1949; she admitted she was infatuated with him, and wondered whether she might even be a little bit in love. For his part, Bob was not what he calls a 'typical Wellesleyite' and, although he lived on a large estate, his stepfather worked there as the caretaker. 'Neither he nor my mother, who was employed as a billing machine operator, were college graduates and I was the first in my family to graduate from college,' he says. 'I knew Sylvia was interested in writing, [but] I had no idea she was going to become famous as a major American poet. I thought she was good looking, but also what attracted me to her was her intellect, and we shared a common interest in reading. Sylvia and I frequently talked about what had taken place in our English classes – we both were in Wilbury Crockett's class, but in different years. Certainly, we enjoyed each other's company while it lasted.'[43]

On 19 December, she was entertaining Bob at her home in Elmwood Road, when she saw her former boyfriend John Hall's beach wagon pulling up outside. Although Bob said he would hide in the basement, the couple decided to endure the embarrassment of the meeting and Sylvia spent the next hour or so trying to make awkward conversation, all the time digging her nails deep into her palms.

Even at this stage in her life, Sylvia suffered from occasional bouts of anxiety. The thought of failing at something as inconsequential as a tennis competition filled her with fear – winning really was a matter of life and death for her – and it was obvious from the letters to her mother that the teenage girl had already become dependent on sleeping pills. She realised that, at the age of seventeen, she still did not have any real insight into her identity. She was, as she wrote in her diary, scared of ageing and frightened of getting married. She loathed the idea of routine, a life where she had to cook food for a husband and children. 'I want to be free . . . I want, I think, to be omniscient . . .' In the deleted text, indicated by the final ellipses of this diary entry – which was published in the preface to *Letters Home* – she also expressed her desire to be a little bit insane. She bemoaned the fact that so few people had what she described as a kind of fire of divine insanity, a quality that had the power to transform the everyday into something extraordinary. The 'girl who wanted to be God' (as she called herself in the same entry) aspired to transform herself into a psychotic deity. In many ways, Sylvia Plath did just that.[44]

At the end of September 1949, Aurelia Plath wrote a letter to Smith College, the elite women-only university in Northampton, Massachusetts, asking for information about the application procedure for her daughter. In her reply, Ruth W. Crawford, the director of admissions, outlined the process and enclosed an application card and a request for a ten-dollar administration fee. Sylvia should expect to take two sets of tests (achievement and scholastic) and also be prepared for certain evaluations of the candidate's mental health. 'The College is interested in psychological tests [. . .] the American Council Psychological Test is also urged whenever possible,' wrote Crawford.[45] Next to this, Aurelia wrote in red pencil one word: 'Inquire', a note that implies she suspected all was not well in her daughter's inner world.

Sylvia knew she had set her sights high and admission depended on a wide range of criteria, 'the school record, the principal's recommendation, the College Board tests, the results of psychological tests which the student may have taken [. . .] Before the student is finally admitted, she must submit to the College Physician a full history of her health,' a phrase that Aurelia also underlined in red pencil, 'together with the results of a complete examination made by her home physician.'[46]

Sylvia was confident of her academic record – she achieved a string of As (the only exception being a B in gym class) – yet she didn't want to appear, as she wrote in 'America! America!', 'too dangerously brainy'.[47] It wasn't good form to be seen to acquire a mass of top marks and nothing else. She realised the importance of seeming like a fully-rounded person – she knew that colleges were looking for good all-rounders not just academic high achievers – and it was lucky, she said, that by this time she had already read and studied the work of Machiavelli.[48] So, on her application form, in addition to outlining the books she had read and owned – a list that included the poets Robert Frost, Stephen Vincent Benet, T. S. Eliot, A. E. Houseman and Edna St Vincent Millay (the last two she identified as her favourites), novels by Austen, Willa Cather, Tolstoy and Sinclair Lewis, plays by Shakespeare and Eugene O'Neill and essays by Toynbee, Emerson and Thoreau – she went on to describe the wide range of activities that she pursued outside school: she was a member of the basketball team; enjoyed participating in debates and listening to various visiting speakers as part of the Jefferson Fellowship; loved taking an active part in the Decorations Committee (for which she created decorations for the gym for the school dances); contributed in her own small way towards global peace as part of the United World Federalists; looked after children in her spare time; and worked on the staff of the school newspaper,

The Bradford. When the announcement of her position as co-editor (with Frank Irish) was made, the newspaper said that it was confident that, 'Sylvia will be an exceedingly able editor because of her exceptional ability as a writer. Not only has she a keen critical eye, but also the noteworthy reputation of sticking to a task until it is done.'[49] Sylvia applied the same determination to win a place at Smith; this obsession with getting into college she later defined as a 'subtle, terrifying virus' that infected many of her friends.[50] After all, she and her immediate circle had bought into the American dream: that if she worked hard enough she could transform herself into anything. The key was education.[51]

This was all very well, but Aurelia worried about how she would finance her daughter's college education. If Sylvia had chosen to enrol at Wellesley College, she would have received a full scholarship from the town; a four-year course at Smith was an expensive proposition. The only way that Aurelia could afford the tuition would bc if her daughter won one of the highly competitive scholarships, which varied from $250 to $850 a year. It was also possible for some girls to work in the co-op houses: for instance, one hour a day working in the kitchens or waiting on table could shave $250 a year off the average board and lodging fee of $750. On top of this, she would have to find tuition fees of $850 a year.

'To the student whose income is decidedly limited, a college education may be possible with the aid of scholarships and self-help work [. . .]' read one leaflet from Smith that was sent to Sylvia at this time. 'Only a student who is physically strong and whose academic standing is satisfactory should ever try to take on extra work for the sake of decreasing expenses. Without these advantages a girl risks a physical or nervous breakdown and may in health and energy pay a greater price than a college education is worth to her.'[52] Sylvia, it seems, took no notice of the advice; throughout her time at college, she felt she needed to try to sell her stories and poems in order to contribute towards her rising expenses.

Sylvia was constantly made aware that she was not in the same economic class as many of her friends. In October 1949, she had to resign herself to the fact that while her fellow 'Crocketteers' were looking forward to a biking trip through Europe the following summer, she would have no choice but to stay at home (and try to earn some money for college expenses). A month later, she wrote to her German pen pal Hans that she would have given anything to be able to go on the educational tour – her friends were going to cruise down the Rhine, attend the music festival in Salzburg and go to the Passion Play – but the cost was prohibitive. Yet she sustained herself with the thought that, if she were fortunate, she would be accepted at one of the East Coast's top women's colleges.

By February 1950 she had completed her application for a scholarship, an award that was 'considered on a competitive basis [according to] scholastic ability, financial need, and personal qualifications'.[53] On a scrap of paper that is now in the Smith archives, Aurelia jotted down a series of figures that helped her work out whether she could afford it; even if Sylvia did win a scholarship her mother would still have to make a substantial contribution. Aurelia's annual salary was $3,662; the house had cost $9,250, and its present value was $10,000; she had $250 in savings and a life-insurance policy worth $2,000 at maturity, and which at present stood at $850. Her outgoings over the course of a typical year included a mortgage of $1,650 and taxes of $250. From these intricate scribblings, Aurelia managed to calculate that she could afford to give her daughter $400 a year. A later note, on the same piece of paper, said that actually

Aurelia gave Sylvia at least $600 a year during the first three years at Smith.

'Sylvia is a superior candidate for college,' wrote the principal of her high school, Samuel M. Graves, to Smith's admissions department. 'She has a keen, analytical, well-disciplined mind and her intellectual interests and power reflect a superior family background as well as her own high standards of achievement [. . .] Following her father's death and her mother's becoming a college instructor, Sylvia has carried many home responsibilities and has taken care of children whenever she could be spared from her home duties [. . .] May college mean some "fun" for her as well as intellectual accomplishment!'[54]

Other references were supplied by her Unitarian minister, her family doctor, Dr Francesca Racioppi, and a number of teachers, including Wilbury Crockett – who said that he had never come across her equal, 'in terms of intellectual acumen, lively spirit of inquiry, and ability to think and work creatively'. He added that Sylvia appeared to be 'exceptionally well-adjusted' and that she was able to mingle easily with a wide range of people.[55] Her neighbour, Elizabeth Cannon Aldrich, also wrote of Sylvia's seemingly well-rounded personality. 'On several occasions over the past two and a half years, we have entrusted the care of our four young children to Sylvia,' she said. 'She has applied her talents of music and art for the children's enjoyment, but they have always been most impressed by her calm and gentle manner. On the occasions when Sylvia has had to meet strangers at our home she has been well poised and gracious. Given a job to do, she has proved herself capable and resourceful.'[56]

Yet these testimonies related only to the surface Sylvia, not the many different and at times conflicting identities that she hid under the veneer of her 'uniform' of normality, a look that she defined as comprising a neat skirt and sweater, topped off by a 'squeaky clean' pageboy haircut.[57] A darker, more disquieting Sylvia was beginning to emerge from the shadows.

For Christmas 1949, instead of the usual gifts of velvet hair ribbons, watercolours and chocolate creams, Aurelia gave her daughter an altogether more subversive present: a copy of Friedrich Nietzsche's *Thus Spake Zarathustra*. The philosophical text, which Nietzsche wrote between 1883 and 1885, expresses a range of ideas that contradicted (and still continues to contradict) accepted notions of morality, decency and conventional behaviour. The seventeen-year-old girl thrilled to Nietzsche's playful, paradoxical prose and, in 1950 or 1951, she went on to write a poem, 'Notes on Zarathustra's Prologue', based on a segment in Nietzche's introduction; 'The earth hath then become small and on it there hoppeth the last man who maketh everything small. His species is ineradicable like that of the ground-flea; the last man liveth longest.'[58]

Leafing through the contents page of her copy of the book – which is now held by Smith College and which was heavily underlined throughout by Sylvia – one could easily mistake the names of Nietzsche's chapter headings for the titles of some of Plath's later poetry: 'The Three Metamorphoses'; 'The Famous Wise Ones'; 'The Dance-Song'; 'The Grave-Song'; 'The Sublime Ones'; 'Redemption'; 'The Stillest Hour'; 'The Vision and the Enigma'; 'Before Sunrise'; 'The Three Evil Things'; 'The Honey Sacrifice'; 'The Shadow'; 'The Song of Melancholy'; 'The Awakening'; and 'The Sign'.

As Sylvia started to read, she became fascinated by Nietzsche's idea of the *Übermensch*, the self-mastered, self-created individual. Not only was Plath an intellectual snob – she couldn't bear people who had not bothered to improve themselves by a constant stream of educative reading – but, from early on, she also had a vision of herself that was at odds with her immediate circumstances. At the time, American society certainly didn't expect girls from lower-middle-class homes to transform themselves into radical poets and novelists – and indeed throughout her life she would continue to struggle to free herself from these constrictions and assumptions. She viewed Nietzsche's book – with its series of impassioned mantras declared by the prophet Zarathustra – as an anti-Bible or a kind of self-help text that schooled her in the art of the will to power.

Even before reading *Thus Spake Zarathustra*, Sylvia viewed herself as a thing apart, as can be seen from her diary entry of November 1949 (later reproduced in *Letters Home*), in which she called herself the girl who wanted to be God. She admitted that she did have 'a terrible egotism.'[59] Yet, at the same time, Sylvia wanted to free herself of her identity so as to assume the perspectives of the people she wanted to write about. She was afraid when her attempt succeeded.[60] Faced with this seemingly insurmountable problem, she turned to Nietzsche for advice. 'I love him,' said Zarathustra, 'whose soul is so overfull that he forgetteth himself, and all things are in him [. . .] I tell you: one must still have chaos in one, to give birth to a dancing star.'[61] Despite her groomed appearance and perfect manners, inside Sylvia lurked confusion and disorder. As she wrote in a letter in August 1950, most people did not realise 'the chaos that seethes behind my exterior'.[62]

Nietzsche also had a piece of advice for aspiring writers, 'Of all that is written, I love only what a person hath written with his blood. Write with blood.'[63] During the course of her short career, Plath sacrificed everything for her writing: her mental health, her close relationships, her life. As she would write two weeks before her death, in the poem 'Kindness', 'The blood jet is poetry/There is no stopping it.'[64] No doubt

Nietzsche, who loathed the concepts of pity, compassion and mercy, would have approved of Plath's subsequent use (and betrayal) of her friends and family in *The Bell Jar*. After all, he loved 'the great despisers'[65] and was in favour of an individual who was 'hated by the people, as the wolf by the dogs [. . . he] is the free spirit, the enemy of fetters, the non-adorer [. . .]'[66]

It would be an overstatement to say that Plath used *Thus Spake Zarathustra* as a literal guide on how she should live and write. Yet there are a number of unsettling parallels between the text and the personal mythology she created. She particularly responded to the lines in the section 'The Sublime Ones', where Nietzsche writes, 'Calm is the bottom of my sea: who would guess that it hideth droll monsters! Unmoved is my depth: but it sparkleth with swimming enigmas and laughters.'[67] Of course, the great enigma of Plath's life was her dead father, whom she often imagined as a kind of sea-god figure. 'Ah, I cast indeed my net into their sea and meant to catch good fish; but always did I draw up the head of some ancient God,' wrote Nietzsche in the chapter 'Poets'. 'Thus did the sea give a stone to the hungry one. And they themselves may well originate from the sea.'[68]

One of the most chilling chapters in the book, in respect to Plath's story, is the one that carries the title 'Voluntary Death'. Here, Nietzsche writes that the will to power – the concept of self-determination – should be brought to bear on the manner and timing of one's demise. 'Die at the right time: so teacheth Zarathustra [. . .]' writes Nietzsche. 'My death, praise I unto you, the voluntary death, which cometh unto me because I want it.'[69] In the same chapter, Nietzsche touches on the relationship between dying at the most appropriate moment and long-lasting fame. 'And whoever wanteth to have fame, must take leave of honour betimes, and practise the difficult art of

– going at the right time.'[70] Plath was fascinated by the idea of death and rebirth and would work many of its symbols into her poetry. Her most famous poem dealing with the subject was, of course, 'Lady Lazarus', in which she writes of her 1953 suicide attempt and subsequent rising from the world of the dead. In *Thus Spake Zarathustra* Nietzsche states, in 'The Grave Song', 'And only where there are graves are there resurrections.'[71] Plath would view herself as a woman reborn, a being who emerged from the subterranean world of the family's basement at her home in Elmwood Road, her so-called 'grave cave', to live again.[72] As Nietzsche said in the 'Poets' chapter, 'Many a poisonous hotchpotch hath evolved in our cellars: many an indescribable thing hath there been done.'[73]

The 1950s in America can be seen as a decade of conformity and consumerism – its poster child being the figure of the unthinking, television-watching suburbanite – yet it was also a period of paranoia and interior panic. The triumvirate of horrors, the Cold War, the Korean War and McCarthyism, unsettled the country's body politic, yet Plath for one could not understand the public's unquestioning nature. On 2 January 1950, Sylvia wrote a letter to her pen pal Hans about a recent dance at the University of New Hampshire, which she had attended with her boyfriend Bob Riedeman. Although she felt she could talk openly with Bob – luckily he was just as interested in the world of ideas as she was – she was appalled by the strange blankness in many of the faces of her contemporaries. Girls were obsessed with nothing but their appearance, she said, while the boys cared only for money and sex. Parties had a surface appeal – sure, there was a great deal of laughter and fun – but underneath she found everything all so meaningless. The sound of the music and the chatter would never be able to drown out the awful hollowness that lay beneath the surface, she said.[74] It was no wonder that people were scared of turning their gaze inwards, she observed, what with the constant stimuli supplied by radio and television. After all, it was so easy to let oneself be lulled into a soporific, half-conscious state by the comforts of the entertainment industry. She would, she said, rather read a book – and let her imagination do the work – than go to a movie. She knew she had to keep her creative instincts sharp, her imagination fresh.[75] There were too many things that made her angry, too many things that unsettled her, for her to sit back and accept life blindly, unquestioning.

In February that year, in response to the news that the United States had pledged its continuing commitment to the development of the hydrogen bomb, Sylvia and her friend Perry Norton wrote to the *Christian Science Monitor* to express their outrage. The following month their letter was published under the title 'Youth's Plea for World Peace'. What they could not understand was the paradox that a weapon of mass destruction had been created as a way of bringing about peace and security.[76] The arms race – the struggle to develop the most powerful, most destructive weapon – was short-sighted. Although they did believe, at first, that the atomic bomb did have a part to play in world stability, now that the Russians had also developed the technology the situation was becoming dangerous. Where would it all end? Would America not simply go on to try and create even more terrifyingly destructive weapons? And then surely Russia would follow suit? The arms race, they surmised, would have dire consequences for the whole world, a world that had already witnessed the deaths of hundreds of thousands of people in the name of war and peace.[77]

They went on to outline that although they believed in the ideals of democracy and capitalism – to say anything else would be tantamount to treason in anti-communist America – they wondered whether it might be better to try to achieve peace not through 'dread or repulsion' but rather through 'the power of attraction'.[78] Sylvia and Perry, both still in high school, postulated that this state might be brought about by the spread of world federalism. 'We both joined the World Federalist Society in high school because we were convinced that, in our youthful minds, the movement was the way to prevent future world wars,' recalls Perry. 'Our belief was that the reason that nations went to war was because they had no restraint imposed from above, as compared to the various states in America which did not have conflict because of its federal government. We thought a similar model would be the best way to prevent wars.'[79]

The Korean War – a battle of ideologies between South Korea (supported by the United Nations) and North Korea (backed by the People's Republic of China), which started in June 1950 – particularly distressed Sylvia. Each time she opened a newspaper and read about the conflict she confessed to feeling sick; there was nothing heroic about this struggle, she said. And as for the word 'communism'? What did it mean? Although the general public did not seem to know how to define it they were certain that they loathed everything to do with it, she told Hans.[80] In the same letter, she quoted Thomas Hardy's poem 'The Man He Killed' to illustrate her point about how war destroys man's common humanity. After the narrator of the poem has just killed an infantryman in battle he stops to reflect on the futility of war. The last lines read: 'Yes; quaint and curious war is!/You shoot a fellow down/You'd treat, if met where any bar is/Or help to half a crown.'[81]

In an earlier letter to Hans, Sylvia had written of her enthusiasm for Thomas Mann, particularly his novels *Buddenbrooks* and *The Magic Mountain*, the latter of which ends with the onset of the First World War. Sylvia would have been particularly drawn to Mann's themes of decadence and purging, suffering, illness and death. In 1953, the year Plath tried to commit suicide, Mann would say of the novel's protagonist, Hans Castorp, 'what [Hans] came to understand is that one must go through the deep experience of sickness and death to arrive at a higher sanity and health.'[82] In *Buddenbrooks*, Sylvia read the words, influenced by the philosophy of Arthur Schopenhauer: 'Where shall I be when I am dead? [. . .] I shall be in all those who have ever, do ever, or ever shall say "I" [. . .] Who, what, how could I be if I were not – if this my external self, my consciousness, did not cut me off from those who are not I?'[83] Sylvia expressed remarkably similar thoughts in her journals and letters.

Instead of getting her to write an extensive paper on Mann, her teacher Wilbury Crockett asked her to deliver an hour-long presentation on the author, a talk that she clearly enjoyed. In the countdown to graduation, her schoolwork – together with preparation for her college entrance exams, which she took in March, her duties on the school newspaper, her election to the National Honor Society and her role as Lady Agatha in the school production of J. M. Barrie's *The Admirable Crichton* at the end of April – left her with little free time to pursue her own writing. Despite her frantic schedule, she still managed to compose a number of fine poems, particularly 'The Invalid', which deals with the psychological pain of awaking in the early morning, the sting of returning to consciousness after the bliss of sleep.[84] In this way, 'The Invalid' foreshadows the opening lines of her 1958 poem 'The Ghost's Leavetaking'.[85] 'The Invalid' also introduces the fantasy of the drowned man into Plath's poetry, a motif she would go on to explore in poems such as 'Full Fathom Five', 'A Life' and 'Daddy'. In another poem – 'Midnight Snow', also written in 1950 – Plath writes of the wish to simply fade away and disappear into the white, snow-covered landscape, until she is at one with the air.[86]

Perhaps it was this interior hollowness that prompted her need to compete in such a spectacular fashion. She was addicted to achievement in the same way an alcoholic is hooked on booze; the winning of awards, certificates and prizes were all concrete markers of her accomplishments, signifiers of attainment that helped boost her self-esteem. On 10 May she heard from Ruth Crawford that she had been accepted at Smith; she was also thrilled to learn that she would receive a good scholarship. The news took a while to sink in, and often she found herself walking around the house in a daze.[87]

On graduation day, 7 June 1950, as Sylvia collected her raft of high-school awards – the Sons of American Revolution History Prize, an *Atlantic Monthly* writing-contest award, three gold keys in the Regional Scholastic art contest, the Wellesley Club award for best English scholar, and three prizes from the *Boston Globe* (best news story, best poem, best write-up of editors' convention), plus a watch as a gift from her proud mother – it appeared as though the young Sylvia Plath had not a worry in the world. Her entry in the yearbook includes comments such as, 'Warm smile', 'Energetic worker', 'Bumble Boogie piano special', 'Clever with chalk and paints', 'Those fully packed sandwiches', 'Basketball and tennis player' and 'Future writer'.[88] The jaunty lyrics she composed for the 1950 graduation song, performed in the alumnae hall on graduation night, speak only of the collective memories of the students as they came together for one last time.[89]

Yet in private Sylvia, who really did stand alone, was penning material of a rather different nature.

Four

IF I REST, IF I THINK INWARD, I GO MAD

In July 1950, Sylvia started a new journal, a chronicle of important incidents and conversations; a memoir in which she could record fragments of experience that she thought she might use in her writing; a document that served as a tool through which she could better understand what she saw as the mysteries of her self. The book has a maturity of tone lacking in her earlier diaries; it is less a straightforward list of activities pursued on certain days of the year – indeed, the majority of the entries are not dated – and more literary in its scope and ambition.

Sylvia had always been aware that her journal was vulnerable to prying eyes, which perhaps forced her, at times, to censor her writing. This fear found expression in her unpublished story 'The English Bike', a strange tale about an unnamed girl who feels uncertain and anxious about the sharing of information. At the end of the story the girl learns that her mother has read the letters that she has written to a boyfriend, documents that contain a myriad of little secrets she wanted to keep just between the two of them.[1]

Despite these concerns, and now that she was getting ready to move away from home, Sylvia began to write in her journals with a new freedom. She recorded encounters in detail that she had not already related (and perhaps never would relate) to her mother. She described unkind thoughts, bodily functions and wild sexual fantasies that would have been decidedly frowned upon had they been made public at the time. For instance, at the beginning of the journal she writes of the joy of being a virgin. Yet next to this entry she wrote, with a different pen, of her wish to be raped.[2]

Indeed, rape fantasies make more than one appearance in the journal. Later, she writes of wishing she could be taken in a car to the mountains where she would be trapped inside a cabin, the wind howling outside, where she would be raped like a 'cave woman'.[3] Although this may sound facetious we have to remember that Sylvia was a young woman overloaded with a huge store of sexual energy that she was not allowed to express, living in a society that wanted to contain female eroticism within the confines of marriage. The anger that she felt about this – and the rage that she was not born a man, free to sow innumerable wild oats before settling down – would find expression throughout her journals.

The first entry in the new journal – in her neat, schoolgirlish handwriting that sloped towards the right as if on a constant journey of discovery – describes her sense of physical satisfaction after coming home from a day's labour at Lookout Farm, where she worked as a crop-picker. She found the hard physical work satisfying, she said.[4] Each day, she rose at six and cycled the five miles to the farm in South Natick. There, her duties included weeding the land, setting strawberry runners and picking peas, spinach, beans and radishes; by the end of the day her hands were so dirty she had to wash them in bleach to get them clean. Although the pay was low, the bonus was that the farm was staffed by a range of fascinating people, many of whom she thought were ripe to step from reality on to the blank page. Lookout Farm certainly provided rich pickings for the keen-eyed writer: it became the inspiration for a piece of reportage she wrote for the *Christian Science Monitor* for $5; the poem, 'Bitter Strawberries', which she sold to the same newspaper for $4; and a couple of unpublished stories that centred on Ilo Pill, an Estonian refugee whom she claimed had tried to seduce her. After a day in the strawberry fields, Ilo, who wanted to be a painter, invited Sylvia into a barn to show her a sketch of a fellow farmworker. In her journal, she wrote how he clamped his mouth on hers and how he pulled her towards him.[5] Although she managed to pull away from him, she was left feeling so full of desire that she found herself physically shaking.[6] Back at home, she met her mother – who was in a reproachful mood[7] – and, instead of telling her about it, she rushed upstairs to write it down, keen to try to capture the episode in all its complexity. From this raw material, Plath wrote two stories, 'The Estonian', dated October 1951, and 'The Latvian', in February 1952. 'You have an interesting setting, once the reader understands what it is,' wrote one of her professors, who gave her a mark of B-plus. 'Establish it more quickly and more clearly [. . .] Your greatest fault [. . .] is a tendency to overwrite. Simplify your writing and test your figures of speech.'[8] Sylvia duly reworked the story, in which she cast herself as the figure of Lisa but didn't bother to change the identity of Ilo; a rewrite that earned her an A-minus and the commendation, 'You have improved this story in every way. The setting is given at once, the order is clearer and you have simplified your writing enormously. An excellent job. But condense.'[9]

In August 1950, *Seventeen* published 'And Summer Will Not Come Again', for which they paid $15. One would have thought that Sylvia would have been thrilled to see her first story in print at last, but, according to a letter written by Aurelia to a family member, she was perturbed because she had not disguised 'the character of friends upon whom the story is based'.[10] Aurelia maintained that Sylvia had given some thought to the 'significant "errors"'; indeed '"lessons [had been] learned" from the experience', yet she went on to repeat this 'offence' – the lifting of people straight from life into her literature – throughout her career. One positive effect of the story's publication, however, was a curious fan letter from a twenty-one-year-old English major from Chicago named Eddie Cohen.

'Normally, I do not collect autographs, write letters to the editor, nor play hunches,' he wrote to Sylvia on 3 August. 'Indeed, previous to this moment, I doubt very much whether I would have admitted, even under extreme pressure, that I read "Seventeen" magazine. But at the present, I am grateful enough to you so that I am willing to ignore a principle here and there [. . .] The stories in "Seventeen" are generally so much drivel. On one occasion, though, I ran across a story which moved me enough so that I had to repress myself from crying out "Eureka", or something equally unlikely [. . .] Why it should have so captivated me, I don't fully know. In part though, it was because I felt there was a thought behind the story which was expressed rather more subtly than the usual "Seventeen" hit-'em-with-a-brick technique, and also because it seemed that the author (or authoress, as it developed) had an insight into people which was a little above average.'[11]

After flicking back to the first page of the story Eddie had come across Sylvia's high-school graduation photograph (a picture she disliked) and read her mini-biography. 'Sylvia Plath loves being seventeen,' it said. '"It's the *best* age." [. . .] She plays a lot of basketball and tennis and she pounds the piano "strictly for my own enjoyment". Jazz makes her melt inside, Debussy and Chopin suit her dreamier moods.'[12] As he read this he admitted that his eyebrows arched slightly and that his curiosity had been piqued, 'so in lieu of a formal introduction you can accept the quite adequate chaperonage of 1500 miles and the postman, perhaps you can find time to write and tell me a bit more about yourself, or even let me read some more of your writing. I will spend a good deal of time the next few weeks in peering anxiously into the mailbox, so please don't let me down.'[13]

Sylvia wrote back a cool, ironic letter in which she managed to describe the basic details of her life without appearing too sincere or earnest. From the letter that Eddie had sent her, she could tell that he was fun, impulsive and possessed a certain writing technique that he could put to good use. If he was prepared to let down his guard – his cynical sense of humour which he used like a form of defence[14] – then she would be overjoyed if he could take on the role as an informal critic of her writing. Yet she wouldn't send him samples of her work just yet, as he had asked for; this she would do only after he had mailed some writing to her. At least now he should be aware that she was far from naïve, she said.[15]

Over the next four years, Eddie Cohen assumed the role not only of informal literary critic but also of fantasy boyfriend, agony aunt, sex counsellor and psychotherapist. Sylvia's letters to him – letters that are, by turns, open, funny, heart-felt, angry, perplexed and, at times, despondent – served as a kind of alternative journal, a diary that functioned as a repository for her innermost fears and desires but also had the power to answer back, to advise, joke, worry and warn too. From the beginning there was an intimacy between them, an intimacy that was forged by, and to a certain extent depended on, their status as strangers. 'I feel like a guy who has just weathered his first date with A New Girl,' Eddie wrote after receiving Sylvia's first letter. 'Now I can loosen my tie, open my collar, and begin to enjoy myself. And I do think that I will enjoy myself, because if your first letter is any indication, my hunch has paid off with a pretty sharp kid. (You may blush now – nobody is looking).'[16]

Eddie proceeded to tell her a little more about himself: he was a student at Roosevelt College, Chicago, but before that he had been forced to drop out of the University of Chicago and take a 'six month breather' in order to recollect his 'somewhat scattered wits'. It was obvious that Eddie had experienced, or was still in the process of experiencing, something of an existential crisis. He told her that, over the course of the last two years, he had been exploring 'the deepest crevasses of my mind in search of the answer to who am I? what am I? and what am I doing here?'[17] These questions were very much on Sylvia's mind too.

Unlike Sylvia he did not care what people thought of him; often, he did not shave, he had unruly hair and heavy eyebrows – 'but the purtiest blue eyes and long lashes,' he joked – and he liked to walk around with a cigarette permanently in his mouth, 'so that it's almost one of my features'.[18] Although he was born into a wealthy family who lived on Lake Shore Drive, he preferred to hang out with creative types; in the evenings, he would go to parties in the black areas of Chicago, loved to go swimming in the lake at night, and enjoyed arguing about politics at various jazz joints in the city. Sylvia tapped into his sense of alienation, anger and injustice.

'Underneath it all there is quite a troubled, restless spirit,' he wrote. 'I'm the little boy who woke up one morning to find out there ain't no Santa Claus. In other words, I have learned to look the world square in its ugly puss, and I don't always like what I see. And for all that, I'm still a strong idealist and have quite a burden of principles to carry around with me. True, my principles are sometimes at right angles or worse with the conventionally accepted ideas of right and wrong, but at least I stick to mine. Do I sound bitter? In a way, I am. I'm a cynical idealist, and if that isn't an ice cream and pickles combination, I don't know what is.'[19]

Sylvia recognised herself in the description, particularly the phrase 'ice cream and pickles', believing that it summed up the paradox of her character pretty accurately. On the surface she may look sweet and appetising, but dig a bit deeper and you would encounter her acidic and sour side. There is no doubt that Sylvia was intrigued by Eddie, fascinated to learn that such a character existed. Sure, she had known her fair share of intellectuals – men who could talk about philosophy and science for hours, but who were inept on the dance floor – and guys who were perfect physical specimens, but who were so inarticulate they had to depend on one word to describe almost every feeling or situation. However, in her short life – she was nearly eighteen – she said that she had never chanced upon a person with such a range of fascinating, and at times, contradictory personality facets. She too, she told him, had a 'mercurial disposition'; she thought of herself as quite unorthodox and idiosyncratic. Perhaps this had something to do with the fact that she had spent the early part of her adolescence trapped in a prison of awkward self-consciousness, she explained. While her contemporaries were busy taking their first steps at junior dances, she was grappling with the complexities of Aldous Huxley's *Brave New World* or drawing portraits of herself in pencil. Looking back, she said, she was pleased that she had experienced troubles at this time and she was aware that she still carried with her a vulnerability that often could be mistaken for insensitivity. She was afraid of being hurt, she said, and so protected herself with a sheen of cynicism, an aura of indifference. Like many egoists, she said, she carried around inside her a vulnerability that she tried to keep hidden.[20]

The correspondence led to a confession of infatuation, at

least on Eddie's part. He was convinced that they were so alike they could be psychological twins. Sylvia responded to his letters because she transformed him into a symbol. In her journal she wrote of her attachment to him, how she viewed him both as an alter ego and as a reflection of her own writerly self.[21]

Eddie told Sylvia that, as a child, he had spent most of his time in bed fighting off a range of illnesses and described how he had immersed himself in the world of books, forever trying to perfect his writing technique. He also told her that he had wanted to train as a psychiatrist – he said that he never got around to it as he was too lazy to do the study and the endless exams. Yet he possessed a remarkable ability to read people. 'You are original and unconventional, and as such naturally gravitate to people of your temperament,' he said.[22] Her latest letter struck him as something that he could have written himself.

'Take the style of your letter first,' he wrote on 19 August. 'Easy, breezy in tone, almost conversational rather than written. Long complicated sentences mixed with ones that are so short as to be grammatically barbaric. A powerful vocabulary and slang hashed together. Parenthetically poking fun at yourself. Serious statements covered by little jokes at the end [. . .] And then there was the part about the fun-loving individual who seethes inside.' He told her that, remarkably, his two roommates recalled him saying the exact same thing about himself around six months previously. 'If you don't stop building yourself up to me,' he warned, only half-jokingly, 'you are liable to wake up some morning and find me sitting in a tent on your front lawn.'[23]

Eddie Cohen's understanding of Plath's personality was uncannily accurate. Using her letters as a kind of tarot pack, he was able to read her shadow side, teasing out hidden aspects of her personality that perhaps she was not yet conscious of. Even at this early stage of their relationship he interpreted her as something incomplete, a fragment, an observation she later made in 'The Stones', in her sequence 'Poem for a Birthday'. 'That absorbing combination of characteristics which you spoke of (which I think applies to myself as well) is the result of a sincere, if sometimes misdirected effort to be a whole human being,' he wrote to her.[24] He amazed her by taking off by car to Mexico, where he sent her updates on his sex life, including the offer of a prostitute who approached him with the line, '*Mi amigo, desea usted un poco fuckee*?'[25] He had also mailed her a story he had written about his relationship with his girlfriend, Bobbe, which he described as having 'as much fact as fiction', a comment that could equally apply to Plath's stories.[26] Eddie told her that the piece revolved around 'the refutation of the line, "Five thousand years of what? We're still nothing but animals",' a line that resonated with Sylvia and one she would use in chapter seven of *The Bell Jar*.[27]

Throughout the autumn, Eddie responded to Sylvia's tentative questions about sex with a refreshing frankness. First of all, to what extent should one indulge? While he did not believe in promiscuity for its own sake, he reasoned that if a couple were in love, or thought themselves to be so, surely they should be allowed to express those feelings? Plath then asked about contraception, as she had heard that some girls had become pregnant even while using it. 'I know of not one single case where contraceptives have been used where the couple have been caught,' he said. Would she catch VD? 'I think you just threw that in for kicks,' he replied, referring back to her letter. 'The chances of that with someone you know are just about so nil as to be laughable.' If she had sex would it spoil her chances of getting a good or 'idealistic' husband? 'The only thing I can say to that is just plain old-fashioned B.S. [. . .]' he said. His attitude was not one of proscription – it was up to the individual to decide what was best for him or her – and he advised Sylvia to make up her own mind about just how far she was prepared to go. 'Some need the fullness that only living together can bring, the constant, everpresent sex,' he wrote. 'For some, once a week, in a hotel, where there are no interruptions to worry about will do [. . .] Some will do with only petting to orgasm. Some, with kissing. For some, only marriage can be the answer.'[28]

In another letter, Eddie advised her on the many factors involved in lovemaking; it was not, he said, simply a case of achieving orgasm. One also had to take into account 'the strength of the sexual urge, or how easily a person is aroused; timing, or how quickly a person reaches climax; capacity, of the amount of sex one is capable of within a given period of time; and attitude [. . .]' Whereas he and Bobbe were capable of having sex four or five times a night, this depended on the stamina and compatibility of the couple. 'Add to this the mechanical aspects, which is mostly a learned process, of being able to touch ones partner at the right places, of doing the correct things at the correct times, and perhaps you can get some idea of the complexity of the factors which make for happiness or none in a sexual relationship. They make the difference between orgasms which are momentary flashes of pleasurable sensation and those which leave the room spinning wonderfully for hours.'[29]

Around this time, Sylvia felt sexually attracted to a local boy, Emile, who was not only handsome and dark-haired, but also had a killer smile[30]. He had invited her out on a double date to Ten Acres, a local dance hall. Waiting for him to arrive, she luxuriated in dressing herself slowly, relishing the sensation of applying clouds of powder and touches of perfume. In her journal she wrote of the complex ritual of preparing herself for the arrival of her date. But while it was all very well to make herself look attractive, what was the point of it all if at the end of the night she was left feeling dissatisfied?[31] Still a little weak from having two wisdom teeth extracted that morning, she accompanied Emile into the dance hall, where they started to talk about the boy's sister who had died of pneumonia when she was just twelve and his twenty-year-old cousin who was paralysed for life after breaking his back. 'Good lord, we're morbid tonight,' he said, changing the subject. Sylvia told him that she dreaded getting old; she hated the thought that she could not be as self-reliant as a young person. As the conversation progressed, she noted that the air was thick with 'the strong smell of masculinity'.[32] On the dance floor – an area in which a young couple could express their sexual desires but hardly fulfil them – Sylvia felt his erect penis push against her stomach. For her part, Sylvia felt like she was drowning in a sea of desire. Later that night, at the house of his friend, after kissing his 'sensuous and lovely' mouth, she told him what she had been thinking all along: that he didn't give a damn about her except physically. He couldn't deny it, but he wished that she hadn't said it as 'the truth always hurts.' After he had dropped her back home, she was left thinking of Eddie's line about the fact that, for all of the developments in civilisation over the course of history, humans were nothing more than animals.[33]

On their second date, Sylvia felt even more attracted to Emile.[34] He placed his hand on her stomach and kissed her 'hungrily', but when he whispered to her that he liked her, but not too much – he didn't want to fall into the trap of liking anybody too much – she blurted out her true feelings: that she was an all or nothing sort of girl. In that instant, their brief relationship was over. He wished her well at Smith, she told him that she hoped he had a nice life, and then he walked down the path and away. In her journal she writes of how she stood there, all alone, crying in the dark.[35]

The experience with Emile inspired Sylvia's story 'Den of Lions', which won third prize in the *Seventeen* short-story competition. In it, she is Marcia, a young, inexperienced, socially anxious girl who goes on a couple of dates with a boy named Emile. She is worried about being seen drinking ginger ale instead of beer and self-conscious that she is not as witty or charming as the rest of the older, more sophisticated group. When one of the boys, Peter – based on Emile's friend of the same name – tells a dirty story, she feels ill at ease, like a Christian thrown to the lions. At the end of the evening, Emile whispers the same line that his real-life counterpart uttered to Sylvia, at which point she makes the decision to stop seeing him. The last lines of the story – which was published in *Seventeen* in May 1951 – were lifted virtually word for word from her journal entry.[36]

As Sylvia was working on the story – which she described as having been wrenched out of her life – Eddie Cohen wrote her a letter that made the point that there was quite a difference between sex in the real world and romance as promulgated by *Seventeen*. In a funny skit he wrote of the magazine's production code, he said that a heroine of a *Seventeen* story should not be both beautiful and popular at the beginning of the tale, as readers would not be able to identify with her. She should not have breasts, but 'in circumstances of extreme duress she may heave her chest in a sigh [. . .] Legs are permissible,' but no female character 'shall in any circumstances be possessed of the organs of reproduction, nor of the desires which accompany them'. This was probably not strictly necessary, he added, as the heroes featured in the stories were mostly lacking sexual urges. A girl should neither drink nor smoke, unless she regrets it at the end of the story, but she could have differences with her parents, who always act with the best of intentions. 'No heroine,' however, 'must permit herself any expression of anger or futility stronger than those used in Little Orphan Annie.'[37]

As Sylvia prepared to enter Smith, the anger she felt would not go away. One night, while babysitting for a neighbour, she wrote in her journal that her unexpressed sexual desire was driving her to the point of distraction. She was, she said, sick with longing'.[38]

In mid-September 1950, Sylvia travelled for the first time the hundred miles from her home in Wellesley to Northampton. She walked along the quiet streets up towards Observatory Hill and looked back at the Smith campus, with its mix of pretty, traditional clapperboard houses and elegant late-nineteenth-century neo-classical buildings, and watched the sunshine dance across the roof of the glasshouse that sat next to the splendours of the aptly named Paradise Pond. As she gazed upon the college, she felt a quiet exhilaration run through her. Until this moment, the college had remained within the realms of the unreal, a mere fantasy; although she knew she had been accepted, Smith was nothing more than a dream to her. Then, she walked back down to the campus, stopped outside Haven House and stared up at one of the windows. Suddenly it was all very real: from the following week this would be her home for the next year. She was going to be a Smith girl.

The independent liberal-arts college for women, standing in the picture-postcard town of Northampton, had been founded in 1871 (opening in 1875) with a $400,000 bequest left by Sophia Smith, a Massachusetts' spinster. Although she had been going to leave her fortune, which she had inherited from her father and brother, to fund an institute for the deaf (she had lost her hearing at the age of forty) Sophia was persuaded that the money could be put to better use educating women. By all accounts, Sophia had led rather a sheltered, quiet existence. Her friend the Reverend John M. Greene recalled, 'There were no startling episodes, no wild romances' in her life. 'She built few castles in dreamland or in love-land. Life was serious, real, to her. She walked with her feet on *terra firma*, not in the clouds.'[39] By the time Sylvia arrived, the academic reputation of the college was outstanding; alumnae have included Margaret Mitchell (who left after one year); Julia Child (who graduated in 1934); Betty Friedman (1942); Nancy Reagan (1943); and Barbara Bush (1947).

What was the role of Smith? According to English professor Mary Ellen Chase – who taught at the college from 1922 until her retirement in 1955 – it was a place where individuals could meet, learn and interact. She was wise enough to acknowledge that its students would probably not change the world; more important, she thought, was the contribution each of them made to the intellectual and social atmosphere first at Smith and then in communities they would encounter in their lives. 'I like the idea, which I think is prevalent amongst us, that four years at Smith College are not so much a preparation for a larger life as they are in themselves a larger life here and now,' said Chase, who during the course of her career wrote more than thirty books, 'a life filled with opportunities for new excitements in study for its own sake, for fun in new friendships and pastimes, for the discovery of values and loyalties both in books and in people, in short for those enduring satisfactions in human life, thought, and aspiration which, quite literally, "cannot be shaken".'[40]

Although many people assumed that the women's college was a cloistered environment this was far from the truth. 'Too many absurdities have been uttered concerning the ivory towers and sheltered walls of a college,' said Chase. 'We have no such nonsense here. We are a quite unsheltered community of some 2,500 fellow-students, some teaching and some being taught, all, let us hope, studying and thinking together. As in any such community we have the superior and the average, the grave and the frivolous, the rich and the poor, the potential scholar and the charming hostess, the rural and the urban from every state in the Union and from foreign countries as well. We look daily upon faces that might well "launch a thousand ships" and upon faces, which alone will never startle or waylay; we associate daily with some minds which are second to none and with others which surely need refurnishing, not to say redecoration.'[41]

The general stereotype of a 'Smithie' was a girl who was eminently sensible, highly intelligent, charming and often quite wealthy; a perfect wife for her male counterpart at Yale or Princeton. Although Sylvia was a scholarship student, the continuance of her grant depended on her earning top grades; if her marks slipped, her money would be withdrawn and she would be forced to leave. Within a couple of days she mentioned her money worries to a girl who lived in Lawrence House, a cooperative building that accommodated girls who paid reduced fees in exchange for work, and she also started to keep a record of exactly how much she spent. She deposited $180 in the bank, and noted (slightly guiltily) in a letter home to her mother that she spent $4 on a table. During her first academic year, she spent $30 on books; $25 on art supplies; $25 on her room; $25 on food; $50 on clothes; $15 on entertainment; $25 on transportation; $25 on dues and fees; and $50 on miscellaneous items.

From the beginning – and not for the first time – she also felt socially inferior. Many of the other girls in Haven House, where she was the only freshman on the very top floor, were from families that were not only rich but socially well connected too. Excised from one of her letters to her mother published in

Letters Home, written on 26 September 1950, was a sarcastic comment Sylvia made to Aurelia about the girls' upper-class accents.[42]

She also felt insignificant, disorientated by the sea of faces that she encountered on her freshman evening. Standing there, on the steps of the Scott Gymnasium, watching six hundred women walk by, she felt herself slipping away. Would she ever feel more substantial than simply a name typed out on a card?[43]

At times Sylvia felt empty, blank, in need of an identity. She knew it was up to her to fashion a life for herself at Smith and to construct a personality to match.[44] To her mother, however, she wrote a steady stream of jolly-sounding cards and letters. Her room, she said, was like a New York apartment and she adored the touch of her wooden desk.[45] All the girls in her house were so jolly and amenable, she said.[46] Her first assembly – in which she saw the staff, dressed in all their finery march across the stage - was so moving that she felt on the verge of tears. 'I still can't believe I'm a SMITH GIRL!' she wrote.[47] She even managed to make a joke about her embarrassing 'physical', which involved stripping off, and then, once swathed in a sheet, passing from room to room where she was told to drop her covering. She said she was so used to hearing the words 'Drop your sheet' that she had to remind herself to put on clothes each morning. A picture was taken of her posture – she stood at five feet nine inches tall and weighed 137 pounds – but she concentrated so hard on keeping her ears and heels in a straight line that she 'forgot to tilt up straight'. The result was the comment that although she had quite a good posture she was seriously in danger of falling flat on her face, a diagnosis that would be proven to be true.[48] 'I remember that she seemed to be all elbows,' says Ann Hayes (neé Davidow), a tall, freckle-faced Jewish girl, whom Sylvia met in Haven House in her first few days at Smith. 'She was a startlingly attractive, but somewhat physically awkward kind of person. I saw her as quite ungainly, but at the same time she was something of a blonde bombshell. She had this blonde hair that she draped over one eye. She really was quite a stunner.'[49]

From the beginning the two young women – whose birthdays were only one day apart – hit it off; Sylvia said that 'she is the closest girl yet that I've wanted for a friend' and described Ann as a 'free thinker'.[50] Ann recalls, 'Sylvia was the first person I met at Haven House and we became close quickly. She was one of those people who fused with other people very fast and our relationship instantly took off. We had a very, very intense friendship and she was very kind to me. I couldn't type, but Sylvia insisted on typing all my college papers for me. I always thought that was a darn nice thing to do. She had this garret room right at the top of Haven House and I remember going up to see her in the attic, which was a very intimate, personal space. She was very effusive and she did have at that time a manic quality to her personality; she had an incredible "upness" and exuberance. One could not just be a friend, one had to be "the most wonderful friend", which is how she saw me. Even then, she was fascinated by the concept of the double – that we were the same person – and although we had a few things in common, I wanted to say to her, "Just cool your jets". I was not quite the soul mate she was looking for and I thought somebody needed to slow her down at times. She was very aware of which other girls were cliqued off – she thought everybody belonged in some sort of group and she felt left out. She worried about building friendships – she wanted to forge close relationships with other girls – but did not want to pay the social cost of being friends with too many people.'[51]

Sylvia's policy of social isolation had its consequences; the other girls in Haven House viewed her with suspicion and often made catty remarks not only behind her back but also to her face. One day she walked down the stairs of Haven to the ground floor to pick up a letter from her pigeonhole, and, overhearing the murmur of voices coming from the living room, felt immediately anxious and paranoid: surely the girls were talking about her. Instantly, she remembered, a ragbag of unpleasant remarks which, looking back, she now knew were directed towards her. Yet often the verbal and psychological attack was so subtle that both antagonist and victim pretended there wasn't a problem. Sylvia was so overwhelmed by 'fear and inadequacy' that she could not respond to barbs that were designed to insult and humiliate her; all she did was keep her mouth shut and smile.[52]

At the beginning of October, Ann organised a blind date for Sylvia. It was, in fact, a triple date, with three girls meeting three boys from nearby Amherst College. When she arrived at the campus Sylvia was relieved to see that the one marked out for her, Bill Gallup, was six feet tall, slim and fresh-faced. Immediately, the couple separated from the crowd and went to his room, where they talked about religious belief and the concept of the ego. He told her that she seemed like a girl who lived intensely, that she was rather theatrical in her manner and occasionally talked like a young girl 'reporting a theme'.[53] They went on to enjoy a dance at one of the houses and then proceeded to walk around the campus at night. She felt comfortable with Bill and was relieved she hadn't had to spend the night sitting in a room filled with smoke trying to keep a false smile on her face; rather, she was able to simply be herself, she said. At the end of the night, as the other couples were kissing each other outside Haven House, he turned to her, commented on the lack of people's inhibitions and lightly kissed the tip of her nose.[54]

A couple of weekends later, Sylvia went over to Amherst

again with Ann. Yet her night out consisted mostly of sitting on Bill's red sofa, where she dozed for two hours. This, however, was better than being in the midst of a group of people, pretending to be someone she wasn't.[55] By this point, however, her initial enthusiasm for him had dissipated. 'It [. . .] was,' as Eddie Cohen pointed out, 'something in your mental attitude towards him' that had changed;[56] it seemed Bill had simply served his purpose. At that moment in time, Sylvia needed a quiet, sensitive boy – a young man who reminded her of her brother – and Bill had played that role to perfection. She realised that she easily outgrew men – before arriving at Smith she had already decided that Bob Riedeman no longer suited her. 'My feeling is that Sylvia found a life at Smith that was very stimulating, but it could not include me,' says Bob more than sixty years later. 'I've often said that she went on to bigger and better things.'[57] Yet Sylvia was also conscious of the dangers involved in the dating game: if she regularly cast men aside then she had to be aware that one day it could happen to her. If somebody did jilt her in the same kind of fashion, she wrote in her journal, she was sure this would be some sort of 'poetic justice'.[58]

Soon after Sylvia's relationship with Bill Gallup ended, Ann managed to set up another blind date for her with 'a very straight-laced young man' from Amherst, Guy Wilbor, who had been a classmate of Ann's at high school.[59] By this point Sylvia was so desperate to be seen to be enjoying herself on a Saturday night – rather than face the snide comments of her fellow housemates – that she said she wouldn't have cared if he were only five feet tall. Luckily, he was six feet two and sweet-natured. Although there was, as she said, no 'spark', at least he seemed wholesome and pleasant.[60] 'My first impressions of her was that she fit the type that went to Smith,' recalls Guy. 'She was very interesting to talk to, seemed knowledgeable, erudite and interested in what I was saying. I remember I did a lot of the talking, about the stock that I owned and making money from the stock market, and she seemed interested in that. We went on another date – I think she came to dinner at Valentine Hall, Amherst – and I recall enjoying talking to her. I think she said that she would like to become a writer – she already was one at the time, but she kept that secret. I didn't think she was a raving beauty or anything; she was quite a plain girl, not made up or anything, and we had no real physical contact apart from holding hands. You've got to remember everything proceeded so much slower in those days and the 1950s was very much an age of innocence.'[61]

Sylvia, however, was not quite as innocent as she appeared: during that night's date with Guy she proceeded to use him as a means by which she could bolster her self-image. It was important for her social standing, she said, to be seen to be accompanied by an eligible man; her moment of triumph was greeting Bill Gallup. She was, as she wrote in her journal, so pleased he saw her enjoying herself with another boy. Later, Bill rang and asked whether he could give her a ride home at Thanksgiving; as she accepted, she reflected on her slow rise up the social ladder. She knew that she was capable of academic achievement and she was aware that she was more than adept at attracting the attention of males. Things were looking up, she observed. In the future, when faced with difficulties, she had to remember to view things from a balanced perspective and try to keep her robust sense of humour intact. After all, she believed in Heraclitus' aphorism 'Character is fate'. Could she now dare to hope that her outlook was an auspicious one?[62]

At the end of October, Sylvia was called in to see Mary Elizabeth Mensel, the director of scholarships and student aid at Smith. Although she was nervous about the meeting – she even wrote to her mother to ask her what to say – when she sat down in front of the older woman she found herself enthusing about the college, its courses and environment, with a natural passion that dispelled any awkwardness. During the conversation, Mensel revealed to Sylvia the identity of her 'benefactress', the woman who had endowed her $850 scholarship and who had, in effect, changed the course of her life: the novelist Olive Higgins Prouty. Prouty – who had been born in Worcester, Massachusetts, and graduated with a bachelor in literature degree from Smith in 1904 – had made a fortune by writing lush, bestselling melodramas such as *Now, Voyager* (1941). Sylvia wrote home to tell her mother how rare it was for a freshman to win the scholarship, but it had been awarded to her because of her proven writing and publishing success. She also told her mother that Prouty would be keen to hear more about her progress at Smith.[63]

Plath later said that when she discovered the identity of her benefactress she felt 'a magical kinship' with her; throughout her childhood Prouty had been a household name. In a piece of reportage that she wrote later, titled 'Tea with Olive Higgins Prouty', Plath related how as a girl she would listen to the radio serial *Stella, Dallas*, adapted from the novel of the same name. And now, years later, Prouty was 'personally responsible' for her presence at Smith.[64]

A month later, Sylvia wrote a letter to Prouty outlining what Smith meant to her. In the letter, which she wrote easily and speedily,[65] Plath described the sense of joy and disbelief at hearing the news that she had been accepted to the college, and outlined the reality of her day-to-day life. It was, without a doubt, the most challenging experience of her life; later she would describe her time at Smith as a series of 'rapid idea-inoculations'.[66] To Prouty she wrote of how she felt stimulated by the education she was receiving at Smith.[67]

Each week Sylvia had twenty-four hours of classes, comprising English, Introduction to French Literature, botany, art, physical education and General European History. She said she loved each of her subjects in turn and told her mother that she was being 'stretched' in directions she never thought possible,[68] but found history the most challenging. There were 600 other girls in the lecture hall and, because she had never studied European history in any detail before, she found the work difficult; each night she had to force herself to plough through forty pages of dense text about the past. English, if anything, was a little too easy. The freshman course did not include any creative writing and, on one occasion, her teacher told her that she should let others in her class 'work at a story analysis once in a while'. However, it was annoying to observe people wrestle with techniques and aspects of fiction writing that she grasped with ease.[69] In her mid-term exams she received a string of good results: A in botany, A-minus in both French and history, B in English and B-minus in art.

Particularly satisfying was the cross-fertilisation of ideas across many of her favourite subjects. For instance, in art she sketched the same trees that she analysed in botany. And when she bicycled across campus she didn't just see trees; rather, she saw inside the trees to the cellular structures that she had studied in the laboratory.[70] She told Prouty that she had always been introspective and, especially in her teenage years, she had felt a need to try to express herself. Interestingly, one section of the letter, excised from *Letters Home*, focused on the development of her writer's technique: how she often observed incidents and conversations involving herself from the perspective of the third person. She always felt a compulsion to wrench chunks of experience out of her life and write them down on paper, she said. Sylvia also told her benefactress – who would play an increasingly important role in her life – that, since arriving at Smith, she had been impressed by the 'dignity and capacity of women'. She adored hearing about her fellow students' backgrounds, especially learning about the lives of those young women who had been born and brought up outside New England. She felt that the country – indeed, the whole world – was waiting for her. There were so many little details of her life at Smith that enriched her existence, she wrote; she adored the view of Paradise Pond from her window, the sound of the chapel bells pealing on Sunday afternoon, and the sight of the lights of the campus houses contrasted against the night sky. At the end of the letter she stopped to thank Olive Higgins Prouty once more; she realized that the scholarship had the power to transform her life. Sylvia emphasized that her benefactress was responsible for 'the formation of an individual'.[71]

There is something more than a little uncanny about the last sentence; indeed, in many ways Sylvia could have stepped straight out of one of Prouty's books, particularly *Now, Voyager*. The novel – made into a Hollywood melodrama in 1942 starring Bette Davis in the lead role – tells the story of Charlotte Vale, a repressed, fatherless, rather bookish woman who attempts to free herself from the unhealthy grip of an over-possessive mother. The toxic relationship between mother and daughter, both of whom live in Boston, results in Charlotte's complete mental breakdown, and she is forced to spend a couple of months in an upmarket psychiatric hospital set in its own grounds. Like Charlotte, Sylvia questioned the reality of her own existence and often felt separated and distanced from the immediacy of her life. The two women – the fictional and the real – experienced, as Prouty writes in the novel, a 'sensation of detachment' from their own personalities, a symptom that, in both cases, would culminate in a nervous breakdown.[72] In Charlotte's case her mental collapse was caused by a lack of independence from her mother and an overwhelming sense of failure; similar factors contributed to Plath's own breakdown and suicide attempt in 1953. Prouty wrote *Now, Voyager* from experience: she had suffered two nervous breakdowns – one in 1894, when she was only twelve years old, and the other in 1925, after the death of a daughter. It seems likely that she drew on the confusions and crises of adolescence in the creation of the anxious Tina, the daughter of Jerry, Charlotte's love interest in *Now, Voyager.* Tina suffers from an abnormal devotion to her father, a love that makes her mother jealous of their relationship; was this another parallel that Sylvia saw reflected in her own life when she read the novel? Certainly, as Prouty writes, 'One cannot evade one's personality by running away from it.'[73]

Sylvia knew this all too well. One day, while sitting in the library at Smith, she took out her journal and wrote about feeling lost, leached of identity. What did she consist of, she asked herself as she looked at the room packed with girls. Was Smith nothing but a glorified centre for conditioning? She was sure that Aldous Huxley, the author of *Brave New World*, would appreciate the observation. If she stopped to think she felt herself going insane. 'If I rest, if I think inward, I go mad,' she wrote in her journal.[74] She continued to regularly depend on sleeping pills and by the time Thanksgiving came she felt so exhausted that she was looking forward to a few days' rest at home in Wellesley. On her return to Smith, at the end of November 1950, she felt gripped by a deep depression. In her journal she wrote about a sense of loneliness that enveloped her, a malady that she compared to a disease of the blood, an illness that had spread its contagion throughout the body.[75] Although she could have tried to escape the cloud of melancholy that seemed to cling to her, by simply walking out of her room and involving herself in a light conversation with some girls on the ground floor, she wanted to confront these unpleasant feelings and begin to analyse them. What was the point of it all, she asked? Why carry on when she could just as easily commit suicide? She felt unsettled by a sense of self-hatred, 'torn between I know not what within me'.[76] No doubt the loneliness would pass when she began her classes the next day, but still the sickness in her soul would remain.[77]

Sylvia's spirits were boosted, however, when she received a letter back from Olive Higgins Prouty, in her near-illegible handwriting, thanking her for her letter and informing her that she was having copies of it made so she could send it to a few of her friends. 'I think there is no doubt that you possess a gift for creative writing,' said Prouty.[78] The novelist also invited her to tea at her home in nearby Brookline, Massachusetts, over the Christmas vacation. To prepare for the visit, Sylvia read her way through most of Prouty's oeuvre and she observed how her characters seemed to stand in stark contrast to the 'bitter, depressed' protagonists that peopled the novels of her modern-literature course. As she read Prouty's work she felt 'the same warm heart' that she had sensed in the letter the author had written.[79] Yet on the bus to Prouty's mansion Sylvia found herself gripped by worries. How could she justify the scholarship? What would happen if she never realised her dreams of becoming a good writer? Would Prouty be disappointed in her? Would her college withdraw the scholarship and give it to an older girl who was already in the process of writing a best-selling novel? Dressed in her best wool suit, and holding her white gloves in her hand, she walked up the curved driveway towards the enormous white house and rang the doorbell. From inside, she heard the yap of a dog and the approach of footsteps. A maid wearing a white apron opened the door and told her to enter; Mrs Prouty would be down in a few minutes. Sylvia was shown into a large room with blue walls, gold curtains and French doors that opened onto a delightful terrace. As she was admiring the author's taste, a voice surprised her with the words, 'You must be Sylvia!' A tall, handsome, blue-eyed woman, who looked to be in her late sixties, stretched out her hand as she walked towards her; at that moment all Sylvia's 'misgivings' disappeared. Over tea and cucumber sandwiches Prouty asked Sylvia about her background; she told her that after her father had died her mother had taken a teaching job. Had she ever written about her family? Sylvia told her she had not: after all, she came from such an ordinary home. 'For you, perhaps,' Prouty smiled, 'but not for me, not for others. Think of the material you have there!'[80] Later, when Plath ransacked her own life – and indeed included caricatures of Aurelia Plath and Olive Higgins Prouty in *The Bell Jar* – the author would have cause to regret this piece of advice.

For the next hour the bestselling novelist and novice writer talked about the craft of writing, with Prouty telling Plath how she had begun her career by drawing inspiration from her own environment. As she left the Brookline mansion, Sylvia felt confident to be able to follow Prouty's guidelines. After all, she observed, a trip to the local store could be just as interesting as a journey to Tibet; the skill lay in the storytelling, the development of narrative and drama. Plath felt inspired by Prouty's advice to search for material in the everyday stories of human interaction and experience. Whenever she felt discouraged or bored with her writing she said she would remember Prouty's words, 'Take life!'[81]

In November 1950, *Seventeen* published Sylvia's poem 'Ode to a Bitten Plum', for which she received ten dollars. Soon the clipping from the magazine found its way onto the bulletin board in College Hall. 'By the way, I'm almost famous!' wrote Sylvia to her mother.[82] Two months later, she learned that the magazine had awarded her a third prize of $100 for her story 'Den of Lions'. 'It seems my love affairs always get into print,' she said, remembering how her encounter with Emile had inspired the story.[83] Again, the news of her success quickly spread around the college; later, Sylvia would write that the only silent woman is a dead one.[84] One day a senior girl turned to her and congratulated her on appearing on the College Hall bulletin board for the second time in the space of a few months. Sylvia rushed over to the hall and found a cartoon by Stookie Allen that had appeared in an Illinois paper under the heading, 'Born to Write'. The feature – which had been published without her knowledge or input – was so overwrought it reduced Sylvia to fits of laughter. 'To get atmosphere for a story about a farm she took a job as a farmhand,' it said. 'Now she's working on a sea story,' for which she was apparently prepared to get a job on a boat. The preposterousness of it all delighted her, as was evident in the letter she wrote home to her mother.[85] The newspaper also stated, accurately, that a national magazine had printed two of her stories, or 'brain children'; after all, publication was 'the real test of being a writer'.[86]

Not all her critics were so laudatory, however. When Eddie Cohen read 'Ode to a Bitten Plum' in *Seventeen* he found it disappointing. 'You tried to make too much out of the subject,' he said, 'with the result that it was somewhat overdone.' He did note, however, that Plath seemed to have a special attraction to colours. 'I notice that all your poetry is liberally splattered with chromatic references.'[87] Eddie admitted he had felt a twinge of satisfaction when he read in one of her letters about a date that had disappointed her, and also pangs of jealousy when she reported that she had enjoyed a night out with a man. For a couple of months he had toyed with the idea of turning up on her doorstep, but he reasoned that perhaps this was not such a good idea. 'Maybe two writers could never get along anyhow,' he wrote. 'They are apt to commit double homicide over each other's criticisms of their work.'[88]

Eddie also pointed out that she had not had enough experience of life, or of love, to be able to write convincingly of its complexities. Although she did have quite an unusual insight and understanding of 'the world in terms of ideas and groups of people', she did not grasp the reality of the individual in conflict with either himself or herself and society at large. 'This results from two things: never [having] had the experience of facing demanding personal situations on your own; and never having had a really compelling, overwhelming love affair.'[89] He praised her for her highly developed sensitivity – and the fact that she reacted more intensely to ordinary stimuli such as the patter of rain or the crunch of leaves underfoot – but warned her that her emotional range was still quite narrow. She had, he maintained, never suffered from unrequited love, serious financial difficulties or messy parental conflicts. 'The last year,' he said, 'I have seen many of my friends, all of whom are hard-headed, clear-thinking people, driven to sanatoriums and asylums because of such influences. And the more sensitive a person is, the more likely affected he is.' He recollected the first story he had read of hers, 'And Summer Will Not Come Again', the one that had compelled him to write to her a few months before. This was, he said, only a 'fractional thing', expressing only a few facets of her personality, a mere fragment of her talent. 'When you have experienced a full, complete love, and the searing that accompanies its break-up, then you will understand,' he wrote. 'Then, too, I think, you will be a great writer. Now, you have the eyes and ears and soul of a great writer. Then, you will have the heart of one.'[90]

Five

WHO IS SYLVIA?

The Christmas vacation of 1950 was not a happy one for Sylvia. Although she had been looking forward to a little rest and recuperation, within a few days of being back at Elmwood Road she had fallen into a deep depression. She realised that one of the factors that contributed to her low mood was that she felt she had to pretend to be happy in front of her mother. As she wrote in a letter to a friend, her mother's *raison d'être* was the knowledge that Sylvia and Warren were happy and fulfilled. Aurelia had worked like a slave and sacrificed her health for the sake of her two children; the least Sylvia could do was to try to convince her mother she was enjoying life. Yet the strain of keeping up appearances was not conducive to her mental health. She also acknowledged that she could no longer turn to Aurelia in moments of emotional crisis and she realised that she was afraid of taking on the responsibilities of an adult. Her mother admitted that she had cosseted her; indeed Aurelia called Sylvia the prima donna of the family. 'We freed her from the chores the rest of us shared to keep a home running when I had to teach and travel to my post each day in order to support us,' she wrote, 'for we felt Sylvia had more talent than the rest of us and should have the opportunity to develop it.'[1] Now, as Sylvia was striving to become more independent, she felt anxious about the everyday aspects of life such as cooking, cleaning and, most frightening of all, the necessity of earning one's living.

Often, she looked back at her own childhood with a sense of longing, nostalgia for a time of romanticised certainty and infantilised escapism. One senses from reading her journal entries that Sylvia found the journey from innocence to experience a far from easy transition. Many aspects of life angered her, she said, and she went on to make a long list of all the difficulties and anxieties that she encountered in the adult world: words such as 'fairy', once so lovely and untainted, now seemed soiled with smutty meanings; fraternity parties where the threat of sexual assault hung heavy in the air like cigarette smoke; the reality of competition, in which she had to participate without having the luxuries of riches or extravagant good looks; the limits of her background, which she said proscribed and narrowed her chances of achievement in the creative world; the gap between her ideal of a mate and the awful actuality, that a man really wants a woman for nothing more than sex and housework; and the ominous spectre of the mental hospital on the hill in Northampton. She wondered why children were conditioned to grow up in an idyllic, magical world 'only to be broken on the wheel as we grow older'.[2] She also questioned the construction of her own personality, the enigma of her identity. If she had been born of Italian parents who lived in the caves there is little doubt she would have grown up to be a prostitute at the age of twelve, she said. By contrast, if she had been born into a wealthy, cultured New York family she would enjoy a life that was richer intellectually and she would already be equipped with an address book overflowing with useful and important contacts. The multitude of different egos spread across the planet was too problematic to think about. So intrigued was she by the idea of individual consciousness that she wrote out the letter 'I' several times in her journal, a symbol perhaps of her fragmented, or multiple, identities. She constantly aspired to be cleverer, more beautiful, more skilled than she was and admitted that she was envious of those 'who live better, who love better than I.'[3]

Over the vacation she also took steps to finally sever contact with Bob Riedeman, telling him, in rather harsh terms, that she felt full of hatred for everything and everyone and cared only for herself. She also informed him that a war veteran who had taken her out on a blind date had tried to force her to have sex. Although she had managed to fight him off – and make very clear how much she loathed the inequalities that existed between the sexes – she had been shocked to find that he still wanted her to masturbate him. The combination of the verbal onslaught, together with this rather unsavoury revelation, repelled Bob Riedeman for good.

Then, just before New Year's Eve, she came down with sinusitis, an infection that she had suffered from ever since she was a child. During the vacation her mother had warned her to try to look after herself, but too many late nights took their toll. Whenever Sylvia came down with sinusitis, she felt, as she confessed in a letter to her mother, like a 'depressive maniac'[4] and Eddie Cohen suspected that the illness was purely psychosomatic. As he wrote to her: 'every cold which you have written me about has come on the heels of a breakup or other unfortunate experience with a male.'[5] Intriguingly, the first occurrence of the illness came in the week after her father had died. It seems probable that her repeated attacks of sinusitis were physical expressions of separation anxiety.

When she returned to Smith in January her spirits didn't recover. Dosed up on penicillin and nose drops she felt devastated by the news that her friend Ann Davidow had withdrawn from the college and would not be coming back. Sylvia knew that her friend had had problems – in December, Ann had become so depressed that she had suicidal thoughts. She could not cope with the workload; she couldn't sleep; she felt a failure; she thought she was just not bright enough for Smith. In a letter to her mother Sylvia confessed that she became frightened when Ann told her that she had been building up a secret stash of razor blades and sleeping pills and that she often dreamt of ending it all.[6] Sylvia had tried to talk to her in order to boost Ann's self-image, but nothing seemed to lift the blackness that seemed to oppress her. Sylvia had thought about writing to Ann's parents, but she knew that the girl's mother refused to believe there was anything wrong with her daughter. 'I didn't adjust to Smith at all, and I think my lack of adjustment resonated with her,' says Ann.[7] With Ann, Sylvia felt like she could 'face anything'; without her she was 'bereft'.[8] Now, Sylvia noticed that the girls in Haven House were forming into cliques: one girl, Blanton, was in the process of transforming herself into a socialite and running about with the upper classes, while the trio of friends Maureen, Diana and Reggie had grouped themselves into a snobbish little gang and who continually made snide remarks.[9] She desperately missed Ann Davidow and admitted to feeling jealous of her friend's newfound happiness – Ann adored her art school and her new boyfriend. In a letter to Ann, Sylvia wrote of the crucial psychological role her friend had played in her life, outlining how she felt so totally empty she almost wished she had never met her. She told her that her friend played a key role in balancing her; without her she felt disoriented and out of kilter.[10] On hearing the news of Ann's departure from Smith, Eddie Cohen wrote to Sylvia to say that the two Chicagoans must meet up, provided Ann had 'not already placed her head in an oven or something like that [. . .] Anyone with suicidal tendencies should fit neatly into the group of neurotics and semi-psychotics with whom I surround myself.'[11]

Sylvia's despondent mood was reflected in her journals; entries written at the beginning of 1951 express her sense of alienation from the world and her terror of a nuclear war. She was horrified to learn of the atomic bombs being tested in Nevada and recalled a harrowing description of the victims of Nagasaki, in which the injured were compared to lizards crawling up the hill. As she watched snow fall outside her window, she tried to imagine what life would be like if America was attacked by atomic weapons. A vision of the countryside being bombarded flashed into her mind, and she could almost hear the cries of the innocent victims.[12] In the post-nuclear world there would be no such thing as democracy or freedom, concepts so beloved by modern America. She wondered, once again, about the double standards involved in warfare – and why it was acceptable to award a medal to someone who had slaughtered hundreds of people in battle and then electrocute a man who had killed another individual. She had heard that her old high-school English teacher, Wilbury Crockett, had been questioned by the authorities on suspicion of being a communist; in fact, as he went on to explain to the Town Board in Wellesley, he was simply a pacifist. In today's paranoid world that obviously constituted a crime, she observed.[13]

She surmised that she was living in an age of decline and went on to compare the United States to the Roman Empire in its final stages. Perhaps this was the beginning of a new 'dark age', she surmised.[14] All of us were living on the edge of an abyss, she wrote, and it took a great deal of courage to be able to step towards the precipice and look down to see what lies beneath. She was conscious that she could investigate the darkness further, by using writing as a tool of analysis.[15] Plath did just that, constantly feeling compelled to move closer to the edge – an impulse that carried with it adverse consequences for her mental health.

January 1951 was taken up with hours of studying for exams. Sylvia pushed herself hard and on 1 February she wrote to her mother of the stress she had been under. Although the tone of the letter was unmistakably upbeat – she made a black joke that she would either hang herself with her typewriter ribbon or join Alcoholics Anonymous – the tangle of names and dates that she was expected to memorise for her history exam left her feeling tense. Again, she self-medicated, turning to her trusty stock of sleeping pills to try to relieve her anxiety. She also admitted that her depression and tiredness might have been caused by the onset of her period, the first that she had had for five months.

Her hard work paid off when she learnt that she had received As in history and botany, A-minuses in French and art, and a B-plus in English. Constantly she challenged herself, yet no matter how much she achieved she felt disappointed. She knew she could never get through all the books she would like to read, neither could she satisfy her desire to inhabit a myriad different personalities.[16] She realised she had advantages, and she was conscious of how much she had already accomplished, yet still felt dissatisfied and melancholic.[17] She traced this malaise back to her inability or unwillingness to choose between alternatives. After all, if she wore the mask of a number of different personalities no one could blame her for 'being I'.[18]

After the departure of Ann Davidow, Sylvia was on the lookout for another student whom she could claim as a soul mate. The role fell to Marcia Brown, a short, ebullient fellow freshman who lived on the first floor at Haven House. Looking back over her close female friends, and analysing each in turn, she realised that Marcia, from New Jersey, combined many of their best qualities; in future letters, Sylvia would address her as 'Angel Child'. 'She was really tall – I'm barely five foot – and she had a wonderful blonde page hairdo, and she was a bit gangly,' remembers Marcia. 'She wanted to talk with everyone in our dorm and she was fun to be with.'[19] Marcia liked Sylvia's 'eager enthusiasm, [her] absolute attentiveness to one, intelligence, [and] interest in all manner of things, and we shared many interests and concerns'.[20]

Marcia defines their friendship as that of 'two young, starry-eyed women who were embarking on adventures of study and learning and being away from home. It kind of set the tone of how we communicated with each other [. . .] There was a bond between us and a real kind of love between us that had nothing to do with her creativity necessarily or her success as a poet. It was just that, a really wonderful friendship.'[21]

At the beginning of February, Marcia invited Sylvia to come and stay at the house of her Aunt Harriet in Francistown, New Hampshire. From there, Sylvia wrote a letter to her mother, describing how she had fallen in love with Marcia's aunt's home: with its dark grey floors, simple white walls, green woodwork and dusty rose-patterned curtains, the house appealed to what she called her puritanical nature. After Sylvia had spent the night in Marcia's room, with its modest bunk beds, the two girls decided to share a room at Smith; for Sylvia, who always had to watch how much she spent, this meant a saving of $50 a year. Marcia remembers her friend's elaborate bedtime routine. Sylvia had, she recalls, 'this long, blonde hair [. . .] and every night she got into an aqua-blue bath robe, and then she had to put up her hair', using pieces of torn cloth. 'And then she put Noxzema on her face, thick Noxzema which I think has one of the worst odours ever. I almost moved out after the first three days just because she smelt so awful.'[22]

Sylvia's spirits were raised in February by the arrival of a letter from Dick Norton, the elder brother of her friend Perry. Sylvia had always viewed him as a cousin figure – indeed, she addressed Dick's parents as uncle and aunt – which is why she was somewhat surprised that Dick, who was in his senior year at Yale, was inviting her down to the college for a weekend. The letter was polite in tone, but it was difficult to discern whether he wanted to move their relationship forwards or merely keep it on its existing plane. However, when Sylvia told him, in a 'sparkly' note,[23] that she would be free on the weekend of 17 February – it was Yale's annual swimming carnival – he allowed his reserve to drop a little. When she asked what she should bring down for her stay, he wrote back, 'Just please Syl, no firearms, pet alligators; you know how old-fashioned we are here.'[24] Sylvia told Ann Davidow the exciting news about the forthcoming date and, although she tried to remain cool and disinterested – after all, the meeting did not guarantee the development of a romance – she did confess that Dick, a medical student who was handsome, blond and intelligent, did seem rather perfect. What was particularly intriguing, added Sylvia, was the fact that he had invited her down to Yale again for another weekend in March – and they hadn't yet even had their first date.

The Plath and Norton families had known each other for years. In fact, when Dick's mother, Mildred, had been an undergraduate at Boston University she had studied German under Otto Plath. William Bunnell Norton, Dick's father, after graduating with a BA and a PhD from Yale, taught history there from 1927; he later recalled that he first met Aurelia – and a very young Sylvia, age two or three – at a Christmas party organised by the Faculty Wives' Club. Yet it wasn't until after Otto's death and Aurelia's move to Wellesley that the two families became closer, 'but not really intimate,' said Dick's father, 'though a couple of miles apart in the same town and connected with B.U. through separate colleges, we discovered similar interests and came to have numerous other friends in common.'[25]

On their first weekend together, Sylvia and Dick spent a great deal of time talking in his room; there was precious little else to do since it rained all day. That Saturday night they went to the swimming meet, and later he accompanied her to the female-only set of rooms where she was to spend the night. On Sunday they dressed in old clothes and took a bike ride to a nearby hill where they could look back over New Haven. Throughout their time together, she felt rather overawed by Dick's scientific approach to life: according to his world view only things that could be measured, analysed or cut open had any value. He also appeared so adept at swimming, skating and dancing – and seemed blessed with a whole raft of practical skills – that she felt more than a little inferior in his presence. He had already secured a place at Harvard Medical School for the next academic year and seemed worldly and grown up (he had worked temporarily at a mental hospital and had interviewed twenty-five married couples for a sociology class).

When she returned to Smith – after missing the 9:05 train on the Sunday evening, which resulted in an appearance in front of the Judicial Board and a penalty of having to sign in by nine each night for the following week – Sylvia vowed that she would try to learn more about the basics of the natural world. In some respects it seems as though Dick had brainwashed her into thinking that 'knowledge comes through science'; so keen was she to try to impress Dick that she thought she should buy some books on chemistry, physics and maths and read them over the spring vacation.[26] She acknowledged that, although she felt inclined towards poetry and art, there should be no reason why (as she told her mother) she couldn't grasp the basics of the physical world so as to root her in reality.[27] Excised from this same letter in *Letters Home*, Sylvia also wrote of Dick's character; the parts of his personality that she liked most stemmed from his mother, while the traits she disliked, such as his habit of emitting a hearty laugh, he had unfortunately inherited from his father.[28] It was, she wrote to a friend, a shame that he hadn't kissed her once, not even in a friendly manner, over the weekend.

She had high hopes for their next date, however, as he had invited her to the Yale prom in March. Sylvia had a mild panic about her wardrobe: although she could depend on her old favourite, a white formal off-the-shoulder dress, she was deficient in the accessories department. Her mother sent her a pair of gloves, but when Sylvia received them she saw that they had holes in them. Turning to her friends at Smith she managed to borrow a Mouton fur coat, a black leather handbag, a crinoline and a pair of silver sandals that she said were as comfortable as bedroom slippers. As a result, she felt a little like Cinderella, she said, as she walked into the basketball court of the Yale gymnasium, which was decorated with blue netting and filled with the music from two dance bands. Dick was a vision of respectability, dressed in his best tuxedo, complete with white shirt and black bow tie. Later, in an unpublished letter to Ann Davidow, Sylvia wrote of how, that night, their romance had segued from the platonic to something more romantic in nature. The attraction was strongly physical, almost as inevitable as magnetism or another law of nature. After the dance, Dick accompanied her to her boarding house and as the couple walked hand in hand through the deserted streets, the icy wind whipping about their heads, Sylvia felt like she was living a moment that seemed crystalline in its brilliance. Dick and Sylvia stopped for a second and looked up at the stars. Dick told her that the experience reminded him of being in a church.[29] He kissed her and then, without saying anything, Sylvia went inside, where she proceeded to get undressed. In bed, in the dark, she was aware that her body was still responding to Dick's light touch. In her journal she wrote of the deep eroticism of the moment, a sensation that continued to envelop her as she fell asleep.[30]

The next day, Sylvia and Dick took a long bike ride through the countryside and that night walked up the hill to gaze at the lights of the town. She told herself to make the most of the experience, as there was a possibility she might never see him again. Yet, as she admitted to Ann Davidow, she had never felt such a strong sense of admiration for any of her previous dates. She vowed that she would try and work hard, both at her studies and on improving herself, so that he would appreciate her. Some of her friends, however, were not quite so easy to delude. Eddie Cohen, for instance, most probably motivated by jealousy at Sylvia's new romance, warned her of her tendency to try to adapt too much; as he saw it, she was in danger of forging false identities of herself just so she could fit in with other people's expectations of her. 'People can accept you for what you are, or they can accept you for mirroring themselves,' he said. 'As for the second kind, if you try to please all of them, you will become a shapeless, amorphous personality.'[31]

Sylvia confessed, again to Ann Davidow, that her problems stemmed from a sense of insecurity that she was capable of attracting anyone – whether a man or a female friend – over a long period of time. She traced this back to her teenage years when she felt inferior, a 'gawky mess', a girl with bad hair and poor skin exiled by her peers from the coveted circle of popularity. Being forced to live for five years in this state of hell made her naturally cynical, she said. How could anyone possibly like her, she often asked herself. Yet the realisation that she was now quite popular and not that bad-looking – she had, after all, gone on a few dates, had been admitted into Smith and had achieved some success in her writing – perhaps explained why she found herself prey to sudden attacks of manic over-enthusiasm and emotional high spirits. Her hopes and dreams were being fulfilled, so why shouldn't she be happy about it? The problem, she added, was one of balance: the sudden shift from outsider to insider status had left her feeling out of sorts.[32] Of course, this was only part of the explanation; the reality was much more complex and disturbing.

At this point, those close to her were unaware that they were about to be cast as fellow participants in a psychodrama of Sylvia's making. In March 1951, when Dick Norton wrote to her from Yale, enclosing a couple of his own poems and an excerpt from the 'Who is Silvia?' speech from Shakespeare's *The Two Gentlemen of Verona*, he had no idea that the search for Sylvia's identity would be the central quest of her creative journey and the dominant pursuit of her brief life. He was innocent of the strength and force of Sylvia's visionary imagination, a creative power that attracted – and nearly destroyed – many of those who strayed into its path.

One of the people who would later claim to have fallen victim to Plath's imaginative vampirism was Jane Anderson. Born in Wellesley in 1931 into a prosperous family (her father was an investment banker and a member of Wellesley Country Club), she had gone to the same Unitarian church as Sylvia as a girl; she had attended the same junior high school; and, in 1946, she had served as associate editor of *The Phillipian* when Sylvia, then in eighth grade, sent in her poem 'Winter Sunset' for publication. In many respects, Sylvia regarded Jane – or

'Andy', as she was known at college – as her 'double': not only did the two young women attend Smith (where Jane was in the year above) and date Dick Norton, but both of them experienced severe mental illness and found themselves in the same psychiatric hospital at the same time. Later, Sylvia would use Jane as a basis for the character of Joan Gilling in *The Bell Jar*; in fact, in the draft version of the novel Plath named her Jane. In the novel Plath paints a decidedly unflattering portrait of Jane/Joan, with her 'starey' eyes, 'gleaming tombstone teeth' and a frame the size of a horse.[33]

The book – which ends with Joan's suicide – had such a devastating effect on Jane that, much later, she sued both the Plath estate and the makers of the 1979 film for libel and invasion of her privacy. 'I'm concerned about what people think of me personally and professionally,' Jane Anderson told reporters during the 1987 trial. 'I have made bordering on a heroic effort to get my life together,' she said, after experiencing a number of 'very serious' mental-health issues when she was at Smith. The appearance of the novel, and then the subsequent film, had, she said, resulted in her suffering from persistent bouts of 'extreme anxiety'.[34] As she related in court documents, bequeathed to Smith College by Anderson after her death and previously unpublished, 'the precipitating events leading to my admission to McLean were extremely similar to those described in the book [*The Bell Jar*].'[35] Jane also went on to state, in another unpublished document, 'I felt the way she [Sylvia] used me as the basis for the Joan Gilling character was a very hostile thing to do [. . .] also [an] angry thing to do.'[36]

When Jane first started to date Dick at the end of December 1949, neither of them could have any conception of how their lives would be channelled by Sylvia Plath. Their relationship was, by all accounts, a chaste one. 'The 1950s [was] an age of enormous innocence,' Anderson said later, 'everything was very uptight, straight-laced.'[37] Certainly, as was considered right and proper, she had 'never had sexual intercourse. And I had never consciously masturbated.'[38]

In Dick's first letter to Jane he described her as having a 'tempered' outlook and told her that he was touched by the hospitality of her 'fine family'.[39] The couple enjoyed outdoor activities such as skating, bicycling, skiing and walking, but their recreational activities had to be put on hold after Joan fell ill during the early part of 1950. When Dick returned from Yale to his home on Cypress Road, Wellesley Hills, for six days at the end of January, he hoped that she had recovered her health so that she could join him on a walk through the Massachusetts countryside, or at least a few bouts of ping-pong or a trip ice-skating. He continued to pursue her, asking her to the Yale prom – the same event he would invite Sylvia to the following year – and Derby Day, held on the last Saturday in April. He warned Janc that thc previous year the celebration, which marked the day of the first big spring regatta, had been something of a 'riot' because of the current craze for water pistols.[40] 'Donning inventively outlandish costumes, Yalemen and their dates pile into trucks, horse-drawn wagons, old jalopies and chartered buses, driven ten miles to Derby, Connecticut [. . .] on the banks of the Housatonic,' observed one contemporary commentator. 'There they drink beer, play ball, smash each others' straw boaters, throw their girl friends into the river and generally have a loud time. Some time during the afternoon there are intercollegiate crew races, the ostensible reason for the whole celebration.'[41] Indeed, the event – a custom of the last thirty-one years – became so outlandish that in 1951 the Yale committee decided to ban it, because there were 'too many fights, too many girls dumped in the

Housatonic, too many truckloads [. . .] of beer cans and other litter to be hauled away afterwards. One special cause of complaint: Yalemen and their dates had taken to filling water pistols with beer, discharging them at elderly ladies on Derby street corners.'[42]

Dick and Jane continued to date, and to write to one another, throughout 1950; Dick's letters to her often began 'Dear Sugar and Spice'. Indeed, there was a great deal more to Jane Anderson than perhaps met the eye. She had a sharp intellect, was elected president of her class, served on the electoral board and recommended books by Erich Fromm to Dick. Yet, in June 1950, when she returned home and told her parents that she wanted to switch to be a pre-med student in her sophomore year so that she could eventually train to be a psychiatrist, her news was met by icy disapproval.

'I think I had notions [. . .] around 16 or 17 that I would be more attractive to [my father] in certain ways and I don't mean sexual as much as intellectual than my mother,' said Jane. 'My father and I up until the time I went to college had enjoyed intellectual interchanges and a shared interest in subjects such as Latin, and I think I did go through a period of thinking that I could be more of a companion to him in certain ways than my mother could [. . .] It was very upsetting to me when his attitude towards my intellectual activities seemed to change very suddenly [. . .] when I was in college.'[43]

Jane's parents made it perfectly obvious that they did not approve: a girl of her situation should not have a career. Why couldn't she just enjoy a more general course at Smith, perhaps take a secretarial job and then marry well? Once, when she told her father about her high grades at Smith, he told her he wished she would get all Ds; studying hard, he said, was not the way to secure a good marriage.

By the summer of 1950 Jane had decided that Dick was not

the man she was going to marry. 'During the winter of 1949–50, the spring of 1950 into the summer of 1950, I thought I was very much in love with him,' she said. 'And then I met during the summer another man, whom I cared about more [. . .] And I shared my thoughts with [Dick] when I saw him again in early September 1950. I think [he] was disappointed. But he and I [. . .] did [continue to] see each other.'[44]

Jane first started to suffer what she classified as 'exhaustion' during the end of the summer of 1950, when she spent a period of time with her new boyfriend, Earl, a divinity student, in Philadelphia. When she returned to Smith, she felt unable to cope; she was gripped by anxiety and plagued by the thought that she had made a mistake in choosing to major in the history of art. Uncertain about what she should do, she turned to Smith's resident psychiatrist, Dr Marion Booth, and began to confide in her. During that summer in Philadelphia – where she was working in a factory to earn spending money – a workman had sexually assaulted her. 'He came up behind me and pressed his genitals against me,' she said. 'I was standing at the end of the conveyor belt where boxes were coming off, and I had to pick them up at certain intervals and pile them in a larger box.'[45] The assault in turn triggered off earlier, more disturbing memories of sexual abuse when she was five or six. She recalled a maid introducing her to a male relative, most probably the help's brother, who then led her into a large walk-in closet, where he proceeded to touch her body. 'The image is that I had my clothes on and that he probably touched me in the genital area,' she said.[46]

In September 1950, at the house of a family friend in Nantucket, she also had a heated argument with her father about the nature and existence of God. While he believed that there was only one, Christian God, she maintained that it would be more helpful and less divisive if one interpreted the world as if there were a fight between the god of good and the god of evil. As the discussion escalated, she retired to her room, shortly followed by her father. 'He did try to start talking to me and I was still feeling angry,' she recalled. 'I felt my father was putting me in a bind where I was not supposed to disagree with him.'[47] This was, in fact, the first time in her life she had stood up to her authoritarian father. 'He did strike me as being out of control with his aggression because he was a very discreet man and to come up into my room was a very intrusive act [. . .] On some level I was worried what further aggressions he was going to direct towards me. And that [. . .] could have possibly been tinged with some worry about some sort of aggression expressed through sexuality.'[48] Later, on another occasion, after her father had told her that he would like her to get all D grades, he came into her room when she was in bed, and he 'grabbed my arm and kissed it up to about the elbow. And then he left.'[49] Jane felt confused, upset and angry, not only with her father but with her mother too, whom she felt reinforced his narrow view of their daughter's abilities and potential. 'I felt upset that I couldn't talk very well with her, either [. . .]' she said. 'And that she seemed to agree with my father in the positions that he had taken.' As Jane started to question her own place in society – and the stiflingly limiting series of expectations surrounding her own future – she became increasingly frustrated. Although there were role models around – she looked up to Phyllis Williams Lehmann, an art historian and archaeologist at Smith who was married to Karl Lehmann, professor at New York University's School of Fine Arts – these were few and far between. 'It was the first time I knew a woman who was combining a professional life with a marriage, and that was very important to me, to see that you could combine these two parts of one's life,' she said. 'Before I tended to perceive it as an either/or.

All my teachers in elementary school were single women, except perhaps one, and certainly at that time there was very much an attitude in society you either got married and gave up all professional activities, or you were single and you were a professional woman.'[50]

Like Sylvia, Jane was an angry young woman whose method of revolt would find expression in madness.

In March 1951, Sylvia wrote to her mother about Dick's visit to Smith to attend the sophomore prom with Jane. Three months later, Sylvia was obviously still feeling anxious about the relationship between Dick and Jane, even though the couple had ceased corresponding in April. In June, while working as a mother's helper in Swampscott, Sylvia had a nightmare in which both Dick and Jane appeared. The dream – described in an unpublished letter to Marcia Brown – centred on her decision to break a date with Dick so she could steal off with a more dangerous, rebellious male. After returning home, she was greeted by her mother and Dick – who had taken Jane to the prom – who expressed disappointment in her. At the end of the dream, Dick said repeatedly, 'Oh, Syl', as he disappeared into the ether never to return. Sylvia was left knowing that she had behaved badly: how foolish of her to lose a perfectly nice, respectable mate for the sake of a night's pleasure with a cad. She compared herself to one of her favourite fictional heroines, Scarlett O'Hara, knowing that 'playing fast and loose' had ruined her. Perhaps there was something to be learnt from the dream after all, she said.[51]

The conflict between outward respectability and inner desire was a very real one in Sylvia, a tension that came to be symbolised through a series of opposing figures whom she sought out and then exploited throughout the course of her life. During the spring of 1951, Sylvia could not have found two men more different than Dick Norton, the sensible, conventionally minded Yale student and Eddie Cohen, with his greased-back hair, denims, leather jacket, and a cigarette or pipe permanently hanging from his mouth. What especially fascinated and thrilled Sylvia was the contrast between their letters, documents that would often arrive on the same day. For instance, on 18 March, Dick wrote to her about his loathing of the work of Ernest Hemingway, whose material he thought was degenerate. The next day, Eddie reflected on the nature and power of their correspondence; after all, it was Sylvia's writing that had first attracted him to her. 'What peculiar force was there which caused me to sense the essence of your being by reading a few lines in a magazine, and which sends the blood pounding behind my eyes every time I receive a letter from you?'[52] Eddie went on to wonder about their future together, noting that he had yet to fully commit himself to his new girlfriend, Rita. 'I have a lingering suspicion that much of the reason for my being unable to wholly give myself to Rita has been my unconfirmed idea of what might possibly exist in points east,' he said.[53]

On the last day before spring break, Sylvia was in her room when a girl called to tell her that there was a boy downstairs waiting to see her. Sylvia did not have a clue who it could be. Dick was spending the vacation in Florida with his grandparents – from there he sent her a card, addressed to 'Beauty and Kindness', and a letter enclosing a specimen of Spanish moss – and she was not expecting any other dates. The figure standing at the bottom of the stairs, with a pipe gripped between his teeth, was Eddie Cohen, who had driven from Chicago to Northampton on a whim. 'This is the third dimension,' he said, referring to the fact that previously they had known each other only through the two-dimensional form of the letter. Eddie offered to drive her home and Sylvia was too shocked to refuse. It was one thing to express one's innermost desires and secrets to a stranger, quite another to see that person in the flesh. From the beginning the encounter was an awkward one. Sylvia felt on edge and nervous and Eddie, despite his rebellious image, was somewhat timid and shy. As the three-hour car journey progressed, Sylvia became increasingly worried about what her mother would say if she saw her daughter with the rather louche-looking Eddie. To try to put him off, she told him that she was in love with a young man from home and could not consider dating anyone else. Then, on arriving at Elmwood Road, she thanked him, in rather a cold manner, for the lift, briefly introduced him to Aurelia, who had come out to greet them, and then dashed upstairs to her room. Eddie had no option but to turn around and make the thirty-hour trip back to Chicago. Inside, Aurelia gave Sylvia a stern talking to about her selfish behaviour.

'Your mother was quite right – you were incredibly rude,' wrote Eddie, who had at this point decided to enter therapy. 'I was no end angry at the reception I received.' The rejection could have prompted him to behave in a rather different manner had the long drive not sapped him of all his energies. 'The incident could have been much different – nastier, perhaps – had my physical condition at the time been different from what it was,' he said. As for her mother, the one she had warned him about? 'One look at your mother was sufficient to tell me that here was a sympathetic creature, despite the stern and foreboding account which you had given me beforehand.'[54]

After spring break – which involved a stay with Marcia Brown at her New Jersey home, together with frequent trips into New York City – Sylvia returned to Smith. She wrote to her mother that it was strange to be back at college but she was looking forward to seeing Dick, who was due to visit for a weekend in April. On the surface the date seemed to go well. On Friday, the young couple enjoyed hamburgers and milk on the lawn outside the Davis student centre and a long walk around Paradise Pond, while the next day they went on a bike ride with Marcia to Look Park. On their return, after wading across a stretch of cold water, they both took hot baths (separate ones, of course). By this point, Sylvia confessed to feeling extremely odd and dizzy, possibly due to what she termed excitement.[55] Whether Dick noticed Sylvia's manic behaviour is hard to say – his letters, at this point, are models of discretion and decorum – yet, he did not spend every moment with her, maintaining that he needed some time to himself so he could study. Sylvia burst into tears and sobbed on Marcia's shoulder; ever the faithful friend, Marcia rustled up some breakfast and brought it to her in the room. Sylvia was puzzled about Dick's reaction. Obviously something had disturbed him. But what?

Although he was too polite to address the issue, perhaps the answer can be found in a coded letter he wrote to Sylvia a few days after that weekend. Dick related that, in their American studies lectures, the professor continually stated the fact that modern man lacked direction and purpose – he quoted from Thomas Wolfe's novel *Look Homeward, Angel*: 'O Lost, and by the wind grieved, ghost, come back again' – and wondered whether Sylvia was what could be described as a modern woman. Norton, in his own way, was trying to fish for clues about both Plath's literary ambitions and her status as a suitable candidate for marriage as, according to Jane Anderson, Dick 'wanted a woman to be a full-time wife and mother'.[56] The idea that Sylvia might write about unsavoury matters such as mental instability and messy personal emotions *and* seek a professional role outside the home would not have impressed him.

Plath sensed that Dick was not altogether at ease with her – in another unpublished letter to her mother she describes him as having two different personalities and surmises that he often displayed a mask of joviality to cover up what he really felt about her. Even so, there is little to suggest that Dick could have ever, at this stage at least, discerned the true state of Plath's mind or the violence of her imagination. A few days after their date, Sylvia was in class when she felt inspired to write a poem – in effect a letter she could not send to Dick. The poem 'April 18' encapsulates Sylvia's sense of self-loathing[57] and articulates the sense of regret she felt after she expressed certain thoughts and feelings to Dick.[58] Sylvia was fearful that the words – which obviously hurt Dick enough for him to make an excuse why he couldn't see her the next day as planned – would affect their relationship, a future lost as easily, as she said in the poem, as 'a tennis ball at twilight'.[59]

Whereas Dick was unable or unwilling to look into Sylvia's dark heart, Eddie Cohen was only too capable of seeing what lurked behind the young woman's polite and controlled exterior. The man whose transformation from abstract absence to physical presence had disturbed her so much had no qualms about telling the truth. He was intrigued by her decision not to answer his last letter – in which he had accused her being rude when he had hinted their encounter could have turned nasty – and wrote that actually he now thought more of her; 'By behaving in a manner somewhat less than perfect, you have become considerably less of a goddess and more of a human being in my eyes,' he said.[60] After her short story 'Den of Lions' appeared in the May issue of *Seventeen*, he wrote to her with a detailed critique of her work and her personality. Whereas

Dick wrote to congratulate her on her use of similes, Eddie questioned their validity. 'A girl trying to decide about a boy does not make similes in her mind (at the moment of the decision, at any rate) about Christmas tree ornaments,' he wrote. He also wondered whether she had given enough background to Marcia's resolution, at the end of the story, to cast Emile from her life. Perhaps what she needed, he surmised, was to suffer more. 'I actually find myself wishing at times that some guy comes along – the one who looks like the right one – and then in the end steps on you so hard that you ache for months afterwards, down where I don't think you have ever really hurt,' he said.[61]

Sylvia wrote back telling him that she was not in love with Dick – in fact, she did not believe in the word – an opinion that prompted a furious invective from Eddie. 'Read this first,' he wrote in red, warning her that the enclosed letter was 'vicious' and that it was 'filled with bitterness and hostility [. . .] and that you are the target'. Cohen couldn't believe that she was so self-centred as not to allow someone to get close to her; rather, he suspected that she was 'unwilling to surrender completely because of the emotional damage which would result from failure after that surrender. The philosophy would seem to be that if you don't wade in too deep you can't possibly drown. Which is true enough [. . .] but you can't get to the other side, either.' His letter continued, 'I know full well that I have gotten ahold of your most sensitive spot, and I am only too eager to drive the knife in right up to the hilt.' He closed by questioning his own role with regard to Sylvia: why did they keep writing to one another? 'The psychiatrists have a term for it – or rather a couple of them – acting-out and projection. And beyond that – who knows what?' He left it at that, leaving the letter unsigned.[62]

Instead of cutting him off, Sylvia carried on corresponding with Eddie, partly because it seemed she enjoyed living vicariously through him. On 19 May, he wrote her a letter in which he described a wild party that had got out of hand. During the gathering he had accused one girl, who had obviously taken a dislike to one of his stories, of penis envy. Affronted by the insult her boyfriend tried to take a swipe at Eddie. In contrast, on the same day, Sylvia received a letter from Dick describing in detail a faculty club lunch, a quiet supper with Perry, his reading list over the summer and his travel arrangements to the Cape, where he had secured a summer job. That afternoon he had taken his bicycle out to Savin Rock, where he had sunbathed for half an hour and then stopped off at Dairy Queen for a cone.

There is no doubt that Sylvia admired and adored Dick – she told her mother that he was 'the most stimulating boy I've ever known'[63] – but she was also rather afraid of showing him her whole, true self, in all its contradictory, messy glory. She was particularly concerned about her general lack of co-ordination and her inability to act in a graceful fashion while skating, swimming or doing anything else remotely athletic. One day in May, after she came back to Haven House from a shopping trip with Marcia she started to feel ill. She took some pills and went to bed, but by the time Dick appeared for a date with her on the Saturday afternoon, she felt like she was burning up. Determined not to let him down, she went walking in the hills and then, later that night, tried to enjoy a meal at Wiggins Tavern; the only thing she could swallow was ice cream. Although she had planned another date that night – after saying goodbye to Dick – she had no choice but to cancel and check herself into the infirmary, where she stayed for a week, a victim of her annual spring attack of a sinus cold. Then, just as she was recovering, she met with her advisor, Kenneth Wright, to talk about her academic programme for the following year – she decided to major in English. On the way out of his office she slipped on the smooth stone floor and fell on her ankle, 'which gave a nasty and protesting crunch'.[64] Wright, also Smith's professor of botany, carried her down the stairs to his car; although she worried that she had broken her ankle, after an X-ray it was discovered to be only a sprain. Yet the sight of her foot – which had swollen to three times its normal size – distressed her, as she wanted to look her best for Dick. She was, as usual, in a quandary over money as the college had decided to award her a grant of only $400 for the forthcoming year, while the board of trustees had raised annual room and board fees to $1,650. In addition, she felt that, once more, she had become unpopular within Haven House.

Sylvia wrote to Ann Davidow outlining her worries. She felt unattractive – the heat of the day had made her hair limp and sweat clung to her body, despite having a series of cold baths – and talentless; she felt disappointed that her art teacher had told that one of her recent works was as vulgar as the worst kind of wallpaper. Acutely attuned to Ann's predicament – the former Smith student had been to see a specialist in Chicago – she wished that one day she too could see a therapist who could help illuminate certain aspects of her childhood.[65] She continued the self-analysis in the same letter, outlining how hard she found it to share herself with too many people. Not only was she introspective she was also plagued by a series of what she described as rather strange thoughts; the combination made her wonder whether anybody apart from the small group of people she loved and trusted would understand her.[66] She was also aware, as she wrote in an unpublished journal entry, that she lived by extremes: people were either gods or devils and experiences were cast either in the light of romantic ecstasy or shadowed by doubt and negativity.[67] The thought of having to choose one type of life made her question the nature of existence itself. She felt frustrated that she only had one life and that she didn't know when it would come to an end. How on earth could she construct an identity knowing that it might all be taken away from her in an instant?[68] One day, she knew she would die and 'rot in the ground' but who would mourn her. Fundamentally, she did care about the direction and quality of her life, a life which she knew would never be easily defined. With this in mind, she was, she said, determined to fashion as many varied lives as possible and live them all to the full.[69]

As Sylvia's first year at Smith came to an end, she busied herself with a round of exams. By the end of the stretch she felt like she deserved a Purple Heart for sheer endurance, she said, but her grades reflected the huge amount of work she had done: As in botany, French and art; A-minus in European history; B-plus in English (which frustrated her); and (not surprisingly, considering her gawkiness and awkwardness) a C in physical education. She spent the morning of her last day of the academic year organising her possessions and clearing her room, stuffing things into her suitcase and tying string around piles of books. After she had finished her chores, she spent the afternoon thinking about the peculiarities and absurdities of life. The Norton brothers arrived to drive her home and on the journey back to Wellesley Dick talked about the wonders of chemistry – he seemed fascinated by the carboxyl and hydroxyl groups – a subject that Sylvia was hard-pressed to comprehend. Later, after supper at Elmwood Road, Dick dropped by to show her the new coat of paint on his two-wheeler bike. As they walked around the streets near her home, Dick started to talk about the complexities of the international political situation, another issue that Sylvia felt so unsure of that she deftly changed the subject. Although she knew she was ignorant of certain things, she didn't want the summer to be taken up by reading textbooks or taking notes. Rather, she wanted to expand her knowledge of twentieth-century literature. In Wellesley, while shopping for a graduation present for Dick (she settled on a record of César Franck's Symphony in D Minor, recommended by her mother) she bought a selection of books for herself, including Steinbeck's *The Grapes of Wrath* and *In Dubious Battle*, Faulkner's *As I Lay Dying* and *The Sound and the Fury*, Knut Hamsun's *Growth of the Soil*, Pearl S. Buck's *The Good Earth* and Hemingway's *The Sun Also Rises*. She noted that some of the covers of the novels in the Pocket Book edition – particularly the works by Hemingway and Faulkner – were quite lurid, but neither author had a reputation for being the shy and retiring type.[70]

On her way home from shopping, she stopped by the town's tennis courts – a place she jokingly referred to as somewhere she stalked her prey[71] – where she saw her friend Philip McCurdy. His new attractiveness impressed her and, although he was young – at this point the baby-faced boy was still in high school – she admired his handsome, athletic form. She informed her friend Marcia of how she had placed a maternal hand on his shoulder and told him, in Mae West fashion, to come up and see her some time.[72] She suspected that the young socialites from well-off Wellesley families looked down on her for spending time with what they thought of as the socially inferior Philip, as she wrote to Marcia, but she didn't care. As long as a person was interesting who really worried about a person's colour, age or education, she asked.[73] This was not entirely true, as Sylvia had already written to Eddie Cohen about the so-called 'aristocracy of ability', her view that only those who had bothered to educate themselves were worthy of her attention. 'I find it hard to believe that the people who must interest you are those who have either high intellects or great creative powers,' wrote Eddie. 'Surely you know and enjoy people who are neither artists, painters or musicians, and whose IQs are less than 150.'[74]

Sylvia had a week and a half at home before she was to start work as a mother's helper in Swampscott, Massachusetts. One day, after she and her old friend Patsy O'Neill had visited Wilbury Crockett, she entered her house and she noted that the air smelt of 'warm stagnant human flesh and of onions'.[75] In her journal, she described her grandfather as a white-haired old man, even-tempered, and admiring of everything she did. Her grandmother was 'spry, with a big fat bosom and spindly arthritic legs', a messy eater, who dropped crumbs of food down her dresses, and who slurped her soup.[76] Although she loved her dearly, Grammy did not escape further criticism: in her journal, Sylvia recorded a series of notes that she thought she might one day use in a poem about a 'fat, greasy and imperfect grandmother'.[77] She recalled snatches of memories of her father, remembering that, as a child, she used to dance in front of him as he lay on the sofa in the living room after supper. She wondered whether the absence of a father figure in her life helped explain why she desired male company and wished that someone had taught her the basics of science when she was younger. As a result, she 'leaned abnormally to the "Humanities" personality' of her mother. At times, in the midst of a conversation, she'd notice that she was talking like her mother, a similarity that frightened and disturbed her. In her journal she wrote of the unsettling image of Aurelia living inside her and of how, at times, her face bore the same expressions as her mother.[78]

It was clear that the Nortons occupied a higher position within the class structure, and Aurelia would have been thrilled if her daughter had the chance to marry into such a respectable family. Indeed, that summer, Dick's father informed Sylvia that they would consider it a privilege having her as a daughter-in-law, an announcement that nearly reduced Plath to tears. Yet the relationship between the young couple was far from easy going, even at this early stage, and Sylvia often felt as though she were merely playing a part.

Before Dick's Yale commencement in June, Dick and his parents, together with Sylvia, were invited to tea at the headmaster's house, an event that dragged on for two hours. Sylvia said that by the end of it she had become so sick of making small talk with the mothers of young men, and their fiancées or wives, that she felt her smile had become fixed on her face. In a letter to Marcia, she joked that she even considered drowning herself in the bowl of iced tea. At the ceremony she had fallen out with Dick because she had refused to endorse his position about the essential meaninglessness of the event. No doubt trying to adopt a position of cynical sophistication, Dick dismissed Class Day as trite, an opinion his father disagreed with. Sylvia sided with Mr Norton and, as a result, Dick went off in a sulk. His spirits recovered enough to bash out a few tunes on the piano while Sylvia and Mr Norton played ping-pong at New Haven's 'Y', where Mrs Norton and Sylvia were due to spend the night.

That summer Sylvia hoped to be able to see something of Dick, who had secured himself a job as a waiter at Latham's in Brewster. But soon after arriving at the house of the Mayo family, situated at 144 Beach Bluff Avenue, she found that she had hardly any time for herself let alone Dick. The Mayos lived in an enormous white house that stood on a grassy hill overlooking the sea, complete with tennis court and a yacht moored nearby. Their lifestyle reinforced Sylvia's awareness of her lowly place within society. 'I'm only the maid,' she said.[79] Sylvia thought of the house as a 'mansion'; its grand scale dwarfed the modest proportions of Elmwood Road. She was to work fourteen or fifteen hours a day for six days a week, for which she was paid $100 a month, and her duties including looking after the Mayos' three children – Frederic, seven, Esther (or Pinny), four, and Joanne, two – cooking, cleaning, washing the dishes, managing the laundry, making beds and ironing. 'My grandmother, who had graduated from Smith, wanted two helpers – one for us and one for my cousins,' recalls Frederic Mayo.[80] Sylvia worked for his parents, Dr Frederic B. Mayo, a physician, and Anne Blodgett Mayo, while Marcia was employed by Anne's sister, Esther Blodgett Meyer.

On her first day at the house, the rather impractical-minded Sylvia felt so overwhelmed by her new job that she spent most of the day in tears. She had never learnt how to use an oven or a broiler – the kitchen had always been the domain of her mother and grandmother – and she couldn't rustle up anything more ambitious than scrambled egg and cheese. She felt isolated and depressed, and she wrote to her mother of how she couldn't imagine staying at her new employers for more than a week. All she wanted to do, she said, was cry on her mother's shoulder.[81] She resented the fact that she had no time for creating her own work or thinking in an intelligent manner; her life seemed subsumed by housework and the practical demands of looking after children. The more she thought about her situation the more frustrated she became; in the first few weeks she felt a mix of emotions including anxiety, fear and unease; she was also angry with herself for getting herself in this awkward position in the first place.[82] She missed regular contacts with boys, without whom she felt lost and ill-defined, but on her days off at least she could see Marcia, who worked at the Blodgetts' grand house nearby. When Sylvia learnt of Marcia's relatively easy life (she had several hours a day off) she admitted, in an unpublished section of a letter to her mother, that she had to fight the urge not to feel angry, indignant and jealous.[83]

After three weeks in the job, she and Marcia decided they'd had enough. They were tempted to quit. In her journal she confessed to feeling on the verge of rebellion. It wasn't just the fact that she had a mountain of chores to do or that she had to bear witness to seemingly endless fits of rage by the children. She felt like she wasn't recognised, that her true talents and abilities were being ignored. It all seemed so unjust somehow.[84] One day, Sylvia was allowed to take a cruise around the ocean on the family's yacht, the *Mistral*; it was her job to keep an especially close eye on Joanne. In an unpublished letter to her mother, she noted both the opulence on board that – the yacht could sleep twelve people, there was a table at the back of the boat that could seat ten, there were two toilets, a crew of three – and the fact that the family seemed to take all this for granted.

The inequalities that she witnessed so rankled her – the sight of the Mayos enjoying themselves on their yacht, drinking cocktails, hosting dinner parties, socialising with their equally rich relatives – that ten years later she wrote the poem, 'The Babysitters', about the experience. In it she describes the family's yacht with a set of stairs made from polished mahogany that one used to lower oneself into the sea. Whereas she didn't know how to cook, the Mayos had a cabin boy who was an expert at cake decoration.[85] She confessed that at nights, she wrote 'spitefully' in her journal, her fingers bearing the burn marks from ironing the clothes of the three children, one of whom, Freddie, was so particular about his dress that, as she said in 'The Babysitters', he wouldn't step foot outside the house unless the stripes of his sweater were the same design as the stripes on his socks.[86]

Today, more than sixty years after that summer, Frederic Mayo has fond memories of Sylvia. 'I remember that she was pretty and that we trusted her implicitly – we never thought not to trust her,' he says. 'Her function, as we saw it, was to play with us. I don't know whether she liked it. I do remember that she needed her own space and her own time – I was not used to that as a kid. Looking back, I can see how it must have been quite a shock for a girl like her, a scholarship student, to find herself in our world. The house, originally a summer home, had been winterized – so the outside sun parlour became the living room – and the scale of it was extraordinary. There were acres of hallway and the living room was thirty-five feet by twenty-five, while the dining room was a similar size. Her bedroom, which was separate from all the other rooms, had a walk-in closet, a tub and a sink and toilet. It had huge bay windows that looked out towards the sea, a bureau and a desk and bedside tables. Even though it was a small bedroom I think it was huge compared to her own room back home.'[87]

His mother, Anne, described Sylvia, in a note to Smith's vocational office, as 'an intelligent, honest, well-mannered girl with a pleasing disposition'.[88] In private, however, she expressed a rather different opinion. 'She did not find Sylvia easy-going or easy to manage and my mother thought that she did not give her the support that she needed,' says Frederic.[89] Neither did Anne Mayo appreciate the description of her as a sporty wife in 'The Babysitters'. 'That was not one of my mother's favourite lines,' he admits.[90]

Sylvia may have found the situation difficult to adapt to at first, but over time she came to love the three Mayo children. She particularly enjoyed putting the children to bed, writing tenderly in her journal of washing Joey in the bath, dressing her in new diapers and a white nightgown and placing her gently in her cot, where the baby gurgled away happily, pinching Sylvia's cheeks as she settled down. She foresaw a life of happiness and love for the girl, a life full of only the best things.[91] Pinny – with her blonde hair and large brown eyes – was the next to get ready for bed, followed by Freddie, whom Sylvia thought the cleverest and most interesting of the children; she described him as a boy with the face of a 'Kewpie-doll' and the fashion sense of Beau Brummel. As she put Freddie to bed he kissed her on each eyelid, the mouth, and then the neck. He had to give her neck four kisses, he said, because it was so big.[92]

One day at the end of July, Sylvia and Marcia – their skin the colour of burnt sienna, their hair bleached from the sun – decided to rent a rowing boat in nearby Marblehead so as to explore the ocean. Their destination was, according to Marcia, 'nebulous',[93] but in just under two hours they made it as far as Children's Island, which had once housed a children's hospital but was now, as Plath wrote in 'The Babysitters', nothing but a home to flocks of angry seagulls. The two young women took it in turns to row and Marcia read aloud from Philip Wylie's *Generation of Vipers*. That night, on their return to Marblehead, they met a Canadian man, who invited Sylvia to the Eastern Yacht Club and who got so drunk that she had to drive them home. She was desperate for male company – as she wrote in a letter to Marcia, the occasional compliment about her appearance was vital for her psychological survival. How she longed for the sight of a man waiting for her at the bottom of the stairs, waiting to take her arm, as if she were an equal, not someone who was socially inferior'.[94]

On 16 July, Sylvia and Dick – both of whom had the day off – went to explore a section of the rugged Massachusetts coastline near Marblehead. Sylvia already felt anxious about Dick's status as one of four young men within a company of fifty beautiful waitresses and, although he had maintained that she had no reason to worry, she was still suspicious. While Sylvia does not state exactly what happened during their day together, from her journal one can learn that she felt disappointed and betrayed. She did want him to be aware, she said, of how his revelation had affected her.[95] Dick's confession had resulted in a 'crumbling of faith and trust', and Sylvia felt compelled to outline her feelings for him in an abrasive letter.[96] From one of his letters, one can discern that he had been approached by another woman, whom he told Sylvia he had turned down due to the strength of his own resolve and 'aversion to potentially sordid circumstances'.[97] He did not want to pursue the liaison because of the concepts he held so dear to him, he said, ideals such as 'honesty, healthy living, truth, beauty'.[98]

Almost as soon as she had sent her letter to Dick, Sylvia had misgivings. In her journal she tried to analyse her feelings and persuade herself that she had behaved inappropriately, but as she did so the old anger about gender inequalities – particularly relating to sexual behaviour – began to rise to the surface. The hypocrisy of the situation enraged her: why could a man sleep with many women and yet still get away with demonising promiscuity? Why should women not be allowed to admit that they felt desire too? Why was it the case that women had to serve so many functions – the receptacle of emotions, the carer of children, the provider of solace? She realised that, at the moment of her conception, her destiny had been determined for her. As a writer, she wanted to mix with all sorts – soldiers, sailors, men drinking in bar rooms – yet society insisted that this was unbefitting and unseemly. All she wanted to do was to delve into the souls and experiences of those around her, and yet there was a section of the world that was barred from her view. At the end of the entry, she wrote, 'Being born a woman is my awful tragedy.'[99]

Sylvia's difficulties with Dick continued throughout the summer. In September, after finishing her job with the Mayos, Sylvia and Aurelia were invited to spend a few days in a tourist cabin in Brewster, on Cape Cod, with Dick's parents. On the third day of the visit, Sylvia and Dick managed to escape from their families to spend an hour or so on a deserted beach. Dick – who was still working as a waiter – came prepared for an afternoon of study, with a physics text tucked underneath his arm, and Sylvia became so frustrated by his lack of communication that she said she would happily swipe him around the head with the book. They decided that they would try to sort out their problems by having a 'truth talk' that night. After supper, the couple walked out in the darkness and under the stars sat back to back in a large field. Dick began by outlining how Sylvia's letter made him think that she did not feel affectionate towards him, and, as a result, he felt rejected. He also told her that he wished that she were three years older, and that he felt a sense of longing for her. Although Sylvia was pleased to have talked through their various misunderstandings, at the end of the encounter she was not sure whether Dick was the man for her, and wondered whether she should try to find someone who was less controlling and more relaxed. If she did choose to become a doctor's wife, wouldn't that just be conforming to the expectations imposed by convention? She wrote to Ann Davidow outlining her worries, observing how a young woman's period of attractiveness lasted only eight years before ageing began to take its toll. She was sure that she wasn't the kind of woman who wanted just a man, home and children. She was, she said, too selfish to let herself be crushed by the demands of a man and his career.[100]

Sylvia also wrote of her worries to Eddie Cohen, who replied with the question, 'Where's the conflict?'[101] Was it the case that she didn't know whether she loved her boyfriend or not? 'If you're not sure, then you're not in love, at least by my definition,' he said. And what about her various anxieties about being tied down? 'First – what's the hurry? Apparently he is not in a position to get married at once, so why not let the thing drift on and see where it leads,' he advised. 'Also, why does marriage have to interfere with your chosen career? It might even be a help. And lastly, wherefore will it be any different with anyone else?' Surely she should realise that a man like Eddie – who would be prepared to take his wife trekking across the globe on a series of adventures before settling down to have children – was a rarity, if not an oddity? 'For most of the world a woman has a definite social role in marriage which will not permit the existence which I am inclined to feel you want before you start on the home and kiddies and dinner-every-night stuff,' he continued. 'If I may get bitter for a moment, the nice clean boys of your acquaintance (you know, the ones who want the mother of their kids to be a virgin, etc) would probably faint dead away at the thought of their wife living in the jungles of Mexico or on the left bank in Paris. Which means only this – that the type of individual who believes in what I somewhat contemptuously refer to as conventional morality also leads the type of life which is apt to be somewhat conventional. Literary wise, such a situation is likely to be somewhat sterile [. . .] You can have your career, or you can raise a family. I should be extremely surprised, however, if you can do both within the framework of the social structure in which you now live.'[102]

She could not understand why Dick hadn't yet made more physical advances towards her. Eddie put this down to the fact that Dick – or 'Allan' as Sylvia called him in these letters – was still unsure of himself and of her. 'As time goes on, your attraction to him and vice versa are likely to increase,' he said, adding that he thought that physical gratification was the 'best way ever devised to separate love from infatuation'.[103]

From Harvard, Dick wrote Sylvia a series of loving but strange letters. He called her 'My girl' and 'Princess', praised her as a 'dear, sweet, lovable and beautiful woman', and said he longed to hold her close. He also sent her a number of detailed anatomical drawings of a cadaver that he was dissecting and invited her to lectures on the role of pathology in the understanding of disease.[104] In one letter he asked whether she might, in the future, have any cause to contact the local mental hospital; after all, he observed, it might turn out to be quite a useful experience.

It was obvious from Sylvia's letters to Eddie that part of her felt uncomfortable with and uncertain about Dick. She told Eddie – whom she regarded as her expert tutor in a kind of therapy correspondence course – that Dick was handsome, brilliant, personable, athletic and simply wonderful, but she doubted whether she could 'come up to the subconscious set of standards he expects me to emulate'. Eddie couldn't believe what he was reading. 'Now, look lady, let's come down to earth,' he said. 'Doesn't that ring just some kind of a false note? Doesn't it sound just the slightest bit like a rationalization? I hate to pull rank on you, but I do know a little something about subconscious minds myself, and I didn't get all I know out of a newspaper feature column on psychology. What sounds extremely more probable to me is that Allan does not come up to your standards for some reason or other. But here the reasons are actually subconscious – at least to the extent that you cannot intellectually perceive them. Allan seems perfect, but, for some reason, he doesn't quite measure up. But the mind will not accept orders from the "sub-conscious" without some sort of a reasonable excuse for doing so. What then? So we invent a reason. In this case we decide that the thing will have to go by the boards because you don't measure up to what Allan really wants. Which is considerably better than admitting the reverse and having to decide just why Allan doesn't come up to your ideal.'[105]

Sylvia paid a number of visits to see Dick at Harvard Medical School, where, dressed in a white coat, she saw a number of dead babies in glass bottles and accompanied him to anatomy lessons, where she witnessed the dissection of a cadaver. 'For weeks afterwards, the cadaver's head – or what there was left of it – floated up behind my eggs and bacon at breakfast,' she would write later in *The Bell Jar*.[106] In the novel, Plath also relates a scene between Esther and boyfriend Buddy Willard in which he asks her whether she had ever 'seen' a man – meaning a naked man – and whether she would like to 'see' him. 'I guess so,' Esther replies. Buddy then proceeds to unzip his chinos, lay them on a chair, and takes off his underpants, which Esther observes seem to have been made of a material similar to nylon fishnet. 'Then he just stood there in front of me and I kept on staring at him,' wrote Plath in *The Bell Jar*. 'The only thing I could think of was turkey neck and turkey gizzards and I felt very depressed.'[107] At some point over the Thanksgiving holiday, in November 1951, Sylvia asked Dick whether he had ever had an affair with anybody. He went silent, increasing her suspicions. She rephrased the question – had he ever gone to bed with anyone? She had always felt, as she related in the novel, that he had made her feel so much more sexually experienced than he, when in fact he had just been pretending to be innocent all the time. Under pressure, Dick finally confessed that he had lost his virginity that summer and that he had, in fact, seduced several women. The shock made her sick, she told Ann Davidow. It wasn't the revelation of the sex that disturbed her so much as Dick's hypocrisy. The news skewed her perspective, unsettling her already delicate and vulnerable mental constitution; she described the news and its fallout as a little hell.

Dick too seemed shaken by the encounter. A few days after his confession he wrote to Sylvia to tell her of his disturbing dreams: in one, he saw a plane bombing the White House and destroying the President's office; and in another he had been called to see a patient whose skin had been removed – as he approached he saw that she was holding her skin out in front of her.

She considered two options: ending her relationship with Dick or finding the first available man to sleep with, yet she did neither. Eddie Cohen – in his latest dispatch – said that he doubted whether 'the discovery of the Mr. Hyde in Allan's [Dick's] hitherto sterling character' would entice her to start flinging herself at every man who crossed her path, 'and you really are not in such a hurry to sacrifice your maidenhead upon the altar of Allan's hypocrisy. Sure, you're angry and hurt and disillusioned, but I think that when you've considered it a bit, you'll realize that morality and ideals are really not such awful things after all. But what makes them worthwhile is when they are intelligently and personally arrived at, and not camouflaged behind invalid and hypocritical reasoning. If you wish to remain a virgin until marriage, well and good, so long as you have admitted to yourself that virginity, per se, is not any sort of worthwhile value, and that what holds you back is fear and doubt over whether a pre-marital affair would be fully satisfying on every level.'[108]

Eddie went on to tease her about her misuse of the word 'lie' instead of 'lay'– she had told him of her desire to go and 'lie with someone else'. He advised her that actually it would be better to use 'the Anglo-Saxon Fuck' since it could be used 'as either a noun, verb (transitive and intransitive), adjective, adverb and expletive.' Cohen then went on to address a more serious point: Plath's sexual fantasy involving rape, something he had noticed in one of her previous letters. Why was she so preoccupied with her chastity being taken away by force, he asked. 'You must have used the word rape in this letter five times,' he said. She had also told Eddie that she worried that she would never meet the right guy. He advised her to stop fretting about it, as she was still quite young. He told her to avoid trying to put her men on pedestals, making golden gods of each of them in turn. 'You're a pretty broad individual, and there aren't too many guys who can fit into all the facets of your personality,' he said. He told her to keep circulating; if no one snatched her up, he was tempted to travel east to try his luck with her. 'Don't snicker, kiddo, remember to whom you are speaking,' he said. At the end of this letter he told her to wise up. 'Don't screw up your life because you learned that there ain't no Santa Claus,' he said. 'If you feel you have to indulge yourself, latch on to a guy who'll make it worth your while. (Physically and emotionally, that is, not financially.)'[109]

After a great deal of self-analysis, Sylvia realised that she could trace the strong emotions she had felt after Dick's confession back to her deep-seated resentment of men. Her difficulty was not so much moral as practical, as she told Ann Davidow in an unpublished letter. Rather than being angry with Dick for seducing other women, she felt jealous that she had been denied the same opportunity with other men. Far from being driven by high morals, she had been motivated by fear and cowardice, afraid of getting pregnant and scared of what other people would think of her. The question was, as she wrote to Ann, what should she do with her "burning" desire in the meantime?[110]

Six

I MYSELF AM HEAVEN AND HELL

One day in September 1951, Sylvia travelled into Boston to do some shopping in preparation for the new term at Smith. She found the experience overwhelmingly depressing. She enjoyed dressing well, responding to the textures of certain fabrics on her skin, appreciating the line and cut of particular dresses and savouring the range of new autumn colours, but she knew that she could never afford the fashion of her dreams. Her budget could stretch to the purchase of a simple wool dress, but everything else that went with it – the hat, the gloves, the coat and the shoes – was out of the question. As she wrote in a letter to Marcia Brown, she knew that lusting after such fripperies was reprehensible, but she couldn't help herself. She confessed that, although she tried to remember that in twenty years' time she would have all the physical charms of Eleanor Roosevelt, and as a result she should work on improving her more lasting qualities such as her intellect, she still felt the desire for money. Why, she asked, hadn't she been born into a family that was wealthier and more privileged?[1]

It was a question she was forced to ask herself again when on 6 October, together with Marcia Brown and her fellow house-mates from Haven, she was invited down to Sharon, Connecticut, to the coming-out party of Maureen Lee Buckley. Maureen was the daughter of the wealthy Texas lawyer and oil developer William Frank Buckley Senior. Three of Maureen's elder sisters had already graduated from Smith, while four brothers were graduates of Yale. 'She is fun loving but cooperative, upright, honest and loyal,' one of her referees wrote to Smith. 'She has a sparkling personality and is very adaptable. She is at home in any group socially.'[2] Yet, in a letter Sylvia wrote about the event to her mother, Maureen appears only fleetingly; it's clear that what impressed her most was the lavishness of the occasion. Dressed in a blue bolero suit and a brown coat she described as 'versatile' (a polite term for well-used, something definitely not bought specially for the occasion), Sylvia was driven to Connecticut in a cream-coloured convertible. As she travelled she noticed the New England landscape in all its autumnal splendour[3] and on arrival at the Buckley residence, Great Elm, she was impressed by the estate, surrounded as it was by enormous lawns with majestic trees, with a view of the valley beyond. As the girls got out of their car, they noticed a caterer unloading what seemed like endless cases of champagne. The house was the grandest private home Sylvia had ever seen, with its series of stone steps that led up to white colonial columns; inside she thrilled to the sight of 'a thousand living rooms', the walls covered by a proliferation of art. This was going to be a party to remember.[4]

As the event would last late into the night the girls were advised to rest for a couple of hours. The two friends had been set aside a room in 'Stone House' – another 'mansion' that was 'across the way' – and soon Sylvia lost herself in the romanticised fantasy of the setting. She cast herself as a character in a period novel or as a modern-day Scarlett O'Hara. After the chauffeur had taken the girls to the Sharon Inn, where the Buckleys had provided a buffet supper for thirty, the driver delivered them back to their rooms, where they were given the opportunity to rest once more and dress for the party. On arrival at the Buckley house, Sylvia was greeted by a mass of girls all in 'swishes of taffeta, satin, silk' and a spectacle that took her breath away: a glass-roofed patio in the centre of the house that reminded her of the magnificent courtyard in Isabella Stewart Gardner's mansion-turned-museum in Boston. French doors led to a marquee out on the lawn, which had been decorated with balloons and Japanese lanterns, and set out with dozens of tables covered in white linen. There was a raised platform for dancing, a band, two bars and waiters serving champagne. The lavishness of the occasion left her speechless, she told her mother.[5] Although she told Aurelia that she felt confident that she was beautiful – and that daughters of millionaires complimented her on her appearance – the letter's extreme effusiveness masks Sylvia's very real uncertainties and anxieties. She knew she could play a part effectively and, as she was 'announced' and 'received', she simply followed the other girls through a series of intricate social rituals, customs that must have appeared as alien to her as those of a foreign culture. After dancing with Carl, a philosophy major and Eric, a tall, hook-nosed freshman, Sylvia was sought out by Plato Skouras, whose father was Spyros P. Skouras, the president of 20th Century-Fox. Half-way through a dance, Plato told her that he wanted to show her a painting in one of the drawing rooms. He led her down from the raised platform, through the patio, past the fountains and into a room where he pointed out one of Botticelli's Madonnas. 'You remind me of her,' he said.[6] A few minutes later she was back on the dance floor again, this time with a handsome, dark-haired Princeton senior, Constantine Sidamon-Eristoff. After several dances, the couple walked outside – 'the night was lovely, stars out, trees big and dark', Sylvia observed[7] – and then, after they had regained their energy, they danced Strauss waltzes on the lawn.

'I knew a few people, but not many, but then I saw this absolutely gorgeous girl,' recalls Constantine. 'As soon as I found somebody who could dance and who could dance well – she waltzed beautifully – I don't think I let her alone. That was the start of whatever romance there was. She was absolutely lovely – she was interesting, talkative and gay, in the true sense of the word.'[8]

The two could not have come from more different backgrounds. Born in Manhattan in 1930, Constantine was the son of a Georgian prince who could trace his ancestry back to the fifteenth century, and he had attended the Millbrook School in Dutchess County, New York. 'The Buckley boys had all gone to Millbrook, and in my class we had Fergus Reid Buckley. So we were all invited up to this lovely house in Sharon for Maureen's coming-out party. My memory of Sylvia is of a girl who was opening up, exploring the world intellectually and in every other way. She was great fun, a charming girl. I got the impression that she was happy – she was outgoing, she was meeting new people. That night she met several at the party who gave her a rush, including me. Who wouldn't be happy?

'The culture of dating was completely different. You dated – you went on a date – and after a while if you got really serious you moved to "going steady". If you did that, in some circles, you got "pinned" – which meant you were engaged to be engaged. Then you had your engagement and then came marriage. We all tried, but with a decent girl there was little physical contact – physical contact was a dangerous affair. Those were the days when everybody was feeling their oats, but not quite sure how to sow them.'[9]

The two talked late into the night – Sylvia was proud that she could use 'big' words and formulate intelligent lines of conversation – and soon Constantine was kissing her hand and telling her how beautiful she was, how lovely the skin on her shoulders felt. He offered to drive her back to her room, a journey that seemed to last all night. He talked to her about the legend of Jason and the Golden Fleece – claiming that it had originated in Georgia – and topics as diverse as childbirth, atomic power and love. As he was kissing her, she told him not to suffocate in her long hair, to which he responded, 'What a divine way to die!'[10] Finally, at five o'clock in the morning, he opened the door of the car for her with the word, 'Milady'; as she stepped out she replied, 'Milord'.[11] The next day, after a luxurious brunch at the Buckleys' home, Sylvia, Marcia and three other girls were driven back to Smith in a chauffeured Cadillac. 'Back here,' she wrote to her mother. 'I can't face the dead reality.'[12]

The contrast between the two worlds – the gap between the giddy heights of a life that she recognised was out of her reach and the strictly demarcated uniformity of her day-to-day reality – plunged her into a depression. As was often the case, her illness started with physical symptoms: sneezing, waves of high temperatures, and a head clogged with mucus. On 15 October, she checked herself into Smith's infirmary, where she was dosed up with nose drops, sleeping pills, privine and pyrobenzamine, which left her feeling slow-witted and groggy. 'Sinusitis plunges me in manic depression,' she wrote in her journal.[13] She realised that she had wasted her time in the hospital by flicking through old copies of the *New Yorker* magazine, when she should have been studying for her courses: an introduction to politics that she said had 'thrown' her completely: Introduction to the Study of Religion (she had 'fouled' up her first written paper and was a week behind); art (she thought she had missed at least ten hours of work); Nineteenth- and Twentieth-Century Literature, which she maintained was 'plainly above' her unless she set time aside for extra reading and attended lots more seminars; and creative writing, which 'demands what I love – work and time'. But how could she do it all, what with weekends with Dick, work, and a social life? And would she ever find enough time to work at the mental hospital? 'Now I know why Ann left,' she said.[14] She also had an upcoming lunch with a scout from *Mademoiselle* magazine, a woman who was touring the colleges and meeting all the girls who wanted to apply for the prestigious annual College Board Contest, which Plath would win in 1953. Again, she was worried about what the hell to wear. All her clothes were, she observed, brown or navy or velvet, and she knew she did not have any matching accessories. She felt angry with herself for spending so much money on an array of items that simply did not look right together. In her journal she lambasted herself for her lack of style. How on earth could she criticise one of America's most popular fashion magazines when she looked as bad as this?[15]

Money – or the lack of it – was a constant obsession. In an unpublished letter to her mother she wrote of a shopping trip to Northampton, just before Christmas. She had felt exhilarated by the sights and smells of the shops and wished she could buy lots of things if only she had a few thousand dollars. Next to this sentence, Aurelia scribbled in pencil the words, 'Desire for things'.[16] Although she had $130 in her bank account at the beginning of the new term, Sylvia knew that all of this would be used for essential expenses. During the year, she spent a total of $35 on books, $35 on art supplies, $25 on food, $140 on clothes, $50 on transport, and $20 on dues and fees. She was so short of cash that she even considered selling stockings: for every pair she sold for ten cents, she would receive one cent. The problem as she saw it was that in order to keep up her reputation as a top-grade student – which in turn guaranteed her scholarship status – she would need to set aside a large chunk of time for studying. Earning money to help supplement her grant was a necessity, but she worried it would have a detrimental effect on her grades. What was she to do? In another unpublished letter to her mother, written at the end of October, Sylvia drew a picture of her own grave and joked about her brief life being over.[17] Although the drawing had been sent in a spirit of fun, it symbolised the various opposing demands and stresses that Sylvia had to cope with even at this stage of her life. She realised, as Eddie Cohen wrote to her that month, quoting the *Rubáiyát* of Omar Khayyám, 'I, myself, am Heaven and Hell.'[18]

Her spirits improved when she received a letter from Constantine, inviting her down to Princeton at the beginning of November. She thought the handsome 'Russian oil magnate to be',[19] as she called him, would disappear like the champagne bubbles that had fizzed about her mouth on the night of the Buckley party, and so she was heartened that it seemed as though he was keen on pursuing her. She was tempted to accept his offer, but anxious about the consequences. The journey – five hours by train – was not only long but also expensive. She had already accepted Dick's invitation to Harvard and if she accepted Princeton as well she would be away from Smith – and her routine of studying – for two weekends in a row. She had important written papers due on 6 and 7 November. Although all the girls at Smith encouraged her to disregard reason and head down to Princeton – he was, she told her mother, the one man who compared favourably to Dick.[20] – she made what she called a mature decision and decided to politely reject the offer. She wrote to Constantine, excusing herself, telling him that she had already had a social commitment that weekend (she didn't, of course, but this was easier than going into the complicated details of why she would have to turn him down). It was not as if she did not want to see him, she wrote, and hoped that he could suggest another time when they might see one another again. She signed herself a contrite but somehow optimistic Sylvia.

The couple continued to correspond throughout the latter part of the year and Sylvia's letters to Constantine are wonderful illustrations of her intelligent mind, quirky sense of humour and lively writing style. In one letter, dated 8 December, she included a charming drawing of herself writing a letter to 'Dear Connie', a sketch of herself holding a suitcase and staring in amazement at the dizzying heights of a skyscraper (she had been invited by Marcia to spend a few days with her friend at her mother's home in New Jersey and thought that she could easily travel into Manhattan to see Constantine) and a quick still life of a table setting complete with fruit and a bottle of wine (a hint, perhaps, of the type of entertainment she would enjoy with her so-called gallant Georgian while in New York). Constantine, in turn, wrote back, formally inviting her out on a date, including the opportunity to meet his parents in the city. After a couple of days at Marcia's mother's home on Cottage Street, in South Orange, where she arrived on 18 December, Sylvia travelled into Manhattan and met Constantine at the Hotel McAlpin. She felt guilty about the expense, as she wrote to her mother in an unpublished letter, but justified it on the grounds that she was actually quite frugal in many other respects and that she was sure that the experience could prove to be valuable for her. 'After she had come in from New Jersey, I met her and introduced her to my parents – my mother thought she was terrific – and then we went to my normal stomping ground, a little place on 14th Street called the Two Guitars,' recalls Constantine. 'It had been set up by a Russian refugee and his wife. There was a kind of gypsy orchestra and a couple of dancers and for a few dollars you could have a bottle of wine, a blini or two and you could dance.'[21]

The relationship, however, did not progress; and, although Sylvia invited Constantine up to Smith, he never made the journey. 'I just didn't have any time – my mind was focused on getting through college, and then as soon as I graduated I went straight into the army, the Reserve Officers Training Corps, after which I went to Korea. And so we lost touch. I suppose it could have been a romance, but it never was really – it was more of a delightful interchange. But she was a real sweetheart of a girl.'[22]

Sylvia continually tried to expand the limits of her poetic technique. She loved the strict discipline of the sonnet, but her subject matter was anything but comforting. In November 1951, no doubt inspired by one of her visits down to Harvard to see Dick Norton, she wrote a sonnet – later titled 'Sonnet: To Eva' in the *Collected Poems* – that expressed the enormous gap between the young couple's personal ideologies. Whereas men like Dick thought that it was possible to dissect a skull the way one would take apart a clock – viewing its individual components like a series of mechanical parts[23] – women like Sylvia believed that it was impossible to reduce everything to the scientific, the logical and the empirical, a reductive method that ignored or rejected the whimsical images that might be found inside the woman's anatomised skull.[24] She likened the mind, when it was functioning, to a well-oiled machine; yet when one analysed each of the component parts it seemed somehow ridiculous and incoherent.[25] A week or so later she wrote Sonnet: 'To Time' or 'Today we move in jade and cease with garnet', which she said was about the contrast between the natural world and the machine age. Sylvia enclosed the poem in a letter to her mother, asking Aurelia to take note of the new rhymes she had used: 'garnet' and 'car yet', and 'olives' working as a juxtaposition next to 'all gives'. She said she hoped that the new rhyming scheme was a move away from the clichéd and the hackneyed.

Influenced by T. S. Eliot (on 15 November, she sat down with a group of friends from the Unitarian Young People's group and listened to a recording of *The Cocktail Party*), she believed, like him, that it was the poet's business to express the 'greatest emotional intensity' of one's time.[26] Certainly, Plath's 'To Time' can be seen as an expression of Eliot's desire to describe the arid spiritual life experienced by men in modern cities. In a series of notes that she took during one of Elizabeth Drew's lectures on twentieth-century literature, Plath scribbled down the professor's comments on Eliot, Jung, D. H. Lawrence, Ezra Pound, Yeats, Joyce and Virginia Woolf. Certain ideas and concepts stood out as being particularly worthy of note: the idea that artists were, in Pound's words, the antennae of the race; the belief that man was a symbol-making animal and that the writer explored the inner territory where thought and feeling translated themselves into signs and symbols, the so-called 'logic of the imagination'; Lawrence's image of mankind as being like a great uprooted tree that has been torn away from the nourishment of the natural world; the consequences of the Machine Age that destroyed huge swathes of culture, leaving nothing but what Matthew Arnold called 'poor fragments of a broken world'; and the on-going quest towards insight and self-revelation, a journey that often resulted in the exile of the writer from his or her country of birth.

These ideas permeated Plath's early fiction, pieces she wrote both for herself and for the creative-writing course taught by Evelyn Page, whom Sylvia described as an ugly but fascinating woman who had written a number of murder mysteries and had at one point lived in sin in Greenwich Village. In mid-November she wrote a story entitled 'Suburban Nocturne' – a version of which exists in her journal – which described a walk alone she had made at night. Heavily influenced by the imagery of the moderns, particularly Eliot, she compares herself to Ulysses, a character destined to wander, a person who is part of everything and everyone he or she has ever encountered. Destined to journey down the pathways of her own mind she saw herself as a continual searcher, but she knew that there would be no end, no final answer. At the end of the story, Plath returns to her home, repeating a line that she had first written in her journal to the effect that her umbilical cord had never been cleanly cut. She realised that her closeness to Aurelia was psychologically damaging, but she was also only too aware that the topic was a dangerous one; she would have to set this particular psychic quirk to one side, leaving its poetic and fictional exploration to a time in the future when she felt braver, or at least when she felt she could examine it from a more distanced perspective. After writing 'Suburban Nocturne', Sylvia realised that she couldn't hand it in to her teacher – she described it as too squalid to submit – and so she composed another, less controversial piece about her summer job.[27]

The following month she turned yet again to autobiography for inspiration for a story about her relationship with her old friend Mary Ventura, whom she had met in high school. For this piece, Sylvia didn't even bother changing the name of her heroine; it was, as she no doubt saw it, a slice of real life, unmitigated by polluting factors such as invented characters or imagined details. Evelyn Page gave her a B-plus for the story, praising the subtle development of character of Mary Ventura. From the beginning, Sylvia had 'let the reader see those qualities in her and in her environment which will prevent her from becoming the person she wishes to be,' wrote Page. 'Your dialogue is excellent.' But the creative-writing teacher warned her to try to avoid 'trite descriptions such as "rich, vibrant appeal" [and] "plain, drab little woman".'[28]

In addition to her heavy coursework, Sylvia took on extra responsibilities such as co-chairman of decorations for the house dance, membership of the decoration committee for the charity ball in February 1952, and an active member of the Press Board.

Her main duty for the latter was to report on activities (such as lectures or speeches that had been arranged on the Smith campus) for out-of-town newspapers, such as the *Springfield Daily News* – a job that netted her $10 a month. For one assignment for the Press Board, in December, Sylvia went to a talk given by Margaret Morrison, a Christian Scientist from Boston. During the lecture, as the elderly, grey-haired lady expounded on the idea that the mind could conquer the flesh – followers believed that illness could be cured not through the prescription of modern medicine but the banishment of doubts and fears – Sylvia had to do everything in her power to stop herself from having hysterics. Although she did her best to hide it, Sylvia had a sarcastic streak; the sardonic, often acerbic tone of voice she adopted when writing poetry was an expression of a side to her personality that could be snide, scornful and scathing. Dick Norton addressed her as an 'imp', a word that implies merely a mischievous nature, yet there was a darkness to her personality that even he recognised. In the same letter he also classified her as a demon, a devil, a fiend, a spirit and a sorceress, descriptions that actually capture her strange essence.[29]

Sylvia herself was having difficulties trying to define just exactly what was wrong with her. Did she have schizophrenia? Was she suffering from an inferiority complex? And surely she had penis envy? These were just a few of the labels that, in a letter she wrote to Eddie Cohen, she mentioned as possible explanations for her strange thoughts and, at times, odd behaviour. Eddie advised her to stop trying to analyse herself in this way as it was doing nothing but causing her increased anxiety. 'My own judgement would be that whatever the nature of your difficulty is, it has nothing to do whatsoever with either schizophrenia, inferiority, or the lack of a male sex organ,' he wrote back. 'If you must concern yourself about your personality, do it in terms of concrete facts, and stop agitating yourself about your sub-conscious, about which by definition you can discover nothing.'[30]

Sylvia had been feeling depressed after another sinus infection over Christmas and New Year – it took her a month of cocaine nose packs (then a common treatment for sinusitis) and penicillin shots to help her feel normal again. She turned to Eddie for emotional support. He did his best to bolster her low opinion of herself: she was dissatisfied with her writing, felt conflicted about her relationship with Dick, and didn't seem to have a clear idea of her future. What disturbed her most, it seemed, was that she did not have an outlet for her strong sex drive. 'You are further disturbed because you are frank enough to admit to yourself that you have a physical drive towards sex,' wrote Eddie. 'The fact that you have no satisfactory outlet for this stems from the fact that society is maladjusted to the welfare of the individual, and not because there is anything wrong with you [. . .] You can hardly expect, at nineteen, to reject a Bostonian background in mores and arrive immediately at an objective compromise.'[31] Sylvia expressed an interest in psychoanalysis and asked Eddie to describe his own experiences on the couch. This begs the question: could her future problems have been avoided if she had undergone intensive therapy at this stage in her life? Jane Anderson – whom Sylvia recognised as her psychological twin – certainly believed that the poet and writer would have benefited from psychoanalysis as she herself had. The issue, of course, was a hypothetical one – her mother would have dismissed the idea as foolish (no doubt asking: what exactly was the matter with her anyway?) and it was completely out of the range of her limited budget.

After a meeting with Mary Mensel, Sylvia learnt that she would receive a scholarship of $900 for the forthcoming year. There was also the possibility that she could increase this by

$300, the majority of the sum coming from the money she would earn by living in a cooperative house, where the girls paid less for their board and lodging in return for duties such as the preparation of food or waiting on table. This still left a shortfall of $600, which would have to come from Aurelia. In a letter she wrote to her mother in early March, Sylvia described how out of all the "crazy" things, money was the worst.[32] In order to earn extra cash Sylvia embarked on a plan to write for the extremely lucrative *True Confessions* magazine. In Sylvia's copy of the 1952 *Writer's Year Book* she put a tick next to the entry for the magazine, which was published by the Fawcett group in New York. Established in 1922, *True Confessions* had a circulation of 1,711,000 and paid five cents a word; as it regularly ran stories up to 10,000 words, Sylvia saw the potential of earning $500. 'Stories are based on very strongly dramatic life situations,' advised the journal. 'The heroine must be no mental worrier but must actually have a sin to confess. She must have made a real mistake, seen the consequences of her deed, and be telling others so that they may avoid committing the same sin. In other words, there must be a reason why this woman would sit down to write her story for others to read.' The style of writing should be 'exciting, emotional, introspective' while the heroine must show that she has reflected on her behaviour and 'the mistakes she has made'.[33] When Sylvia told Eddie Cohen that she was thinking of trying to enter this highly competitive but also highly lucrative market, he wrote to her, 'The prospect of Sylvia Plath, girl tear-jerker, writing for True Confessions is no end fascinating. After all, though, it isn't a hell of a jump from Seventeen, since in both cases Virtue always emerges triumphant in the end. TC heroines, though, being of a more practical nature, manage to sate themselves on sex and liquor before they settle down to the straight and narrow and tedious routine of housekeeping.'[34]

Sylvia also drew inspiration from top short-story writer Sarah-Elizabeth Rodger, the mother of Clement Moore Henry, Warren's roommate at Exeter and, later, at Harvard. In the same issue of the *Writer's Year Book*, Sarah outlined the secrets of her success. After being contacted out of the blue by a literary agent who saw potential in something she had written, she went armed with a number of stories that she thought would impress him. Yet she wasn't prepared for the bluntness of his response: what exactly did she know, aged nineteen, about murder, suicide, insanity or miscegenation? Nothing, she responded. 'He was too kind to make any other comment than the suggestion that I try writing about something in the realm of my experience,' she related. 'I objected that I'd had practically no interesting experiences and wasn't likely to have any, ever, since I had a very conservative rearing and now that I was through school there was no escape from my deadly fate – that of a depression debutante.' The agent suggested that she should explore the fictional possibilities of that subject, and soon, after writing a story about a debutante who eloped during the Christmas-holiday balls that immediately sold to *McCall's* magazine, she found that she had created a market of her own. 'The important thing about my beginning was that I learned young to write about what I *knew*,' she said. She went on to explain that she had used the basis of her experience – whether it was being a debutante coming out in the 1930s, working as a junior hostess at an officers' club, or living in Europe for three years after the war – in her writing. 'Every interesting thing that happens to me, or to my friends – in either case, well disguised – is grist to my typewriter. I have an inordinate curiosity about other people's love affairs, for instance.' Plath placed a mark next to this section, but obviously did not take notice of – or deliberately ignored – the advice about the importance of changing certain essential details of character and setting. 'Writing is an outlet, a steam-letting process, and a richly rewarding profession!' wrote Sarah, prompting Sylvia to add the handwritten comment in the margin, 'Ah yes'. She went on to recommend the profession of the freelance writer as being the perfect career choice for a woman – 'in that you *are* at home when the baby falls on his nose and has to be taken to the doctor, when the thermostat goes into a snit, when the Siamese kitten licks all the whipped cream off the pie you'd intended serving for dinner [. . .] All these things, annoying as they are, require instant measures – and the woman in an office wouldn't be on hand to cope.'[35]

Sylvia may have gained some practical advice from Rodger's feature, but the underlying message about writing taking second place to homemaking infuriated her. In December 1951 she had received a box of fudge, brownies and cookies from the mother of her childhood friend Ruth Freeman, along with the message, 'The home is woman's paradise'. As Sylvia wrote to her mother, the message was no doubt intended as a kind of rallying call to convert her from her spirit of independent waywardness. She didn't want merely a corner of her own – the title of Rodger's piece in the *Writer's Year Book* – but a whole room of her own. If she couldn't achieve the Woolfian ideal of supporting herself by writing – and forging a space for her own creation – then at least she wanted a job of her own. At the end of February 1952 she went along to a talk given by the president of the Hampshire Bookshop about the publishing business. She wrote a letter to her mother outlining her enthusiasm for a career in publishing – working her way through secretarial and editorial departments, trying out publicity, reading of manuscripts, the juvenile section. She reassured her mother that her education would see a financial reward of sorts. She was sure that her degree in English, backed up by the experience of working for the Press Board, could have a practical application. It would be helpful, she asked her mother, if Aurelia could teach her shorthand.[36] The thought of becoming a wife and homemaker filled her with anxiety, as she told Ann Davidow. In an unpublished letter she outlined her belief that, at that moment, her store of suppressed sexual energy was being sublimated, channelled into her creativity; she worried that once she was married, the urge to write or paint would disappear altogether and she would be left feeling like a mute mannequin, nothing but a silent, stupid imbecile.[37]

In fact, the whole complex business of sex before marriage vexed her. Although she insisted she was not in love with Dick Norton – he was too short and too puritanical in nature, she told Eddie – that did not prevent her from being sexually attracted to him. One Friday in March she travelled over to see him at Harvard Medical School – the first time they had seen each other in three weeks – and (as she related to her pen pal Hans Joachim Neupert) while they were talking in his room, he threw himself down on the bed beside her, pulled the quilt over their heads and they stayed in each other's arms for seven hours until it got dark. The great question that now occupied her was whether she should give into her desires and sleep with him or whether she should resist her physical urges just for the sake of the hypocritical standards set by society. Eddie, for one, confessed that he would be jealous if she did have sex with Dick (or 'Allan' as Sylvia still insisted on calling him). 'I could not help but feel that it is my arms that you belong in, and my kisses and hand that should be caressing your body,' he wrote.[38] Sylvia asked Eddie for his advice on the pros and cons of heavy petting versus sexual intercourse. His reply, with its series of points set out in a list, must have intrigued – and entertained – Sylvia:

1. Intercourse is a helluva lot more fun, as well as more satisfying.
2. Having petting supposedly makes it difficult to achieve adjustment to the intercourse situation later in life. Personally, I discount this. My own belief would be that petting experience, if the female is an active participant, tends to make for better and more considerate sexual partners later.
3. Petting, if it does not culminate in orgasm for both parties, will increase rather than alleviate frustrations. To my mind, this is the most important argument against it.
4. Simultaneous orgasm is almost impossible to achieve by petting, an important factor in the sense of unity and oneness which ideal sex should bring.
5. Petting, by virtue of the fact that it can be carried on while fully dressed, lends itself to participation in movies, hallways, automobiles etc., where sex can achieve an atmosphere of haste, furtiveness and shoddiness which is psychologically bad. Avoid this sort of thing, and reserve your petting for moments when you and Allan are alone and can have unlimited time and a desirable environment.
6. Inasmuch as you want to be pragmatic about this, I might mention that the male emission is a rather messy thing, and that the vagina provides a more convenient and neater receptacle for it than bedding, clothing, hands or any of the other devices that I can remember having used during my petting days.[39]

Of course, he added, it was only natural that she should worry about getting pregnant – in his own experience, out of the three girlfriends he had slept with, each of them at one point or other thought she had been pregnant, and one of the women actually had conceived. 'Right or wrong, though, sweating out a period is a rough go [. . .]' he said. 'It seems altogether likely that eventually you will "go all the way" before marriage, but there is no point in rushing into it or worrying about it. You're sharp enough to wait until you are fully prepared, mentally and emotionally as well as experience-wise.'[40]

From reading Dick's love letters to Sylvia it seems that by May the couple had started to indulge in intimate sexual contact, if not actual intercourse. In a letter dated 13 May, Dick expressed his erotic feelings for Sylvia in a stream-of-consciousness style, a form reminiscent of Molly Bloom's monologue at the end of Joyce's *Ulysses*. Two days later, Sylvia wrote a piece of self-analysis in her journal examining how she had changed over the course of a year from being somewhat timid and introverted to being more outward-looking and dynamic. She listed her achievements: her election as secretary to the Honor Board (a group comprising students and faculty members that judged infringements of the academic honour system); her work on the Press Board; her joy at being elected on to the editorial board of the *Smith Review*, a post that would start in the new term – before outlining her main problem: sex. She felt jealous of some animals that simply went into heat and then reverted back to normal. The problem, as she confessed to her journal, was that human beings felt desire all the time, but too often they felt imprisoned by petty conventions and old-fashioned traditions.[41]

She described a recent walk with Dick down to a river beach where they had come together in a moment of mutual physical stimulation, pressing up against one another. Sylvia then tried to analyse the significance of such feelings. What was the underlying meaning of desire? Was it an urge to kill the other person? Was it a drive to lose identity? There was something destructive about the process, a game of domination and submission. She was sure that she didn't want to fall into the conventional role of the married woman – rather she was determined to carry on living as a perceptive human being open to new experiences.[42] She could not see herself as simply an individual wholly contained and, in some ways, imprisoned within the confines and expectations of her husband. In the same entry she made a series of drawings, a type of Venn diagram that illustrated how she thought she might live, with two circles that overlapped, one that represented herself and the other representing her future mate. Total fusion or total containment was an impossibility and, although Dick had accused her of battling for complete dominance, she rejected this idea. She went on to address the issue of why Dick was so afraid of her being a strong and assertive woman. Did he have a mother complex? From her point of view, it seemed as though Mildred Norton performed the role of a mother to her husband. Was Dick trying to break this pattern and, in doing so, taking the role of the dominant male to the extreme? Certainly it seemed as though Dick had a superiority complex, which manifested itself as a series of rather disdainful attitudes that she found somewhat offensive.[43] Recently he had stated that a poem was nothing but 'inconsequential dust', an incident that found its way into *The Bell Jar*. Dick's comment depressed and angered Sylvia even further. By this point she had realised that writing was a way of life for her; she could not imagine giving it up. Yet she knew that if she were to be the wife of a respected doctor society would expect her to renounce her career in favour of her husband.[44] Yet she worried that perhaps Dick was the best she was going to get. What if she rejected him and then did not meet anyone else? She likened the situation to swallowing a rich oyster attached to a piece of string, the oyster symbolising the prospective partner, the string a sign of reserve or fear of commitment. Both of them might experience a little sickness, but at least neither would then suffer from the full horrors of poisoning. Taking the analogy further, Plath said that if either found the oyster indigestible at least they had the option of pulling up the string before it was too late, before the toxins had seeped into their systems.[45]

Sylvia expressed the polarities between Dick and herself in the short story 'Sunday at the Mintons'', which she wrote over the spring vacation of 1952. The story started life as a piece of literary revenge, a way of venting her toxic feelings for Dick after he had denigrated her creative aspirations. Although the two characters in the tale, Henry and Elizabeth, are brother and sister, it is obvious that they are based on none other than Dick and herself. On the back of the first page of a draft of the story, Plath drew a dividing line. Under one column, headed 'Henry', she made a list of words that described his – and Dick's – character: persistence, industrious, sturdy, dogmatic, calculating, plodding and so on. The other column, entitled 'Elizabeth', contained words that illustrated the personality traits of her heroine and herself: wanton, frivolous, spontaneous, skittish, whimsical, capricious, volatile, erratic and fitful. Sylvia described the story as a 'psychological type thing, wish-fulfillment'[46] and as such it conveys Plath's fantasy of the end of Dick's domination and her own liberation. One day, after dinner, the fastidious Henry and the illogical Elizabeth, who occupies something of a 'twilight world', take a walk along the boulevard by the sea. As they are walking on the pier, Elizabeth drops her amethyst brooch and Henry ventures down on to the rocks to retrieve it only to get swept away by a large wave, while she is carried off by the wind, her deliverance complete. At the end of the story, however, when Henry tugs at her sleeve and tells her that it is time to return home, the incident is revealed to be nothing but one of Elizabeth's fanciful daydreams.

Plath's creative-writing tutor loved the story and gave her an A: 'A fine job. This shows a great deal of imagination, a fine command of language – and the story is extremely amusing. You almost completely avoid trite phrasing.'[47] Although the story had been inspired by her own life, Sylvia hoped that by making the protagonists brother and sister, she had disguised Dick's character sufficiently so he wouldn't recognise himself. When she heard the news that the story had won a $500 prize from *Mademoiselle* magazine, Plath wrote to her mother about her fear of Dick's reaction. Looking back on all her work she realised that her best pieces all had one thing in common: they all shared a certain 'germ of reality'.[48]

After sitting her end-of-year exams Sylvia travelled down to Cape Cod, where she had secured a job at the Belmont. Initially, the concept of a summer working at the hotel in West Harwich thrilled her. Not only would she be near Dick – who had taken a job for the vacation in Brewster – but she also hoped that she would earn enough money to pay her expenses for the following year at Smith. Yet, on 12 June, after only a couple of days at the hotel, she felt exhausted, disappointed and angry. She discovered that because she had no waitressing experience, she would not be working in the main dining hall after all and, as a result, would lose out on potentially lucrative tips. Instead she was confined to the side hall, where she had to wait on the senior management of the hotel. Her day started at eight in the morning and her duties – washing dishes, polishing silver, lifting furniture, scrubbing tables – left her irritable and depressed. She wrote to her mother about how anxious she felt about lack of money, but miraculously at that moment a telegram arrived announcing the fact she had won $500 from

Mademoiselle.[49] Although the telegram lifted her spirits for a moment – when she heard the news she flung her arms around the head waitress – the sight of a mass of beautiful, confident girls who worked in the main hall left her feeling jealous and insecure. At the Belmont, there were ten men to twenty-five women, a ratio that did not please her, especially when all the other women were so gorgeous. She realised, compared to some of these young women, she was on the retiring side, a trait that would not do her any favours when it came to dating.[50] She also had her period and, despite taking aspirin, the cramps were so bad that she was unable to sleep. She worried that Smith would learn about the $500 prize and reduce her scholarship. In addition, now that the story would soon be in print – it was scheduled for the August issue – she felt guilty about using Dick. Yet, at the same time, she had no qualms about seeing the flock of fellow waitresses – wisecracking, heavy-drinking young women – as nothing more than subjects ripe for fictional exploration.

By 15 June, less than a week into her summer job, Sylvia was reaching breaking point. When her mother arrived for a visit, Sylvia's repressed anger burst free and she snapped at Aurelia. She was, as she later wrote to her mother, so weary and worn out that she felt on the verge of tears. Her boss at the hotel had told her she had to work at suppertime, but after dismissing her mother with harsh words she learnt that she could have had the night off after all. Furious, she ran into her room and burst into tears. Dick arrived and drove her to Brewster and even though after going for a walk and picking some wild strawberries she managed to swallow what she described as a kind of awful nausea,[51] she still felt anxious and uneasy. She wouldn't be surprised if her mother wanted nothing more to do with her, she said.[52] She asked Aurelia to forgive her for behaving so strangely and questioned why she couldn't cope when she encountered a group of attractive young women. Interestingly, the following June in New York, Sylvia would be faced with the same situation: during her stint as one of the guest editors of *Mademoiselle* (the episode that proved the central backdrop for *The Bell Jar*), she would begin to experience the signs of a total mental collapse. Sylvia had constructed herself to be the best; anything that encroached on her fixed view of herself as a winner threatened her sense of identity.

She wondered whether she should resign from the Belmont after a month, yet she hated to be seen as a failure. She felt unable to think about anything more than the practical details of her day-to-day existence and the number of eggs people wanted for breakfast. She hated her cheap black uniform – which she had to change into three times a day – and the feel of the stockings that she had to wear. In order to try to cheer herself up she went on a number of dates – in her letters she referred to Dick as being too nice, too clinging – and some nights she stayed out until dawn, partying on the beach and going to dances. During this period she became particularly close to Ray Wunderlich, a skinny, highly intelligent young man from Florida who was studying medicine at Columbia University in New York and worked at the Belmont as a dishwasher and occasional waiter and bellhop. 'She overflowed,' he said years later. 'She had her quiet times, meditative. But everything was abstruse and interrelated, the interrelationship of the world and things, so much so she couldn't fathom it.'[53] They talked about literature and took long walks along the Cape at night. 'There was nobody there to watch us – we took a blanket with us and became very close,' he says. 'I could retrace those steps today, and see those big bushes we used to sit by and lean against. Let's just say we filled each other up.'[54]

Sylvia's mental vulnerability manifested itself in physical illness. One Saturday, at the end of June, she started to suffer a sore throat – a usual indicator that she was coming down with an attack of sinusitis. That night, in an effort to try to take her mind off her illness, she accepted a date with Phil Brawner, a boy from Wellesley who was studying at Princeton. At eight o'clock she rushed into her room and stripped off her uniform, replacing it with a light-blue cotton dress, and spent a lovely evening dancing at the Mill Hill Club. She had promised Phil that she would play tennis with him and some friends the next day, but on Sunday morning she felt so ill that she had to go to the doctor, who advised her to return home for a few days of rest. She met Phil at the agreed time, but asked whether she could accompany him and a couple of his friends in his car back to Wellesley. The boys thought she was joking – after all she looked so tanned and healthy – but on the journey home she lost her voice. On reaching Elmwood Road she had to go straight to bed and the next day felt so ill that she had to be injected with penicillin, a course of treatment that continued for three days. When her boss from the Belmont telephoned to ask when she would be returning to her job, Aurelia told him that Sylvia was probably too ill to return – a story conjured up by mother and daughter – and that it would be better if they looked for a replacement. Although Sylvia felt an immediate sense of relief, within a matter of days she began to suffer from another depression brought on by the fact that she missed her old job. She compared the feeling to being hit over the head by a large hammer.[55] She yearned for the proximity of a group of lively young people, the knowledge that she would see Dick once or twice a week and the beauty of the beaches and the ocean. She wished she had told the Belmont that she would be back in two weeks. Stuck in Wellesley – which she described as stultifying[56] – she dreamt up various plans for how she could return to the Cape and scanned the small ads in the hope that she might spot a suitable position.

She felt release from the nasty depression only when she received a package of forwarded letters – a couple from friends she had met while working at the Belmont, who told her that they missed her, and one from Harold Strauss, editor-in-chief at Knopf. Cyrilly Abels, the managing editor of *Mademoiselle*, had forwarded him the advance proofs of Plath's story 'Sunday at the Mintons" and he wrote to say how impressed he was with her work. 'This struck me as an extraordinarily deft and mature story, far better than the average prize-winning short story,' he said. He added that he would be interested in reading a novel by her, if she ever felt so inclined to write one. 'I must tell you that I find it most unwise to push gifted young writers into a full-length novel before they are fully prepared to tackle so ambitious a project,' he added. 'Shall I put it that I should like to watch a very gifted nature take its course?'[57]

Back home, with nothing to do but sunbathe and read, she attempted to analyse her contrary feelings. Why did those young women – so full of energy and élan – make her withdraw into herself? Was she scared of life? What was the problem?

She said that because she was suffering symptoms of both physical and mental illness she felt compelled to distance herself from life, especially those people who exhibited a certain boisterousness. She just couldn't deal with the jangle of noise and energy that emanated from the girls at the Belmont.[58] Home, was a stultifying environment that obviously bored and angered her in equal measures and she felt at a loss about how to fill her time. She needed some kind of routine to anchor her overactive, free-floating mind. The contrast between the stimulating ambience of the Belmont, with its clearly demarcated schedule, and the sluggish, routine-less environs of Elmwood Road made her think that someone had lifted off a bell jar from a vessel that contained a functioning community to reveal a mass of scared, powerless little people.[59] She asked herself what was the best course of action. What should she do? To whom should she turn now that she felt in this kind of limbo with its suffocating atmosphere?[60]

Desperate for something to give her a sense of purpose, she considered jobs including file clerk, typist, painter of lampshades, and assistant to a local real estate agent, before she came across an advertisement in the *Christian Science Monitor* asking for a mother's helper in Chatham, on Cape Cod. After an interview she was given the job, a prospect that filled her with joy. Fresh from a weekend spent camping with Dick Norton and his family at their cabin in Brewster, Sylvia arrived at the rented house of Michael and Margaret Cantor in mid-July. Her day started at seven in the morning and her duties consisted of looking after the Cantor's three children – Joan, who was thirteen, Susana, five, and Billy, three (the eldest daughter, Kathy, who was seventeen, was studying in Holland). She told friends that the Cantors seemed like a nicer couple than the Mayos, her employers of the previous summer, and she appreciated the fact that she could eat with them in the evenings, something she had rarely done in Swampscott. With her healthy appetite, she relished the delicious suppers – the steaks, lamb chops, salads, one lobster per person, melon for dessert – and the luxury of being able to drive Mrs Cantor's wood-panelled green station wagon down into nearby Oyster Pond. Instead of being excluded or feeling like a hired help, Sylvia felt like one of the family. Yet, despite this newfound happiness, she still felt the need to take her regular sleeping pill, a habit that had been sanctioned by her mother. Sylvia wrote to her friend Marcia Brown, that one of the reasons why she had taken the job with the Cantors was that she wanted to get away from Aurelia. Although she loved her mother, she confessed that Aurelia seemed to feel her depressions more deeply than even she did. It was almost as if Aurelia absorbed her daughter's misery through some sort of invisible placenta. Surely it was better if Sylvia absented herself from her? Wouldn't that be a good way of protecting her mother from her quite violent mood swings?

On 25 July – a fortnight after she had first written about the concept of the bell jar in the journal – Sylvia revived the concept again in a letter to Marcia. She talked about how, for most of her life, she had felt contained in a bell jar – she had a schedule mapped out for her at college, certain goals she wanted to achieve – never having more than two or three weeks' time when she had to think for herself. In this respect, the bell jar is something quite comforting, an enclosing structure that helps to demarcate and regulate one's time and behaviour, rather than the terrifyingly claustrophobic image of the bell jar in the novel. As she told Marcia, although she had experienced the sudden removal of the lid of her own bell jar – when she had left the Belmont never to return – she hoped that soon she would settle back into her own routine. She desperately wanted to return to the core of herself (a concept she knew was shaky), she said.[61] Interestingly, in the same letter Sylvia talks about how she has spread herself too thinly and about her determination to try and gather her 'selves' together, before going on to correct herself by changing this to the word 'self'. She knew that she was a splintered personality, but she had to keep up the pretence that she was whole, complete, unfragmented.

She saw Dick only once a week at the most – twenty-five miles by bike was quite a journey, she said – but managed to continue seeing some of the friends she had made at the Belmont, including Art Kramer, an unattractive but intelligent Yale graduate and law student who was working as a night-attendant, earning $100 a week, for a rich local family. Although she liked Mrs Cantor, she found her rather puritanical approach old-fashioned and patronising; one day when her employer asked her how on earth she had met such a steady stream of boys, Sylvia felt like shouting back, asking her did she really think she was a character that had stepped straight out of a fairy story?'[62]

She loved talking to Art about literature – he recommended that, if she was interested in mastering the art of the short story, she read *Dubliners* by Joyce and Hemingway's *The Sun Also Rises*. On 1 August, Sylvia was fascinated to meet the local author Val Gendron, who ran the Bookmobile service in Chatham. Gendron – a tiny, dark-haired, sallow-skinned woman whose real name was Ruth Fantus – was unashamedly populist in her approach. Sylvia admired her discipline – Val wrote four pages, or around 1,000 words, each day – as well as her ability to switch between genres: she churned out Westerns, Western love stories and books for juveniles and also had broken into the highly lucrative *Ladies' Home Journal* short-story market. The established author and the novice started to chat and when Val learned that Sylvia went to Smith she told her that the college would always open doors for her as it had 'snob appeal'.[63] A week later Sylvia went to see her again and, after talking about writing, Val told her that, if she had written something substantial in a year's time, she would introduce her to a good agent. Unable to wait that long, the ever-ambitious Sylvia dropped off a copy of the August issue of *Mademoiselle* which contained 'Sunday at the Mintons''. She realised that, after reading it on publication, the story was far from perfect – she spotted a number of artistic errors, she said – but when she mentioned this to Val the author told her not to be so apologetic. After all, how many people could dash off a prize-winning story? On 21 August she wrote to her mother about her 'wonderful' evening with Val at her shack set among the pinewoods in Dennis.[64] After being driven over by Margaret Cantor, Sylvia entered what she described as her vision of 'an artist's Bohemia', what she described as a 'half house', painted barn red, with only two windows. After making coffee and serving grapes and a cake, Val, dressed in dungarees and a plaid shirt, led the way up a flight of stairs to her work room, a ramshackle space that she had constructed herself. At 12:30, after five 'wonderful' hours, Sylvia accepted Val's offer to drive her back to the Cantors'.[65] When she returned to Chatham she felt exhilarated. In her journal she wrote how, in ten years she would be thirty-years-old. How much would she have achieved as a writer by then, she wondered.[66] She reflected over what Val had told her regarding technique: it was essential to get the plot down on paper, that was the most important thing. After this, one could inject life into the story by means of detail and emotion. 'Then write the damn thing,' she said.[67]

One day in August the Cantors took Sylvia to a Christian Science Sunday school, a meeting that prompted the same division between outer expression and inner feeling that she had experienced when she had earlier reported on the organisation for the Press Board at Smith. In an unpublished letter to her brother, Sylvia wrote that she deliberately contrived a sweet and devout face while all the time laughing inside, convinced that the devil himself was lodged in her heart, chortling away with her. Through the Cantors, Sylvia met another Christian Scientist, Bob Cochran, a seventeen-year-old senior at the Clark School, Hanover, New Hampshire. Sylvia loved his youthful idealism and his innocence and in her journal she wrote tenderly of how one day, after taking a boat out into the bay, they enjoyed a picnic together on a deserted beach where they read from Mary Baker Eddy's book *Science and Health*. She was aware of the paradox at the heart of their brief romance: while he didn't believe in matter – in Christian Science everything was determined by the mind – he still enjoyed the physical sensation of caressing her, calling her 'cream and honey'.[68] She experienced the joy of the moment with Bob – whom, together with Art and Dick, she called one of her 'pets', a trio of boys who between them prevented her from having to spend more than four days in Chatham without a date – but she knew a future with him was impossible. She was a believer in matter – the here and now – while he had become fixated by a 'spiritual monism' that left her cold.[69] She wanted to try to capture his essence in a short story, but she thought it would be too cheap to sell him to *Ladies' Home Journal*. No, she would aim higher, she told herself, for the *Atlantic*. Although she did not yet have a plot, she did have a title, 'The Kid Colossus'.[70] The concept of the colossus would haunt her throughout her poetic career and the first, and only, collection that Plath would publish during her lifetime would bear the same title.

In addition, she became infatuated with Attila Kassay, a Hungarian man studying business administration at Northeastern University who came to stay with the Cantors for a weekend. It seems that the twenty-four-year-old was equally captivated with Sylvia, who at this stage of the summer sported a golden brown tan and light-blonde hair bleached by the sun. At Nauset beach – which Sylvia believed to be most beautiful of all the beaches on the Cape – the couple played ball and wrestled on the sand, Sylvia noting Attila's tight blue trunks and his powerful thigh muscles. That night, back at the house, Mrs Cantor walked into the kitchen as the couple were dancing. 'You are holding her too close, Attila,' she said, with a strange look on her face. Back in Wellesley, Sylvia dated Jim McNeely, a classmate of Perry Norton's from Yale. On 17 July, Jim called Sylvia and invited her out to the Charles River esplanade in Boston. 'She was all dressed up and looking queenly,' wrote Jim in his diary. 'We lay on the blanket and she seemed so warm. Later we walked all over Beacon Hill and talked. Then the long way home by the River and she was so close and I wonder what Dick would think?

Watermelon on the porch. She's so sweet, so excitable, so talkative, so appreciative and so Nortonish.'[71]

Each of these men was important to Sylvia because, as she stated in her journal, she believed herself to be part of everything and everyone she had ever met. Yet, at the same time, she wondered how she could seemingly adapt to a diverse range of people, changing her mode of behaviour, facial expressions and conversational themes with ease. 'How can you be so many women to so many people, oh you strange girl?' she wrote in her journal.[72] Was this something she could explore in fiction? Conscious of the fact that she should start to think about another short story or even a novel – on 17 September she received a letter from an editor at Dodd, Mead & Company asking if she was working on a longer piece of fiction – she wrote to Eddie Cohen asking for the return of her letters. After one of their infrequent meetings, Eddie remembered Sylvia behaving as though she were pretending to be someone else – 'she was all mask' he later said.[73] It was almost as though she was either too scared of showing her true personality or unable to conceive of a coherent sense of self-identity. 'There was no spontaneity,' he added. 'She seemed incapable of an impulsive remark,'[74] and she had appeared 'rigid and fearful'.[75]

Eddie had assumed that the lapse in communication was due to one of three things: either Sylvia had married Dick, or she had started to seek treatment with a psychiatrist, or she had put him on her 'Shit list for one reason or another,' he wrote. 'The latter theory is obviously correct. Brrrr! It's the first time winter ever blew into town on an east wind.'[76] Eddie told her that he was reluctant to part with the letters, documents that he said gave 'a pretty full picture of Sylvia as she appears to herself, Sylvia as she would like to believe she is.' Eddie knew that Sylvia was ruthless when it came to her work, and so, for the time being, he had no choice but to refuse her request, 'first because I understand that the personal letters of great authors bring tidy sums on the open market, and secondly because you mentioned dovetailing them with mine, and I am a little dubious about the role I am to play in this venture [. . .] I am liable to be utterly ruined by turning up one of these days, big as life, in *The Ladies' Home Journal*.'[77]

Sylvia tried to persuade him by saying that she thought their edited correspondence – which she considered calling 'Dialogue of the Damned' – would appeal to a wide readership as she conceived herself as everywoman and Eddie as everyman. She could not be more wrong, Eddie told her. 'We are a couple of hyper-IQed eggheads whose thoughts on the world are considerably different from those of the masses,' he wrote.[78] Quite honestly, he resented her view of him as merely as a character ready to snatch from real life and channel into her fiction. Wary of her vampiric tendency, he forbade her from drawing on anything relating to him or his writing without his express permission. 'I have ceased to be as I once was, a real person, with thoughts, feelings and reactions, in your mind, and have become instead, as have so many other of the males you have told me about, material for one of your future books.'[79] In another letter he wondered whether she was capable of falling in love with an actual person; rather she seemed drawn by the dramatic potentialities of the situation. He told her that it was essential that she begin to talk about her psychological problems and foresaw that she would have 'troubles far deeper and more important' than those she had outlined in any of her letters.[80] His prediction was about to come true.

Seven

DROWNING IN SELF-HATE, DOUBT, MADNESS

On the drive from Wellesley to Smith, where she was due to begin a new academic year, Sylvia began to feel more apprehensive by the minute. She felt anxious that she would not know many of the other girls in Lawrence House and worried that she hadn't even seen her room. In an unpublished letter to her mother, she told Aurelia that she was feeling drained and disoriented by unfamiliar faces – there were sixty-three other young women in her new house – and likened herself to a displaced person.[1] Although she liked her room – it had three windows that looked out over the shops of Green Street on one side and on to a large tree on the other – she was far from enamoured of her new roommate, Mary Bonneville, a sensible, rather plain girl who was majoring in science. 'Sylvia had nothing in common with her at all,' recalls Janet Rosenberg, (née Salter). 'Mary was an early riser and would go to bed early too, while Sylvia and I were night owls. Sometimes, when her roommate was ready to go to bed, Sylvia would come into my room and sit on the armchair and we would talk into the early hours. By that time she had done most of her important work as she was much better organized than I.'[2]

The two girls had met in the library's stacks at the end of their sophomore year. 'I was not a very gregarious person – I wasn't inclined to approach people – but Sylvia, who was very ebullient, asked me what I was looking for,' says Janet. 'When I found out that she would be moving into my dormitory, we went out for coffee and she told me an enormous amount about herself. She told me about her father having died – that she was devastated by his death – and that she didn't get on very well with her mother, but she was non-specific about what the problem was exactly. She seemed fascinated by the fact that I was adopted and interested in my background – my father was a book-jacket artist, she had seen the name Salter on the credits of a number of books. Later, I had a feeling that everything people said to her was grist to her mill – everything was material – and I began to feel that I had to listen more to what people said to me. In our creative-writing class we were instructed to collect material for our stories and I knew Sylvia had kept a journal for years. She also told me that she regularly wrote home to her mother, letters she said that she was writing for posterity. She expected that if she became famous – which is what she told me she wanted to be – then one day someone might want to publish them. She wrote those letters as carefully as she wrote her short stories. And, although I knew she wanted fame – at this point she told me that she wanted to be a poet, dramatist or novelist, that she was trying out every form – I assumed that money would be part of that. I had very little idea of her financial situation and none of us talked about what kinds of scholarship we had been given.'[3]

In exchange for a reduction in her board-and-lodging fees of $250 a year, Sylvia had to don an apron and wait on tables at lunchtime. Within a few weeks her initial anxiety about her new environment had disappeared: she described Lawrence House as an extremely pleasant environment and the other girls as delightful. As it was a cooperative house, she no longer had to worry about feeling socially inferior – there was, as she wrote to her mother, a wonderful communal atmosphere in which no girl felt ashamed of saying she couldn't buy something or go somewhere because she had no money.[4] She told her new friend Janet Salter that in her old house, 'the biggest problem any of the girls had was which fur coat to wear on a Saturday night.'[5] As Janet recalls today, 'Our house was a co-op and most of us were on scholarship, we didn't have fur coats. Unlike the other houses at Smith, we didn't have maids and so each of us was expected to work – some people did prep to help the cook, then there were others who waited on tables, those who did the dishes. We also had what was called "Bells", where two women sat by the door of the house in two-hour shifts. The door wasn't locked except at night, and so it had to be manned for safety purposes and also to answer any questions. Boys would come by to pick up the girls and, of course, if you were sitting on Bells on a Friday night you met a lot of boys. Although I had my doubts about whether she was a virgin or not, I would never have asked her. There was an assumption that everyone was a virgin – we weren't all that far removed from the Victorian age. Our mothers had brought up us as if that age still existed, telling us all kinds of things that we accepted as truth, and it took a lot of people years to get over this upbringing.'[6]

Sylvia had shared her worries about her relationship with Dick with his younger brother, Perry. One day, after the two friends had fallen asleep together on a double bed, she woke up to see him sleeping. His innocence touched her and the thought came to her that actually Perry – not Dick – would make the ideal husband. She even went so far as to write in her journal of her view that Perry was the perfect man for her.[7] The problem with Dick, she realised, was that they were always destined to compete. As she knew she couldn't try to compete with him sexually – he had far more experience than her – she said.[8]

In October, Dick wrote to her from Harvard Medical School with the news that a shadow had been found on the upper part of his left lung. Medics had taken an X-ray and had ordered further tests. Although the college doctor said he was sure there was nothing to worry about and another test showed that he was free from tuberculosis, eventually it was discovered that Dick was indeed suffering from the disease and by the end of the month he had been sent to Ray Brook, a sanatorium in Saranac, New York. Sylvia too had to have a test to see if she was a sufferer, but thankfully she was pronounced healthy. Up in Saranac, Dick, in addition to his drug therapy, was prescribed a period of rest, and, with his newfound time, he embarked on a course of extensive reading. Over the next few weeks he read his way through Dante's *Inferno*, Tolstoy's *Anna Karenina*, Steinbeck's *To a God Unknown*, Lawrence's *Women in Love*, Gertrude Stein's *The Autobiography of Alice B. Toklas*, Salinger's *Catcher in the Rye*, Boswell's *Life of Johnson* and a play by Pirandello. This was the kind of freewheeling reading list Plath aspired to, but she felt too bogged down by the demands of her academic courses – she had two papers to write each week – and her extracurricular activities to even consider opening a book that wasn't a set text or the subject of a forthcoming essay. 'Don't you envy me?' asked Dick, unaware of how his programme of self-improvement would affect Sylvia.[9] Indeed, Plath was, she confessed in her journal, 'sick' with envy, jealous of the fact that he had the time to lie around and read books and explore any aspect of learning that took his fancy.[10] Her jealousy reached such a toxic level that it threatened to overwhelm her. In her journal she confessed that she was close to committing suicide. She felt hollow, empty, directionless. There was, she said, nothing behind her eyes but a bare and desolate cave, 'a pit of hell'.[11]

Around this time, Sylvia heard of the suicide of one of Warren's classmates at Phillips Exeter, news that had prompted her to telephone her mother in distress. She tried to persuade herself that reality was what she made it – her old belief that it was possible to alter one's life by changing one's perception – but when she tried to examine her life she could see only a 'hell', a reality poisoned by emotions such as fear, envy and hate. She was losing herself in an endless tide of 'self-hate, doubt, madness,' she said.[12] She listed her achievements: her position at Smith, a handsome, clever boyfriend, and the fact that she had earned around $1,000 from writing over the past three years. Although she knew that hundreds of girls would kill to be in her place, she still could not be happy. Was it something to do with wanting to be a writer, she asked herself, before noting in her journal the tragic fate of Virginia Woolf and Sara Teasdale, both of whom who had committed suicide. Had these two women killed themselves because they had been forced to sublimate their drives and desires?[13] Or were female writers innately self-destructive? The question was posed by Sylvia's creative-writing tutor Robert Gorham Davis, who, during one of their morning classes, told his students, 'I hope none of you is planning to be a writer because women writers are usually very unhappy.' Classmate Janet Rosenberg recalls Sylvia's anger when she heard this remark. 'Sylvia and I were both furious about the comment,' says Janet. 'We walked home from the class together and we tried to figure out what he meant. Both of us thought that he believed that writing produced unhappiness in women. It made us furious.'[14] This issue was later articulated by the poet Anne Stevenson – who herself wrote an authorised and highly controversial biography of Plath – in an essay titled 'Writing as a Woman'. 'Sylvia Plath implies all the way through that the roles of "writer" and "woman" are in some way incompatible [. . .] The tension between the two roles – the woman and the writer – is a source of energy in her poems, but it is also, I think, a source of their self-destructiveness. What seems most self-destructive in Plath's work is a haunting fear of failure.'[15]

Sylvia tried to imagine her future, but the roles expected of her by conventional society only depressed her further. If she married

Otto Plath, Sylvia Plath's father. In her poem 'Daddy', Plath wrote, 'At twenty I tried to die/And get back, back, back to you'.

Sylvia Plath as a baby with her mother Aurelia and her grandmother, taken in July 1933.

Sylvia with her mother at Winthrop Beach, Massachusetts, the summer of 1936. Later, Plath would describe Aurelia as a 'walking vampire'.

Sylvia with her younger brother Warren in Winthrop, August 1940. 'Somehow I have a special place in my heart for the ocean', she wrote later.

When Otto was ill Sylvia would dress as a nurse and take fruit and cool drinks to him. After being told of her father's death, in November 1940, the girl said, 'I'll never speak to God again!'

Sylvia with her two best friends from childhood, Betsy Powley and Ruth Freeman. 'She was not a morbid child – it was all fun and laughter', says Ruth.

After Otto's death Aurelia moved with her parents and her two children to a house in Wellesley, Massachusetts. The house was so small that Aurelia and Sylvia had to share a room.

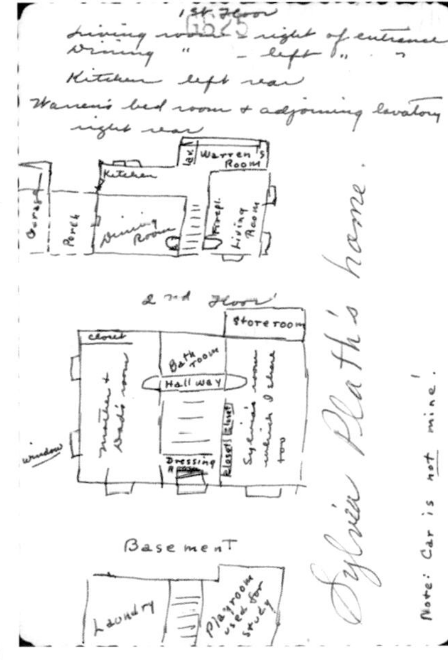

Sylvia in her Girl Scout uniform. Plath was addicted to achievement from an early age.

Sylvia, almost seventeen, with her brother Warren and mother in September 1949.

When Sylvia heard that she had been accepted by Smith College she was thrilled. 'I went about the house for days in a sort of trance', she said.

Sylvia in November 1952. 'Look at that ugly dead mask here and do not forget it', Plath wrote in her journal.

According to Philip McCurdy, Sylvia tried to cut her throat when she was ten and her face when she was fourteen. The two friends would later have a sexual encounter, one he describes as 'fitful' and 'awkward'.

Eddie Cohen wrote to Plath after one of her stories appeared in *Seventeen* magazine. Cohen assumed the role of informal literary critic, fantasy boyfriend, agony aunt, sex counsellor and psychotherapist.

The Norton brothers, Perry, David and Dick. Plath was good friends with Perry, and dated Dick, but would later use him as the model for Buddy Willard in her novel *The Bell Jar*.

Sylvia with boyfriend Myron Lotz, the inspiration for her poem 'Mad Girl's Love Song'.

Plath with Gordon Lameyer. The two were unofficially engaged in August 1954. In his unpublished memoir he writes of how a friend described Plath as 'a time bomb that seemed always about to explode'.

Sylvia's great love Richard Sassoon. 'He is so much more brilliant, intuitive and alive than anyone I've ever known', wrote Plath.

Jane Anderson, one of Plath's 'doubles'. Later, Plath would use Jane as the basis for the character of Joan Gilling in *The Bell Jar*.

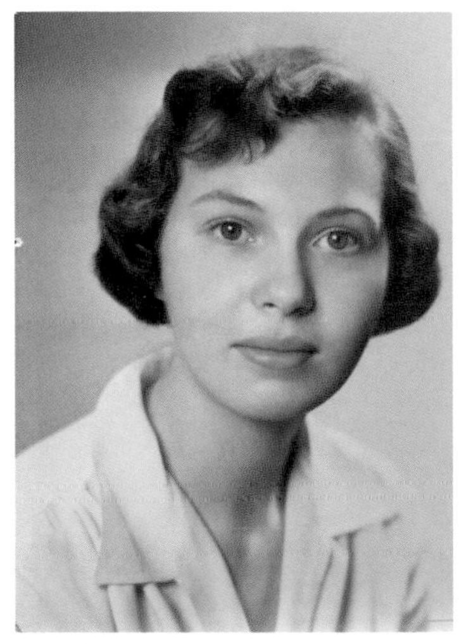

'We started to call Sylvia Plath "Silver Plate"', says Janet Rosenberg. 'That was as much an indication of what we thought of her as anything – that she wasn't real'.

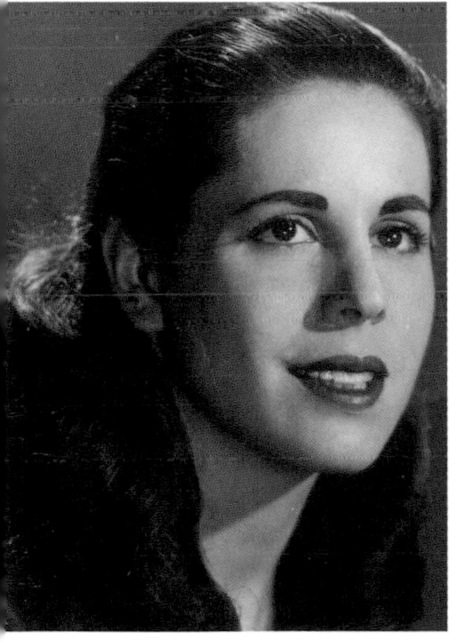

Elinor Friedman. 'Like Chekhov, everything she saw touched her', says Elinor of her friend, Sylvia.

Nancy Hunter. The two young women were, she said, 'Siamese twins, joined at the ego'.

Sylvia with Gordon Lameyer in Venice. By the spring of 1956 their relationship had deteriorated to such an extent the two were barely speaking.

Sylvia with her husband Ted Hughes, whom she married in June 1956, four months after they had first met.

'I shut my eyes and all the world drops dead' – the first line of Plath's poem 'Mad Girl's Love Song'.

would she spend the rest of her life festering a deep-seated resentment of her husband, jealous of his ability to have a career while she had no choice but to stay at home and play the part of the perfect housewife? If that was the case would she deny to herself that she had ever wanted more from life than this? Surely if that was the case the result would be insanity, she surmised.[16] Perhaps she should, as Eddie Cohen had suggested, seek the advice of a psychiatrist, but the services of a mental-health professional cost money, money that neither she nor her mother had. So her only choice, as she wrote in her journal, was suicide. Until she had the strength to do it, she would, she said, cultivate a mask and pretend that she was 'gay, serene' and not 'hollow and afraid'.[17]

In contrast, up in Saranac, Dick was undergoing some kind of psychological rebirth, attempting to transform himself into a more honest individual. He wrote to Sylvia about his plan to tell his parents about his non-virginal status – a confession he hoped would result in a greater independence of spirit. When presented with the opportunity he did not tell Mildred and William of his sexual history – that would have been too shocking – but he did taunt them with the threat of taking up smoking a pipe or joining the navy. He told Sylvia that, instead of pursuing his dreams of becoming a doctor, he might try his hand at being a writer. Experimenting with the form, he wrote out reams of stream-of-consciousness prose, much of it highly sexual, which he sent to Sylvia. He also tried to impress her by including sexually explicit snatches of dialogue he had heard in the sanatorium, such as 'A hard is about the most useless thing I know of in this place'; 'I was only interested in sex when I went with her. I watched her boobs all the time and didn't notice what she was saying'; and 'Boy, did I fill her full of shit.' In case Sylvia didn't know, Dick decoded the sentences for her: a 'hard' was slang for an erection, while 'shit' was shorthand for semen.[18]

Just as Sylvia was distancing herself from him so Dick found himself feeling closer to her. In November he spent two days analysing himself and came to the conclusion that, in the past, he had been more in love with himself than with her. Now, he felt his attitudes were changing and that he could honestly say that he loved her with all his heart. The revelation did not help Sylvia's delicate frame of mind. She already felt that she was unable to cope with the demands of her science course, an interdepartmental course that concentrated on the world of atoms, and although (in a letter home to her mother) she isolated this as the sole cause of her mental breakdown – she said she had even thought of ending it all in order to escape attending[19] – the truth was much more complex. In her mind, Sylvia associated the world of science – with its rules, regulations, formulas and fixed truths – with Dick. Yet here he was, a newly liberated man of leisure, in the process of reinventing himself as a part-time literary critic and writer of racy, modernist prose. 'Do you suppose I could make my living writing?' he asked her.[20] She felt threatened by Dick's attempts to steal into her territory, angry that he assumed he could just take on the mantle of a writer without putting in the same amount of effort – and suffering the same process of rejection – that she herself had experienced. After trying to repress her emotions – a process she likened to the suppression of 'pus-bloated sores'[21] – they finally came to the surface during a conversation with Marcia Brown when she unburdened herself. She confessed to her journal how hearing about another person's happiness resulted in her feeling possessed by hate and jealousy.[22]

After suffering from a bout of insomnia, on 15 December Sylvia went to see the psychiatrist at Smith to talk about her problems – again just blaming them on the demands of her science course – and asked the doctor whether she could spend a few days in the college infirmary. She was sure the rest would not only help boost her spirits but also relieve her of the symptoms of a sore throat and a sinus infection. Sylvia also confessed to her mother, in a segment that Aurelia excised from *Letters Home*, that, on 15 December, she had started her period for the first time in three months. The onset of her period meant that she couldn't go biking with her new date, Myron Lotz, a twenty-year-old classmate of Perry's at Yale whom she had met at the Nortons' house in Wellesley over Thanksgiving. Sylvia was infatuated with Myron, whom she would also call 'Mike': not only was he slim and strong (he had pitched for the Detroit Tigers, reputedly earning $10,000 during one summer), he also was exceptionally bright (the son of poor Austro-Hungarian immigrants, he was first in his class at Yale and would enrol in at Yale Medical School in the autumn of 1953). Sylvia shared with him, so she told her mother in an unpublished letter, a spirit of ambition and an ability to find beauty even among the most aesthetically unappealing of subjects. He also was one of the few people she had met at college who, like herself, knew all the words to a wide range of popular songs.

In December, Myron visited her at Smith. On the way to a college cocktail party – one daiquiri was, said Sylvia, enough to make her high for an hour – they passed the mental hospital in Northampton. As the sun was setting over the black hills, the couple heard the screaming of the patients inside – a sound Sylvia described to her mother as a 'terrifying, holy experience'.[23] She also wrote of her desire to learn '*why* and *how* people cross the borderline between sanity and insanity.'[24] The next day, on a drive through the Massachusetts countryside, Sylvia and Myron spotted a group of small airplanes in a field. After chatting with one of the owners, Sylvia was invited to fly in one of the two-seaters, a journey that she found ecstatic, especially when the pilot turned the plane over in mid-air and she found that the ground had swung above her head.[25] As the airplane flipped, she shouted at the top of her voice that the experience was better than God, religion, 'anything'; a moment later, she took the controls and flew the plane higher and higher into the air. After half an hour in the sky the pilot returned her back to the ground; the contrast between the heavens and the earth served as a neat symbol of the space through which she passed as she fell from the heights of her manic behaviour to the horrors of her depression.

Throughout her life, Sylvia attempted to cast herself as a female Icarus, desperately aspiring upwards towards a perfection – an abstraction – that she knew was impossible to achieve. It was almost as if she was trying to transform herself into a metaphor, a metaphor that she realised was destined to fall flat. This process was played out for real when, just after Christmas, Sylvia went to Saranac to visit Dick. On 27 December, using borrowed skis and boots and uncertain how to turn, Sylvia, who had never skied before, was persuaded by Dick to tackle a tall slope at Mount Pisgah. At the top of the mountain, looking across to the other snow-covered peaks and down towards the green-coloured river below, she felt the same thrill she had experienced when she had been up in the air in the plane above Massachusetts. She of all people knew, of course, that one couldn't feel real ecstasy until one had endured the agony. She pushed herself off and sped down the hill at a good speed, but halfway down the slope she began to wobble and she fell, cartwheeling, into a bank of snow. She pushed the ice off her face, clambered upwards and, with a grin, started to walk away until she realised there was something wrong with her left leg – later doctors confirmed that she had broken her fibula. Sylvia subsequently made light of the incident – she sent a telegram to her mother that included a joke about how difficult it might be to Charleston with her leg in plaster – and it didn't take long for her, creative opportunist that she was, to incorporate the experience into her fiction. In the first draft of her story 'The

Christmas Heart' – which she rewrote as 'In the Mountains' – she is Sheila and Dick is Michael. Plath recounts the skiing accident in great detail, describing it as a final challenge laid down by Dick, a physical and psychological fight to the death. The story also includes details about Dick's infidelity, his time in the sanatorium, flashbacks to the time when Sylvia visited her boyfriend in hospital to see a baby born, and reworked extracts from some of his letters to her. After its rejection from *Woman's Day* magazine, Plath reworked the story: in 'In the Mountains' she becomes Isobel and Dick is called Austin, and the skiing accident is deleted to make way for a more detailed examination of life in the sanatorium and the impact of tuberculosis on the couple's relationship. At the end of the story, Austin expresses his frustration at not being able to kiss his girlfriend – intimate contact increases the risk of catching TB – and Isobel feels the wetness of his tears on her neck.

Plath would also write about the Mount Pisgah incident in *The Bell Jar*, describing it as a symbol of an innate death wish. Logically, she knew that since she didn't know how to ski, she should walk down the side of the slope back to safety, but the 'thought that I might kill myself formed in my mind coolly as a tree or a flower.'[26] As she skis down the mountain she sees herself travelling back in time through various scenes from her life, 'through year after year of doubleness and smiles and compromise, into my own past.'[27] Here, the fall is associated with a stripping back of the masks of the self and, in Plath's imagination, the incident became the means by which she could, in a psychological sense, 'die' in order to be reborn. Already, at this early stage of her career, Plath was fascinated by the idea of resurrection. 'You are twenty,' she wrote at the end of 1952. 'You are not dead, although you were dead. The girl who died.'[28]

Sylvia's rebirth, at the beginning of 1953, was brought about by a kind of mental resetting. Taking on the role of a psychological self-healer, she decided to try to click the various fragments of her disordered mind back into place. After all, if a doctor could mend her broken leg by the means of a cast she could surely resolve her mental-health issues by readjusting the parameters of her perception. The first thing she did to help herself recover from her black depression was admit that she could never marry Dick. She no longer found him attractive – if anything, his tuberculosis rendered him, in her eyes, 'unclean'[29] – and the realisation liberated her. Feeling newly empowered, she set about changing other aspects of her life that made her miserable. She submitted a petition to audit her dreaded science course – attend the lectures, but not depend on it for credit, taking a unit in Milton instead – a proposal that was accepted by the college authorities. On 9 January she wrote to her mother about her newfound happiness, describing how breaking her leg made her acknowledge that her problems of late last year were subjective. If she suffered from any mental imbalances in the future, she said, she would try and approach the illness with the same practical consideration with which she had faced her physical difficulties.[30] After all, she managed to get around campus easily enough on her crutches – she wrote to Myron Lotz of her joy at seeing the trail she left behind her in the snow – and she liked the extra attention her temporary disability brought her. In her journal she wrote how her leg had become a 'passport', something she could use to her advantage.[31] Her paper comparing Piers Plowman to Chaucer's Plowman, Gerard Manley Hopkins' Harry Ploughman and Thomas Carlyle's Peasant Saint was described as 'brilliant' by Howard Rollin Patch, Plath's professor who taught the medieval literature course. According to Sylvia, such praise was better than a bouquet of exotic flowers, she said.[32]

Then, at ten o'clock on Sunday 18 January, Sylvia was called to the telephone in her house. Ignoring the college rules, she rushed downstairs in her bathrobe and picked up the receiver, delighted to hear Myron's voice. 'How's the invalid?' he said.[33] She tried to control her joy, recalling the awful time when Dick Norton had called only to tell her that he was at Smith not to see her but to visit Jane Anderson. Could he drop by later, Myron asked. For the next seven hours Sylvia existed in a kind of ecstatic anticipation. She wanted, she said, to stash away the time with Myron like she would guard a huge store of money.[34] Later that day, sitting in her room working, one of her housemates announced that there was a man to see her downstairs. Myron was early. Sylvia confessed that she was so excited that she could hardly dress herself – she selected a black velvet skirt, an aqua-coloured cashmere sweater and a string of pearls – but this was nothing to the euphoria she felt when he invited her to the Yale Junior Prom.[35] The invitation – the latest in a series of 'highs' – edged her into what can only be described as a manic state. She knew that this wasn't good for her mental health as she realised that she was edging ever nearer towards a dangerously high-pitched level of obsession.[36] She acknowledged that she was in the habit of creating a fantasy image of her boyfriends and told herself that she must not transform Myron into an accumulation of her own projected desires. She had, she said, gone without any kind of sexual interplay for quite a few months now[37] and, while it was normal for her to transfer her fantasies onto Myron, she had to stop herself using him as an 'engine' for her 'ecstasy'.[38]

Although Sylvia attempted to expand the limits of analysis outwards from her self to more generalised philosophical subjects, such as perception and the nature of reality, her focus was forever drawn back inwards. In 'Dialogue', a paper she wrote for her English course in mid-January, she cast herself as Alison, a serious-minded, ambitious girl, who answers a series of questions posed by her friend Marcia. Why didn't she just enjoy herself like any of the other girls at the college? From Marcia's point of view it seemed as though her friend always turned seemingly insignificant incidents into major events, transforming the harmless words uttered by those around her into weapons that had the power to harm her. Alison felt so anxious and tired that one day she thought she might just crack open, so overwhelmed was she by the words that rose inside her that she felt they might consume and destroy her. She confessed that, while sitting at the dinner table surrounded by other girls, she occasionally felt so confused by the voices around her that she thought she would go quite mad. She compared their pointless chatter to the clucking of a flock of brainless birds.[39] Each of us, she said, had various strategies that helped us avoid the agonies of free will, whether political ideology, religion, television and films, or alcohol. She went on to compare the construction of reality to a children's game that involves its participants pulling out various unrelated items from a paper bag, objects which you then had to include into an overarching narrative. From this seemingly senseless jumble one had to construct some kind of meaning, she said.[40] She saw life as made up of a series of tensions and relaxations, and explained this process by using the model of the dialectic: thesis being a time of happy, antithesis as the shadow of death, with synthesis the everlasting, overriding problem. The idea of choice – confining one's options, forever cutting off one's potentialities – horrified her and she visualised this as a kind of tree with many branches, various offshoots that one had to reject in order to carry on climbing. This was an image she would go on and use in *The Bell Jar*: she saw herself sitting at the base of a fig tree (a tree that represented life), starving to death because she was unable to choose which of the fruits to pick. She also included in 'Dialogue' a passage that expressed her dark thoughts of the previous autumn when she considered that her identity was composed of nothing more than an artificial shell. Inside, she felt as though some kind of awful disease had eaten her away, leaving her empty and hollow. And, although she continued to pretend to be 'normal', she was afraid that people would be able to see the 'rot' inside her, that the poison would seep out of her, something that was symptomatic of her falseness.[41] Robert Gorham Davis gave the paper a B; though he said the work was 'thoughtful and intelligent', its tone disturbed him somewhat. He concluded that the paper didn't 'do justice to the quality of life experiences' to which her abstractions referred – the result, he said, was a 'lessening of meaning, since your images, incidents and theoretical constructions are not adequate to what you are discussing.'[42]

The following week Sylvia received another critique, this time a personal one: another letter from Eddie Cohen, who cut through her rhetoric and stripped away the delusions of her recently acquired happiness. Although he was pleased that she was feeling more relaxed, he believed that she should still seek psychiatric treatment. 'If need be, I shall fly out there and seize you by your pretty hair and drag you, caveman style, into the office of the nearest available witch-doctor,' he wrote.[43] At one point, she had thought that it would simply be enough to show her letters to a therapist, but no, that wasn't enough, he said. 'You gotta go in and talk, talk, talk – even though it tears your guts out to do so at times,' he told her. If she really did feel that attracted to Myron, she should make her intentions known, he advised, as there was little to be gained by pretending to be coy. And as for the skiing accident? He had his suspicions that this was nothing more than an expression of her tendency to associate emotional trauma, usually of a romantic nature, with some kind of physical breakdown. 'You are going to be a mighty maimed sort of person if you make a habit of substituting broken legs and other forms of violence for the colds which have been your psychological catharsis in the past,' he said.[44]

* * *

One of the first literary critiques of the work of Sylvia Plath came from an unlikely source: Dick Norton. Confined to the sanatorium in Saranac and still in the process of undergoing a creative renaissance, Dick, writing in the objective style of a professional literary critic, dissected a number of stories (such as 'Den of Lions', 'The Perfect Set Up', 'Initiation', and 'Sunday at the Mintons''), a couple of essays she wrote for college (including the recently written 'Dialogue') and the sonnet 'Twelfth Night' (which was published in the December 1952 issue of *Seventeen* and which is included in the *Collected Poems* under the title 'Cinderella'). In the resulting paper, 'Individualism and Sylvia Plath: An Analysis and Synthesis', which he sent her at the end of January 1953, Norton classified her writing as 'lyrical, inquiring, defiant, intellectual, self-analytical'.[45] One of the most conspicuous themes that he could see running through all her work was, in his opinion, the struggle of the individual to fulfil her own full potential within society. This often manifested itself by characters rebelling or revolting against the expected order, a process that resulted in a greater degree of self-knowledge. 'The writings show a steady progression to deeper insights and greater resourcefulness on the part of the central character,' he continued.[46] If he did have any criticism of her work he confined it to 'Dialogue' – the beginning of the essay was weak, he said, while many of 'Alison's sexual peccadilloes appear unexplained and de trop.' However, he congratulated on her power of description, and concluded, 'It remains for her [Plath] to explore her many-faceted potentialities, assured of a fascinated audience.'[47]

In a letter that accompanied the essay, Dick asked her whether she had read Virginia Woolf's *To the Lighthouse* before writing 'Sunday at the Mintons'', as he noticed a number of similarities between Lily Briscoe and Elizabeth and Mr Ramsay and Henry. One line from Woolf's novel struck him as being particularly influential on Plath's story: 'She set her clean canvas firmly upon the easel, as a barrier, frail, but she hoped sufficiently substantial to ward off Mr Ramsay and his exactingness.'[48] Of course, Sylvia could not bring herself to tell Dick of the true source of inspiration – that the story was based on her relationship with him. Although Sylvia tried to maintain a friendship with Dick, in private she found his letters lamentable and felt nothing.[49] She dreaded having to go and see him over the spring vacation in case he tried to extract some sort of promise from her, an assurance that she no longer felt capable of giving. Physically, she wanted a 'colossus', she said, while mentally she wanted a man who wasn't going to be jealous of her creativity. Mildred Norton had arranged a summer waitressing job for her at Saranac – so the couple could spend some time together – but when Sylvia politely rejected the position Dick's mother turned on her. The Nortons had assumed that Sylvia would marry their son, but now this looked increasingly less likely. Certainly, Sylvia told her mother, she wasn't ready to sacrifice her intellectual and creative freedom at the altar of marriage. Her ambitions, such as attending graduate school and travelling around the world, were not going to be forfeited by any 'squalling, breastfed brats,' she said.[50]

In early 1953, Sylvia relished the prospect of reading and learning from the modern classics, particularly Joyce, whom she considered writing about for her thesis. In February she started *Ulysses* and *Portrait of the Artist as a Young Man*, and in March – with money she had earned as a correspondent from the *Springfield Daily News* – she bought a copy of *Dubliners*, as well as the Modern Library edition of *The Basic Writings of Sigmund Freud*. She became progressively more interested in psychology, particularly the study of the abnormal mind, and spent hours with Myron Lotz poring through his textbooks. As she wrote to her mother in an unpublished letter, she was heavily influenced by her creative-writing tutor, Robert Gorham Davis, and his interest in psychology, especially its relation to concepts such as mythology, poetry and symbolism.[51] Sylvia's copy of her Freud anthology is heavily annotated and underlined. From the quantity of her markings, it seems that Sylvia was fascinated by the source of neurosis and mental illness, highlighting sentences such as 'the psychosis in this case represented a conflict between the ego and the outer world [. . .] The dream is a hidden fulfilment of a repressed wish, or a direct attempt to obtain in phantasy what is denied us in reality [. . .] The psychosis exhibits alone no compromise with reality, turns its back on reality, as it were [. . .]'[52] She also underscored passages about dreams of the deaths of loved ones and the words 'If anyone dreams that his father or mother [. . .] has died [. . .] the dreamer has wished them dead at some time or other during his childhood.'[53] The words she chose to pick out from the book's index make for an intriguing but far from healthy mix: animism, delusions, dementia praecox, demoniacal hallucinations, demons, dream sources, dreams (hallucinatory), forgetfulness, narcissism and paranoia. In Freud's view, neurosis was caused by a conflict between the ego and the id, unresolved tensions that existed between the rational mind and unconscious urges. Presumably Sylvia thought the same: next to the passage in the introduction outlining this idea she drew a big pointed star.

She was fascinated by duality, the contradictions that existed in the minds and souls of each individual. 'We are at loggerheads with our own lives,' wrote W. H. Auden in his poem 'Kairos and Logos'. Indeed, Sylvia highlighted these lines in her copy of Auden's *Collected Poetry*. She annotated her edition with analyses of rhyme schemes, notes to herself and quotations from other writers, such as this one from Montaigne: 'We are, I know not how, double in ourselves, so that what we believe, we disbelieve, and cannot rid ourselves of what we condemn.' She felt particularly drawn to Auden's '*The Sea and the Mirror'*, his long poetic response to Shakespeare's *The Tempest.* In the margin of the poem, where Auden deals with the duality that exists between the characters Ariel (the creative imagination) and Caliban (a symbol of the base and the brutal), Plath wrote of the special relationship that exists between the two. It was impossible for Ariel or Caliban to ignore one another as the two facets were inextricably bound: together they formed the enigma that is the human personality. And although the airy spirit of the imagination may often try and forget its animalistic counterpart, it was important to remember that the creative spirit could often draw inspiration from it.[54]

As Sylvia read – or rather devoured – Auden's work, she became convinced that he was a genius. In the flyleaf of her edition of his *Collected Poetry* she noted that she had found her "God"[55] while she told a boyfriend that he was an 'angel'.[56] One night, in April 1953, Sylvia invited Auden – who was serving as a visiting professor to Smith – to her house for dinner. 'It was a feather in the cap for Sylvia, and she behaved obsequiously,' says Janet Rosenberg. 'He was quite outrageous – I remember he arrived late and said, "I'm sorry I'm late, the zipper on my pants was broken," or something like that. He proceeded to say all kinds of indiscreet things throughout dinner.' Janet also remembers him behaving inappropriately during a Smith College symposium attended by literary and artistic figures such as Allen Tate, Ben Shahn, George Boas and Lionel Trilling. 'Auden and Ben Shahn, both of whom had had too much to drink, kept passing notes to one another during the event, and it was obvious that Auden was the ringleader. The president of the college, Benjamin Wright, was so furious about their behaviour that he said he would never invite Auden to the college again.'[57]

From Plath's point of view Auden could do no wrong and, in an unpublished letter to her brother, she described him as being like a brilliant, extremely funny, naughty boy. Like the

English-born poet, she believed it was an artist's responsibility to disenchant – to unsettle, disturb and force people to see the world from a fresh perspective – a role that found expression in Auden's 'The Composer': 'Rummaging into his living, the poet fetches/The images out that hurt and connect.'[58]

One day in early February 1953, after she attended a lecture by Theodore Greene, a professor of philosophy at Yale, on Protestantism in an age of uncertainty, Sylvia made way back to Lawrence House on crutches. When she arrived home one of her housemates told her that there was a boy waiting for her. As quickly as she could, she hobbled up the stairs and changed into a red sweater and skirt and returned downstairs, into the living room, to see a young, brown-haired man with movie-star looks who introduced himself as Gordon Lameyer. Gordon, a senior studying English at Amherst College, had first heard about Sylvia the previous year from his mother, who had heard her speak at a Smith Club event in Wellesley. As he had been going steady with another Smith student at the time he hadn't done anything about contacting her, but after becoming 'unpinned' (slang for breaking up), he made sure that Sylvia was the first girl he called on. From the first moment, there was a strong rapport between them – they lived only a mile apart from each other in Wellesley; both of their mothers had married Germans; both of them had been brought up Unitarians; and, perhaps most important, they shared a love of literature.

'I was startled when a large girl with a curled-in page boy hobbled down the stairs on crutches,' recalled Gordon of that first meeting. 'Intense she was and animated, with brown, mischievous eyes.' They walked from Lawrence House to nearby Green Street to enjoy a drink, with 'Sylvia swinging along like a pendulum between her two crutches.' Later he wrote, in an unpublished memoir, 'That first evening she seemed to me rather young, full of enthusiasms of a college girl on a first date. On the surface she was very sunny and energetic; I was unaware of her depths.' He was struck by how critical she seemed about her face – she said that it was 'too mobile' and that she did not have what she described as 'classic features'. 'When I told her my nose was broken she complained about her own bad bone structure,' said Gordon. 'Also, her lower lip was a mite too full like the petal of a slightly overblown rose.'[59]

On 10 February, she wrote to her mother to confess her interest in her new date, describing Gordon as extremely handsome.[60] The couple travelled to Amherst, where they talked about religion, Unitarianism and James Joyce, and after a chicken dinner in the community eating hall they went back to his room, where he read some of his own poetry to her. He remembers being impressed that she could quote large chunks of Dylan Thomas – she adored his villanelle 'Do Not Go Gentle into That Good Night', which she knew by heart – and her language, he recalled, occasionally 'verged on the extravagant, displaying a vast enjoyment for the sound of words as if they were exotic fruits, to be tasted and relished'. Although the physical contact between them was, in those first few days, limited to only kissing, he later said he thought that her manner was perhaps a little too forward, 'as if she were being a little too solicitous of me, a touch too flattering. Her enthusiasms seemed to me at that time a little too forced and sophomoric. She tended to idealize men, especially her teachers or any man she thought knew more than she, especially writers.'[61]

At this stage Sylvia was only superficially attracted to Gordon. Her real passion, during the first few months of 1953, was still directed towards Myron Lotz. In her journal she wrote that Myron, or Mike, was the only man she would consider marrying. He was physically strong, lean and healthy (he neither drank nor smoked); he was ambitious, and could provide her with the means through which she could continue to enrich her appetite for cultural pursuits such as theatre, concerts, art exhibitions and travel; and, while he had a photographic memory, he was still sensitive to the power of the written word. She knew, at this point in her life, that it would be dangerous for her to marry a writer or an artist, as she could not bear the inevitable conflict of egos that would result. On 18 February she wrote to her mother to tell her of her excitement at seeing Myron at the weekend – he was supposed to be driving to Smith in a new car, a vehicle that represented to Sylvia a symbol of their new freedom together. She had felt so oppressed and restricted – by the plaster cast on her leg, by the strictly demarcated nature of her studies, by her responsibilities towards Dick – that she wanted to indulge herself. After all, her marks were good enough – A in medieval literature, an A in her dreaded science course, and an A-minus in creative writing – that she thought she deserved a period of unrestrained enjoyment. In her journal, however, she went one step further, fantasising of being taken in a car and driven into the mountains where she would be raped like a cavewoman. She started to obsess about the date with Myron on the forthcoming Saturday to such an extent that it began to consume her. She couldn't wait for him to see her without her cast, which had been removed by the doctor on 19 February. In her journal she wrote of the procedure in a style that prefigures some of her later poetry, especially her 1961 poem 'In Plaster', comparing the removal of the white plaster cast by the doctor to a gravedigger opening a coffin. The exposure of the 'corpse' of her leg, withered and discoloured and covered in curls of black hair, shocked her, and the doctor told her that as the fracture had not completely healed she would need regular whirlpool baths at the hospital.

Back at Lawrence House, Myron called to say that he wouldn't be able to visit that weekend after all because his new car still had not been delivered. The news upset and unsettled her, likening its effect on her mind to the destruction and collapse of a building. She felt claustrophobic, and she found it difficult to catch her breath[62] and this state inspired her to write the villanelle, 'To Eva Descending the Stair', about the paradox between the transience of physical beauty and the inevitable passing of time. Myron's continued absence from Smith inspired another villanelle, 'Mad Girl's Love Song', which she also wrote around this time. 'He didn't come and didn't come and didn't come,' she wrote in her journal.[63] Was he dead? What was the problem? Where was he? Each ring of the phone jangled her nerves in anticipation and eventually after four hours of waiting she flung herself on her bed in a rage, determined not to eat, resolved not to look out of her window for him. The resulting poem, she said in an unpublished letter to her mother, captured the thought that the two were preordained to never see one another again,[64] and included the repeated line, 'I think I made you up inside my head',[65] a line that Olive Higgins Prouty found particularly brilliant: 'It reverberates in my consciousness, not only its sound but its connotation.'[66] The writing of the villanelles lifted her spirits a little: not only did they take her mind off her immediate worries and anxieties, they also were concrete proof that she was talented writer. She recognised that the poems were the best she had written and she sent them straight off to various literary magazines. In March she heard back from the *New Yorker*: an editor at the magazine said that, while there were many things they liked about her work, the two poems she had submitted, 'Mad Girl's Love Song' and 'Doomsday', another villanelle, just did not make the grade. 'We were somewhat bothered by the two rhymes that break the scheme – especially "up" which is not even an assonant rhyme here,' wrote the editor. 'Do try us again.'[67]

The following month *Harper's* offered her $100 for the two villanelles 'To Eva Descending the Stair' and 'Doomsday' and another poem, 'Go Get the Goodly Squab', which she had written the previous spring. Russell Lynes, the editor at the magazine, wrote to her to apologise for taking so long to reply to her submission but said this had not been because they didn't like her work. Rather it was because 'we don't seem to be able to make up our minds which one we like best.'[68] The best solution to the problem was to buy all three poems, 'which isn't just weak-mindedness on our part but real enthusiasm,' he added.[69] On 24 April, the day she heard from *Harper's*, she sent a telegram to her mother wishing her happy birthday, the news serving as a present. She was so thrilled by the acceptance – her first from a non-teenage, literary magazine – that she could not sleep that night. In fact, it seemed like fortune was smiling on Sylvia. Also in April, she was elected editor of the *Smith Review* for the forthcoming year and learned that she had been awarded $10 from *Mademoiselle* magazine as a runner's-up prize in the third assignment for the annual guest-editorship contest.

Mademoiselle described itself as the 'quality magazine for smart young women', but it was much more than that.[70] Founded in 1935 by Street & Smith, it carved out a niche for itself in an age when, according to the company's marketing information, not a single magazine (and there were 701 published in America that year) devoted itself to the interests of young women. The magazine, was, according to the publisher, 'edited exclusively for the 18-to-30 age group above average in education and taste.' Its typical readers were 'college girls [79 per cent of its readers had college degrees], career girls and young-marrieds' and for them the magazine strove to be 'guide, philosopher and friend, to offer good taste in everything from fashion to fiction, from grooming to sound vocational advice, from philosophy and art to entertainment and travel.' By 1953 its circulation stood at over 500,000 and the magazine boasted, without any apparent irony at the contradiction, that it was both the first magazine to run makeovers, turning 'an ugly duckling into a swan', and the first 'to recognize the career girl, first to have a special department devoted to her needs.'[71] Yet, under the helm of editor Betsy Talbot Blackwell and fiction editor Margarita G. Smith (the sister of Carson McCullers), the magazine had developed a reputation for publishing the work of significant literary figures including Albert Camus, Paul Bowles, Katherine Anne Porter, Shirley Jackson, Truman Capote, William Faulkner, Tennessee Williams, Jean Stafford and Dylan Thomas. Plath, in a letter, wrote of her admiration for the fiction featured in the magazine: *Mademoiselle*, she said, offered a rare opportunity for young writers like her who did not always want to conform to the genre expectations of more mass market publications.[72]

All year Sylvia had been submitting assignments to the magazine in the hope of securing one of twenty, month-long placements starting that June. One task involved a critique of the August 1952 issue of *Mademoiselle*, which contained her story 'Sunday at the Mintons" and which also featured a couple of other Smith girls (who had been photographed modelling clothes on the steps of Seelye Hall). She particularly liked the balance of features, which covered topics such as the purpose of a college education and the difficulties and joys of being a young woman with a high intellect. The latter was written by Paul Woodring. She had been thrilled to read Woodring's statement at the end of his article, which said that a young woman could have it all – 'love, romance, sex and the expanding horizons of intellectual companionship'.[73] But was this a realistic prospect?

Although America was experiencing an explosion in the female labour market – the number of working women increased from 18 million in 1950 to 23 million ten years later – they were largely confined to clerical and secretarial positions, domestic service, assembly lines, teaching and nursing. 'Only about one-third of the women who entered college during the decade actually graduated,' writes one commentator. 'As a result, although an unexpectedly large proportion of American women worked, they were conspicuously absent from high-level jobs [. . .] Just over ten per cent of working women entered a profession, and a minuscule six per cent had management positions.'[74]

These were the days when a college education was regarded as a preparation for marriage and motherhood; aspiration above and beyond this was seen as venturing into hazardous territory. 'A liberal-arts education in the 1950s tempted us transitional women to overdevelop in one way, without fortifying us against underachieving in another,' observed Jane Truslow, a contemporary of Plath's at Smith, who would under her married name of Davison write the book *The Fall of a Doll's House: Three Generations of American women and the houses they lived in.* Plath, she writes, 'more dramatically than I illustrates the dangerous illusion we shared, a belief in unlimited possibilities that was, I fear, closer to greed than to innocence.'[75] Part of the problem, according to Davison – who would go on to win one of the *Mademoiselle* guest editorships in 1955 – was the fact that they compartmentalised so many aspects of their lives. 'Ornamental matters of the mind were kept in an upstairs guest room, or relegated to attic storage, while a canny ability to deal with practical exigencies worked in the kitchen,' she wrote. 'We might read Virginia Woolf, discourse on her, but we didn't absorb her counsel: we didn't, as she advised, try to "think poetically and prosaically at one and the same moment, thus keeping in touch with fact." We alternated instead of integrating, and someone should have insisted on our sorting out priorities with ruthlessness, with realism. But we weren't even aware that selection was necessary.'[76]

Plath – like so many of her contemporaries – wanted, as Jane Davison pointed out (in an allusion to Rona Jaffe's 1958 novel), 'the best of everything'. She saw no reason why she couldn't have a stimulating career *and* a husband and family, and, in her mind at least, surely it was possible to write for both *Ladies' Home Journal* and the *New Yorker*. While this literary mix-and-match may seem incompatible today, in the 1950s it was much more acceptable to sell one's work across the spectrum of the marketplace. If she was ever in doubt about this Plath turned to the example of self-proclaimed 'housewife poet' Phyllis McGinley, a college graduate who had managed to combine domesticity – a husband and two children – with an extremely successful writing career. Her name may no longer have a place in the literary canon, but for a thirty-year period from the 1930s to 1960s McGinley – who did publish in both *Ladies' Home Journal* and the *New Yorker* – was a much-loved and much-respected author. 'So popular was her work, and so canny were her portraits of middle-class matrons, their hapless husbands and conniving children, that for two generations McGinley's work – her books flew off the shelves, tens of thousands of copies at a time – was as well-known and as well-heeled as anyone's,' notes one critic.[77] In letters home to her mother, Plath wrote of her admiration for McGinley, who in 1961 won a Pulitzer Prize for poetry for her collection *Times Three*, a book that contained an introduction by Auden. One day, she stated, she was sure the famous Phyllis McGinley would read her work.[78]

Plath knew that winning one of the guest editorships on *Mademoiselle* was an important step towards fulfilling her literary aspirations. The competition was fierce – 800 applicants, with twenty girls applying from Smith College alone – and she did not think she had much of a chance. In addition to her academic record, work experience, publication history, and the quality of her assignments, the magazine had to make sure that she had the right personality. 'One of my assignments was buzzing up to Smith College and chatting with Sylvia Plath to determine whether she would make a good guest editor,' recalled Gigi Marion, who then worked in the magazine's college department. 'Although I thought she might be awfully good, I was on the cusp a little on how she might fit in. Her behavior was almost a performance, which I found a bit of a problem. You might be there another day and find an entirely different personality.'[79]

Yet, at the beginning of May, Plath heard from Marybeth Little, the College Board editor, that she had won one editorships. Sylvia wired back her acceptance immediately, confirming that she would be available to start work in New York at 9 a.m. on Monday 1 June. She adored New York. At the beginning of May she had enjoyed a wonderful weekend in the city with old flame Ray Wunderlich, entirely at his expense. There she had tasted her first oysters on the half-shell and attended her first opera, *Carmen*. She described the trip – which included visits to see Arthur Miller's *The Crucible* and Tennessee Williams' *Camino Real* – as the most wonderful weekend of her life, and she couldn't wait to return to Manhattan. However, she worried about her wardrobe – she had had to borrow a smart black coat to take with her to New York – and she must have been thrown into a minor panic when she received a letter from the magazine advising her on what clothes to bring.

'It can get very hot in New York in June, and you will want clothes which can look as fresh at 5:00 p.m. as at 9:00 a.m. – after a day of visits to manufacturers, luncheons and office work,' wrote Marybeth Little. 'You might include dark cottons, nylons, shantungs, silks or light-weight suits – cool, dark clothes preferably. You'll want to bring along a bathing suit for your weekends [. . .] we plan one "do-dress" party so you should bring along an evening gown, and don't forget hats – we're afraid they're necessary for all the public appearances you'll make.'[80]

Plath – along with the nineteen other girls from all around America – would be expected to perform many roles while at *Mademoiselle*. 'You will be observer, watchdog, errand clerk, editor, typist, writer [. . .] Magazine deadlines are as final as exam dates, and must be observed religiously.'[81]

The salary for the month would be $150, out of which she would have to pay for her room and board. She would have to watch every cent she spent and she was constantly on the lookout for cut-price fashions. At the end of February she had spotted the perfect outfit to wear to the Yale Junior Prom with Myron Lotz in March – a full-length dress with a strapless silver top and a skirt with a nipped-in waist and covered by a swoosh of white netting. Best of all the dress – which today is held by the costume department at Smith College – had been reduced from $50 to $30. When, at the end of April, she did splash out and spend $85 on a pair of white linen French heels, a black silk shantung dress, and a brown, white and black Mexican-print linen suit dress, she wrote to her mother pleading with her not to scold her, adding that she would try to sell more of her poems.

Over the spring vacation, Sylvia tried her hand at writing a story for *True Story* magazine. Motivated purely by money – if it was accepted she could hope to net at least $100 – Sylvia bashed out the 13,500-word 'I Lied for Love', about Jenny Martin, a farmer's daughter who becomes pregnant by a man, Phil, from a higher social class than her own. During the course of the story, Phil dies in Korea and when Jenny tells her father the news of her pregnancy he dies of a heart attack. At the end of the 'confession', Jenny settles down with Ivan – a blond refugee from Estonia, whom she modelled on Ilo Pill – who brings up the child as his own. The twin themes of the story are sex and money, or rather the lack of it. Jenny, like Sylvia, had grown up with the knowledge that her opportunities in life were limited by her family's low income, compared to other girls who came from wealthier backgrounds and whose fathers had enough spare cash to buy their daughters anything they wanted.[82] Jenny thinks that she could become friends with girls from a higher social group than her, but one day she walks into the powder room hears the clique talking about her, describing her as a mere farm girl. Jenny sets out to change herself, so that she could imitate the behaviour of the girls from a higher class and hopefully one day enjoy the same kind of costly possessions.[83]

Sylvia was acutely conscious of her mother's tight economic situation and she constantly worried about her. In May she wrote to Warren – who had just received a coveted National Scholarship to Harvard – outlining how she hoped Aurelia would not have to pay anything towards his tuition as she had reached 'rock bottom' financially.[84] She knew their mother was suffering from ulcer problems again – the condition was so serious that Aurelia had to eat baby food – and she didn't want her to worry about money. Sylvia outlined the rather unnerving situation to her brother: how Aurelia would rather sacrifice herself than let her children suffer. Their mother, she said, was so unselfish that this spirit of altruism could be interpreted as some kind of illness.[85] She told her brother that she planned to work during the summer so her mother would not have to – she couldn't bear to think of Aurelia slaving away in the heat of the day just so she could support her. She wanted to go to Harvard summer school – ideally to study elementary psychology and take Frank O'Connor's short-story course – and applied for a scholarship to help cover the costs. However, she told her mother that if lack of funds meant she was forced to choose between attending Harvard or her mother going out to work during July and August she was prepared to sacrifice summer school.

Over the course of the past year, Sylvia had earned a little over $1,000: $500 from *Mademoiselle*, $250 from *Seventeen*, $100 from *Harper's* and $170 from the *Daily Hampshire Gazette*. Why didn't Aurelia try and do the same, she suggested. After all, she could write about various aspects of her life – for instance, her teaching job, medical shorthand – for women's magazines and Sylvia said she would be more than happy to edit the features for her before she submitted them. If one was out of practice, it was always difficult to start writing again, she said.[86] She wanted to take Aurelia on holiday to the Cape that summer – preferably the week after Labor Day, when the rental rates were reduced – and she wrote to Warren to tell him of the plan. Perhaps they could share the cost of a week in a cabin near Falmouth or Brewster? Although both of them had their problems, it seemed as though, so far at least, their journeys through life had been relatively smooth. Success came easily: by the end of the academic year, Sylvia had not only won two poetry prizes from Smith – the Ethel Olin Corbin prize and the Elizabeth Babcock award, which netted her $120 – but she also had been commissioned by *Mademoiselle* to interview Elizabeth Bowen in Cambridge and write a feature on five young male teacher-poets for the magazine as part of her role as a guest editor. She just hoped, as she wrote to Warren, that the world wasn't destroyed by war before both of them were able to enjoy the fruits of their labours.[87]

An implosion – rather than an explosion – was on the horizon. Sylvia's pretend-perfect world was about to be nearly destroyed, not by an external enemy but by forces much closer to home.

Eight

THE BEGINNINGS OF THE BELL JAR

On 31 May 1953, Sylvia travelled by train from her home in Wellesley to New York City. Accompanying her on the journey to Manhattan was fellow *Mademoiselle* guest editor Laurie Totten, a junior at Syracuse University. 'We lived only two blocks apart in Wellesley and so, when I heard that she had won it too, we got in touch and travelled to New York together,' says Laurie. 'We hit it off right away, but I must say I thought she was a typical co-ed – at that first meeting I thought there was nothing remarkable about her.'[1] At Grand Central Station the two young women – with the help of a couple of soldiers they had enlisted to carry their suitcases – fought their way through what Sylvia described as a rather threatening crowd.[2] The yellow cab honked its way through the glass and steel canyons of Manhattan and pulled up outside the Barbizon, a women-only hotel on the corner of Lexington Avenue and 63rd Street.

By 1953 the Barbizon – described as a cross between a charm school and a dormitory – had built up a reputation as a safe haven in a dangerous city, a place where the daughters of wealthy parents could ensure that their darling girls were cloistered away from the temptations of New York. Fellow guest editor Adele Schmidt – who took on the role of advertising director during the month of June – describes the Barbizon as being 'like a dorm and a minimum security prison';[3] men were not allowed above the level of the lobby and particularly anxious parents could even request that their daughters sign in and out of the hotel each day. Yet its name was also a talisman for success, a symbol of the glamour, excitement and allure of self-reinvention that came to be associated with mid-century Manhattan. 'It was relentlessly marketed and written about in gossip columns and in the back of fashion magazines, feeding the fantasies of girls who dreamed about becoming, in the words of a breathless advertisement, one of the "ambitious, discriminating young women" who became "Barbizon girls",' wrote one commentator.[4] By the time Plath walked through the doors of the pink-coral-brick building and into its expansive lobby with its café-au-lait woodwork, Persian carpets and lush pot plants, she knew she was literally following in the footsteps of a range of famous residents such as Joan Crawford, Eudora Welty, Edith Bouvier Beale, *Titanic* survivor Margaret 'Molly' Brown, Grace Kelly and literary agent Annie Laurie Williams.

Plath's single room – with its green carpet, beige walls and pink and green curtains – had a view over rooftops, gardens, the 3rd Street elevated railway, and a sliver of the East River. If she strained her neck she could just make out the United Nations building. Although the room had a desk, a built-in radio and a telephone by the bed, it did not have a private bathroom – all the girls had to share facilities on the corridor. The next morning, together with her fellow guest editors, who all had rooms on the same floor, Sylvia took breakfast at the drug store downstairs, noting that she could order a fruit juice, eggs, two pieces of toast and coffee for fifty cents. The expense of living for a month in New York preyed on her mind and her letters home read, at times, like an account book. Before leaving Massachusetts for Manhattan, Sylvia had asked her mother to transfer $100 from her savings account to her checking account – she had the grand sum of one dollar in the account at the time. In an unpublished letter to her mother, Sylvia wrote that she hoped to meet some interesting men while in New York so they could take her out to dinner or the theatre so she could enjoy these luxuries without having to pay for them herself.[5] She realised she wasn't like the vast majority of residents of the Barbizon – rich girls who, as she wrote in *The Bell Jar*, were either enrolled at or who had graduated from fancy secretarial schools and were hanging about Manhattan in the hope of meeting a man and marrying well. In the novel, Esther – Sylvia's fictionalised self, who lives at a women-only hotel called the Amazon – recalls talking to one such girl and observing how bored she seemed by her gilded life, flitting between skiing in Switzerland at Christmas and vacationing in Bermuda and Brazil. 'Girls like that make me sick,' Plath wrote. 'I'm so jealous I can't speak.'[6]

On the morning of her first day at *Mademoiselle* she dressed in a smart suit, but just as she was about to leave her room she suffered a nose bleed; drops of blood splattered on to her outfit, forcing her to change into a brown dress. From the Barbizon she walked the eight blocks to the offices of *Mademoiselle* at 575 Madison Avenue. At 9 a.m., in the magazine's dark-green and pink conference room, she met the magazine's legendary editor, Betsy Talbot Blackwell – 'the force which propels and inspires the magazine forward'[7] – who had been with *Mademoiselle* since 1935. 'She took plain young women to New York, where she put them in stylish clothes, restyled their hair and makeup and then put their pictures in her magazine,' wrote one observer.[8] According to Edith Raymond Locke, who worked on *Mademoiselle* as associate fashion editor at the time, Blackwell saw the magazine as something that 'nourished young women inside and out'[9] and indeed her first words of welcome to the twenty guest editors on that June morning included a plea to put 'health before genius'.[10]

Sylvia was delighted to meet the rest of the guest editors – four of whom she said were so beautiful they could have been models in Paris – but less than thrilled when she discovered her new position. Plath had been chosen as the guest managing editor – under the supervision of the real managing editor, Cyrilly Abels – a decision that disappointed her. 'Sylvia wanted to be the guest fiction editor, and I know that she was unhappy with Cyrilly Abels,' says Laurie Woolschlager, (née Totten), who had been appointed one of the art co-directors. 'Cyrilly Abels was a hard task masker – she was always crabby because she was constantly on a diet.'[11] According to the information sent from the magazine to its guest editors, Cyrilly Abels was 'the boss of the deadline' and it was her job to make sure that 'everything goes off with precision. Her wide reading experience in the magazine field and her personal contacts with leading writers, publishers and agents enables her to pick original newsworthy subject matter and the right author to do each article.'[12] That morning, Abels informed Sylvia that her feature, 'Poets on Campus', about five up-and-coming poet-teachers – George Steiner, Richard Wilbur, William Burford, Alastair Reid and Anthony Hecht – would have to be rewritten in a style that was more suitable for the magazine. After lunch Sylvia continued to work on her rewrite and then, in the afternoon, she waited her turn to pose for a picture taken by the German-American fashion photographer Herman Landshoff to illustrate the 'Jobiographies' feature, an overview of the guest editors. Landshoff asked Sylvia to sit on a sofa and hold a rose in her hand. In *The Bell Jar*, Plath describes Esther trying to avoid having her photograph taken – even going so far as to hide in the powder room – because she knew she was going to cry.[13] After the photographer persuades her to try and look a little more cheerful, Esther opens her mouth but feels it forming into something as false and fake as the smile of a ventriloquist's dummy and she bursts into tears. Indeed, when you compare Sylvia's photo to the ones Landshoff took of the other guest editors, there is something rather unsettling about it. Plath's eyes burn with a manic intensity lacking in the other young women, her expression seems contrived and artificial and her smile looks fixed, almost a rictus.

'What sort of girl wins a MADEMOISELLE Guest Editorship and comes to New York to work for a month on the August College issue?' ran the opening lines of the 'Jobiographies' feature. Sylvia couldn't answer this, because she was undergoing the first stages of yet another crisis of identity. 'Life happens so hard and fast I sometimes wonder who is me,' she wrote to her mother from the Barbizon.[14] *Mademoiselle* had commissioned a graphologist to analyse the guest editors' handwriting and above Sylvia's photo and signature ran the line: 'Sylvia will succeed in artistic fields. She has a sense of form and beauty and an intense enjoyment of her work.' This was rather different from the original, unedited analysis sent in by Herry O. Teltscher, which read: 'Strength: Enjoyment of working experience intense; sense of form, beauty and style, useful in fields of fashion and interior decoration. Eager for accomplishment. Weakness: Overcome superficiality, stilted behavior, rigidity of outlook.'[15]

Cyrilly Abels certainly noticed this particular aspect of Plath's personality. 'There was a surprising lack of spontaneity in one so young,' she recalled. 'Although her emotions were deeply felt, she gave little of herself, except perhaps to very close friends.'[16] Did Abels push Sylvia a little too hard? 'Sylvia got what I thought was a more prestigious position, but it did not take advantage of her artistic writing talents,' says Janet Rafferty, (née Wagner), one of the jobs and futures guest editors. 'She most certainly was not a "manager". I often found Sylvia hiding out from the rest of us crying over some mishap with her editor, Cyrilly Abels.'[17] In *The Bell Jar*, Abels is cast as Jay Cee, a woman with a fine mind and first-rate literary connections but an ugly face, who calls Esther into her office and makes her cry by questioning her about her seeming lack of interest in her work at the magazine. Throughout the month of June, Cyrilly Abels sent Sylvia a string of memos, inviting her to meet a number of important contacts, including Vance Bourjailly, co-editor of the new book magazine *Discovery*, and supplied her with a steady stream of manuscripts to critique by such famous writers as Rumer Godden, Elizabeth Bowen, Noël Coward and Dylan Thomas. After being on the receiving end of the rejection slip, Sylvia took guilty pleasure in typing out letters declining the work of a number of established authors and journalists, particularly one to a staff member of the *New Yorker*, the magazine that had repeatedly rejected her poetry. As she signed the rejection letters with her own name she did so with a certain wicked sense of satisfaction.[18]

Although Sylvia became quite close to a couple of the other guest editors, particularly Laurie Totten, with whom she took a walk through Greenwich Village and Central Park, others found her behaviour objectionable. Janet Rafferty, who was then studying at Knox, the liberal-arts college in Galesbury, Illinois, became the basis for the character of Betsy in *The Bell Jar*. 'They imported Betsy straight from Kansas with her bouncing blonde pony-tail and Sweetheart-of-Sigma-Chi smile,' wrote Plath.[19] Today Janet remembers Sylvia as an Ivy League snob. 'Sylvia was the first person I asked to meet when we arrived that first morning at 575 Madison Avenue,' she says. 'She, it turned out, was anxious to meet me, because we had both won in the writing category. We both laughed a lot, but it was obvious to me that she thought nothing existed in the USA west of Lake Placid but American Indian reservations. She thought Knox was way out in the boonies and always introduced me as being from Kansas. Sylvia continued to be friendly with me, but let it be known that she thought Knox was really a "backwater" school, and thought I had won in spite of it.'[20]

On one of the first days at *Mademoiselle* the guest editors were treated to a lunch at an upmarket restaurant. Ann Burnside Love, who was studying at the University of Maryland and who worked as the guest merchandise co-ordinator at the magazine, recalls being astonished by Sylvia's behaviour in the restaurant. 'It was a lunch designed for the girls to get to know one another a little better and we were at that stage where we were watching one another very carefully, all of us groping to see what we should do, how we should behave,' she says. 'Very shortly after we were seated – at this nice table with a white tablecloth – a large bowl of caviar was served. The caviar was supposed to be for everyone on the table, but Sylvia reached out for it, pulled it in front of her and began eating. She proceeded to eat the whole bowlful of caviar with a spoon. I remember thinking to myself, "How rude", but she didn't seem to be paying attention to anyone else. I thought she was as impolite as anyone could be. After that, I stopped paying attention to her, and I'm afraid to say that I could not find reasons to like or admire her.'[21]

In *The Bell Jar*, Plath writes about the caviar incident, incorporating it into a scene in Chapter Three of the novel when the guest editors attend a lunch at the fictional *Ladies' Day* magazine. That morning, Esther had not had time for breakfast and, ravenous, she devours the whole bowl of caviar herself. The cut-glass bowl of caviar is also a symbol of Esther's future prospects – her grandfather, the head waiter at a country club (as was Plath's) had always promised her endless supplies of caviar on her wedding day. But, as Esther confesses in the novel, she never planned to get married. Even if she did, Plath writes, 'my grandfather couldn't have afforded enough caviar unless he robbed the country club kitchen and carried it off in a suitcase.'[22] For Esther, as for Sylvia, the caviar became a symbol of everything she desired but had so far been denied her: money with which to enjoy a stress-free education and the ability and freedom to express her sexuality. It's not surprising then, in that instance, when the bowl of caviar was placed before her, Sylvia felt so angry that she forgot, or chose to ignore, the normal rules of etiquette that governed and restricted the behaviour of educated girls in the 1950s. Plath was hungry for experience outside the limits of her class and background. It was a small gesture, but nevertheless it served as an outlet for her rebellious, deviant spirit.

On the morning of the 3 June, the twenty guest editors posed for a group photograph in the shape of a star. The shoot, taken by Herman Landshoff, proved complicated, recalled Edith Raymond Locke, who was in charge of its styling. She was the one who 'kept running between the photographer on a bridge over that brick terrace and the 20 of you below, adjusting a cap here, an arm a quarter of an inch there. The photographer was a perfectionist and terribly demanding.'[23] Sylvia – who stood at the top of the star formation – was responsible for the copy that ran beneath the image. 'We're stargazers this season, bewitched by an atmosphere of evening blue,' she wrote. 'Foremost in the fashion constellation we spot MLLE's own tartan, the astronomic versatility of sweaters, and men, men, men – we've even taken the shirts off their backs! Focusing our telescope on college news around the globe, we debate and deliberate. Issues illuminated: academic freedom; the sorority controversy; our much labeled (and libeled) generation. From our favorite fields, stars of the first magnitude shed a bright influence on our plans for jobs and futures. Although horoscopes for our ultimate orbits aren't yet in, we Guest Eds. are counting on a favorable forecast with this send-off from MLLE, the star of the campus.'[24]

In many ways, the New York offered by *Mademoiselle* was like a stage set, an artificially constructed world that Sylvia knew was a sham. On 10 June, Sylvia and her fellow guest editors were invited to a formal party at the terrace room of the St Regis Hotel on 55th Street and Fifth Avenue. On the surface it was all rather lovely – in the restaurant, with its ceiling painted the colours of a sky at sunset, Sylvia enjoyed the music from two alternating bands. As each course of her dinner – shrimp, chicken, salad, then parfait – was taken away she was whisked on to the dance floor and, with a daiquiri in her hand, she could look down from the roof terrace across the glittering skyline of Manhattan. Yet there was something not right about the evening. For a start, all the men, albeit young, handsome specimens, had been hired for the occasion by the magazine. As she went on to write in *The Bell Jar*, from an outside perspective a witness would assume she was having the time of her life. Wasn't this the perfect example of the American Dream? For nineteen years a girl from a poor background had lived in some nondescript town, wins a scholarship to a top college and 'ends up steering New York like her own private car.'[25] The truth was more complex. As Plath writes of her fictional persona, Esther, she wasn't capable of steering anything, let alone herself. She knew she should have been excited about the month in New York, but there was something wrong with her reactions. She felt hollow and lifeless, and compared herself to the calm centre of a tornado, 'moving dully along in the middle of the surrounding hullabaloo,' she writes.[26]

Indeed, life in Manhattan seemed to have speeded up, taken on an intense quality that Sylvia found unreal. On 11 June, as Sylvia and her fellow guest editors were being taken by taxi to the New York City Ballet, the car got stuck in traffic. As the young women were waiting, a tall man walked over from another car and introduced himself as the disc jockey Art Ford. There were, he told the young women, too many pretty girls for one taxi, and after he had paid the fare he treated them all to a cocktail. He also proffered an open invitation to the women to meet after his show ended at 3 a.m., when he would show them Greenwich Village at night. In *The Bell Jar* Plath uses Ford as the basis for the character Lenny Shepherd, the DJ who goes on to date Doreen, the society girl with platinum hair whom she based on guest college editor Carol LeVarn. 'I met the original Lenny,' recalls guest editor Laurie Levy. 'He [Art Ford] was well known at that time and the girl after whom Sylvia patterned her "Doreen" character did continue to date him after the original pickup described in the book. I had theatrical ambitions and she arranged an audition. I arrived at his apartment to find him wrapped in a towel, period. He told me to start singing, and proceeded to ignore me as he went off to shave [. . .] After a bit I walked out.'[27] Looking back, Ann Burnside says that 'Sylvia really did a number on Carol LeVarn. I thought she was the one whose life was rather smashed around by *The Bell Jar*.'[28]

After enjoying a quick cocktail with Art Ford, Sylvia made her way to West 55th Street to see the New York City Ballet. During the intermission she bumped into Melvin Woody, a sophomore at Yale and a friend of Marcia Brown's, and, after the performance, the two of them went for drinks in a couple of bars around 52nd Street and 3rd Avenue, where they discussed philosophy. 'I remember that night she was incandescent,' says Mel, now professor emeritus of philosophy at Connecticut College. 'She was radiant – when she was "up" she really glowed. We had a wonderful time that night – we were soul mates – but she was in a manic or hypomanic phase. I first met her because she wrote to me when I was a senior in high school – she had read my poetry, which I had sent to her roommate Marcia Brown. She said she liked my poems – I didn't think they were that good – but from that time on we had similar enthusiasms.'[29]

Sylvia maintained that she enjoyed New York, yet the more time she spent in the city the more she realised that she had led a relatively sheltered existence. In a letter to her brother – whose graduation from Exeter in mid-June she couldn't attend because of lack of funds – she compared her relatively simple and straightforward life at Smith to the hyper-charged intensity of Manhattan, populated with people who seemed, to paraphrase D. H. Lawrence in *Women in Love*, like 'dead brilliant galls on the tree of life'.[30] In the same letter, Sylvia said that, over the course of only a few weeks, she had witnessed at close quarters the world split open before her eyes and 'spilt out its guts like a cracked watermelon.'[31]

The image had its roots in a physical purging that Sylvia experienced as a result of ptomaine poisoning that she had contracted on 16 June, during a lunch at an advertising agency. 'The incident happened in *The Bell Jar* pretty much as I remembered it,' says Janet Rafferty. 'Batten, Barton, Durstine & Osborn had us all for a tour of their agency and served what I thought was a delicious lunch of crab salad. We all ate a lot because it tasted good. It was a hot day and the mayonnaise must have gone bad while they were waiting to feed us. I did take a cab back home to the Barbizon with Sylvia and remembered her starting to vomit, but the cabbie saw what was happening and quickly pulled over to the side so we opened the door and Sylvia did it in the gutter of the street, just below the curb on 63rd and Lexington. I got sick just after and I went upstairs to lie down. We did not have private bathrooms so the one on our floor smelt terrible all day and night. By the next morning we were mostly all okay.'[32]

Sylvia's sickness took on an existential dimension when she learnt of the imminent execution of Julius and Ethel Rosenberg, Communist Party members who were sent to the electric chair at Sing Sing prison in New York for passing secrets about America's atomic-weapons programme to the Soviet Union. On 19 June, the day of their execution, Plath wrote in her journal that the news, splashed over the day's papers and relayed constantly over the radio, made her sick to her stomach. What she found particularly appalling was the overwhelming sense of apathy that surrounded their deaths, the fact that people didn't seem to care that America was about to snuff out the lives of two of its citizens. She described one day at the offices of *Mademoiselle* when one of the guest editors, a beautiful girl with large green eyes, woke up from a nap on the divan in the magazine's conference room, said that she was glad the Rosenbergs were going to die and then went back to sleep. The pronouncement symbolised the response of the American people to the news, 'a rather large, democratic, infinitely bored and casual and complacent yawn'.[33] Plath would write about the deaths of the couple in the opening lines of *The Bell Jar* – 'It was a queer, sultry summer, the summer they electrocuted the Rosenbergs, and I didn't know what I was doing in New York'[34] – and later, after she had suffered her own form of psychic and creative execution by means of electroshock therapy that same summer, Plath would claim to feel a natural empathy with them.

Despite her inner turmoil, Sylvia continued to play the part of a busy, happy-go-lucky single girl in New York. Although she had to miss a tour of *Vanity Fair* magazine and a movie preview of *Let's Do It Again* due to her food poisoning, she did enjoy meeting Gary, or Igor, Karmiloff, a Russian-speaking simultaneous interpreter who worked at the United Nations. In a letter to her brother, Sylvia described Gary in typical overly exuberant terms: he was the most 'brilliant', 'wonderful' man on the whole earth, the most fascinating, charming person she had ever met.[35] She was so enamoured of him that she suspected she would be searching for his alter ego for the rest of her life. In *The Bell Jar*, Plath recasts the UN employee as Constantin, a man a little too short for her liking but who was nonetheless handsome, with light brown hair, dark blue eyes and a lively expression. He had good teeth, and a tan, and he could pass as an American, but as Plath writes, he was in possession of that quality that eluded every American man she had ever met: intuition.[36] On the night of their date, Gary and Sylvia went to a sidewalk café for an Italian meal, and then retired to his penthouse apartment in Greenwich Village where they listened to music. Gary was proud of his studio on the twelfth floor of the only tall apartment building on Christopher Street, with a terrace that overlooked the Hudson River on its left and the skyscrapers of midtown on its right. In *The Bell Jar*, Plath describes Esther, after dinner, going up to Constantin's apartment with the intention of letting him seduce her. After sitting on the terrace, listening to the tug boats on the Hudson, Esther goes to lie down on his bed. She wakes up at three in the morning next to him, but nothing happens between them and she returns to her hotel. Apart from holding her hand, 'Constantin showed no desire to seduce me whatsoever,' writes Plath.[37] So what happened in real life?

'Sylvia Plath was not described as anyone special [to me],' says Igor, 'just a Smith College student not well acquainted with NYC. I agreed [to meet her] as I wanted to see what other students at Smith were like: I had already dated one, Margaret, who was an assistant with Simon & Schuster and interesting in many respects. Sylvia Plath was not as attractive [as her] – too big and heavy for my taste. She was not seductive enough – a bit too provincial and [she] should have shown me some of her own literary tastes and work over dinner, before we retired to my pad on Christopher Street. I recall that Sylvia Plath did not appreciate, as she should have, my couple of Chinese carved furniture pieces, nor my vicuna bedspread, which had cost me a week's salary to acquire. I can't remember anything that was negative about Sylvia, certainly not that she was disturbed, just "heavy-going". She didn't express her feelings to me in the way she wrote home[in the letter to Warren] [. . .] Much of what she said of Constantin is pure fantasy that she should have shared with me.'[38]

Sylvia described her time in New York as a deadly mix of 'pain, parties, work' and it's interesting to speculate on the significance and source of her suffering.[39] We know that she endured extreme discomfort from the ptomaine poisoning – in addition to the food poisoning itself the treatment involved injections with hypodermic needles – and she found the heat of the city in June oppressive and energy-sapping. The agony she wrote about in this entry in her journal could refer to the psychological anguish she felt when faced with a city that she found alienating and altogether too modern for her sensitive soul. In a letter to her brother, she described one day in Manhattan when she got lost on the subway, where she saw a number of beggars, disabled men with amputated limbs, holding out cups for small change.[40] She recalled what she had seen in the zoo in Central Park and posited that the only thing that differentiated men from the beasts was the fact that there were bars on the windows of the cages. When she tried to think of everything she had witnessed, and experienced, she felt like her mind would split open. In the same letter to Warren, she also compared the train that would take her home from New York to Wellesley to a coffin; and, although a spirit of black humour runs through the lines, there is no doubt that by the end of June Sylvia was feeling seriously disturbed. What had she experienced to make her feel so ill at ease? On 20 June, at a country-club dance in Forest Hills, she had met a Peruvian man, José Antonio La Vias, whom she described in her journal as 'cruel'.[41] She did not expand on this, nor did she detail how his cruelty manifested itself. All we know, from the brief entries she made on a 1953 calendar – which featured idyllic scenes of the cities and landscape of Austria – is that Sylvia returned to his apartment on the East Side. What happened there we will probably never know, but if we take *The Bell Jar* as our guide it seems as though Sylvia could have been the victim of a rape or a near-rape.

In the novel, Plath provides a devastating description of a sexual assault at a country club in the suburbs of New York involving Esther, her alter ego, and Marco, a wealthy Peruvian, and a friend of the disc jockey Lenny Shepherd (the fictional counterpart of Art Ford). On their first meeting Esther cannot take her eyes off Marco's diamond tiepin, which he hands over to her with the promise that, in exchange, he would perform some of kind of service 'worthy of a diamond'.[42] As he gives her the jewel, his fingers digging into the underside of her arm, Esther realises that Marco is a misogynist. 'Women-haters were like gods: invulnerable and chock-full of power,' Plath writes.[43] Later that night Marco hits her, repeatedly calls her a slut, rips off her dress and then forces himself upon her. In the novel Esther manages to beat him off, but is left dirtied, humiliated and abused, and on her return to the Amazon goes up to the roof of the hotel and throws all her clothes off the parapet. As she stands there, in the hour before dawn, she watches her outfits – the outward symbols of her false self – disappear into the dark heart of Manhattan. 'I heard she did do that – she went up on to the roof of the Barbizon and threw her clothes off,' says Ann Burnside Love.[44] It wasn't just a few items either, but 'her entire wardrobe, dress by slip by gown, on the last night of her residency there as a guest editor,' she adds.[45]

Sylvia had spent that last day in New York with her former date Ray Wunderlich, who took her on a ride on the Staten Island Ferry. During their time together in the city Ray had noticed her behaviour begin to change. 'She was ashamed of herself really,' he says. 'She was ashamed because she had met indomitable things that she could not conquer, things that were conquering her. She felt that she should be better than that. She told me that there were certain people who bothered her, people whom she did not like. She wouldn't tell me who, but she would talk about them as strange figures. I spent a lot of time trying to mentally stabilize her.'[46] Ray's recollection is verified by Wilbury Crockett, Sylvia's high-school English teacher, who, at the end of June, received an odd letter from his protégée. 'I had a letter from Sylvia from New York – this was just before she came home – she said, "You'll never want to see me again, Mr Crockett, I've let you down."'[47]

On her return from 'Babylon', as one of her Smith professors described New York, Sylvia was met by her family at the station.[48] Her mother described her as looking 'tired' and 'unsmiling' and, as a result, Aurelia dreaded telling her daughter the news that she said had come that same morning – that Sylvia had not been accepted on to Frank O'Connor's short-story class at Harvard summer school.[49] Aurelia, in her account, tried to tell Sylvia in as casual a way as possible, informing her that the class was full and that she would have to reapply the following year. She recalled looking into the rear-view mirror of the car and seeing Sylvia's face turn pale, 'and the look of shock and utter despair that passed over it alarmed me.'[50] From that moment on, Aurelia noticed a change in her daughter, recalling that Sylvia's normal *joie de vivre* seemed to have left her. Aurelia went on to relate that her own mother, Grammy, said she was sure that all Sylvia needed was a period of rest: after all, the girl had been under a great deal of strain during the last year. 'There had been no respite at all, so we encouraged her to "just let go and relax",' she said.[51]

Aurelia's account has gone unquestioned and, over the years, it has been reproduced in various critical studies and biographies. The problem is that her story does not quite ring true. We know that Aurelia Plath had an obsession with collating, and keeping, every single scrap of information that related to her daughter. From Aurelia's point of view, nothing was deemed too insignificant – whether it be a note from a radio quiz show thanking Sylvia for a question she had submitted when she was a child; a ceramic tile sent from *Seventeen* magazine wishing her holiday greetings; or an old shopping list written on a scrap of paper. As a result of Aurelia's curatorial zest, the Plath archives serve as one of the most complete records of any writer in existence. In the light of this, it seems odd that she did not keep such an important letter from Harvard. (Frustratingly, records of such things are apparently not kept by Harvard either.)

Could the document have been lost or deliberately thrown away in a fit of anger? Perhaps, but that still does not explain an odd letter that Aurelia wrote to Sylvia's friend Marcia Brown in the summer of 1953. Marked 'confidential', it outlines how Sylvia returned home 'to a house that was in a state-of-emergency tension. Grammy was seriously ill; and with us, Grammy is the center of our life.' Aurelia's account of the crisis, published in *Letters Home*, states that her mother accompanied her in the car to pick Sylvia up from the station. But would Grammy, a woman considered to be so unwell her family thought she might die at any moment, really have made the trip in the car? In addition, Aurelia suffered from a flare-up of her 'old ulcer' problem, and she had been forced to rest to avoid a 'serious and costly' operation. Aurelia told Marcia – who was living in Cambridge, Massachusetts, in an apartment that Sylvia had planned to share while she attended the summer school – that her daughter had given up the idea of attending Harvard that summer because of these problems at home. She asked Marcia to remain her old 'sunshiney' self, but begged her, for the sake of Sylvia, not to be too enthusiastic about her own experience in Cambridge. 'My girl is run down, too, somewhat,' she said, and what she needed most, she believed was 'outdoor exercise and young people.' Interestingly, Aurelia did not mention Sylvia's rejection by Frank O'Connor.[52]

Aurelia was literally worried sick. Not only was she plagued by ulcer trouble, she also believed that she was about to lose her mother. Perhaps she thought that it would be better for the family if Sylvia remained at home that summer. What was the worst that could happen? Her daughter would have the time – and the freedom – to write; she could teach Sylvia shorthand (a useful practical skill that she could use to support herself in lean times) and she could save money (something the family never had enough of). Also, it was obvious from Sylvia's demeanour – and her letters home – that her experience in New York had exhausted her. 'That summer of 1953, when she came back from New York, I had a sense of her being distracted,' says Peter Aldrich, who lived across the road from the Plaths. 'She was not the kind of smiling girl I was used to.'[53] Staying home for the summer would give Sylvia the chance to rest and ready herself for the heavy demands of the forthcoming academic year.

Certainly Sylvia always believed that she *had* been rejected by Frank O'Connor, surmising that it had been because of the weakness of the story she had submitted, 'Sunday at the Mintons". Yet, during the first few days of July, she debated over whether she should still go to Harvard and take another subject, such as elementary psychology or O'Connor's twentieth-century novel course. Her main worry was the money, as she estimated that the experience would cost her around $250. In her journal she wrote again about the fact she did not come from a rich family and how she only had limited resources to cover the following year's expenses.[54] She was also concerned that, if she did go to Harvard to take another course – and, in effect, earn nothing over the summer – it would reduce her chances of getting a good scholarship from Smith when she returned in September. She resolved that, instead of going to Harvard, she would read Joyce, whom she considered writing about for her thesis, and try and write for *Seventeen*, *Ladies' Home Journal*, perhaps also the *New Yorker* and *Accent on Living*. She knew she would have to stop herself from feeling jealous of Marcia and she needed to formulate a routine for herself. Although she was tempted to retreat from life, she realised she would have to force herself to live in as an imaginative way as possible. Such a task required not only creative thinking but some kind of clever strategy too.[55]

She tried to take her mind off her immediate anxieties by spending more time with Gordon Lameyer, who was living with his mother in Wellesley while he waited to enrol in the navy's Officer Candidate School in Newport. Sylvia and Gordon saw each other almost every day for the next two weeks, visiting his aunt's house in Jaffrey Center, New Hampshire, listening to the symphonies of Beethoven and Brahms and recordings of Frost,

e. e. cummings and Dylan Thomas reading their own poetry and ploughing their way through sections of *Finnegans Wake*. 'We both felt that Joyce's final work was a great compilation of enigmas, a Chinese box, a labyrinthine puzzle, a Gordian knot which seemed impossible to cut.'[56]

With Gordon, Sylvia acted as though nothing was wrong and he had no inkling about the private hell that his new girlfriend was suffering. By 6 July she started to regret her decision not to take one of the other courses at Harvard summer school and she felt trapped by a stifling negativity that threatened to consume her. She recognised that she was 'sick' in her head and told herself that she had to stop thinking about self-harming by cutting herself with razor blades, even the possibility of ending it all.[57] She started to suffer from insomnia so severe that by 14 July she was managing to get only two hours' sleep a night. She was plagued by visions of ending up in a strait-jacket, locked away in a mental asylum, and felt so full of murderous rage that she even considered killing her mother, with whom she was sharing a room. In 'Tongues of Stone' – an autobiographical short story she wrote in 1955 and which she entered for the *Mademoiselle* fiction contest – Plath wrote of how her main character lay in her bed listening to her mother's breathing, a sound so annoying she felt like getting out of bed and strangling her. By doing so at least she would stop the awful process of decay that she witnessed, something that 'grinned at her' like a 'death's head'.[58]

Later, after a great deal of therapy – and permission given to her by a mental-health professional to hate her mother – Plath would articulate the clutch of negative feelings she harboured against Aurelia. But in the summer of 1953 she was disturbed by both the murderous desire itself and her inability to understand its origins. What was the source of her anger? Was it because she suspected that her mother had been far from honest about her rejection from Frank O'Connor's Harvard course? Did she feel aggrieved that Aurelia had manipulated her into staying home during the summer? In a letter she wrote to Gordon in August, she said that she had been forced to give up the idea of Harvard summer school because 'life at home demanded attention'.[59] The phrase reeks of unspoken resentments.

According to Aurelia, Sylvia also felt guilty at using an unnamed friend – whom we now know to be Dick Norton – as the inspiration for the character of Henry in 'Sunday at the Mintons''. 'This reaction might be considered a foreshadowing of her emotional recoil from *The Bell Jar* when that autobiographical novel appeared in London in 1963, shortly before her death,' said Aurelia.[60] In *Letters Home*, she also tells us that, in an effort to try to 'pull herself together', Sylvia encouraged her mother to teach her Gregg shorthand, but after only a few unsuccessful attempts she gave up. 'Later, I regretted that we even attempted it,' said Aurelia, 'for the abortive experience just added to her increasing feeling of failure and inferiority.'[61]

On 15 July, when Sylvia came downstairs, Aurelia noticed that her daughter had a couple of partially healed scars on her legs. After being questioned about them, Sylvia told her mother that she had gashed herself in an effort to see if she had the guts. Then she took hold of Aurelia's hand and said, 'Oh, Mother, the world is so rotten! I want to die! Let's die together!'[62] It's significant that Sylvia's psychological crisis manifested itself not only in a desire to end her own life but also in a wish for her mother to die with her. Aurelia took her daughter in her arms and tried to reassure her that she was simply exhausted and that she really did have everything to live for. Within an hour, the two women had booked an appointment with the family doctor, Francesca Racioppi, who recommended immediate psychiatric counselling.

After a session with a psychiatrist – whom Sylvia did not like, and who soon left for vacation – she was taken on by Dr Kenneth Tillotson. Unknown to mother and daughter, Dr Tillotson, whom Aurelia described as 'an older man, gentle and fatherly'[63] had been fired by McLean Hospital, the psychiatric hospital in Belmont, Massachusetts, after a sex scandal involving a young brunette. In October 1947, a twenty-eight-year-old nurse, Anne Marie Salot, had filed a complaint with the State Department of Mental Health alleging that Tillotson's 'amorous attentions were endangering her health.'[64] After the allegation became public, and Salot maintained she had been forced to leave her job, the head of McLean asked for Tillotson's resignation. Yet the scandal could not be contained and in May 1949 Tillotson and Salot appeared before the grand jury accused of moral turpitude. Both parties pleaded guilty – the couple had been having an affair before Salot registered her complaint – and the married psychiatrist was fined $750. Although the state Board of Registration suspended him for three months, he went on to open a private practice at his home in Belmont.

Tillotson – who saw Sylvia at the Valley Head Hospital in Carlisle – recommended a course of sleeping pills for his new patient. Perhaps it would also be a good idea if she found a job that would take her mind off her own troubles? In theory, it sounded like a good idea and, at first, Sylvia was pleased to help out each morning at the Newton-Wellesley Hospital. One of her duties was to feed patients who were too sick to do it for themselves. While she was there Sylvia spoon-fed her old art teacher, Miss Hazelton, who was dying. In a letter to Gordon, which she wrote on 23 July, she described the range of cases – children born with Down's Syndrome, old people suffering from senility, people who seemed healthy enough but who returned to the hospital a few days later unable to recognise her. The experience, she said, gave her an insight into what we all could expect at the end of our lives.[65] In *The Bell Jar*, Esther gets a job at the local hospital on the suggestion of her mother – the cure for thinking too much about oneself was to help someone else worse than you – and how, one day, she causes a scene by mixing up all the patients' flowers in the maternity ward. After the women turn on her, she flees the hospital never to return.

Sylvia did not last long as an employee at the Newton-Wellesley Hospital either, because soon she was receiving treatment there as an outpatient. Gordon noticed that 'she began to buy paperbacks on psychology at a local drugstore. Retreating into herself, she felt she was gradually but progressively losing her mind. She confessed that it was a dangerous thing to have so little knowledge.'[66] Gordon also recalled that, one weekend in late July, when the two of them were necking she accused him of being 'lascivious'.[67] Did the intimate contact between them bring back memories of the sexual assault she had suffered in New York? 'It seemed to me that Sylvia, being very forthright and loving to play roles, pretended to being more sensuously involved than she was willing to be,' says Gordon. 'Like Zelda before she was married to Scott Fitzgerald, Sylvia enjoyed giving the impression that she was sexually more knowledgeable than she actually was.'[68]

In order to try to shake her out of depression, Dr Tillotson prescribed a course of electroconvulsive therapy (ECT) beginning at the end of July. Sylvia was driven to the hospital by Aurelia's friend Betty Aldrich, who lived across the street. 'I can remember my mother telling me that Sylvia really hated to go, but she knew she had to,' says Peter Aldrich. 'Sometimes Aurelia had to force her into the car. I thought, "What are they doing to her?" I had visions of an electric chair. My only glimpse of her after a treatment was one day when she was coming out of my mother's car and she seemed uncharacteristically lifeless. It was just not like her and I thought to myself, "That's not Sylvia. What had they done to her?" It was almost as if the life had been sucked out of her.'[69]

The treatment had been developed in the 1930s, when Italian neuropsychiatrists Ugo Cerletti and Lucio Bini had carried out a series of experiments on animals to induce seizures by the application of electric shocks. In 1937, the doctors tested their new technique on a person, and by the 1940s the procedure had been introduced to America and Britain as a treatment for depression. At this time, ECT was often administered in an 'unmodified' form – without the use of muscle relaxants – and, as a result, patients suffered from convulsions so severe that dislocations or fractures occassionally occurred. Sylvia's own experience – as related in *The Bell Jar* and in her poetry – reads like something from a modern Gothic novel; later, Olive Higgins Prouty would take Dr Tillotson to task for the badly managed ECT, blaming him for Sylvia's suicide attempt. In 'Sylvia's flamboyant imagination, the EST [electric shock treatment] gear resembled some kind of medieval torture equipment,' says Gordon Lameyer. 'Because this psychiatrist did not give Sylvia a drug or a shot to anesthetize her before exposing her to this gear, Sylvia felt so traumatized by these EST electrodes that were attached to her temples that she felt, not so irrationally, as if she were being electrocuted for some unknown crime.'[70] Sylvia believed that she was being punished, but for what? What had she done? Had she been too ambitious? Set her sights too high? Was it because she was a woman and a writer?

The badly administered ECT fractured and erased her already fragile sense of identity. According to Aurelia, 'after the first poorly conducted shock therapy in 1953, her own powers of accurate recall, factually and emotionally were impaired. The most joyous past experiences became shadowed by implanted doubt and cynicism.'[71] In another private note, Aurelia wrote, 'The breakdown after Mlle led [to] electric shock therapy, poorly administered – this split her into "the double".'[72]

Even after enduring the frightening sessions of ECT, Sylvia tried to carry on as if nothing had happened, still subscribing to her mother's view that one had to show a brave face to the world. Yet she was not feeling any better; if anything, she felt sure that she would spend the rest of her life in a mental asylum. Sylvia could not bear the shame of it; neither could she countenance the fact that her mother, already short of cash, would be economically ruined as a result. In a letter to Olive Higgins Prouty Aurelia said that Sylvia 'wished her life to end for one reason – to spare us the long anguish and expense. You see, the daughter of a friend of ours had had a breakdown, necessitating four years of commitment, during which time the parents became completely poverty-stricken in their efforts to give their daughter the best kind of private care. Sivvy wished to spare us that.'[73]

By mid-July Sylvia had stopped writing a journal. Her diary, such as it was, consisted of just a few notes on a calendar and was limited to entries such as a note saying she had visited the Totem Pole on 11 August, and a reminder to ring Marcia on 17 August.[74] After this entry there is nothing but blank space for the rest of 1953. All that summer, 'Sylvia was depressed due to her inability to write, concentrate and accomplish mental work in connection with her senior thesis – or any other written work,' recalled Aurelia.[75] Sylvia confessed that she felt as though she could neither read nor write, and as a result she felt frightened by the prospect that if she couldn't write no-one would find her of interest.[76] The woman who defined herself through her writing had become an empty page.

That summer, Sylvia had now decided, would be her last. On 22 August, Sylvia went out with her friend Marcia Brown on a double date to a beach with Dick Linden and Melvin Woody. In *The Bell Jar*, Plath disguised her friends' names – Marcia is Jody, Dick is Mark and Mel is Cal – but little else. 'I am Cal in *The Bell Jar*,' says Professor Woody, 'and what she detailed in the book is what roughly happened.'[77] Plath describes Cal as a highly intelligent young man, with a baby face and a mass of white-blond hair – 'the description fits me at that age,' says Woody.[78] In Chapter Thirteen, Cal and Esther discuss the moral implications of Ibsen's *Ghosts*; she recalled it because it was about a boy who had gone insane and 'everything I had ever read about mad people stuck in my mind, while everything else flew out.'[79] The conversation moves on to the best method of committing suicide. How would he kill himself? Cal responds to Esther's question by saying that he would blow his brains out with a gun. Later, Dick Linden would tell Gordon Lameyer that Sylvia had been 'probing them about the best way to commit suicide. At the time they had no inkling she was headed in that direction and thought it was only an academic interest.'[80] In *The Bell Jar*, Esther, accompanied by Cal, swims out to sea, with the intention of drowning herself, an incident that Plath lifted straight from real life. 'I remember we started swimming out into the sea,' says Professor Woody. 'As we swam, I had an intuition that she would keep going out to sea and I told her that I had to get back.'[81] Yet, despite Sylvia's best efforts to drown herself, she was unable to do so – each time she dived under the sea the water spat her out again. Later, Plath would write in her journals of that she tried to imitate the way Virginia Woolf had committed suicide – 'Only I couldn't drown.'[82] If she really wanted to end her life, Sylvia knew that she would have to be a lot more methodical.

On the oppressively hot day of Monday 24 August 1953, Aurelia left her daughter – who that day seemed a little better – with her grandparents while she went into Boston to see the documentary *The Queen is Crowned*, about the coronation of Elizabeth II in June. Waiting until she had the house to herself – Warren had gone to work, and her grandparents sunbathed in the backyard – Sylvia crept upstairs, where she broke the lock of her mother's steel case and took out a bottle of fifty sleeping pills. She scribbled out a note to say that she was going for a long walk and that she wouldn't be back for a day or so. Then she carried a glass of water and the bottle of pills to the basement, removed a pile of logs and kindling that blocked the entrance to the crawl space, crept into this makeshift cave, diligently replaced the wood and proceeded to swallow the tablets. In *The Bell Jar*, Plath writes of what happened next: as she downed the contents of the bottle of pills she began to see blue and red lights flashing before her eyes. The bottle fell from her hands and she lay down in the cramped space. 'The silence drew off, baring the pebbles and shells and all the tatty wreckage of my life. Then, at the rim of vision, it gathered itself, and in one sweeping tide, rushed me to sleep.'[83]

Meanwhile, in the Exeter Street Theater in Boston, Aurelia was feeling increasingly ill at ease. In the middle of the film Aurelia felt gripped by a terror such as she had never experienced before in her life. 'Cold perspiration poured down on me; my heart pounded,' she said.[84] Although she wanted to leave the theatre and return home, she remained in her seat to the end of the documentary, at which point she asked her friend to drive her back home. When she walked into the dining room and found Sylvia's note she knew something awful had happened. Grammy said she had wished she had never left Sylvia alone, while Grampy started to cry. 'The nightmare of nightmares had begun,' said Aurelia.[85] She phoned the police to report her daughter missing, and soon the local community came together to try to find Sylvia. On Tuesday the Wellesley police, after searching the Plaths' home, carried out a detailed search of the heavily wooded area that lay at the back of Elmwood Road and the shores of nearby Morses Pond and Lake Waban. The police were helped in the search by the Boy Scouts and a group of concerned neighbours. 'It sounds peculiar,' Aurelia told reporters that day, 'but she had set standards for herself that are almost unattainable. She's made almost a minor obsession of fulfilling what she believes to be her responsibility to her sponsors, and I am gravely concerned for her.' The night before, Aurelia, together with Colonel Rex Gary, a family friend, and Warren, had travelled into Boston in the hope that they might spot Sylvia at one of her favourite haunts in the city, such as the trail by the Charles River, Boston Common or the Public Garden.[86] 'The Wellesley police had us kids in long lines combing the woods looking for her,' recalls neighbour Peter Aldrich, who was nine years old at the time. 'I was so worried and frightened for her. I knew, through my mother, that Sylvia was sick and very troubled. I remember walking through the woods that stretched up to Wellesley Hills, walking in a line, and both at the same time hoping I would find her and then also fearing I would do so.'[87]

On Wednesday it was reported that, despite another day of searching, Sylvia had still not been found. 'Mrs. Aurelia S. Plath, mother of Sylvia Plath, 20 [. . .] said she believed her daughter's behavior was due to a temporary nervous affliction linked with her creative writing,' said the *Boston Daily Globe*. The same report quoted Aurelia as saying, 'She recently felt she was unworthy of the confidence held for her by the people she knew. For some time she has been unable to write either fiction, or her more recent love, poetry. Instead of regarding this as just an arid period that every writer faces at times, she believed something had happened to her mind, that it was unable to produce creatively any more. Although her doctor assured her this was simply due to nervous exhaustion, Sylvia was constantly seeking for ways in which to blame herself for the failure, and became increasingly despondent.'[88]

Back at Elmwood Road, the mood was growing darker and more sombre. Aurelia, in particular, must have been in agony. She didn't so much worry about the shame that scandal would bring on her family – by now, Sylvia's disappearance was a national story, being reported in newspapers such as the *Baltimore Sun*, *Chicago Tribune*, *Los Angeles Times*, *New York Herald Tribune* and *West Palm Beach Post.* All she cared about was finding Sylvia safe and well.

At noon on Wednesday 26 August, while the family was eating lunch, Warren heard a moan coming from the basement. He rushed downstairs and quickly cleared away the pile of firewood blocking the entrance to the crawl space. He saw Sylvia, returning to consciousness, a near-empty bottle of sleeping pills by her side. 'Call the ambulance,' he shouted.[89] Sylvia was helped out of the dark hole and, in daylight, her family could see that she had suffered an injury to her face. 'There was an angry-looking abrasion under her right eye and considerable swelling,' said Aurelia.[90] 'Sylvia told me that she had woken up and smashed her head against the wall,' says Elinor Friedman Klein, a friend from Smith.[91] According to close family friend Richard Larschan, Aurelia told him 'that the wound was infested with maggots: fly spawn is attracted to meat, it was an open wound, Sylvia had been in a part of the house where insects lived and, as it was August, it would have been warm. Knowing that, the image in her poem "Lady Lazarus", where she talks about people having to pick worms off her like sticky pearls, makes sense.'[92] The ambulance took her to a private room at Newton-Wellesley Hospital, where doctors treated her wound and tried to reduce a high temperature brought on by the infection. When Aurelia was allowed in to see her daughter, Sylvia said weakly that the suicide attempt had been 'her last act of love'.[93] She also said, according to Gordon Lameyer, that when 'she awoke from her overdose of sleeping pills, one of the first things she asked her mother was, "Do we still own the house?"'[94] In the days following her suicide attempt, Sylvia made a number of 'frantic inquiries' as to how her medical care could be paid for.[95] Obviously the economics of life still haunted her even after she had been brought back from the dead.

On Thursday 27 August, Gordon Lameyer's mother telephoned her son to tell him what had happened. Was she dead, he asked. 'There was an awful moment of confusion when I thought that my mother said yes,' he recalled. He went to visit the Plaths, but Sylvia, distressed at the swelling and bruising on her face, did not want to see him. 'You have no idea how very, very happy I am to know that you are recovering from your illness,' Gordon wrote to her. 'Please believe, dear Sylvia, that I feel the very same toward you as I always have. I only wish I had been more communicative before to let you know how extremely fond I am of you.'[96] Sylvia felt well enough to write back, thanking him for his letter and the flowers that he had given her mother to present to her in hospital, but she gave no indication of the seriousness of her continuing psychiatric disorder. Survival was one thing, recovery quite another.

Since Dr Tillotson was on vacation, the Plaths' family friend and pastor of the local Unitarian church, Dr William B. Rice, recommended Sylvia see Dr Erich Lindemann, a senior Boston psychiatrist who was famous for treating the survivors and relatives of the Cocoanut Grove nightclub fire in which nearly 500 people died. His resulting paper 'Symptomatology and Management of Acute Grief', published in 1944 in the *American Journal of Psychiatry*, opens with the lines: 'At first glance, acute grief would not seem to be a medical or psychiatric disorder in the strict sense of the word but rather a normal reaction to a distressing situation. However, the understanding of reactions to traumatic experiences whether or not they represent clear-cut neuroses has become of ever-increasing importance to the psychiatrist. Bereavement or the sudden cessation of social interaction seems to be of special interest because it is often cited among the alleged psychogenic factors in psychosomatic disorders.' Lindemann goes on to explain that grief is a definite symptom with certain psychological and physical symptoms and that it can occur either immediately after a crisis or manifest itself many years after an individual has suffered a trauma. The psychiatrist cites the case of a thirty-eight-year-old woman who suffered a 'surprisingly severe reaction' to the death of her mother. After a consultation, it was discovered that the woman was only 'mildly concerned' about the loss. The real source of her grief stemmed from the fact that she remained 'deeply engrossed with unhappy and perplexing fantasies concerning the death of her brother, who died twenty years ago under dramatic circumstances from metastasizing carcinoma after amputation of his arm had been postponed too long.'[97]

Could Sylvia's suicide attempt have been a delayed reaction to her father's death? Certainly Sylvia later thought so, as she wrote in 'Daddy': 'At twenty I tried to die/And get back, back, back to you.'[98] At the time, however, no one – not even the mental-health professionals – seemed to have a clear idea of the complex matrix of memories, desires, fantasies and experiences that lay behind her breakdown. Francesca Racioppi, the Plath family doctor, said that she could find no trace of psychosis in Sylvia. But there was obviously something seriously wrong. If anything, in the days following her return from the dead, it seemed as though Sylvia was getting worse. In a first draft of a letter to Olive Higgins Prouty written on 29 August, Aurelia wrote in the margin: 'Sylvia is retreating inwardly. Her speech and comprehension has slowed down – I am thoroughly frightened.'[99]

For Aurelia the episode was both terrifying and terrifyingly expensive. Sylvia needed round-the-clock care, but after a few days, she had no choice but to dismiss the private nurses and take on some of the duties herself, working shifts, split with Warren, from seven in the morning until eleven at night. 'This is a nervous breakdown – the one illness I several times jokingly said that we could not afford to have,' she wrote to Olive Higgins Prouty.[100] Aurelia outlined to Prouty the stark reality of her situation. She had an income of $3,900 – she was due back at work on 14 September – and a reserve of emergency funds of $600, which she hoped would pay for the recent spell at Newton-Wellesley. But what after that? 'It has been the pride of my life to stand on my own feet and manage for my family with own earnings,' she said, 'but this now is larger and more complex than I can handle or even understand.'[101] Aurelia said that her daughter was afraid of people and that she wanted to get well away from Wellesley for a time. One of her friends, who had nursed two people with psychiatric disorders, offered to take Sylvia to her summerhouse in Provincetown, where she would look after her, but Aurelia did not know what was the best course of action. 'I am so fearsome of mental hospitals with their locked doors and other patients,' she confessed to Prouty, 'who, I feel would have such a detrimental effect on my sensitive Sylvia. I believe [what] Sylvia needs most [is] quiet, sunshine, exercise in increasing measure, and the reassurance of love.'[102]

Olive Higgins Prouty told Aurelia not to worry – she would take care of the hospital bill up to a sum of $500. If the amount was any less then Aurelia could keep the remainder to help pay Sylvia's future psychiatric-care costs. 'No illness is so hard for the family of the patient, so difficult to deal with wisely, and no suffering is so deep for the one afflicted,' she told Aurelia. 'I speak from experience.'[103] Although she thought that Sylvia would benefit from going to stay with Aurelia's friend in Provincetown, in her opinion it was important that the girl receive the very best specialist care available. Prouty recommended Silver Hill, a psychiatric hospital in Connecticut, which was overseen by Dr William Terhune. She knew that the hospital had a 'foundation' fund, money it could bestow on deserving patients who couldn't afford to pay their own way. If Aurelia agreed, Prouty said she would certainly be willing to recommend Sylvia. That turned out not to be necessary because in September it was decided to transfer Sylvia first to Massachusetts General Hospital psychiatric ward, where Dr Lindemann was in charge, and in then, at his suggestion, to McLean Hospital in Belmont, Massachusetts.

Founded in 1811 and originally called the Asylum for the Insane, it was renamed the McLean Asylum for the Insane after its benefactor John McLean, a wealthy Boston merchant, endowed it with a large amount of money in 1823. In 1895, the hospital moved from its original site in Charlestown (now part of Somerville) to Waverley Oaks Hill, in Belmont. There the landscape architect Frederick Law Olmsted – responsible for designing Central Park in New York and the Emerald Necklace in Boston – created a tranquil space of 240 acres. When Plath arrived here in the autumn of 1953, the complex functioned as a kind of upmarket country club for the mentally ill. Upham

Memorial Hall was nicknamed the 'Harvard Club', as it was said that at one time Harvard graduates occupied each of its corner suites. 'We catered to patients,' recalled one former steward. 'If the patient did not like the lamb we served for dinner and asked for lobster, we gave lobster. They could afford it. Appleton House [one of the houses for women] was the Ritz Carlton.'[104] Some female patients, according to those who worked there, would ask the nurses to make arrangements to have their mink coats signed in and out of 'Filene's storage facilities according to season.'[105] Ruth Tiffany Barnhouse Beuscher, Sylvia's psychiatrist at McLean, would later describe the hospital's main building as containing 'old-fashioned Victorian parlor [rooms] with books, and the patients had tea there every Sunday afternoon with cucumber sandwiches and various goodies to eat.'[106]

Yet, at the same time, patients were allowed to have access to money – even insignificantly small amounts – only if they had the permission of the physician in charge. 'Staff members recall the irony of belaboured discussions over whether or not patients, a few of whom were practically zillionaires and most came from far more luxurious origins than any of the psychiatrists, ought to be allowed to carry around 50 cents in their pockets,' writes Silvia B. Sutton, McLean's historian.[107]

Although it had developed a reputation for attracting patients such as the brothers of Ralph Waldo Emerson, William James, and the man responsible for designing its grounds, Frederick Law Olmsted, when Plath arrived at McLean the hospital was suffering from an image problem. Not only was it still tainted by the scandal involving Dr Tillotson, but the hospital also was short of staff and it housed a disproportionate number of elderly, chronic patients, many of whom would die within its walls. 'McLean at mid-century was a struggling organization, barely able to keep abreast of progressive treatment concepts,' states Sutton, 'let alone serve as a model for other hospitals.'[108] One psychiatrist who worked there in the early 1950s said that although the hospital had 'wonderful grounds and potentially good facilities' the problem was that everything centred around its director Franklin Wood, who was not a psychiatrist. 'The atmosphere is almost medievalistic or feudalistic in that respect,' he observed.[109]

Even though the hospital was expensive – Plath's fees ran to more than $800 a month – Wood, a gifted administrator, worried about balancing the hospital's books and, in order to keep to a strict budget, underpaid his staff no matter what their expertise. In one of his annual reports, Wood complained of the difficulty of finding health professionals who would work for low wages. 'No longer does the feeling of satisfaction in a job well-done and the helping of others serve as a goal,' he wrote. 'Money seems to be the predominant aim of today.'[110]

The malaise that surrounded McLean was symptomatic of the state of mid-century psychiatry. As Ruth Beuscher, Plath's own psychiatrist, recalled: 'McLean was still in the nineteenth century. But that wasn't surprising – it was 1953.'[111] Jane Anderson, a fellow patient at the time, who later became a psychiatrist, recalled that 'the premise was that all the problems were in me, that there was no attempt to see that part of what I was struggling with was caused by my relationships with my family, [rather] that everything was turned back to me [. . .] there was no family therapy, [as] family therapy had not been conceived of [at] that time [. . .] This was the end of the old era of psychiatry [. . .] At that time there were no drugs for emotional states [. . .] there were no anti-depressants.'[112]

On arriving at McLean, Sylvia was assigned a young psychiatrist only nine years older than her, Ruth Beuscher, whom Plath described in *The Bell Jar* as 'a cross between Myrna Loy and my mother.'[113] For her part, Beuscher felt immediately drawn to Plath, as she later told the psychoanalytic psychologist Karen Maroda. The women 'considered themselves two of a kind: Both were child prodigies with high IQs; both were ambitious and determined; both considered themselves "intellectual snobs".'[114] However, unknown to the Plaths or Olive Higgins Prouty, who continued to pay for Sylvia's treatment, Beuscher was only a psychiatric resident, in effect still a trainee. 'Sylvia was one of my first patients at McLean,' said Beuscher. 'I don't think they knew I was that inexperienced. It was McLean and I was the doctor assigned to her. That was it.'[115] According to Beuscher – who appears in *The Bell Jar* as Doctor Nolan – Plath's depiction of her experience in McLean in the novel is 'pretty accurate'. Doctors prescribed regular injections of insulin, which was designed to shock Sylvia out of her depressive state but only resulted in excessive weight gain. 'I never seemed to get any reaction,' Plath wrote in *The Bell Jar*. 'Just grew fatter and fatter.'[116] In the novel, Esther meets another patient, Valerie, who after undergoing a lobotomy no longer feels possessed by anger. 'I'm not angry any more. Before, I was always angry,' she says.[117] Sylvia later told a friend that when she realised her initial therapy was proving ineffective, she stormed into the psychiatrist's office and demanded a lobotomy. 'There seemed little reason to go on suffering and little hope that I would ever recover,' she said. 'The psychiatrist laughed at me and shook his head. "You're not going to get off that easily,"' he said.[118]

In her first few weeks at McLean Sylvia seemed almost catatonic. What worried those close to her was that she seemed to have lost the power to read. Wilbury Crockett, her old high-school teacher, would visit her once a week, armed with a word game called 'Anagram'. Using its letters he would spell out simple words for her, but he later recalled that Sylvia was so unresponsive that, at first, she couldn't form basic words such as 'and'.

Olive Higgins Prouty kept a close eye on her protégée's treatment. She acknowledged that as the weeks passed, Sylvia did not seem to be improving. What worried Prouty – who occasionally took the young woman out in her car – was the fact that Sylvia did not seem to have a routine; as a result, she spent hours doing nothing in her room. 'I realize there is occupational therapy available but she hasn't yet the initiative and power to plan her own day' Prouty wrote to Beuscher on 14 October. 'On the drive with me she was interested in the various places we stopped – a mushroom farm, an old house [. . .] conversing naturally with the people we saw. She was not concentrated upon herself. It was not until near the end of our drive that she discussed herself and her present setting. I discovered that she is not mixing well with the other patients, feels isolated, and wants some sort of occupation to make her isolation more bearable [. . .] I advised her to ask for work on a loom. She finds sewing difficult and frustrating. But she would need much instruction and encouragement. She is easily disheartened, she says, if she finds she cannot co-ordinate.'[119] Prouty also wrote to Dr William Terhune at Silver Hill to update him on Sylvia's progress, telling him that she was 'going through a period of feeling terribly inadequate, and inefficient and inferior. Her college honors she believes were undeserved, and she feels that all her former hopes and ambitions are obliterated.'[120]

Sylvia's frustrations came to a head when, on 27 October 1953, her twenty-first birthday, her mother brought her a bouquet of yellow roses, her favourite flower and Sylvia proceeded to dump them into the waste-paper basket. 'I knew in my bones that if I ignored the day, she would write, "Mother saw fit to ignore my 21st birthday" and make much of that,' said

Aurelia later in an unpublished letter. 'So I did what my heart prompted me to do – hoping for the miracle that she would understand that I saw this as an illness to be fought through and conquered and that I loved and treasured her – glad she had been born to me. While it was the last thing she really wanted (in her true self) she resented my freedom to visit her and leave her – she emotionally wished I, too, would have a breakdown so that I would really experience everything she experienced. How far my vicarious sharing of her agony went, she never knew – I didn't want to show her.'[121] Aurelia was in a lose-lose situation. She did not want to burden her daughter with any more problems and so kept her anxieties to herself. As a result, her old ulcer flared up once more – she suffered regular internal haemorrhages and the following year she would undergo surgery to have three quarters of her stomach removed. Yet Aurelia's selflessness and stoicism were far from rewarded. In 1957, when Plath was writing her poem 'The Disquieting Muses', she thought back to the times her mother stood by her bed in McLean. Why had she written those excoriating last stanzas, Aurelia asked. '"Oh that," she responded airily, "that was because you were so optimistic and serene when you visited me in the hospital. I thought you had no idea of the hell I was going through."'[122]

Dr Paul Howard, the chief psychiatrist at McLean, held the steadfast belief that Sylvia would improve if only she continued with the insulin treatment for the recommended course of three months. Prouty – who seemed to set herself up as a mental-health expert – knew little about insulin therapy, but apparently 'it has an effect similar to that of electric shock treatments.'[123] By mid-November, Prouty told Aurelia that she was going to see her lawyer: if Sylvia had to remain in an institution for a longer stretch of time she believed that her attorney would probably recommend that she be transferred to a cheaper hospital than McLean. 'Do not let this disturb you,' she wrote to Aurelia. 'Sylvia's welfare will be our guide.'[124]

By this point Sylvia had started to undergo psychotherapy under the direction of Ruth Beuscher. And, although Sylvia later lauded Beuscher – calling her 'a permissive mother figure', and 'a clever woman who knows her business & I admire her'[125] – the psychiatrist had not yet undertaken full analytic training. According to Karen Maroda, who interviewed her before her death, Beuscher 'was in therapy during medical school with an analyst in training', but she admitted that '"at least a third of the time I didn't show up. I don't think I ever really got into it."'[126] This astonishing admission casts doubt on the effectiveness of Beuscher's method. Certainly, both Olive Higgins Prouty and Aurelia Plath had their doubts. In a note to Aurelia, Prouty said that Sylvia seemed to talk about her '"mother complex", "guilt complex", and what not! I don't think she is ready yet for self-analysis.'[127] Prouty and Aurelia were also frustrated that the psychotherapy sessions were confidential and frustrated that Beuscher would not reveal any details of her conversations with Sylvia. On one occasion when Aurelia visited her daughter, she asked Sylvia about the nature of the therapy sessions. Did she really hate her? 'Why I don't hate you, mother!' Sylvia replied.[128] But this statement only raised the two women's suspicions. 'That reveals what line is being followed,' wrote Prouty to Aurelia.[129] Yet Prouty herself suspected that Aurelia could be the source of many of Sylvia's problems. 'I feel sorry that Dr Beuscher couldn't have included her [Aurelia] in her treatment of your illness,' she wrote to Sylvia at the end of 1954. 'It seems that psychiatrists should treat their patient's nearest relative [. . .] as well as the patient himself – for often he, or she, is the cause of the patient's maladjustment and illness.'[130]

By the end of November, Prouty and Aurelia were so dissatisfied by the treatment that they started to investigate other options, including the Boston Psychopathic Hospital. 'Frankly, I cannot see any marked change in her depression, her attitudes or her ideas,' Prouty told Erich Lindemann, who continued to supervise her case. 'For a brief period, several weeks ago, I thought she was better [. . .] She complains to me of her idleness and long objectless hours of nothing-to-do [. . .] She has no ability at present to carry out a program herself or to initiate activities. She was terribly depressed and discouraged last Monday because she had been ineffectual in all her own attempts to escape idleness. She feels alone and cut off from the other patients [. . .]'[131] Both women objected to the fact that Sylvia was no longer able to leave the hospital, even if she was accompanied, and that her mail was censored. Prouty wrote to McLean's director, Dr Wood, expressing her concerns and informing him that she thought it would be better if Sylvia was transferred to another hospital. Dr Howard, McLean's chief psychiatrist, told Prouty and Aurelia that he had a plan. He thought Sylvia should try another round of electroshock therapy. If Prouty would only continue to pay the fees up to the 1 January – she had already spent around $2,500 – then McLean would meet the expenses from then on.

After her last experience with ECT, Sylvia was naturally terrified. Yet Dr Beuscher viewed it as a procedure of last resort. 'For many years it was absolutely the treatment of choice for somebody who was actively suicidal,' she said. At this point, Sylvia was 'just as depressed as when she had walked in – she was just totally depressed and wasn't getting any better. We had talked about a lot of stuff – I found out that she hated her mother [. . .] But she had been in there for months, and Mrs Prouty was paying the bills.'[132] In *The Bell*

Jar, Plath describes how Esther is taken down into the basement of the hospital and led through a series of underground tunnels to a room with a green door with the word 'ELECTROTHERAPY' printed on it in black letters. She climbs up on to a high bed, with its 'white, drumtight sheet', where a salve is placed on her temples and the electrodes are fitted to either side of her head. Then 'darkness wiped me out like chalk on a blackboard.'[133] When she regains consciousness she is aware of a change in her mood, feeling surprisingly at peace. 'The bell jar hung, suspended, a few feet above my head. I was open to the circulating air.'[134]

Dr Beuscher had expected Sylvia to undergo a course of at least ten ECT sessions and she was astonished when her vulnerable patient seemed to show signs of recovery after only two or three treatments. 'I don't know what happened,' said Beuscher later. 'Nobody can explain why Sylvia got over her depression [. . .] She just didn't want to have any more shock treatment [. . .] I never saw it happen with anybody else.'[135]

Ruth Beuscher did not have to look far to find the key to Sylvia's supposed psychic recuperation. Ironically, it stemmed from the unlikely source of Jane Anderson, Dick Norton's old girlfriend, who had been admitted to McLean in February 1953. Although she had been suffering symptoms of anxiety, depression and the inability to cope since 1950, matters came to a head in the early part of the year when she received a letter from her boyfriend in Philadelphia breaking off the relationship and also discovered that she wouldn't, after all, receive a Woodrow Wilson fellowship. 'I walked around Northampton [for] two days crying,' she said in an unpublished document. 'I was just feeling overwhelmed.'[136] One day in February, she told her parents that she was taking a train from their home in Wellesley into Boston, but while in the city she changed her mind and, in a distressed state, took a bus to Cleveland. When her father heard about her change of plan, he knew something was wrong and he, together with a doctor, immediately travelled to Cleveland to bring her back. On the return journey, on the overnight train, Jane began to have thoughts that somehow she would end up underneath the wheels of the train. 'I had no thought-out plan how I was going to kill myself,' she said. 'I think it was more of an image of a passive victim being run over by somebody, something, a train. And that was very frightening to me.'[137]

After being taken to McLean and interviewed, Dr Francis de Marneffe diagnosed Jane as a 'hysterical personality', a young woman 'who was extremely anxious, who obviously was having a great deal of difficulty in her relationship with her family, her parents.'[138] Jane had run away from the family home in Wellesley in, according to de Marneffe's original diagnosis, a 'fugue state'; she experienced a number of sexual fantasies involving her father, and also feared that she would kill him. Jane had 'tremendous admiration and respect for her father [. . .] and yet [there] was a sense of not being understood by him, of in a way almost abandonment, if you will, [a] lack of support.'[139]

Just before Sylvia was admitted to McLean, Jane experienced a severe crisis that resulted in her smashing her right hand through a window, an incident that is mentioned in *The Bell Jar*. In the novel, Plath compares the scar on Joan Gilling's hand to a 'miniature mountain range',[140] and later Jane said that 'there was a bright red, wheal-like scar along the outer edge of my right wrist when Sylvia first saw me at McLean in September, 1953.'[141] One day, while at Codman House – in *The Bell Jar* it is called Caplan House – Jane told the nurse on duty that she was not feeling well, but the nurse was busy with another patient. 'In a state when I was out of control and feeling that something was happening to me rather than my making it happen, I put my hand through a window, and I very unintentionally cut it as I drew my hand back after it had gone through the window, and I cut it on a jagged piece of glass.'[142]

It was obvious that the two young women shared a dark bond. 'Sylvia and I did have a sense of having shared a unique and difficult kind of experience after we had been patients together at McLean,' recalled Jane.[143] Not only had Sylvia and Jane both dated Dick Norton, but both of them felt frustrated by the narrow gender roles that constricted and constrained them. Plath and Anderson were also haunted by the ambiguous feelings they harboured towards their fathers, they both fantasised about killing a parent and both felt that there was no other escape from their living hell than suicide. The anger they felt towards their families and society had driven them insane. The methods they chose to help them recover differed drastically, however. While Sylvia convinced herself – and other people – that she had made an almost immediate mental upturn after only a couple of sessions of ECT, Jane opted for the slower but, so she believed, more beneficial and long-lasting psychotherapeutic approach. In *The Bell Jar*, Esther mocks Joan for her constant prattling about egos and ids, something which obviously bores her. 'While I was a patient at McLean, I did tell Sylvia I had decided to become a psychiatrist,' said Jane later. 'I did talk about psychology with Sylvia. I did exhort her to put more effort into her therapy, and Sylvia derided my efforts to recover by therapy alone, without shock treatments.'[144]

Jane, like all those close to Sylvia, was amazed by the speed with which she seemed to recover and later she admitted to feeling envy that Plath 'seemed to feel much better after having shock treatments and I still felt in much psychological pain.'[145]

The tension between the two women was observed by the staff, particularly Francis de Marneffe, who went on to serve as the chief executive officer of McLean. In unpublished testimony, he describes the relationship between Plath and Anderson as 'a very complicated one'. While Jane admired Sylvia for her skill with the written word, and for the fact that she was a published writer at such a young age, there were, he said, various unresolved issues surrounding the fact that they had both shared the same boyfriend – in fact at the end of 1953, Dick Norton, who had been finally released from his TB sanatorium, paid a visit to McLean to see Sylvia and Jane. (In *The Bell Jar*, Dick's fictional counterpart Buddy Willard asks Esther, 'Do you think there's something in me that *drives* women crazy?' and she tells him that he had nothing to do with her mental breakdown.)[146]

Yet, the greatest source of antagonism between the two women, said the psychiatrist, was their contrasting methods of treatment. 'I think Jane felt that Sylvia was, in a sense, taking a shortcut to getting out of McLean,' said de Marneffe, who shared an office with Dr Beuscher. 'Jane had [. . .] made a commitment to really make some changes in herself and work and struggle through the pain of her own illness and identity [. . .] to hopefully come out at the other end of the tunnel, whereas she saw Sylvia as not really coming to grips with her personal problems. And, therefore, there was friction.'[147]

According to Ruth Beuscher, Sylvia's recovery was related to the fact that she convinced herself that she was better – that, in her words, 'inside [she] just reorganized so she wouldn't have any more [ECT].'[148] Sylvia's seemingly miraculous psychic reorganisation stemmed from a desire to win. Suddenly, she was back in school again, wanting to achieve, desperate to be top of the class. As Franklin Wood said, Sylvia was an 'accomplisher'.[149] Surely she couldn't let Jane Anderson – who seemed to have every advantage in the world – beat her to it. By

Christmas Day Sylvia felt well enough to go home for the day, where she typed a letter on her brother's typewriter to Gordon Lameyer. She apologised for not writing to him, and even managed to joke that months of treatment had left her feeling somewhat uncommunicative.[150] She described, in a cheery tone, some of the women she had met at McLean, including a girl from Vassar who composed her own songs and the hospital's librarian, who let her type up the stencils for the in-house newspaper. She signed off the letter, 'your rejuvenating Sylvia'.[151] Indeed, doctors at McLean could see no reason why she could not return to college to resume her studies, and on 27 January 1954, at the Smith faculty meeting, the staff voted that 'Sylvia Plath be allowed to return to college[in the] second semester.'[152]

On the surface it looked as though Sylvia was almost back to her normal, sunny self, but in hindsight Francis de Marneffe believed that the writer had merely managed to repress the problems that had previously threatened to undermine her. When Sylvia left McLean she still had an 'unresolved illness', and rather than being cured she had simply 'escaped into some kind of pseudo health'. What was ironic, he said, was that Plath went on to portray Jane/Joan as the sicker woman: at the end of *The Bell Jar* the character commits suicide, while Sylvia/ Esther survives. In the book, Plath describes 'somebody else who was going crazier than she was,' said de Marneffe. 'In other words, the person who ultimately killed herself is not Esther Greenwood [. . .] In many ways, I would say that the book is an incredible projection on to Joan Gilling [. . .] I think Jane Anderson felt it was hostility, and I have to agree with her. I don't think there's any question in Jane Anderson's mind that Sylvia Plath was a very sick girl.'[153]

One day, while she was still at McLean, Sylvia arranged to meet her old friend Philip McCurdy, who had visited her regularly in the hospital over the past few months. After a day trip to

Harvard, where Philip was at college, the couple went out dancing to the Totem Pole. Later that evening, as Philip drove back to Wellesley, Sylvia made it clear that she wanted the night to go on. 'Our relationship had been getting a little warmer each time I saw her,' recalls McCurdy. 'I don't know whether that was because she was lonely or that she was man hungry.'[154] Perhaps Philip was initially taken aback by Sylvia's physical advances; certainly he was nervous, both because it was his own first time and because of the high respect he had for Sylvia. He drove the car to the end of a road, a dead end, where the couple started to kiss. 'She seemed to have a firm, yet sweet and gentle, grasp on what should take place, but my ardour matched hers only intellectually – not, sad to say, romantically or physically,' wrote McCurdy years later. 'One climbs the pedestal uncomfortably and a little fearfully even if one has been the creator of that pedestal.'[155] From Sylvia's behaviour, he says it was, 'obvious that she was more experienced, but it wasn't rape on her part. Either because of nerves or lack of experience I did not perform very well.'[156] The encounter, he says, 'was even more fitful, awkward and inexperienced than one can imagine.'[157]

Sylvia's sudden sexual openness could also be traced back to Ruth Beuscher, who tried to persuade her patient not to suppress her erotic urges. For years Sylvia had attempted to keep her desires in check, but now a health professional whom she trusted and admired had given her permission to free herself of her sexual inhibitions. The mantra that the psychiatrist repeated was that sex would help cure Sylvia of her psychological quirks and make her feel better. One had to remember, said Beuscher two years before her death in 1999, that sex 'was not considered as it appears to be now, a sort of psychological vitamin, without regular doses of which you are prey to the evils of madness. That's not the way it was for anybody, especially not for women.'[158]

Nine

I AM CHAINED TO YOU AS YOU ARE TO YOUR DREAMS

Sylvia's new life – or in her terms her renaissance – started with what she interpreted as a near-death experience. Warren had offered to drive her from Wellesley to Northampton, and by the time brother and sister had reached Smith the weather had turned treacherous. They travelled down Elm Street in a thick blizzard, but at least the main road had been cleared of snow. Then, as they started to drive down the hill by Paradise Pond that led to Lawrence House, Warren lost control of the car. The vehicle started to skid and tilt and Sylvia could see only three possible outcomes: colliding with the car in front, crashing into Smith's botanic garden, which contained the college's outstanding collection of specimen plants, or veering off the road and into Paradise Pond below. As the car span around in a terrifying eddy, Sylvia repeated, 'Oh God, God, God, God' to herself, but eventually Warren managed to bring the vehicle to a standstill.

For the next half an hour, Sylvia remained visibly distressed[1], but, according to Estella Kelsey, the new housemother of Lawrence House, she didn't let the shock ruin the tea that had been prepared for her. When the maid started to serve Sylvia first she made it clear that Warren should take the first cup as he needed it more. 'That was my first indication of what a lovely person she really was,' recalled Mrs Kelsey.

'Her beauty was surpassed only by her lovely voice and gentle manner.'[2] The housemother remembered that, in September 1953, when she had taken up her position at Smith, she came across a large crate marked with the name 'Sylvia Plath' in heavy black letters; she had been informed that the student would not be starting her studies in the autumn after all and had arranged for the box to be placed in storage. The retrieval of the crate from its dark and dank storage space echoed the rebirth of Sylvia herself, who had literally and figuratively decided to go underground. After receiving a long, typed letter from her protégée, Prouty wrote back to say how pleased she was to see Sylvia's words, once imprisoned 'as if in ice' now flowing so freely. The fact that she had managed to somehow reconfigure her perception and behaviour showed, a 'wonderful fighting spirit which your illness hasn't crippled in the least [. . .] though it has added much to your self-knowledge and wisdom.'[3] Your speedy recovery, once you turned the corner, seems little less than miraculous,' she added. 'If there come periods of returning depression, remember it is nature's usual method.'[4] She was only sorry that, as she was vacationing in Mexico, she had not been able to witness Sylvia's release from McLean and subsequent 'emergence from the darkness.'[5]

Sylvia's suicide attempt had made her something of a talking point at Smith. 'If Sylvia could not exactly haunt the room during her absence, she clearly made her presence felt,' said Nancy Hunter Steiner, who lived in Plath's room in Lawrence House during the time Sylvia was in McLean and who became a close friend. 'She was a frequent topic of conversation in the house; as the months passed I grew familiar with the details of the Plath legend through the speculative gossip that raged at the mention of her name.'[6] In her imagination, Nancy formed a mental image of 'this girl-genius' whose room she had usurped, picturing her 'as plain or dull or deliberately dowdy, a girl who rejected all frivolity in the pursuit of academic and literary excellence.'[7] As Nancy later admitted, she could not have been more wrong. The first time she met Plath – at a lunch at Lawrence House organised by Mrs Kelsey – Nancy blurted out, 'They didn't tell me you were beautiful.'[8] Nancy – whom Gordon Lameyer considered 'a handsome, beautiful girl, but self-consciously so, with a high forehead and a black bouffant hairdo'[9] – described Sylvia as 'remarkably attractive',[10] so striking in fact that she could have been taken for a B-movie actress or airline stewardess. She was, Nancy later recalled, 'impressively tall, almost statuesque, and she carried the height with an air of easy assurance [. . .] Her eyes were very dark, deeply set under heavy lids that give them a brooding quality in many of her photographs. Her cheekbones were high and pronounced, their prominence exaggerated by the faint, irregular brown scar that was the only physical reminder of the suicide attempt.'[11] Far from being alienated or tortured, Sylvia seemed, in Nancy's eyes at least, as though she was 'eager to create the impression of the typical American girl, the product of a hundred years of middle-class propriety.'[12]

Sylvia regarded Nancy as her alter ego or mirror image, telling her new friend that her Irish colouring was a perfect counterpart to her own German blondness, adding that certain qualities that were dominant in her personality were submissive in her own. Nancy was just the latest in a long line of young women Sylvia had cast as doubles, women she thought she needed to complement certain absences in her own identity. Later, Nancy would see Sylvia and herself as 'Siamese twins, joined at the ego'.[13] Her function, as she saw it, was to provide Sylvia with a kind of 'filter through which the inspiration passed, qualifying and tempering what she initiated. She was pleased by the neatness of the alliance and suggested that our combined strengths created an impenetrable fortress – that together we were invincible. I did not understand at the time that alone Sylvia felt defenceless and imperiled.'[14] It's not coincidental that Sylvia's quest for a double began when she left for Smith. For the early part of her life, Aurelia (self-appointed creator and curator of Sylvia's identity) had assumed that role. Now that Sylvia was away from home she needed to find replacements. Just as the loss of her father compelled her to seek out boyfriends who could act as substitute figures, so the absence of her mother drove her to search for women who could take on a role that went above and beyond the 'normal' boundaries of the maternal. 'Understanding Sylvia Plath has often seemed to me a little like seeing double through a mirror in which mothers and daughters are twinned [. . .]' writes Plath's cousin and English professor Anita Helle. 'Aurelia's own letters offer an extended example of what I would identify as mother-writing: a type of creative activity in which the materiality of a child's being is transformed into a cultural product which provides both source and justification of a specifically maternal presence. Kinship is in this sense no abstraction, for the metonymies of the "I" and the "other" perpetually remind us of a seemingly "natural" contiguity in which the self often threatens to collapse into the identity of the other.'[15]

Each of Plath's doubles tried her best to soothe and salve these psychological lesions but, to a greater or lesser degree, the result was, inevitably, always the same: failure. According to Nancy Hunter Steiner, Plath formed a 'pathological dependence'[16] on her doubles, a fixation that proved unsustainable. 'Each time I put together the puzzling pieces of Syl's behavior I constructed a picture in which she was driven, periodically, to stage a symbolic salvation with herself as the suffering victim and me as the deliverer, almost as though only by being snatched from the brink of death could she confirm her worth [. . .] She seemed to be saying that, inside the mass of complex, highly developed machinery that was Sylvia Plath a piece was missing – the key that could wind it all up and keep it going.'[17]

Like all the other girls at Lawrence House, Nancy's continued presence at Smith depended on her achieving high marks and, as a result, she, like Sylvia, 'brought to even the most trivial activity an almost savage industriousness – a clenched-teeth determination to succeed that emanated from us like cheap perfume.'[18] Yet Sylvia and Nancy were both 'determined that no one was going to guess we were "scholarship girls" if, with a little ingenuity, we could appear to belong in the mainstream of campus life.'[19] Actually, the spring semester of 1954 was the first time since Sylvia had started at Smith that she had not received a scholorship, a point that obviously rankled Aurelia. In a private note years later, Aurelia wrote 'In Spring Semester 1954, I paid the entire tuition, board and room feeling (after cashing in my insurance) the strain on her would be less – she need feel no sense of obligation [to get high marks].'[20]

The college authorities agreed that, on her return to Smith, it would be better if Sylvia followed a lighter academic programme, taking only three courses that semester instead of the usual five. Yet, in addition to choosing Newton Arvin's early-American literature, nineteenth-century intellectual history with Elisabeth Koffka, and Russian literature with George Gibian, Sylvia decided to audit modern-American literature with Robert Gorham Davis and go to lectures on medieval art. She adored her new courses, especially her Russian literature class with Gibian. 'She was that good looking girl who stared intently, out of the crowd of students, when I was talking to the class [. . .]' he later recalled. 'Sylvia looked to me always as if she had just come back from skiing in Vermont or swimming in Bermuda – healthy, good looking, tall, good posture – like the non-intellectual, un-tormented Smith girl stereotype.'[21]

By necessity, Gibian's course – which included Tolstoy's *War and Peace* and *Anna Karenina* and Dostoevsky's *Crime and Punishment*, *Notes from the Underground* and *The Brothers Karamazov* – often involved talking about insanity, depravity and suicide, and Sylvia felt a little embarrassed at first and conspicuous that the scar on her cheek would mark her out just as Hester Prynne's scarlet letter served as a badge of shame in Hawthorne's novel. She wrote to Jane Anderson to tell her that she had recovered to such an extent that she was even considering writing a forthcoming Russian paper on the theme of suicide. After all, as she had her own experience to draw upon she could now analyse the issue from more than a purely theoretical point of view.[22] No one attempted to ask any probing questions about her suicide attempt; rather, she volunteered the information freely to a small group of selected friends, most of whom had had knowledge or experience of mental illness – friends such as Jane Truslow, who had undergone a series of electroshock treatments at Baldpate Hospital, and Marcia Brown, whose mother was incarcerated in a mental hospital in New York City. To each of these friends, she gave an overview of her experience; it was, as she told Jane Anderson, nothing like the kind of self-analysis she had undergone while at McLean.[23] Later that year, she told fellow Smith student Elinor Friedman that, throughout her whole time at McLean, she had carried a book upside down. 'She said to me, "When you are crazy, that's all you are" – that phrase is stamped on my mind,' recalls Elinor. 'The madness was so all-consuming. She described to me in perfect detail the episode when people forced her on to the table where she had that procedure [the first ECT] done to her. At the same time, she said very openly that she would not go through it again. If it happened again she said she would kill herself.'[24]

Sylvia told Nancy Hunter that the strangest part of the whole episode was waking up in the hospital. '"I don't believe in God or in an afterlife," she said, "and my first reaction when I opened my eyes was, 'No, it can't be. There can't be anything after death.' I was terribly disappointed that even death couldn't put an end to my consciousness."'[25] Plath explored these issues in an essay on Dostoevsky entitled 'The Devil's Advocate', which she wrote in March for her Russian literature course. Since there was no such thing as God or immortality then she could be certain that, if she committed suicide, she would not be punished. When she had regained consciousness and found that her body had not followed the wishes of her intellect and had not perished after all, she felt that she had, somewhat ironically, arrived in her own personal hell, the only one she believed in. This was not a pit of fire and brimstone, but something more tortuous: a place where nothing made any sense.[26] To illustrate her own experience, Plath quotes a segment of Book Eleven of Dostoevsky's *The Brothers Karamazov* in which Ivan debates the nature of life and death with a hallucinatory devil figure. The devil tells the mentally disturbed young man a story about a philosopher who rejects everything, '"laws, conscience, faith," and above all, the future life. He died; he expected to go straight to darkness and death and he found a future life before him. He was astounded and indignant [. . .]'[27]

Certainly Plath saw language, and specifically poetry, as part of her regeneration. In February she sent Gordon Lameyer 'Dirge in Three Parts', the first poem she had written since the spring of 1953. In just twelve lines, this satire dripping with black humour, alludes to Adam and Eve, Alice in

Wonderland, the Wizard of Oz, Dante and John Bunyan. 'The Daliesque surrealistic "vampire clock" prepares one for the wonderful timepiece metaphors of the "unwinding heart" and the "black hands" clapping together at midnight as when Mephistopheles summons Faust,' wrote Gordon back to her. He especially liked the line in the last stanza of the poem in which, at a clap of the hands of the clock, man is converted to excrement. 'I remember last year you told me that "dung" was one of your favorite words when you saw it in a poem of mine . . . You wrote that Auden accused you of being too glib, which I do not think is applicable in this poem.'[28] She dreaded the time when, as she had already experienced in the summer of 1953, she lost the ability to compose poetry. As she wrote to Gordon, she wanted to continue to be able to perceive, understand and create until such a time when she was no longer capable and sonnets turned into gibberish once more.[29] In 1954, Sylvia often placed the subject line 'Cabbages and Kings' at the top of her letters, a reference to Lewis Carroll's poem 'The Walrus and the Carpenter' from *Alice Through the Looking Glass*. In Plath's mind the phrase also signified the transformative power of metaphor, a force that was central to every aspect of her life. Without it what was the point of living? In 1955, Plath wrote 'A Sorcerer Bids Farewell to Seem', a response to Carroll's poem in which she envisages a time when, like Shakespeare's Prospero, she renounces her old magic. Instead of using words as devices to illuminate and transfigure perception, Plath imagines a time when she no longer calls upon her muse Alice to help her create, no longer looks into the Mad Hatter's hat for new metaphors. Plath had glimpsed the alternative – a place where poetry and simile did not exist[30] – and she knew that, for all its attractions, it was not a place where she could live. 'In her work, ugly, distorted worlds exploded and erupted in metaphoric profusion,' says Nancy Hunter

Steiner. 'The paradox troubled me at first; later I could guess at some possible explanations. Sylvia constructed images as an engineer designs a bridge – with painstaking, almost mathematical attention to every detail [. . .] Sometimes she chose words with disquieting connotations for their shock value. Often, however, the poetry reflected the turbulent process that was taking place beneath her placid exterior. At her core, Sylvia experienced a welter of raging emotions and violent impulses, and on the surface, to keep them in check, she wore the mantle of a bourgeois lady, as inhibiting and restraining as a straight jacket.'[31]

Sylvia adored listening to Edith Sitwell reciting 'Façade' – whenever she played it at home in Wellesley, Aurelia insisted that all the connecting doors be shut so she didn't have to hear the modernist poetry being read to the accompanying music of William Walton. Plath particularly relished the physicality and sensuality of Sitwell's vowel sounds and lines such as 'the navy-blue ghost Of Mr Belaker, The allegro Negro cocktail-shaker'. After her written exams in March, Sylvia decided to treat herself to a lecture by the famous English literary critic I. A. Richards, who was due to talk at Smith on 'The Dimensions of Reading Poetry'. After the lecture, Sylvia and a number of other students accompanied him to President Wright's house, where Plath, the supplicant, sat at his feet by a roaring fire and listened to Richards declaiming poetry. Sylvia possessed a steely determination to learn the craft of the poet and no opportunity to mix with the literary aristocracy was passed over. 'When Sylvia was at Smith she carried around a book in which she wrote down metaphors and similes, images she used in her poetry,' says Elinor Friedman Klein. 'Creativity was central to her life – it was a way of being in charge of something you feel when you are able to control nothing.'[32]

Although Sylvia saw Dr Booth, Smith's psychiatrist, once a week, in her own mind she thought that she had completely recovered from her breakdown. She was completely free of psychological problems, she told her mother, and as a result the discussions she had focused more on general philosophical questions rather than the specifics of her mental health.[33] She told Jane Anderson that further psychiatric treatment was 'superfluous' – she felt that, at last, she had found a way to manage and master her emotions. Instead of being gripped by bouts of mania she felt more balanced and calm, she said.[34]

Plath's self-image, however, was not always consistent with how other people saw her. In an effort to try to convince herself that she was fully socialised, Sylvia started dating again and during her first month back at college she went out with eight boys. She felt particularly drawn to Atherton Sinclair Burlingham, a handsome graduate of Cornell who was studying at the Union Theological Seminary in New York City. The problem was that Burlingham, who went by the nickname 'Bish', was dating Plath's housemate Mary Derr. 'Bish looked like Cary Grant except that he was blond,' says Mary. 'He loved being around the girls and I thought he was pretty nice. Sylvia was kind of fickle and she wanted to see what Bish was like and so when she next went to New York she looked him up. She thought he was wonderful – she was stuck on him, wanted to marry him, she said – and it was obvious that Sylvia was trying to steal Bish from me.'[35]

She was guilty of 'bird dogging', fifties slang for trying to lure away another woman's boyfriend, a social crime at the time. Tom Derr, Mary's brother and a fellow student at Union Seminary, who also went on a date with Sylvia in the spring of 1954, recalls that Bish was 'a sweet guy, but not appropriate for Sylvia, who was a dramatic, highly verbal presence'.[36] In a letter to his sister Tom expressed astonishment that Sylvia could fall so quickly for his friend. 'I shouldn't think people with level heads would do that so fast,' he said. 'I mean, doesn't one reserve judgment to discover if the feeling is mutual? [. . .] Anyway, I complained to Bish about Sylvia's self-centeredness, and suggested that even if she were starving for affection it was time to grow out of it, and that people like you (and by inference him himself) shouldn't be expected to have to supply this affection. When do you stop coddling a person and help her to grow up by making her rely on her own resources, etc. That sort of thing. I made it brief. Maybe he will get the idea.'[37]

Sylvia made the trip to Manhattan during the spring vacation of 1954, after she had received an invitation from Ilo Pill, the thirty-five-year-old Estonian she had met on Lookout Farm in the summer of 1950. Aurelia, feeling that her daughter deserved a treat, paid for Sylvia to fly from Boston to La Guardia, where, on Sunday 28 March, she was met by Pill and taken to the apartment that he shared with his mother on the corner of Lexington Avenue and 123rd Street in Harlem. She sat down to a dinner with his aunts and uncles, all of whom spoke broken English, and later he took her out to see T. S. Eliot's *The Confidential Clerk.* The next day, the aspiring artist announced that he had taken the day off work to show her around the city, but Sylvia, reluctant to get involved, made up a story that she was engaged to be married and that their relationship would never progress beyond friendship. On Tuesday evening, Sylvia – wearing in her hair one of the half a dozen red roses that Ilo had given her – met Bish and the couple dined at Asti, after which they took a ride on the Staten Island Ferry. On Wednesday morning she told Ilo that she was going home, but in fact she took a taxi to Union Theological Seminary and woke up Bish. After breakfast they went to a lecture by the theologians Paul Tillich and Reinhold Niebuhr, who both taught at the college, and then, after a spot of piano playing in the practice room, Sylvia made her way downtown to see her friend Janet Salter, who had invited her to stay. Unfortunately Plath had not told Janet of her change of plans; her friend, believing that Sylvia was travelling directly from Boston to New York, waited for her at Grand Central Station.

'I waited for one train and then the next, but finally, after calling my parents, I went back to our place in Greenwich Village,' recalls Janet. 'She had been expected at about one o'clock, and at six we got a phone call from her. She told me that she had gone to the Union Theological Seminary where she had visited Bish, Mary Kerr's boyfriend. The way she approached the phone call was just incredible – all jolly and happy as if she hadn't put us out at all. I'm sure if something like this had happened the year before she would have apologized. When she had visited me before we had done all kinds of things together – we had gone to the Rockefeller Plaza to see the skaters and I had taken her on my own personal walking tour of the Village and I had shown her the house where Edna St. Vincent Millay had lived. This time she had other things in mind – she obviously just wanted a bed to sleep in.'[38]

On 1 April she met Bish again for lunch and a walk in Morningside Park, where they discussed philosophy and theology – Sylvia relished taking on the role of devil's advocate, she said – and then that night she dined with Cyrilly Abels and her lawyer husband Jerome Weinstein, a lawyer, at the couple's Fifth Avenue apartment. She got on so well with the other guest – Weinstein's nephew – that after the dinner they carried on drinking at the Albert Hotel in Greenwich Village. By the time

Sylvia arrived back at Janet's home, an apartment on Tenth Street, it was obvious that she was drunk.

'Sylvia tripped in kind of late and she was pretty high,' says Janet. 'We had put up a cot for Sylvia in my bedroom, but as my parents slept in the living room they couldn't go to sleep until she had come in. Her eyes were all red-rimmed and she was trying to focus but couldn't. She was really drunk – you could smell it on her. And she had lost her wallet – her train ticket was in it and she had no money to go home. The next day we went back to the bar, the Albert Hotel, which in those days was a very unsavoury place and it was rumoured to be frequented by prostitutes, but we didn't find it. Throughout the visit she behaved in what I can only describe as a manic fashion, but also she was so vague about so many things. My mother – who had worked as a social worker and who had had experience dealing with the mentally ill – thought she was schizophrenic. On one level she was so manic and enthusiastic about things, but then when it came to telling you anything specific there was a vagueness about her and a blankness in her eyes.'[39]

According to Janet, Plath's behaviour during her stay in New York only confirmed her and other Smith students' belief that Sylvia was seriously mentally ill. 'All of us thought that she had a split personality and/or she was schizophrenic,' she says. 'The one thing nobody thought of was that she might be manic-depressive, because she was always manic. Maybe she had moments of depression that nobody knew of. In her junior year, the enthusiasm and ebullience seemed genuine, but when she came back to Smith there was something phony about it all. I remember I wrote a postcard home at the end of my senior year telling my parents that we had started to call Sylvia Plath "Silver Plate". That was as much an indication of what we thought of her as anything – that she wasn't real.'[40]

On her way to Massachusetts, Sylvia stopped at New Canaan, Connecticut, to see the popular writer Sarah-Elizabeth Rodger, whom she idolised. After taking one look at her, Rodger, who was the mother of one of Warren's friends, insisted that Sylvia stay overnight in her home. The next day she had lunch in New Haven, where she saw Yale student Melvin Woody. In a letter to Gordon Lameyer, she said that, as she had borrowed so many of the young man's poetry books, she had to force him to accompany her home to Wellesley on the train. Melvin Woody has a rather different recollection of the encounter. 'She persuaded me to get the train back with her because she did not want to have to deal directly with her mother,' says Professor Woody. 'She did not go into any specific details, but it was obvious she wanted to use me as a kind of cushion. She needed me to protect her from her mother – it was obvious she did not want to be alone with her.'[41]

No doubt Sylvia knew that Aurelia would be able to tell that she had spent most of her time in New York partying and drinking. Aurelia still worried about Sylvia's mental health and, despite all the reassurances that she was back to her normal, breezy self. In April she told her mother that she was now a 'well-adjusted person' but Aurelia feared a return to the hell of 1953.[42] She was not the only one. Eddie Cohen, one of the most perceptive of Plath's correspondents, wrote a letter to her at this time questioning the true state of her mental health. 'I must admit that I find your bubbling-over existence rather disconcerting [. . .]' he said. 'In all the constant rush of emotional and esthetic experience which have marked your last two letters, you have been remiss, perhaps deliberating, with the facts.'[43] What exactly had been the problem? Why had she tried to commit suicide? What kind of diagnosis had she been given? And what therapy had she received? 'I realize that these questions probe into still raw points, and may be too difficult for you to delve into now.' Her main problem, as he saw it, was her narcissism, and he defined her as a 'woman who gets a great deal of pleasure from looking into a mirror. A very flattering mirror, at that.' There was no point pretending to herself that she had been fixed or cured – 'when reality intrudes, as it eventually must,' he warned, 'you will merely bounce back to where you so recently returned hence.'[44] Cohen later theorised that his friend suffered from borderline personality disorder. 'While there is no consensus among the professionals as to exactly where that border is, most of them agree that such people make those closest to them angry and uncomfortable a great deal of the time,' he said.[45] Borderline personality disorder – a condition that was not included in the American Psychiatric Association's Diagnostic and Statistical Manual of Mental Disorders until 1980 – manifests itself in symptoms such as an unstable sense of self-identity, highly volatile mood swings, extreme bouts of anger, the formation of intense but problematic friendships and relationships, suicidal thoughts and attempts, all of which Sylvia experienced.

Before returning to Smith, Sylvia had lunch with Olive Higgins Prouty, whom she called her fairy godmother, saw Phil McCurdy at Harvard, caught up with her reading (Melville, Faulkner, Tolstoy and Henry James) and mused over her future. She toyed with the idea of taking a job or immersing herself in further study after graduating. She favoured the latter, she said, because she knew that conventional nine-to-five employment, even for a glamorous publishing house, did not suit her temperament. Looking back at her brief spell at *Mademoiselle* in the summer of 1953, she realised that an office job would sap her creativity. At the end of a day at the magazine all she felt like doing was going to a show, having a drink or going to bed. As she wrote to Gordon Lameyer she felt either too tired or too guilty to do any writing; certainly, her job was nothing that would make the basis of a novel.[46] She was grateful for the extra year at Smith, she told Gordon, because it would give her more time to mature, she would be able to travel in the summer and she had the opportunity to meet a wide range of like-minded people. She wanted to carry on having new experiences and learning about the world. It was essential for her to live as intensely as possible, she said, even if she did suffer along the way.[47]

Twelve days after writing this letter, Sylvia met a man who would help her free herself of her conventional morality, liberate her sexually and expand her intellectual horizons. Richard Sassoon, a senior at Calhoun College, Yale, did not match her physical ideal – he was the same height as her and wiry and, with his black eyes ringed with purple shadows seemed possessed of a haunted quality; in a letter to her mother she said that he looked like an absinthe addict. Yet, from the moment they met, on 18 April, Sylvia felt challenged and stimulated by him. She felt drawn to his sensitive and intuitive character (Plath believed that American men were sadly lacking in this respect), his European heritage (a British citizen, he was a distant relative of Siegfried Sassoon and had been born in Paris in 1934) and his romantic spirit (he frequently quoted Rimbaud, Baudelaire and Verlaine). Sylvia met Richard through his roommate at Yale, Dick Wertz, a former boyfriend of Plath's good friend Nancy Hunter. On that Sunday in mid-April, the two boys travelled up from Yale to Smith in Richard's Volkswagen, and, together with another Smith student, the foursome drove out to Look Park, where they raced each other across the fields, watched the deer and walked by the river. That evening, the group made the trip out to Mount Tom State Reservation, where they climbed the fire tower and stared down at the lights of the Pioneer Valley below. Although Sylvia did not like heights – as she came down she said she felt gripped by a sense of euphoria and fear[48] – she found the whole experience exhilarating. From there, the group moved on to Amherst, where they sat in a panelled bar and Richard spoke French; Sylvia was astounded by how much she understood of the conversation and she felt flattered when the dark-eyed young man complimented her on her accent.

Two days later Richard wrote the first of many letters to her, letters written in a spidery hand and in a stream-of-consciousness style, many of which are in French. 'My dear,' he scribbled in pencil. 'Memories – memories only/ no thought for the future: these are dangerous! [. . .] I am God. I damn you for my pleasure [. . .] Dream? Never – too natural. I make this. I am God! Me + you = me [. . .] I am irrational [. . .] pure bête [. . .] a bientot, enchantress (sorceress).'[49] It was obvious that here was no regular Yale student content to graduate, work his way up the corporate career ladder, marry and have children. 'Dick was an extraordinarily bright guy,' says Melvin Woody, who was also one of his roommates. 'The Yale French department virtually created a curriculum specially for him. He would lounge around for days on end doing nothing and then suddenly he'd go to the typewriter and bash out a paper that would receive an A. It was obvious he came from an upper-class background, although of course he never talked about that in any way. His family was living on income – I don't think his father ever worked – but I got the impression that Dick had trouble adjusting to America, as he had been used to a class hierarchy.'[50]

Richard told Sylvia a little about his childhood: that, at the age of three, he came down with a mysterious illness, a condition that was considered so serious that 'the greatest doctors of Europe' gave him up for dead, and he was saved only by love; at four he wandered from room to room saying, '*Ce n'est pas vrai, ce n'est pas vrai*' ('It isn't true'); and at ten he discovered that he had the ability to control and direct his dreams in a semiconscious state. 'I began an entirely new life and when it came to an end I thought I was going to die,' he said. Between the ages of six and fourteen he was considered something of a genius. 'I was a philosopher and a very great fool, and I meditated for hours upon very important matters,' he said. At Yale, where he was taking a divisional major in History, Arts and Letters, with a focus on French literature, he worked on various literary magazines, wrote a history of his college and served on the library committee. His aesthetic sense was so finely tuned that it pained him to see or experience anything that did not match his high standards of beauty. 'When you have seen a moving forest of classical columns you do not wish to walk down the streets of New Haven, and when you have lived the beauty of Mallarmé you do not wish to read Sandburg,' he told Sylvia. In the same letter he expounded on Plato, Aristotle, mathematics, love and philosophy. 'I believe only two types of person are tolerable and they are those that love passionately and those that are passionately loved,' he said. 'And the former because they are constantly dying and have no life of their own, must rule.' His words and ideas frequently contradicted themselves but that was part of Sassoon's intellectual game, a divertissement that Sylvia found both mentally exhilarating and deeply erotic. The new man in her life was a walking paradox, an ambiguity brought to life. 'I am always two and must always be,' he wrote, reflecting Plath's conception of herself as an identity continually in flux.[51] Sassoon also confessed to a propensity for depression. 'I have tried to hide it,' he wrote to her, 'but you must know this of me – I see strange visions in my depressions and I am impetuous and I wish my will done immediately, because there is a constant fear of an end in me.'[52] Like Plath, he was also attracted to the shadow side of nature. 'I am the only one who has ever pacted with the devil and then spat in his face,' he told her, 'and were it not for you I should be more alone than ever I have been.'[53]

Sassoon was drawn to Sylvia's poetic sensibilities. In April she sent him copies of 'Admonitions' or 'Never Try to Know More Than You Should' and 'Verbal Calisthenics', poems that she had written the year before and that had appeared in the spring 1954 issue of *Smith Review*. He wrote back to say that he thought her work excellent. 'Poetry is a great discipline, a tortuous discipline, a perversion,' Sassoon observed, 'and above all a piece of impeccable logic.'[54] The same month Plath also wrote a sonnet, 'Doom of Exiles', which articulates the agony of returning to one's homeland to find it defiled and decayed, and was overjoyed to see her poem, 'Doomsday', featured in *Harper's* magazine. 'It is Art!' said Richard when he read the poem. 'What an effort it must have been [. . .] I fancy it was written for me, and I know well it was not.'[55] Yet he also believed he had a great deal that he could teach her. 'Darling, darling – I dare not let you grow up without me,' he said. 'I tell you I am the best educator in your country.'[56]

At the end of April, Plath was looking forward to attending the formal dinner for students of Lawrence House who had been nominated for Phi Beta Kappa, but when a couple of girls checked on her they realised that their housemate was ill. Mrs Kelsey went upstairs and found her 'flushed with fever'. Immediately, the housemother arranged for Dr Booth to admit her to the college infirmary and asked the two students to help bring her down the back stairs to a car waiting outside.[57] Although she was diagnosed with flu it seems that she could have been suffering from other symptoms too: bleeding and cramps so severe she wondered, as she outlined in a lighthearted letter to her friend Philip McCurdy, whether she could have been poisoned or whether she had undergone some kind of miscarriage. Whatever had been the cause she had felt decidedly odd, almost as if she had given birth to a batch of babies all at the same time.[58] The mere feel of the sheet on her skin was almost too much for her to bear and she likened the sound of a sneeze to the reverberations of an exploding volcano. While in the college infirmary, Plath, responding to the news of the demise of Philip McCurdy's housemaster at Harvard, thought of the unpredictability of death. If only one could foresee one's own death, what she described as a kind of thrombus in the blood vessel of one's life, then perhaps all of us would proportion our time rather differently.[59]

Plath would have been told to try to take it easy on leaving the infirmary, but she did not follow the doctors' advice. Prompted by her awareness of the transience of life, and the concomitant desire to make the most of every moment, she started to behave with a renewed intensity. She dyed her hair platinum blonde – a makeover that initially shocked Aurelia – and became romantically entangled with Melvin Woody, Sassoon's roommate. 'Sylvia and I made a mistake, in that our relationship became quite erotic at one stage,' recalls Professor Woody.[60] For weeks the couple had experimented sexually, but always stopped short of full sex: Melvin wanted to take the next step, but Sylvia said she was worried about getting pregnant.

The real reason that Sylvia distanced herself from Melvin was that she was infatuated Richard Sassoon. Her feelings were reciprocated: 'I am chained to you as you are to your dreams,' he wrote to her at the end of April.[61] On Saturday 1 May, Richard packed poetry books, chicken sandwiches and a bottle of Bordeaux wine and drove Sylvia out into the Massachusetts countryside. The couple hiked across green meadows to an idyllic spot at the top of a hill, where they enjoyed the afternoon. Then, at twilight, as a wind started to blow, Sylvia and Richard started to make their way down the slope, climbing over several fences topped with barbed wire. After cutting herself on the wire, and getting bitten by 'malicious minute flies', Sylvia was glad for the sanctuary of Richard's car. But then the nightmare began. As Sassoon put his foot on the accelerator pedal, the wheels of the car spun deeper into the ground. Sylvia looked around her – there was nothing but darkness for miles – and then she started to panic. Her overactive imagination immediately spewed out visions of murder in the woods.[62] Luckily, Sylvia remembered seeing an old farmhouse further down the road, and the couple began to walk hand in hand in the dark towards it. As she approached, her mind was again flooded with images of violence – evil farmers armed with guns and vicious dogs and sadistic hired hands who would take pleasure in murdering them – but, after knocking on the door, the young lovers were welcomed into the cosy home. While Richard went off to deal with the tow truck and get the car out of the mud, Sylvia charmed the family to such an extent that they called her 'Cinderella', invited her to a square dance the following week, and treated her like a 'queen'.[63]

At the beginning of May, Sassoon invited her to New York City. He had already arranged to sail to Europe after his exams and so the weekend in Manhattan would have to serve as the couple's last opportunity to see one other for a couple of months. While ruminating on the delights of the forthcoming liaison, Richard wrote to Sylvia, 'I am talking myself into thinking it will be rather fun to play daddy to a naughty girl if you are naughty.'[64] The couple checked into a hotel on 44th Street, where, apart from a brief outing to see an off-Broadway production of *The Seagull* starring Montgomery Clift, they spent the majority of their time in bed. Sylvia confessed in a letter to Phil McCurdy that she had slept for only two hours that Saturday night, an indication that she had, most probably, finally consummated her relationship with Sassoon. On Sunday they woke up at noon and went to Steuben's, where they enjoyed a lunch of onion soup, herrings in sour cream, and ice-cream éclairs, washed down with plenty of white wine. Sylvia was so tired that, on the journey home, she slept on the back seat of Richard's car. 'You will never know how wonderful I feel when you say I make you happy,' wrote Sassoon to her a few days later. 'It is so much better than being a God [. . .] I love you, darling.'[65]

When Sylvia returned to Smith, she had to face the 'reign of terror' of the exam season.[66] Despite this description, it seems as though Plath relished the challenge to prove to the college authorities that her intellect was just as razor sharp as it had been before her breakdown. Plath wrote on Tolstoy and Dostoevsky, Nietzsche, Marx and Hegel, and the theme of egoism in American literature, a question that she said, not surprisingly, she said she had thoroughly enjoyed. Later in May she learned that she had been given an overall mark of an A for English. She also wrote an end-of-year paper for her intellectual-history course, entitled 'The Age of Anxiety and the Escape from Freedom', in which she discussed Erich Fromm's 1941 text and Nietzsche's *Thus Spake Zarathustra*. Sylvia had been meaning to read Fromm's *Escape from Freedom* for four years, and its central idea – that if mankind cannot live with the responsibilities and obligations of freedom it will lean towards authoritarianism – intrigued her.

By this point Sylvia's finances were again in a perilous position. In the second semester she had budgeted $125 for clothes, $15 for books, $50 for transport, $20 for food and $50 for miscellaneous expenses, but she had spent rather more, and now she had only one dollar in each of her two bank accounts. Smith had awarded her 'an unusually large scholarship' for the next academic year: Plath would receive $1,250, plus a guaranteed place in a co-op house, which effectively meant that she would receive $1,500 for a year, leaving only $300 for Sylvia to pay.[67] Yet this did not solve her immediate problem. Her main concern was, as she told her mother, lack of money. She simply did not have a clue about where it was to come from.[68] She had had to set aside $300 for her expenses during the summer when she would be attending Harvard and she knew she would need that sum again in spending money for the next year. In her dreams, she wished she could travel to Europe, but of course this was out of the question; a summer waitressing job was more realistic. No doubt she would owe her mother a great deal of money by the end of her senior year.[69]

Plath returned home to Wellesley to find her mother in poor health. Aurelia still had problems with her duodenal ulcer and in early June Sylvia wrote to Gordon Lameyer to tell him how worried she was about her mother. Writing about herself in the third person, she said that, as a result, she was not only anxious but also more than a little frightened.[70] In the same letter, and again in the third person, she described herself as a girl who hoped to grow as straight and as fast as a bamboo tree; she only hoped that in the process she did not hurt anyone.[71] She told Gordon that she loved him – despite (or because of) the fact she hadn't seen him in months (he had been stationed on the USS *Perry*). Lameyer returned to Wellesley for a weekend in June and was immediately taken aback by the colour of her hair. 'I did not feel her bleaching her hair was typical of her natural attitude toward most things,' he said.[72] Her mother believed that the new look, perhaps borrowed from Marilyn Monroe – whom Sylvia would later dream about, believing her to be a kind of 'fairy godmother'[73] – gave her daughter the opportunity to try out a 'more daring, adventuresome personality'.[74] Yet neither Gordon nor Aurelia could have conceived of how Sylvia's new, more intrepid persona would manifest itself.

At the end of June – after she had attended the weddings of two of her friends, Claiborne Phillips and Marcia Brown – Sylvia drove with Gordon to Provincetown, on Cape Cod, where she was staying with her mother and grandparents for a few days in a rented cottage in Eastham. 'High on the dunes at P-town, we lay on my parents' old car rug on the burning sands,' recalled Gordon. 'Really in touch with each other for the first time, we had a lovely day in the sun, picnicking, swimming and sharing ideas, but I soon came to realize that Sylvia was not ready to let me push our relationship to the limit, and I did not want to hurry her. Although she was game to experiment playfully, I became accustomed to a rather innocent Adam and Eve relationship. It was Eden before the Fall.'[75]

Plath had arranged to sublet an apartment for the summer in Cambridge with Nancy Hunter, who was also attending Harvard summer school, and two other young women from Lawrence House. The four students sublet a one-bedroom apartment – in the Bay State Apartments building at 1572 Massachusetts Avenue. As Sylvia and Nancy had persuaded their friends that they needed quiet to study during the day, the other two girls, who went out to work, were relegated to the dining room, where they slept on a sofa bed. Sylvia had enrolled in Frank O'Connor's Nineteenth-Century Novel and an intensive course in beginner's German, while Nancy chose two classes taught by Hans Kohn, who had lectured on Ibsen at

Smith earlier that year and whom Plath had found intellectually brilliant. During that earlier talk on the Norwegian playwright, Kohn caught Plath smiling as he discussed the promiscuous behaviour of one of Ibsen's characters. He pointed a finger at Sylvia and said, in a knowing manner, how he guessed she had enough life experience to understand.[76] Although Gordon regarded himself as the 'major man in her life'[77] – and Sylvia had told Nancy that she intended to marry him – the two girls decided that their policy for the summer was to date any man who offered either dinner or a theatre ticket, even if she did not find him particularly interesting. 'We had a gluttonous appetite for the attractions of the city and little money to indulge it,' recalled Nancy.[78]

One day in July, after Sylvia had given Nancy a whirlwind tour of the treasures of the Widener Library, the two friends were standing on the steps of the building when they met a tall, balding man in his early thirties. 'He was thin, with bones like broomstraws that poked out here and there along his frame [. . .]' said Nancy. 'The splintery frame stretched up above our heads like a flagpole, ending at a small round head [. . .] behind the thickest glasses I had ever seen, two tiny, watery blue circles masqueraded as eyes.'[79] He introduced himself as a science professor who was visiting Boston on a research project, and, within the space of ten sentences, it became obvious to both Sylvia and Nancy that 'he was probably the most brilliant man we had ever met [. . .] His voice was low and resonant and he used it to fashion a rhetoric that set our heads spinning.'[80] Plath used the man – identified only by his first name of Edwin in previous biographies – as the basis for her character of Irwin in *The Bell Jar*, where he is described as 'a tall young man with a rather ugly and bespectacled, but intelligent face'.[81] However, in one of Plath's scrapbooks she names the professor as Edwin Akutowicz, a mathematics scholar. Akutowicz persuaded the two young women to accompany him to a nearby coffee shop, where he outlined, in terms the liberal-arts students did not understand, his complicated mathematical theorems. Nancy found herself dumbstruck, and she was sure that the professor – whom she regarded as slightly sinister – would call the apartment later to invite Sylvia out. So she was amazed when Edwin telephoned to invite *her* out to dinner, which took place in his rented apartment. After the meal, Akutowicz proceeded to chase Nancy round the brown leather sofa for five minutes while repeatedly bragging, 'I always make the ladies happy.'[82] Finally, Nancy managed to convince the randy professor to take her home, where she fell sobbing into Sylvia's arms. Each time Akutowicz called the apartment Plath refused to let him speak to Nancy, yet over the course of the following few days it was obvious that Edwin and Sylvia had struck up a friendship. 'She began seeing him furtively, as though embarrassed' said Nancy.[83]

Sylvia had started to see Ruth Beuscher twice a month and Akutowicz would drive her to the psychiatrist's office in his convertible. It was most likely Beuscher who persuaded Sylvia to take her sexual experimentation to the next stage. What exactly happened between Plath and Akutowicz depends on whom you choose to believe. The facts are these: Sylvia had spent the night at Edwin's and, the next morning, Akutowicz called Nancy to tell her that her friend had haemorrhaged badly; she had seen a doctor and seemed to be feeling better. Nancy came home from class to find a note from Sylvia saying that she had gone on a picnic with Edwin, but when she returned Plath looked pale and told Nancy that she had been bleeding again. Nancy took her into the bedroom, and sat her on the bed, but when Sylvia got up a large dark stain was visible. 'The back of her skirt was bloodstained and a small trickle of blood ran down her leg like the outline of a jagged tear,' recalled Nancy.[84] After cleaning herself up, she joined the other girls in the dining room; but after a few moments she rushed to the bathroom, where she collapsed and where Nancy found her in a pool of blood 'that spread like a giant wound' across the white tiles. Nancy did her best, with the guidance from a doctor whom she had telephoned, to help stem the bleeding, and Sylvia went back to rest in bed. However, at ten o'clock that night, when Plath got up, the two women were horrified to discover that Sylvia had been lying in a layer of blood that had pooled on top of the plastic tablecloth that had been placed on top of the mattress. 'The back of her yellow nightgown dripped bright red and bits of dried blood were matted in her long yellow hair,' remembered Nancy.[85] Despite Sylvia's fear of hospitals and doctors, Nancy had no choice but to seek medical help for her friend, whom she was afraid would bleed to death. Nancy promptly telephoned Akutowicz and arranged for him to drive them to the hospital, where doctors managed to stop the bleeding. Although the enormous loss of blood may seem suggestive of something serious, according to Nancy, 'The [corrective] procedure took about ten minutes, during which the doctor kept up an easy banter, encouraging us to relax. The metal instruments clanked in his hand like a fistful of silverware, but he seemed to know what he was doing [. . .] The job completed, he flashed us a conspiratorial smile. "Tomorrow you'll be good as new," he remarked. "And don't start thinking you're exceptional. I've seen a number of cases just like yours."'[86] But what had caused the haemorrhage?

It is at this point that the stories begin to diverge. According to Nancy Hunter Steiner, Sylvia told her that Edwin had raped her; meanwhile she maintained to Gordon Lameyer that 'without provocation she had been manually attacked' by Akutowicz.[87] If it had been a rape would Sylvia have chosen to continue to go out on a series of dates with Edwin, as we know she did, even inviting him up to Smith in November? After a certain amount of reflection, Lameyer admitted that his acceptance of Sylvia's story – that she had been damaged by a finger – somewhat naïve. 'I am convinced that the account of Esther's fiasco with "Irwin", when she nearly fainted from loss of blood [as told in *The Bell Jar*], was biographically accurate for Sylvia,' said Gordon. In the novel, Esther seduces Irwin so she can lose her virginity: she wanted somebody, she says, whom she didn't know and whom she wouldn't continue to see in the future. The process had to be detached and dispassionate, almost like a tribal ritual.[88]

As Plath was no longer a virgin, it could have been possible that she wanted to use the highly sexed scientist as a way of expanding her erotic repertoire. 'As in tennis or in skiing, she feared to be seen as an inchoate beginner,' said Gordon Lameyer, who liked to believe that Edwin was her first sexual partner.[89] Or perhaps she let herself be persuaded to see Akutowicz as some kind of father substitute with whom she could act out a long-suppressed fantasy. 'The root cause of her nervous breakdown was, I believe, her fixated Electra Complex [. . .]' observed Lameyer. 'Apparently Sylvia came to the realization that her father's death, when she was eight years old, did not allow her to outgrow her natural Electra Complex. When he died, she felt he was a god who had abandoned her. It caused her to try to find some kind of superhuman quality in all the men in her life who might be seen as replacing him [. . .] Subconsciously she may have wanted all the major men in her life to recapitulate in their actions the trauma of her childhood [. . .] Psychologists have described how narcissists, whose personality development has been defective, due to their love needs in childhood not having been fulfilled, suffer from inner conflicts which sometimes can result in a splitting of the self and the subsequent repressing of the side of the self which is destructive [. . .] At certain times in her life Sylvia apparently felt psychologically pursued not only by her own double but by her father's double.'[90]

In many ways, Plath's poetic vision was formulated by her father – or least her fantasy version of him. As she says in 'Lady Lazarus', addressing the Herr Doktor, Herr Enemy figure, 'I am your opus.'[91] She felt angry that he had been snatched from her and later, after undergoing therapy with Ruth Beuscher, she outlined in her journal the complicated matrix of emotions relating to her father's death. 'I have lost a father and his love early; feel angry at her [Aurelia] because of this and feel she feels I killed him,' she wrote.[92]

Plath seized on Otto's amputation as a symbol of her own loss; his absence was a constant presence, a kind of phantom limb that continued to haunt the peripheries of her consciousness. 'I've come to believe that she carried a serious trauma within – like a long, long pregnancy,' says Olwyn Hughes, the sister of Ted Hughes and Plath's former literary executor. 'All her efforts were to somehow resolve this inner chaos [. . .] Her father was adored and heavily mined [. . .] "Moon and the Yew Tree", "Berck-Plage" and "Little Fugue" were the real matter of her horror at her father's illness, amputation and death.'[93] In 'Berck-Plage', Plath wrote that 'This black boot has no mercy for anybody./Why should it, it is the hearse of a dead foot,'[94] and in 'Little Fugue' she contrasted the innocence of a prelapsarian world with the horrors that came afterwards, a fall she somehow connected with her father. 'The world occurred./You had one leg, and a Prussian mind.'[95] According to the mythology she had created for herself, Plath believed that her truncated relationship with her father had laid the fragmented foundations of her life. Her destiny was set the day Otto died, she writes.[96] In the same poem she states how she is the ghost of an infamous suicide – 'It was my love that did us both to death.'[97] Plath's poetic mission was a writing out of her half-memories, desires and fantasies associated with Otto. In this way many of her poems serve to reify the absent father figure, the words acting as a substitute for the real thing. But the poet knew that her skills stretched only so far: as Ariel she had the power to conjure a whole world full of 'airy spirits', but she realised that she was a mere servant to the controlling father-muse figure of Prospero; it's no surprise to learn that, in 1958, she thought of calling a forthcoming volume of poetry *Full Fathom Five* after Ariel's song in *The Tempest.* 'Full fathom five thy father lies,/ of his bone are coral made,/Those are pearls that were his eyes,/ Nothing of him that doth fade,/But doth suffer a sea-change/Into something rich and strange', echo throughout Plath's life and poetry. Otto never faded from his daughter's imagination; if anything, his image became more alive with time as Sylvia transformed him into something far richer and stranger than anything he had been in life.

She felt compelled to recreate her father in her work, but acknowledged that the task was an impossible one. 'I shall never get you put together entirely,' she wrote in her 1959 poem 'The Colossus'.[98] Plath also admitted to herself that she thought there was a direct connection between the loss and continuing lack of her father and her compulsion to seek out replacement figures. She was, she said, always searching for the 'gigantic paternal embrace of a mental colossus'.[99] While she wanted her future husband to be a 'demigod of a man', she realised that her desires were unattainable. 'I want a romantic nonexistent hero,' she said.[100]

In the summer of 1954, Sylvia started to date Harvard tutor Ira O. Scott Jr, whom she viewed, significantly, as her new godfather. In one of her scrapbooks, Plath described Scott accompanying her on a tour of the gardens of Castle Hill, the grand estate in Ipswich, Massachusetts, and inviting her to various restaurants where he had plied her with champagne and steak suppers, and taking her sailing off Marblehead.

The following year, inspired by her various romances, Plath wrote a nineteen-page story that she entitled 'Platinum Summer', in which she casts herself as Lynn Hunter, a brunette who one day sees an ad in a magazine for a hair dye with the caption: 'Were you a blonde baby?' Lynn, like Sylvia, had indeed been a blonde baby and, after buying the lotion, she applies the liquid each night only to find that the product not only changes the colour of her hair but also alters her personality. Lynn walks with a new confidence and a happy glow encircles her.[101] The story is set at the fictional Oceanview Hotel, where Lynn works as a waitress and focuses on her relationship with two contrasting men – Ira Kamirloff (a combination of Ira Scott, Edwin Akutowicz and Gary/Igor Karmiloff) and Eric Wunderlich, a medical student based on Ray Wunderlich. Each of the men responds to her hair in a different way – Ira finds the blonde hair sexy, whereas Eric thinks it doesn't suit her personality – and by the end of the story, Lynn decides to reject the glamour of Kamirloff for the authenticity of Wunderlich. In a telling aside, Lynn asks Eric whether he would ever want her to act like a kaleidoscope. That is exactly what worries him, he responds. As she is ruled by an impulsive streak she would always need a strong man to stop her running wild.[102]

The summer of 1954 also motivated Plath to write notes for a humorous story provisionally called 'Coincidentally Yours', about two or three girls who share an apartment in Cambridge. The main character would be a young woman like herself, she said, who was fun, quite extrovert and blonde and who, by chance, manages to bag the right man. Characters she could include would be based, she said, on her flatmate Nancy, a girl with Modigliani eyes and extraordinary cheekbones; Edwin, a raging Don Juan imprisoned in a fuddy-duddy exterior; and Ira, whom she describes as a kind-hearted professor. She told herself that she must not try to pack the story with too many incidents just because she had experienced them and because she was, at heart, a realist. It was more important to try to keep to a streamlined, tightly written plot. One detail she thought she would have to include was the time when, last summer, she had contracted ptomaine poisoning (an incident that finally made its way into *The Bell Jar*).

It may be easy to write off stories such as this as nothing more than sentimental slush for the women's slicks, yet Plath used this kind of fiction to explore one of her central preoccupations: what sort of man she would eventually marry. What is intriguing is that the man she indicated who, in her real life, she would most like to commit herself to – Gordon Lameyer – does not appear anywhere in these stories. In a letter that she wrote to him at this time, Sylvia talked about being alone in the apartment in Cambridge, which she imagined that she shared with Gordon and waiting for him to come home. She told him that she would devote herself to him for as long as he was alive.[103]

In August, Sylvia had the opportunity to act out her fantasy when she invited Gordon, who was on leave from the navy, to Wellesley for the weekend. Her mother was away at the Cape with her parents and she had the house to herself. She enjoyed cooking meals for him, reading short stories by J. D. Salinger and Carson McCullers, listening to records, and relaxing. 'Yes, we were intimate [. . .]' said Gordon. 'That brief encounter was our only intimate experience because Sylvia managed always to invest all her major life experiences with trauma, for herself and others. Although she had taken precautions, she feared a week or so later that she might be pregnant. However, her system, still upset by the previous year's insulin injections, caused her periods to be irregular, or sometimes altogether missing. When in early September she called to say that she feared she was going to have a baby, I assured her I loved her and would marry her. I wrote her a long letter, which I asked her to destroy, which this time she did. Sylvia was horribly afraid that she had let down all those who had believed in her [. . .] Fortunately, all her fears were dispelled several days later.'[104]

On 24 August, Sylvia went out on a date with Gordon. The couple planned to attend a number of parties in and around Boston before driving back to Lameyer's home in Wellesley. That night, Sylvia's flatmate Nancy Hunter was at the apartment in Cambridge when she got a panicked phone call from Aurelia. Where was Sylvia? Nancy could not exactly tell her. 'Mrs. Plath was incredulous, reminding me that it was the anniversary of the suicide attempt and that someone ought to be keeping an eye on Syl [. . .]' Nancy wrote later. 'She asked if I could absolutely guarantee that Syl was not off in a secluded corner of Boston that very minute, dying from some self-inflicted wound.'[105] Finally, after a series of frantic phone calls, Nancy reached Sylvia, who called Aurelia to reassure her that she was fine. The crisis forced Nancy to readdress her attitude towards her friend. 'She was not depressed or alienated; in fact, she was racing from experience to experience with a recklessness that asserted her invincibility [. . .]' she said.[106] 'Crisis had followed crisis that summer in a dizzying profusion.'[107]

By the end of the summer, the physical relationship between Sylvia and Gordon had atrophied. Although they occasionally slept in the same bed they never again made love. 'The world had turned and tilted again, and our orbits were out of phase,' recalled Lameyer. 'If Sylvia were telling the story, she would probably say that in her senior year, she "outgrew" me, to use her favorite Alice-in-Wonderland image. After this summer, our relationship was like the radio call-sign of my destroyer: Minor Key.'[108]

Ten

NOW, VOYAGER

Sylvia had long dreamt of travelling to Europe. In 1948, the sixteen-year-old girl had written to her German pen pal, Hans, telling him that one day she hoped she would be able to save up enough money to sail across the Atlantic. The following year, lack of money had prevented her from accompanying her fellow Wellesley High School students on a bicycle trip through Europe organised by Wilbury Crockett. On arrival at Smith, she found that girls from wealthier families were always talking about their vacations in Europe, and all three of her serious boyfriends – Dick Norton, Gordon Lameyer and Richard Sassoon – had spent months on the Continent.

Europe represented many things to Sylvia: independence from her mother; a chance to connect with her family's Germanic and Austrian roots; and an opportunity to situate herself within the tradition of American authors, such as T. S. Eliot and Henry James, who had chosen to leave their homeland and live as exiles. In her second year at Smith, Plath had attended a lecture on modernism by Elizabeth Drew, a professor of English, which discussed this very point. Sylvia had taken copious notes, observing that, while texts such as Homer's *Odyssey*, Virgil's *Aeneid* and Dante's *Divine Comedy* centred around the search of the self, twentieth-century writers expressed this search for self-discovery in new forms. Next to a section on Matthew Arnold, Plath had written that the poet had believed traditional European culture had fissured and disintegrated. What did it mean for a writer to be an exile in a strange country? In another comment on the theme of the quest in literature she observed that most writers ended their careers feeling a certain amount of dissatisfaction and alienation. Fundamentally, the voyage many artists experienced was an interior one.[1]

Plath acknowledged that were she ever to grow as a writer she would need to wrench herself away from her familiar environment. Not only would such a journey give her greater insight into her self, but she was sure that it would provide her with a wonderful range of experiences that she could use in her writing. She wrote to her mother about the endless fictional possibilities provided by Europe: the local customs and traditions, the sights, sounds and smells and the extraordinary array of people.[2] But how could she, a young woman with limited means, ever finance such an ambition?

It seems that the idea of applying for a Fulbright scholarship first occurred to her in May 1952, when she heard that an English major at Smith had received the award. Three days later she wrote in her journal, 'I will still whip myself onward and upward (in this spinning world, who knows which is up?) toward Fulbright's, prizes, Europe, publication, males.'[3] Throughout 1952, despite her glowing academic record, she still felt uncertain that she would ever stand a chance of winning one of the coveted awards – 'only a million people want them; no competition really,' she wrote in her journal.[4] However, one day in the autumn of that year, Plath had a long meeting with her old high-school teacher Wilbury Crockett, who inspired her to pursue her dream. The prospect was certainly a daunting one. Could she dare to dream that one day she would spend a year or so studying at Oxford or Cambridge? The main stumbling block, of course, was lack of money. Yet she knew she had a couple of years in which to research fellowships and scholarships. 'I am young, husky, and eager to work,' she said.[5]

When Sylvia returned to Smith in September 1954, she set about doing all she could to increase her chances. She interviewed each member of the English department, quizzing them about everything pertaining to the Fulbright, and she received particularly strong support from Mary Ellen Chase, who had spent time in Cambridge, England. 'Without doubt,' she said of Sylvia, 'a most talented, even brilliant girl, both as a potential scholar and as a literary artist [. . .] I think, at least in my twenty-seven years here [at Smith], I have not known so obviously gifted a girl. And with her intellectual and artistic gifts she has a really lovely nature. She is simple, courteous, humorous, generous, thoughtful, and charming as well. She has not the slightest trace of conceit or arrogance.'[6] Plath's other academic references in support of a Fulbright were similarly glowing. 'I have known Miss Sylvia Plath intimately as a student for the past three years,' wrote Elizabeth Drew, 'and I have never had a more brilliant and a more charming student to teach.'[7] George Gibian, assistant professor of English and Plath's Russian novel tutor, said that Sylvia had a 'great sense and feeling for words'. His only objection was that, at times, her prose style manifested a certain over-exuberance, a 'defect' of which she was aware. Yet, despite this, he felt 'quite confident that we shall hear further of her as a scholar, short story writer, and poet.'[8] Striking an initial note of caution, Newton Arvin wrote, 'In speaking of Miss Sylvia Plath it is a temptation to resort to the kinds of superlatives of which, in general, one is bound to be (and must be) suspicious.' Yet he added that in more than thirty years of teaching he had not come across a better student. 'She struck me as having a very exceptional quality of mind – both imaginative and controlled, both lucid and intense. Her natural feeling for literature is extraordinarily sensitive and immediate, and her capacity for expressing this is far beyond the mark set by even the typical good student.' Not only was she 'gracious and mature in manner and bearing' but also she possessed a 'fullness of personal experience and a depth of temperament that one does not frequently encounter'. By the end of his reference, his praise is unbounded. 'Whatever limitations she may have, either personally or intellectually, are not known to me.'[9] The only dissenting voice came from Estella Kelsey, Plath's housemother at Lawrence, whose reference was wonderfully two-faced. 'Sylvia Plath is a girl of unquestionable character,' she wrote. 'She has a gracious personality and is most thoughtful and polite when it is to her advantage. Her appearance is quite striking. She has a pleasant voice and pleasing correct deportment.' Yet underneath this – for the eyes of the staff of Smith's vocational office only – she added, 'Sylvia Plath is self centered and very selfish. Her talent for writing has made her difficult for the girls to live with.'[10]

Plath realised that, despite these mostly rapturous reports, nothing her tutors at Smith said could gloss over her period of absence from the college between September 1953 and February 1954. In the run-up to the application deadline, Sylvia wrote to her mother to ask for her advice. Since Marion Booth, the Smith psychiatrist, would be obliged to tell the Fulbright committee about Sylvia's mental breakdown and her spell in McLean, perhaps she should ask Ruth Beuscher for a reference too? The decision was a masterstroke of pre-emption, as Sylvia knew that her therapist's report would assuage any doubts about her mental stability.

'In my opinion, at the time of hospitalization Miss Plath was suffering from a state of mental turmoil which is highly unlikely ever to recur,' stated Beuscher. 'Some of the qualities most obvious in her illness were the very ones which, properly channeled and maturely balanced, contribute to her undoubted superiority as a person. She has a great sense of responsibility, not only to others who may depend on her, but also to herself, and to her integrity [. . .] Her chief fear is that having had an emotional upheaval sufficiently severe to provoke hospitalization will be held against her as evidence of basic instability. While in many cases this might be a valid conclusion, in the case of Miss Plath, I feel that anyone refusing her for a position on those grounds would be depriving not only Miss Plath, but also depriving themselves.'[11]

In the same letter, Beuscher defined Plath's psychotherapy as a 'success', yet by her own admission psychiatrist and patient had seen each other for only twelve sessions since Sylvia had left McLean. This disclosure calls into question the validity of Beuscher's opinion: were twelve sessions of intermittent post-hospital therapy enough to warrant a statement that effectively promised Plath a clean bill of mental health? In some respects it seems as though Plath, the consummate actress, duped Beuscher into believing that she was well and Beuscher let herself be duped. Beuscher – who could not countenance the possibility that she had, in effect, been managed and manipulated by Plath – could see only the positive aspects of Sylvia's character and she remained blind to her patient's faults and weaknesses. A few years before Beuscher died, she was interviewed by Karen Maroda who wondered whether Ruth had been right in maintaining that Sylvia had been stable enough to travel to England. 'How could she not pursue a Fulbright?' Beuscher responded. 'And how could I stand in the way of her doing that?'[12]

Through the American Association of University Women, Plath applied to both Oxford and Cambridge. She had heard that Fulbright scholars were often allocated to participating universities on an almost random basis and so she wanted to make sure she was considered by Oxbridge.[13] Yet she knew that her application to Oxford was likely to be turned down, because the university was averse to students 'with any physical or mental ills in the past.'[14] The sheer red tape – twelve copies of her letters of recommendation, twelve statements of purpose, three health exams – was maddening, as were the two three-hour Cambridge exams that she took at Mary Ellen Chase's house in November. Sylvia found the questions so general – along the lines of 'The art of the novel, what is that?' and 'The importance of metaphor in poetry' – that she felt that to answer them properly would take her at least a year.

In case the Fulbright did not come through, Plath put into action a back-up plan – sending off applications for graduate study to Harvard, the Radcliffe Institute and Columbia University. As she wrote to Gordon, she was sure that her brunette (rather than blonde) personality would take dominance this year – before her return to Smith she had made an appointment for a dye job to rid herself of her shock of peroxide hair. Now was the time to wave goodbye to the rather superficial character who was happy to stay up all night partying, drinking and enjoying conversation over bourbon and water. She did feel rather odd, she admitted, when she first went back to the rather staid uniform of Bermuda shorts, knee socks and loafers and it was strange to see herself surrounded by hordes of young women rather than men.[15] She even switched from bright-red nail polish to the colourless type as she knew, when applying for scholarships, it was better to adopt a more staid and sensible appearance.[16]

This year she was, she said, determined to devote herself to academic pursuits – her new courses included Shakespeare, an intermediate class in German and the twentieth-century American novel. One day in October, Plath was contacted by the *Smith Alumnae Quarterly* and asked to interview Alfred Kazin, the author of *A Walker in the City* and *On Native Grounds*, who that year had been appointed the William Allan Neilson professor. Although he was initially quite frosty towards her – believing that she was just a spoilt rich kid like most of the other girls[17] – when he learnt that she was on scholarship and that she had a few stories and poems published he became 'charming'. Kazin, who was leading a first-semester course in advanced composition, told Plath that his job was to 'release the unexplored talents of the student' and said that, on the question of the best approach to teaching creative writing, 'the important thing is "not to have theories"'.[18] In a letter to her mother, Sylvia described the encounter: Kazin – whom Plath called 'the great winking albatross', due to his nervous twitch[19] – had quizzed her about her writing and had invited her to audit his class. Later, Kazin remembered the conversation quite differently. It was Plath who had implored him to let her take the course. Why, he asked, would she want to audit a class in creative writing when she was already a published author? 'She replied that she was lonesome and she wanted to talk,' he recalled.[20] Her motivation, of course, was much more centred around the fact that she suspected that Kazin, who himself had taught as a Fulbright lecturer in Cambridge in 1951, could serve as a powerful and influential mentor. Thirty-nine-year-old Kazin was obviously impressed by Plath's first appearance in his class. Sylvia was appalled by the apathetic nature of her fellow students – who were either too frightened or too idiotic to venture forth an opinion[21] – and, at the end of the class, after Kazin had turned to her to ask her what she thought, he was so impressed he asked her to stay.[22] Almost immediately, Plath was winning A grades from Kazin, together with comments like this one for her story 'The Day Mr Prescott Died': 'Very nicely done and every word by now, absolutely professional.'[23] In his reference to the Fulbright selection board, Kazin was even more commendatory: 'She is not merely the most gifted student in the class but perhaps the most interesting student writer I have seen in years. Her work is mature, individual, and so deeply perceptive that I have already urged her to send out to magazines several of the pieces she has written for my class [. . .] Miss Plath is top-notch, and I can assure the committee that she is someone to be watched, to be encouraged – and to be remembered.'[24]

One of the more dynamic students in Kazin's creative-writing group was Elinor Friedman, a dark-haired junior who had recently met Sylvia when Plath had given her a prize from one of Smith's arts societies for a play that she had written. 'At Smith you could ask someone from another house for dinner and Sylvia had been invited over,' she recalls. 'We got on immediately to such an extent that we ignored everyone else at the table. My first impression of her was that she was someone I could talk to about anything.'[25] In an article that she wrote for *Glamour* magazine in 1966, Elinor remembered that she was initially rather taken aback by Plath's appearance. Conscious of Sylvia's academic brilliance and aware of her disappearance and suicide attempt, Elinor anticipated a shy, socially awkward, bespectacled young woman, 'clutching her Dostoevsky for dear life. But Sylvia was lovely, willowy-lithe with great soft dark eyes, wide laughing mouth and a tumble of light hair.'[26]

On the first afternoon they spent together, Sylvia took Elinor up to her room in Lawrence House and initiated her into the well-worn ritual that marked the beginnings of a new friendship: the presentation of the pile of rejection slips that she had fashioned into a kind of makeshift altar. 'I've got hundreds,' she said. 'They make me proud of myself. They show that I try.'[27] At this point, 'Sylvia had not become "the thing on the mount".

She was beautiful, open and had the ability to talk about things of interest, such as politics and poetry.'[28]

Elinor also recalled that Plath was an astute listener, that she soaked up detail 'like a blotter' and that she was extraordinarily perceptive. 'Like Chekhov, everything she saw touched her. She was able to refract and reflect the light of her experience as exquisitely as stained glass.'[29] Sylvia had, according to Elinor, a 'false idea of what it was to be glamorous – she was not glamorous. I had the attitude, "Who cares if a bus hits you the world goes on." I was outrageous, I didn't give a shit, but I think Sylvia did. She was a perfectionist, and being a perfectionist is an impossible role to take on. Excellence was central to our culture at the time – we were brought up to be good little girls and we wanted to make our parents proud of us. In those days "good" equalled "married", ideally to a professional. Sylvia was exactly like me in many ways, only with more drive. You couldn't see it, but you could feel it. She wanted to be everything, I think. She was always searching for the self she was going to be.'[30]

In the autumn term of 1954 Plath started working on her thesis, 'The Magic Mirror', a study of the double in Dostoevsky's 1846 novella *The Double* and in *The Brothers Karamazov*, in his final novel published in 1880. As she started to work through the two texts, Plath would have been struck by the parallels between Dostoevsky's philosophical and psychological exploration of split personalities and her own internal battles. After seeing his double, 'a man who was quite himself',[31] the government clerk Golyadkin feels so psychologically undermined that he wants to erase his own identity, 'to be obliterated, to cease to be, to return to dust.'[32] At one point, after fleeing from his evil twin through the streets of St Petersburg, he feels as though he is 'standing at the edge of a fearful precipice, while the earth is bursting open under him

[. . .] the abyss draws him.'[33] Five years before, in 1950, Plath had written something similar in her journal – a passage where she articulated her feelings of alienation and dislocation, and talked of standing on the edge, steeling herself to peer down over the cliff face in order to see the horror of what lies below. Throughout Dostoevsky's novella, Golyadkin – described by one critic whom Plath quotes in her thesis as 'the psychological embryo of all "split" characters created by Dostoevsky'[34] – encounters his counterfeit self and by the end the nightmare is so complete that he believes he is seeing a 'multitude of duplicates' at every turn.[35] Plath herself was conscious of the fragility of her own identity, and the ease with which her self could mutate from mask to mask. Reading her journals is like coming face-to-face with a multiplicity of fragmented selves. At times, when Plath confronted her own double in the pages of her diaries, she must have got as much of a shock as Golyadkin himself when he encounters his 'noxious' and 'unworthy' twin'.[36] In January 1953, six months before her breakdown and attempted suicide, Plath had pasted a photograph of herself into her journal. She told herself to take a good hard look at the image and never forget it. 'It is a chalk mask with dead dry poison behind it, like the death angel. It is what I was this fall, and what I never want to be again.'[37] Like Golyadkin, Plath was always haunted by a fear of what might happen if her own 'unworthy twin' took over.[38] At the end of Dostoevsky's novella, the government clerk is borne away by a carriage towards a madhouse. 'Our hero shrieked and clutched his head in his hands,' writes Dostoevsky at the very end of the book. 'Alas! For a long while he had been haunted by a presentiment of this.'[39]

Plath was even more fascinated by Dostoevsky's mature work, *The Brothers Karamazov.* In her own copy of the novel, Sylvia underlined the words of Marc Slonim, who wrote in the introduction: 'Dostoevsky's main interest lay not so much in the description of environment or in the strangeness of events as in the emotions and thoughts of the individual and his work was centered upon most intricate psychological and philosophical problems.'[40] Plath was particularly drawn to the character of Ivan, who during the course of the novel encounters not one but two doubles: Smerdyakov, who by killing Fyodor Karamazov believes he is simply reflecting Ivan's unconscious desires to murder his father, and the devil, who appears before Ivan one night and who tells him, 'I am only your nightmare.'[41] Like Plath, Ivan had established a 'brilliant and unusual aptitude for learning' since infancy[42] and was 'haunted by a great, unsolved doubt.' As Plath read the novel, did she also draw parallels between Ivan's wish to murder Fyodor Karamazov and her own elaborate fantasies about her father's death? In her copy of the book, in the margin next to Ivan's words 'and afterwards I told you in the yard that I reserved "the right to desire"? [. . .] Tell me, did you think then that I desired father's death or not?'[43] Plath made a note about father killing.[44] Although the physical murder of the father figure is carried out by Smerdyakov, who is rumoured to be Fyodor Karamazov's illegitimate son, Ivan often felt compelled to murder him too. This patricidal desire seeps from one character to another, infecting their psyches like a vicious form of brain fever. Even though Ivan is theoretically innocent of the crime, his guilt eventually drives him mad. 'Who doesn't desire his father's death?' Ivan asks at the end of the novel.[45]

As Plath read the book did she ask herself whether she had ever suffered from a similar form of psychic patricide? According to one of her own 'doubles', Nancy Hunter Steiner, Sylvia adored and despised her father, Otto, in equal measure. 'I probably wished many times that he were dead,' Plath told her.

'When he obliged me and died, I imagined that I had killed him.'[46]

Sylvia became so fascinated by the theme of the double that she read widely on the subject, including James Frazer's *The Golden Bough*, which her mother had given her in 1953, Freud's *Dostoevsky and Parricide* and *The Uncanny*, as well as Kafka, Poe, Robert Louis Stevenson, E.T.A. Hoffman and Wilde. In addition, she tackled heavy-weight psychological studies, essays such as 'The Phantom Double: its Psychological Significance' by Stanley M. Coleman, which had appeared in the *British Journal of Medical Psychology* in 1934, and 'Schizophrenia' by Edward W. Lazell. The one book that she felt frustrated that she could not read was Otto Rank's *The Double as Immortal Self*, a German-language text that had not yet been translated into English. In the middle of working on the thesis, she wrote to Gordon Lameyer about the possibility of writing an 'adolescent story about doubles'; after all, as she examined the realities of her life, every incident and situation seemed to reflect a mirror image back at her.[47] As we now know, that 'adolescent story about doubles' became *The Bell Jar*.

In December 1954, as Plath was nearing completion of her study, Olive Higgins Prouty wrote her a letter and asked, 'Doesn't Dostoevsky's double personality depress you a bit?'[48] The theme was, she said, absolutely gripping as it centred around how the ego was represented by images such as twins, shadows, mirrors, hauntings and reflections. The shadow side, she added, often came to symbolize the conscience, the enemy, the desire for self-destruction or the hopeless quest for immortality.[49] She refused to let the dark subject matter drag her down; she feared, perhaps, that if she allowed herself to become too emotionally involved with the material then her own double might make another appearance. A line in Alfred Kazin's introduction to Dostoevsky's *A Raw Youth* which Plath quotes in her thesis, best summed up her psychological predicament. 'One of Dostoevsky's greatest insights into the disordered personality is his realization that there are people who will do anything to avoid disarranging the fundamental conception they have of themselves.'[50]

On 27 October, her twenty-second birthday, Sylvia wrote to Gordon expressing her love for him. In order to cope with her workload, save money and keep sane, she said that she would have to closet herself away from all social contact. She wanted to see Gordon with all her heart, she said, but it was just not possible. This was, of course, not the whole truth. Sylvia was simultaneously dating not only Edwin Akutowicz, the man who was responsible for the horrific vaginal haemorrhaging, but also Richard Sassoon, who had returned from Europe. 'People have some strange notion that a person is more in possession of his mind than of his body,' Sassoon wrote to her in the autumn of 1954, 'and things which are said to be in the mind are considered to be in control.'[51]

For his part, Gordon said that he would do everything in his power to wait for her. If she needed time, or space, he would, he said, be prepared to give it to her. After the couple went to see a production of *Portrait of a Lady* in Boston, Gordon wrote, 'I see you as a Jamesian heroine like Isabel Archer being exposed to life [. . .]' – in letters that she wrote back to him at this time she signed herself Isabel – 'Your life is yours to lead; if you would rather call it quits because you are concerned about my attitudes, please do. Or if you would rather start seeing other men again, go ahead [. . .] As for myself, I think we have got too much together to give up when the going gets rough. When you prophesy a hard future if we ever get married, you do not exaggerate.' Yet practical problems of house, finances, continuing education and work could easily be solved, he added. 'I love you, I love all of you, and your thorns are the best part of you,' he said.[52] At the beginning of December Sylvia wrote back, insisting that she had no desires to end the relationship. Gordon was, she insisted, the most important man in her life. While she would not turn down the chance of the occasional friendly date with men such as Ira Scott and Richard Sassoon, it was, she said, unlikely that she would ever see either of them again.

Unknown to Gordon, in late November Sylvia went on a date with Sassoon. They drove out to Mount Tom, where they enjoyed a glass or two of cognac, before travelling on to Greenfield for dinner. His letters burnt with an erotic fury that Sylvia found utterly compelling. 'While yet there is something of the child in you,' he wrote to her at this time, 'I shall spank you [. . .] o yes, I will, I quite promise it [. . .] just for the hell of it.'[53] In another letter, also written towards the end of 1954, he said, 'Alas, too, I hurt you from time to time, and say things to you that are plainly unkind [. . .] but it must be soon I see you, for the devil may call for me anytime and you had best be around, my love, if you want to come come come with me.'[54]

In early December, Sylvia told both Gordon and her mother that she was going to spend a few days with an old Smith friend, Claiborne Phillips, who had married and was living in Manhattan. In fact, she spent the weekend in New York with Sassoon. The couple went to see the gigantic Christmas tree and the ice-skating rink at Rockefeller Center; browsed for books at Brentano's and window-shopped on Fifth Avenue; ate oysters for breakfast and snails for dinner; and, on the Saturday night, went to see *Bad Seed* by Maxwell Anderson at the 46th Street Theater. On Sunday 12 December, Richard parked his car on a street just off Fifth Avenue while the couple went for brunch at Steuben's. After their meal they discovered that Richard's car had been broken into and that Sylvia's suitcase, containing some of her best clothes, a number of poetry books, theatre programmes and her Chanel No. 5 perfume, had been taken. They spent the rest of the afternoon at a police station, where Sylvia found herself so fascinated by some of the sordid stories she encountered that she even flirted with the idea of becoming a crime reporter for a year. On her return to Smith, Plath wrote the poem 'Item: Stolen, One Suitcase', which detailed her furious reaction on discovering the loss of her possessions: her lovely blue cashmere sweater, her gold slippers, a necklace adorned with jet-black stones and silver moons. If the poem is anything to go by, it seems Richard became so frustrated by Sylvia's hysterics that he slapped her across the mouth.

Punishment, whether mental or physical, seemed to play a central part in their relationship. 'One time I recall her telling me how this short French-speaking Yalie had taken her to Rahar's in Hamp [a restaurant in Northampton] and, getting mad at her, had slapped her face,' remembered Gordon Lameyer.[55] Indeed, Sassoon's letters are peppered with threats of discipline. In one he writes, 'And I know I teach girls to be women and I teach them to taunt me and then you are far and cannot be punished [. . .] you are the only one I have wished to please and to punish.'[56] On 18 December, in a letter that opened with a joke that he wanted to end their love affair, he said, 'You are naughty and you eternally transgress. If I cannot completely curse you, I must then be very convincing. It is a way of scolding, my love, a new way – one must always be inventing new ways of scolding when one is conceiving new ways of loving, and it is so every day [. . .] I think you will never die or be old, because I love you too much and there is a force and a fire and a fury of life in my love [. . .] My God, I love You, like the rage!'[57]

The couple spent the Christmas of 1954 apart – Richard had to visit his family at their home, the Ramparts in Tryon, North Carolina, while Sylvia had arranged to spend a few days skiing in Vermont with her new friend Jon Rosenthal, an Amherst graduate, before travelling back to Wellesley for Christmas itself. Over the vacation she saw a great deal of Gordon, yet by this point she knew, as she wrote to a friend, that she could not marry him because she suspected he would never be able to keep up with her seemingly insatiable intellectual and imaginative appetites. Yet, during the late part of 1954 and early 1955, as she continued to date him, she refused to tell Gordon the truth about her feelings for Sassoon. Perhaps Sylvia justified her behaviour because she knew that Gordon was, at least for the foreseeable future, married to the navy; in early 1955 he was due to set sail for Cuba. For his part, Gordon continued to hope that they could forge a future together. After Sylvia sent Gordon a Valentine's card, he replied with a letter that included a family tree at the bottom of which was his name, the initials S. P. and a question mark, followed by spaces for eight children. 'As you split your provincial cocoons and spread your butterfly wings, I like to see you fly in many directions,' Gordon wrote to her. 'I will never try to make you pinned and wiggling on a wall. You are too chameleon-like I hope for that. For me the interesting butterflies are those who fly above the nets, whose life is changing in new nets, whose very force is mutable [. . .] Darling, darling, I love you.'[58]

Sylvia had kept the theft of her suitcase a secret from her mother because as she wrote to a friend after the incident, if a girl's family had to pay a large part of her college expenses she didn't go and buy a wardrobe full of new dresses; rather she would have to make do.[59] Sylvia was acutely conscious of the sacrifices Aurelia constantly made for her. In November Aurelia had told Sylvia that she had bought a typewriter, a purchase that meant that her bank account was now perilously short of funds. She would have to be careful, she said, adding in a tone of supreme self-martyrdom, 'Fortunately, I do not need any clothes this winter – not even shoes.'[60] Luckily the theft of Sylvia's clothes was covered by Richard, who sent her a cheque. Yet even when she went shopping with Sassoon's money she was careful, hunting out bargains in the sales: a charcoal-grey long-sleeved wool dress that had been reduced by $20, a necklace that had been knocked down from $22 to just $4 and a caramel-coloured sweater at $12 off. Despite Richard's cheque, she was still in financial dire straits: at the end of January she had only $17 in her checking account and $11 in her other bank account, which meant that she would be $100 short on her expenses for the rest of the year. She had had to pay $20 to get her thesis typed and then there was the $25 she had spent on medicines (she suffered another severe attack of sinusitis in January and had to be admitted to the college infirmary for a week). In addition, her application fees for postgraduate courses came to $25 and she knew she would also have to pay $30 for upcoming expenses such as a cap and gown for her graduation ceremony in June. In a letter to her mother Sylvia explained the situation and even went so far as to tell her that she had been so hard up that she had been forced to sell some of her old clothes and possessions; later, Aurelia learnt the truth about the theft of her daughter's suitcase.

Her mother agreed to meet the shortfall by a monthly loan. Sylvia insisted that she would pay the money back by graduation, but from reading the interchange of letters between them one senses that Aurelia tried to impose a series of conditions. Would it not be a good idea, she suggested, for Sylvia to try to do something practical? Something that could earn her money? What about shorthand? Typing? Perhaps the suggestion of secretarial school brought back the horrific memories of the summer of 1953 when Aurelia had tried to teach her daughter shorthand. In a stern letter – parts of which were excised from *Letters Home* – Sylvia wrote back to her mother to explain the importance of writing in her life. She wanted to write her own letters and manuscripts, not type them for other people. Aurelia also was not keen on Sylvia's plan to teach fifth-grade children at the American school in Tangier, Morocco for a year. Sylvia tried to put her mother's mind at rest, but again the tone was far from friendly. She didn't care about set objectives and career-oriented goals, she said. Surely what was more important was the enjoyment and experience of life itself? She knew she did not have the luxury of wasting time and she was determined to squeeze everything out of each moment of her existence. She wanted to live – and write – with passion. Sylvia realised that the contents of the letter would probably infuriate her mother, as their interpretations of success were so different.[61] On the back of the envelope, Aurelia wrote in pencil one word: 'maneuvering'.

Sylvia had experienced a rather stressful start to the new year. In addition to her exams, she had proofread and submitted her thesis; written a clutch of poems for her teacher Alfred Young Fisher, who had agreed give her private tuition in poetry; sent off the short story, 'The Smoky Blue Piano', to *Ladies' Home Journal* in the hope of it netting her $850; worked on her application for *Vogue*'s prestigious Prix de Paris (which would mean a prize of $1,000); and dashed off a profile of Smith for a Yale Literary magazine. In the midst of all this, she had to go before a panel of four men at Harvard for an interview for a Woodrow Wilson Fellowship, which was worth $1,250. The academics, including Francis Rogers, the dean of the Harvard Graduate School of Arts and Sciences, fired a series of what she thought were quite impertinent questions at her, including whether she intended to get married and have children. On 26 January, she received a letter from Harvard that read, 'I regret to inform you that your name has been withdrawn from the list of nominees who are still being considered for the National Woodrow Wilson Fellowships.'[62] Plath was left disconsolate by the news – it was, as she told her mother, the first time she had been rejected[63] – but the worst thing, as she told her mother, was the fact that Dean Rogers would also be responsible for the decision to admit her to Radcliffe. In addition, the panel informed her that it would be extremely unlikely for her to be awarded a Fulbright for Oxford or Cambridge.[64] She could cope, she said, with the rejections from magazines, but this was something else – 'this, after all, is my life.'[65] However, Sylvia had not lost her sense of humour. Later that same afternoon, she told her mother to keep the letter from Dean Rogers for her grandchildren to see; one day she could tell them how she had enjoyed a brilliant career despite the rejection. 'And they will look admiringly at a picture of me, just elected most popular waitress at Howard Johnson's,' she joked.[66]

In mid-February, Sylvia heard from Mary Ellen Chase that she had been accepted by Newnham College, Cambridge on a two-year BA Honours course, a programme that would automatically award her an MA on completion. She had still not heard about the Fulbright, but she was, she said, determined to get the money somehow. Sylvia was ecstatic at the news – her long-held ambition had finally come true, she wrote to her mother.[67] Aurelia, however, had mixed feelings, as can perhaps be gleaned from a postcard that Sylvia sent her mother in March. The card describes Mary Ellen Chase making the public announcement of Sylvia's entry to Cambridge one evening at an event at the Hampshire Bookshop and then Benjamin Wright, Smith's president, walking over to her and shaking her hand. Red pencil in hand, Aurelia underlined the key points of the missive, but also circled some of her daughter's spelling mistakes. Although she was proud of Sylvia's success, there was an expectation that she could do even better. Throughout this time, Aurelia continued to suffer from the painful symptoms of an ulcer, a condition that Olive Higgins Prouty believed could have been brought on by worry, stress and a fear of separation. 'Ulcers are often psychosomatic – the result of long continued anxiety [. . .]' she told Sylvia. 'It may well be she is anxious about losing you – I mean losing your dependence on her.'[68]

At this difficult time any extra money was welcome, as Sylvia did not want to be too much of a burden to Aurelia, and so she was delighted to receive a telegram from Cyrilly Abels at *Mademoiselle* magazine asking whether she would report on a forthcoming symposium to be held at Smith on the mid-century novel. The magazine was prepared to pay between $10 and $50 for the report, depending on the fullness of the material. The conference, chaired by Mary Ellen Chase and held at Smith in early March, had been organised to honour Alfred Kazin's appointment as the college's William Allan Neilson professor. The panelists included Brendan Gill, William Maxwell, Daniel Aaron and Saul Bellow and Sylvia took copious notes during the conference, writing down key quotes and ideas: 'Desire for happiness, but "Man must learn to bear a certain position of uncertainty" – Freud.' Although each of us went on a journey of self-revelation none of us would ever truly know ourselves. A writer's task was to try and see through the patina of surface reality to the dark motives of the human psyche beneath.[69] At one point, the panellists addressed one of the most pressing literary questions of the day: was Franny – J. D. Salinger's character from his story of the same name – pregnant or not? Kazin turned to Maxwell, the fiction editor of the *New Yorker*, where

Salinger's story had appeared in January of that year, who told the audience that, in his opinion, Franny was not pregnant; rather she was undergoing a spiritual crisis.

The debate about Salinger tipped over into Plath's own life: although she agreed with Maxwell, Gordon maintained that it was obvious that the character was indeed pregnant. The couple began to argue about the issue when Gordon came up to Smith for the following weekend and it soon became heated. 'It was this weekend that we made our first split,' he said. 'I can recall walking disconsolately into some bushes in front of Lawrence House; apparently Sylvia noticed it and worked it into a poem about herself at that time with the ironic title, 'Spinster'. Her reaction to our joint decision was to try to retreat into the pristine coolness of winter.'[70] In the poem, which she composed in 1956, Plath writes of a woman going for a walk with a boyfriend one April day when something odd happens: her suitor strolls into 'a rank wilderness of fern and flower', unsettling the petals. She finds the season of spring too messy and chaotic and longs for the purity and severity of winter, before constructing a ring of barbed wire around her heart so that she could never be hurt by a man again.[71]

Could Plath not see the irony of the situation? It was not she who needed a protection around her heart, but Gordon. At the end of April, Sylvia wrote Gordon a chatty letter, telling him about her busy workload and how much she needed a break. Luckily, she said, one of her friends had lent Sylvia her parents' modern house in Longmeadow, where she enjoyed an evening of cocktails, lamb chops, strawberries and coffee. The experience left her feeling relaxed and happy, she wrote. What she didn't tell Gordon was that her friend Elinor Friedman had provided the house so she could sleep with Sassoon. 'I remember that she came to my parents' house in

Longmeadow with Richard, so she could have an assignation,' says Elinor. 'She left a note on the bed afterwards which read, "Merci chérie".'[72]

Despite the fact that Plath was still writing poems for him – including 'Sonnet for a Green-eyed Sailor' – Gordon realised that Sylvia was no longer in love with him. In his unpublished memoir, *Dear Sylvia*, Gordon wrote of this time, 'April had been the cruellest month, because I realized that Sylvia's "hurricane heart" [a reference to a line in 'Sonnet for a Green-eyed Sailor'] was not in love with me, nor could I desire any longer to love this whirling dervish [. . .] Because most of my energies had been absorbed by my duties on my ship, I had felt as if I had been standing still intellectually, as if on a treadmill, unable to develop. By contrast, Sylvia was exploding with ideas like a pinwheel on the Fourth of July [. . .] Over the past two years I had been fascinated by the mind I saw developing, but I knew I was not the one to try to keep the lid on this pressure cooker.'[73]

In the few months before her graduation from Smith, Plath seemed supercharged by success. Under the tutelage of Alfred Young Fisher, she was writing five new poems a week – poems she wanted to gather together and publish in book form within the year. In April she read some of her work that she had entered for the annual Glascock Poetry Contest to an audience of 200 at Mount Holyoke College. Sylvia adored performing her poetry to a large audience, especially when she felt that they understood her sense of humour. She wrote to her mother about how much she would love to be a public speaker as she delighted in the act of making people laugh.[74] Before the reading, Sylvia together with her fellow contestants had been interviewed for the *Christian Science Monitor* and *Mademoiselle* and she had had her photograph taken with one of the competition's judges, Marianne Moore, whom she described as 'someone's fairy godmother incognito'.[75] Sylvia so admired Moore that she asked her to sign her copy of Moore's *Collected Poems*. 'Sylvia Plath's turned down corners and underlinings make me feel that there was some reason for the collecting of these poems,' wrote Moore on the flyleaf of the book. 'I am grateful to have a reader.'[76]

Almost as soon as she had returned from her overnight stay in Holyoke, Sylvia received the news that she had been awarded the Alpha award for creative writing from Smith's English department and a letter from Edward Weeks at *Atlantic Monthly* informing her that the prestigious literary magazine admired her poems 'The Dispossessed', 'Insolent storm strikes at the skull' and 'Circus in Three Rings'. 'In each case it seemed to us that there were inequalities which made the parts seem better than the whole,' wrote Weeks, who enclosed a cheque for $25. He particularly liked 'Circus in Three Rings', but he believed that it could be improved with some work. 'The second stanza is a perfect beauty, but neither the first nor the third are up to it. My impulse is to send you the enclosed check with the hope that you might take the second stanza and, under the new title of "The Tamer" or "Lion Tamer" do a revision which will win us completely [. . .] I do want to see you included in our next group of young poets which we are beginning to select for our August issue.'[77] Plath was faced with a dilemma. Should she revise the poem, and risk sounding contrived and artificial? Or should she refuse to rework it and possibly incur the wrath of a magazine that had published Edith Sitwell, Dylan Thomas and Wallace Stevens? She drank two martinis, slept for twelve hours and studied Weeks' letter once more. She hated messing with a poem once she had finished with it – a poem , she said, was like a delicate timepiece; if you altered the inner workings of its cogs the whole thing might fall apart.[78] Sylvia politely declined to go ahead with the revision, but sent in five of her other poems as alternatives. A few weeks later the *Atlantic Monthly* wrote to tell her that they had decided to print 'Circus in Three Rings' without any changes.

Compliments seemed to spring from every letter she opened. John Ciardi, one of the judges of the Glascock Prize – which Sylvia won, together with another student – wrote that Plath was a genuine 'discovery' and told her that not only would she continue to compose poetry but that she would become even more accomplished.[79] In addition to the $50 she won from the Glascock competition, in April she received $100 for a story that had won a Christopher Movement contest. The following month she heard that she was an 'honorable mention winner' in *Vogue*'s Prix de Paris, with a $25 prize and a guarantee that she would be given preferential treatment if she ever applied for a job at Condé Nast magazines. She won $40 for the Ethel Olin Corbin poetry prize, $50 as one of the winners of a Marjorie Hope Nicolson prize for her Smith thesis and $100 for an Academy of American Poets prize for a selection of poems she had submitted under the pseudonym Robin Hunter. *Mademoiselle* wrote to say that they would like to publish 'Two Lovers and a Beachcomber by the Real Sea', for which they would pay her $30. The irony was that although in 'Two Lovers and a Beachcomber by the Real Sea' Plath wrote, once more, about the possible failure of the poetic imagination, her own creative powers had never been more productive – or profitable. In a letter to her mother she announced how much she had earned from her writing that year: $470, 'plus much joy!' she added.[80] By the beginning of May she had typed up sixty poems into a book, which she named *Circus in Three Rings*, dedicated to her 'favorite Maestro', Alfred Young Fisher.[81]

Finally, on 20 May, Sylvia received the news she had been

waiting for: news that she had won a Fulbright. She telephoned her mother, in Newton-Wellesley Hospital, where she was, in Aurelia's words, undergoing 'intravenous feedings' to build up her strength for a 'subtotal gastrectomy'.[82] When a nurse answered the phone, Sylvia told her that the news would help her mother more than anything. Aurelia was duly wheeled out into the corridor to speak to her daughter. 'Such joy!' said Aurelia.[83] Sylvia told her new friend Lynne Lawner (one of the contestants of the Glascock contest, whom she had met in Holyoke) that she was walking on air. 'You are about to enter one of the most wonderful experiences of your life,' Alfred Kazin wrote to her.[84] She dashed off a letter to Richard Sassoon, who responded with what seems like congratulations issued through gritted teeth: 'I was so proud of you when I read your letter,' he said. 'I was always sure you would be very successful. Really all of that is wonderful.' However, hadn't she rather forgotten something? What about the trip they planned to New York that weekend? Had that slipped her mind? 'So you understand, my dearest, that I expect you to keep your engagement with me for Friday,' he continued. 'I shall be extremely disappointed in you if you are not able to do so [. . .] You are not a child anymore! Sometimes your actions just amaze me. Dearest don't let my anger spoil your happiness [. . .] You simply can't tell me casually that you'll come Saturday or Sunday.'[85] After posting the letter, Richard regretted his bullying tone. 'I think I wrote a very nasty letter to you,' he said. 'Oh, I am not apologizing. I mean it to be a bit nasty – no not nasty, I don't think it was, because I am never nasty to you anymore really – but I did scold you [. . .] Dearest, I love you dearly and there is not much limit to my love, but there is a rather rigid limit to the way I run my affairs [. . .] What is really rather difficult for me to believe, [is] that this sort of behaviour is quite natural to you [. . .] and I know deep down that you love me – though sometimes you act less like a woman in love than I have heretofore thought possible.'[86]

Sylvia agreed to Richard's demands and they travelled to New York together, where they saw a round of movies, including *Wuthering Heights* with Laurence Olivier, Max Ophüls' *La Ronde*, and William Wyler's *The Desperate Hours* with Humphrey Bogart. The couple also ate at the Three Crowns on East 54th Street, a Scandinavian restaurant famous for introducing smorgasbord to the wider world at the 1939 World's Fair in New York. On her return to Smith, Plath could luxuriate in the knowledge that soon she would achieve her goal of graduation. After all, as she looked back over her academic career there were times – particularly her spell in McLean, when she could neither read nor write – when she doubted that she was capable. Clarissa Roche, a friend who met Sylvia in 1957, later said that she remembers Plath striking a rather cynical attitude towards Smith. Roche 'never guessed that she had flogged herself to that summit and that acceptance into Smith was so terribly important to her,' she wrote. Fundamentally, graduation from Smith was, according to Roche, 'a huge ambition fulfilled.'[87]

On the morning of 6 June 1955 – graduation day – Sylvia woke up suffering from abdominal cramps. She asked Nancy Hunter if she had any medicine – she didn't – but her friend suggested that another girl in the house, 'Gloria Brown', might have some rum that could help settle her stomach. In Nancy's memoir she writes of the tensions that existed between Plath and 'Brownie', the 'leader of the beatnik fringe', a free-spirited bohemian.[88] As Hunter saw it, 'To Brownie, Sylvia was a misguided child who allowed an external force to condition her behavior, even when that force ran contrary to instinct. She seemed certain that Syl would be happier if she weren't constantly torn between her impulses and the set of values she had acquired from society.'[89] Plath had, as Nancy relates in her memoir, already threatened to report Brownie to the college authorities after discovering that she had smuggled rum into Lawrence House. Sylvia relented only 'after a great deal of pressure, and after learning that Brownie, not so easily taken, had amassed a store of incriminating evidence to use against her in reprisal.'[90] When she reads those words today, Brownie – real name Sylvia Scully – can hardly recognise herself. 'The idea that there were two factions in the house, with me and Sylvia as figureheads, is ridiculous,' says Sylvia, the daughter of the *Variety* columnist Frank Scully. 'Sure, I had grown up in Los Angeles, in a house where celebrities and artists were often visiting, and I was a lot more liberal in my views than Sylvia, but the portrait of Brownie is an exaggeration, a composite of several different girls. However, the rum incident was more or less as she describes it in her book, but the rum wasn't hidden under a pile of dirty clothes and I had not smuggled it into the house. A student from another house had left it there and had not returned to pick it up. Nancy did come to me to ask for some Cuban rum for Sylvia and I gave it to her. I think it helped Sylvia and afterwards she did leave me a note and a gift to say thank you.'[91]

Feeling better, Sylvia and Nancy donned their caps and gowns and descended the steps to the quadrangle. The commencement started with the hymn 'Turn Back, O Man', with its moving lines, 'Turn back, O Man, forswear thy foolish ways,/Old now is Earth, and none may count her days [. . .]' followed by the invocation and the Lord's Prayer. The commencement address given by Illinois governor and Democratic politician Adlai Stevenson, who had been nominated for president in 1952. Stevenson – whose wife divorced him in 1949 – took as the theme of his speech the idea that a woman's ideal place was confined to the home.[92] Stevenson seemed to be saying that, as Nancy writes in her memoir, the purpose of a Smith graduate was to go on and use her education to help her husband and children make wise, rational decisions. 'Men, he claimed, are under tremendous pressure to adopt the narrow view,' she wrote. 'We would help them to resist it [. . .]' Plath enjoyed the talk, interpreting it as witty and clever, while Nancy found it 'eloquent and impressive' even though it 'seemed to hurl us back to the satellite role we had escaped for four years'.[93]

Sylvia, however, was enjoying herself too much to care about the underlying sexual politics of the speech. Alfred Kazin waved to her as she returned from collecting her degree – she was one of only four *summa cum laude* graduates that year. Later she told her mother, who had travelled to Northampton on a mattress in the back of a friend's station wagon, 'My cup runneth over.'[94] She would have liked Warren and Olive Higgins Prouty to have been there, but previous engagements prevented their attendance. A few weeks before the ceremony, Prouty had written to her: 'Dr Lindemann always said that you would recover from your illness anyway – in whatever surrounding you were but you'd never have become so warm and alive to me without the scholarship award and the small help I could contribute during your illness. Please keep warm and alive.'[95]

Gordon too would have liked to have been there to see her graduate, but he was on duty on his ship. A couple of days before the ceremony he wrote her a poignant goodbye letter: 'I know no better poet living. And although I am not there to see you pass down that long academic aisle, I bequeath to you my happy ghost who will step out of your magic mirror and smile at you as you pass. As Henry James said at the end of a novel, "We shall never be again as we were," and to that I add "Thank God". My most grievous fault, as I see it now, was confusing life and art. By associating you and me in a crippling Jamesian situation, I helped to paralyze myself. Damn my allusive mind! [. . .] From you I learned the most. I have found a language, a way of looking at life, a beauty in the terrible paradoxes [. . .] I have taken all you had to give – and you gave more than anyone.'[96]

Richard had invited her to the Yale prom, but Sylvia had already promised to serve as an 'honorable maid' at the wedding of her childhood friend Ruth Freeman on 11 June at St John's Episcopal Church in Winthrop. Lynne Lawner tried to tempt her down to Cape Cod for a few days' holiday, but again she had to refuse: she had to look after her mother, who would need constant care after her stomach operation. Duty, at least for the time being, would have to come before pleasure. Yet at home in Wellesley, she enjoyed playing the role of housewife. She did the laundry, cooked, cleaned, weeded around the trees and flower-beds, dyed the rug in the porch, and went out and bought two cans of enamel paint and painted various items of furniture. Aurelia seemed to be improving, and she received her visitors while resting on a chaise longue in the back yard. In her spare time Sylvia read back issues of the *Saturday Evening Post* – which paid $1,000 for a single story – continued to see Gordon, with whom she played tennis and went swimming, and picnicked with her friend George Gebauer, whom she described as the complete opposite in temperament to her: with his scientific mind he just couldn't understand Sylvia's enthusiasm for the everyday. She could never be bored, she told her brother, because she had so many projects that she wanted to complete; in fact, a whole lifetime would not be long enough for her. A future partner would have to be able to experience a range of simple pleasures such as enjoying the taste of a milkshake or an afternoon spent messing about in a rowing boat.[97]

While at home, Sylvia neglected writing to Sassoon, a temporary abandonment that Richard felt keenly: he even questioned the postman who delivered letters to his apartment in New Haven about whether there had been a problem with the mail. But then, at the end of June, he received a letter sprinkled with her perfume. 'Seriously, dearest, I cannot tell you – and it would be almost indecent to – how terribly worried I was about you,' wrote Richard, who after graduating took a job as a salesman for a local heating company. 'I was a bit – oh well, very if you would care to know – unhappy that you did not write – but terribly afraid lest something had happened to you.'[98] She invited him to her house for the July Fourth weekend, where Sylvia cooked him a delicious meal of lobster salad, broiled chicken, date nut bars, tollhouse cookies, steak and peach angel pie. Although Richard thought that he had done his best to come across as a 'being of charming young innocence',[99] and Sylvia assumed her mother had cast to one side her former doubts about his suitability to one side, Aurelia still had a problem with Sassoon. And, it seems, during the summer of 1955, that Sylvia had a problem with him too.

Sylvia couldn't help comparing Sassoon to a new man who had entered her life: Peter Davison, whom she had met in January. Davison – then working as an editor at the publishing house Harcourt, Brace – had travelled up to Smith and had called on Alfred Kazin, who informed him of Plath's considerable talents. Davison, a handsome, well-educated young man – the son of Edward Davison, a Scottish poet who had immigrated to America in 1925 and who was a friend of Robert Frost's – visited Sylvia while in hospital, where she was suffering from sinusitis, and, after a chat, informed her that he would like to be the first publisher to read her novel if she ever wrote one. Sylvia and Peter kept in touch and, in June, when she heard that he had taken a job as the assistant to the director of Harvard University Press, Plath flirted with the idea of one day marrying such a man, a Harvard graduate who had spent a year in Cambridge on a Fulbright.

Now that her mother was in Eastham, convalescing, Sylvia had the house in Wellesley to herself. From there, on 19 July, she wrote to her mother about her forthcoming date with Peter. She particularly adored the sound of his 'Britishy' voice, she said.[100] Perhaps it was Davison who was responsible for the uncertainty Sylvia now felt towards Sassoon. From New Haven, Richard, who had quit his job with the heating company, kept writing to her, calling her, but there was no response. He surmised that she was unhappy because in a couple of months she would be sailing for Europe and leaving him behind. 'You must not be sad, Sylvia,' he wrote on 1 August, 'you will have a delightful time in England – witty and intelligent people, friends you will make easily, writing circles, theatre in London, very good music performances.'[101] It was likely that he would take up a place to study at the Sorbonne in Paris – if so, it would be relatively easy for the couple to continue seeing one another – and she should not worry; she would only have to choose, he said, between him and Mephistopheles.

It's more likely that the real source of Sylvia's unhappiness was guilt. Indeed, she had, at this moment at least, made a choice, but the decision had not been between Sassoon and the devil, but between Sassoon and Peter Davison. According to Davison, the couple slept together after their first night out on 23 July and again on each of the ten occasions when they saw one another after that. On their first night, at Peter's apartment in Cambridge, Sylvia was wearing a white dress and he later recalled that her hair had been bleached blonde by the sun. 'She asked more and more questions, she seemed strangely elevated, and she hardly waited to be asked to slip into my new bed,' he said.[102] When Gordon asked whether he could see her at some point over the weekend of 6 August, she told him that he could not: an editor whom she had met through Alfred Kazin wanted to take her to Martha's Vineyard to meet an important agent. Again, the truth was rather different: although the agent did exist, he lived in New York City and the editor was her new lover, Peter Davison. At the Vineyard, where the couple stayed at the Barn House, a community of artists, writers and bohemians, Plath met the Irish poet and novelist Padraic Colum, a German baron and baroness who hosted a champagne party in the barn, the president of Rutgers University, with whom she did the dishes one day, and an English professor at Williams College, who played Elizabethan folk songs on the recorder.

Plath's deepening relationship with Davison prompted her to write an excoriating letter to Sassoon. It's not known exactly what Sylvia wrote to him – as Richard told me, 'Sylvia and I did correspond a lot and, long ago, visiting my parent's house, I looked in the attic in a trunk where I kept her letters and they were not there, which is a total mystery'[103] – but the letter obviously left him upset and disturbed. By the content and tone of Sassoon's response the same day, it seems most likely that she wanted to bring her relationship with Richard to a close. 'I only hope you know what you do, and what you are about to do,' he said. 'I am sorry you have put me in such a position that I cannot even try to tell you [. . .] It is possible that you strangle as decent, as honest and as faithful a heart as will ever have beat so purely and profoundly for you alone [. . .] Even as this sorrow will last, you have always the concern and the blessing of Your devoted, Richard.'[104]

The next day, Richard wrote again. Sylvia was obviously upset and he tried to lighten the mood, asking her to forgive him for the seriousness of his last letter. Plath blamed her low spirits on the worsening relations at home with her mother. 'I am very sorry there is so much hatred and frustration in your home,' said Richard.[105] Sassoon advised her to try to patch things up with Aurelia, at least superficially – 'Believe me, it is no good to leave a home with a foul taste in the air,' he said.[106] Sylvia also blamed herself for what she saw as a lack of achievement. Despite starting out with such good intentions – looking after her mother, reading, writing, preparing for Cambridge – the summer had been, as she admitted to Gordon, a long stretch of undisciplined hedonism. Apart from the sale of 'Lament' – a villanelle that proved to be the first of her bee poems – to the *New Orleans Poetry Journal* for the sum of $7.60, she had not managed to sell either 'Platinum Summer' (a story she sent off to *Collier's*) or 'Tea with Olive Higgins Prouty', a piece of light reportage that had been rejected by the *Reader's Digest*. She was frustrated by the constant press mentions of poet Adrienne Rich, the twenty-six-year-old poet who had won a Yale Younger Poets Award and a Guggenheim Fellowship and who by 1955 had already published two volumes of poetry. Sylvia began to doubt her own abilities. On her return from Martha's Vineyard she wrote a letter to Gordon complaining about her general ignorance: she knew nothing about history, politics, art and music and she was appalled by the narrowness of her conversation. She would also have to curb her habit of being indiscriminately gushing about everything, she said. In a photograph that was taken at the Vineyard, in which Sylvia sits next to Peter Davison, Roger Baldwin and Eleanor Besse, Plath looks straight to camera, a slash of a smile across her face. In contrast to the others in the picture, who look thoughtful, studied, engaged, there is a look of panic on Plath's face, as though she quickly decided to don a mask of glee in order to disguise the terror beneath.

Davison witnessed both Plath's seemingly insatiable appetite for knowledge and her sense of alienation from herself. 'I felt as though I were being cross-examined, drained, eaten,' he wrote in *Half Remembered*. Yet, at the same time, when Sylvia started to tell him a little about her past, 'it was as though she were describing a stranger to herself, a highly trained circus horse.'[107] The only moment he felt that he encountered any authentic emotion during their brief relationship was the time when

Sylvia told him of her breakdown and suicide attempt. It was, he said, 'a simpler, less poised and more touching story' than what she would later relate in *The Bell Jar*.[108] After dinner at Elmwood Road, on 23 August, Sylvia took Peter out for a walk and told him, in a cold and distant voice, that she did not want to continue the relationship. 'She was on the lookout for a man whose strength and gifts would anchor her instability, and I was at best a leaky life preserver,' he said.[109]

Years later, Davison – who went on to marry Jane Truslow, Sylvia's classmate at Smith, and who was the American editor responsible for commissioning *Bitter Fame*, the 1989 biography of Plath written by Anne Stevenson – wrote a poem about Plath called 'The Heroine', which includes the lines:

> I've seen her love letters – those she wrote
> to other men while she was using me –
> and her hate letters – those she wrote
> to me while she was using them[110]

Sylvia spent the rest of the summer preparing herself for her new life in England. Margaret Cantor took her on a shopping spree to buy a new set of luggage from a wholesaler's that was selling it at half price. She threw herself enthusiastically into a series of private dance lessons that her mother had bought her as an advance birthday present at the Fred Astaire studios in Boston; she particularly enjoyed learning the tango, she said. She endured typhoid and tetanus vaccinations – which the American authorities recommended to citizens travelling abroad.

At the end of August she travelled to Washington D.C. to see her college friend Sue Weller; Sylvia said she loved the city's wide leafy streets and its grand neoclassical buildings. Sue served as a guide, showing Sylvia the Washington Monument, the National Gallery, the eighteenth-century gardens at Mount

Vernon (the plantation home of America's first president on the banks of the Potomac River), and the Lincoln Memorial, which she described as almost a holy experience – 'such a colossus [. . .]' she wrote to her mother. She said she felt a sense of awe as she gazed up at the enormous structure.[111] While in the city, Sylvia also saw David Lean's *Summertime*, starring Katharine Hepburn and set in Venice, a film that made her desperate to visit Italy. From Washington Sylvia took a train to Baltimore and met Gordon, who drove her home to Wellesley. At the end of August, she wrote him a heartfelt letter that expressed both her sense of excitement at the prospects of starting a new life and her fears and vulnerabilities. She told him that she couldn't quite describe the range of odd feelings that she was currently experiencing. It was, she said, the first time in her life when she was forced to turn her back on the comforts and routine of home.[112] She wondered whether the transition from America to Europe would result in her growth or spell disaster. Would she feel creatively inspired or would she want to run back home to everything that was familiar?

On 11 September, Sylvia, Aurelia and Warren met with Olive Higgins Prouty, who the next day wrote to her protégée, 'It was lovely to see you on your last night [. . .] Almost as if you really belonged to me.'[113] As Prouty wrote these words, which she addressed care of the Cunard liner *Queen Elizabeth*, the novelist must have been struck by the superficial parallels that existed between the character of Charlotte Vale – the heroine of *Now, Voyager*, who goes on a European cruise after spending months in a sanatorium following a nervous breakdown – and Sylvia. In the novel, Charlotte falls in love on her journey, a love that proves to be fundamentally healing. Prouty, of course, was in the business of writing romance; it was Plath's tragedy that she expected her life to follow the patterns of the same genre.

Eleven

IN THE DEPTHS OF THE FOREST YOUR IMAGE FOLLOWS ME

Within a matter of days, Plath had initiated a shipboard romance of her own, with Carl Shakin, a twenty-one-year-old physics graduate of New York University's College of Engineering who had won a Fulbright to study at the University of Manchester. The relationship started with the taking of tea, followed by 'long bull sessions' up on deck, but then, after the two started dancing, it became more involved and intimate.[1] Sylvia knew that Shakin had been married for only eight weeks, but that did not seem to concern her. What was more important was that she was young, vibrant and desperate for every new experience that came her way. She wrote to her mother about the magnificent time she had had aboard the ship, an experience made all the more memorable by the presence of Carl. Each night there was dancing and, up on deck, she felt that she was communing with nature.[2]

When the ship docked in Cherbourg, the couple went ashore and, in her typical over-exuberant manner, Plath described this as 'the most enchanting afternoon' of her life: a scene from a Post-impressionist painting alive with turquoise and pink, people on bicycles, workers drinking wine sitting in outdoor cafés, beautiful churches, children playing with hoops and feeding goldfish, flower stalls and fountains. She felt, she told her mother, immediately at home. She did not miss the eight-lane highways and the brash commercialism of America. In France, she said, the streets were designed for young people in love, couples who always seemed to be pedalling around with flowers hanging from their bicycles.[3]

From France the ship continued to Southampton, from where the couple travelled to London, which Plath said was the most magnificent city she had ever seen. Sylvia particularly relished the richness of London theatre and in the course of a week she saw Beckett's *Waiting for Godot*, Rattigan's *Separate Tables*, and Marcel Aymé's *The Count of Clerambard*. During the day she attended lectures at Bedford College, went for picnics with Carl in Hyde Park and browsed in bookshops, and in the evenings she returned to her room at the YWCA, near the British Museum, which cost just $1.50 a night, including breakfast. One night she was invited to a reception at the American ambassador's residence in Regent's Park, a mansion once owned by Barbara Hutton; and, although she enjoyed the cocktails and hors d'oeuvres, she was frustrated to learn at the end of the evening that some of her fellow guests, to whom she had not been introduced, had included influential figures such as the poet Stephen Spender, the novelist C. P. Snow, and John Lehmann, the influential editor of the *London Magazine*. After Carl left London for Manchester Sylvia felt a little lonely, but she knew it would be only a matter of time before she met other men, *British* men.

On 1 October she travelled to Cambridge on an early train and fell immediately in love with the city. On arrival, one of her housemates at Whitstead, an all-female house on Barton Road, took her on a walking tour of the various colleges with their secret courtyards, King's College Chapel with its awe-inspiring stained-glass windows, and the river Cam, with its seemingly endless procession of punts, swans and ducks. 'Situated on the edge of the Fens, Cambridge has a flat landscape which, when the mists rise at twilight, takes on the muted green and silver-gray tones of a Corot painting,' she wrote in an article for the *Christian Science Monitor*.[4] Her letters to Aurelia and to her friends in America overflow with enthusiasm and a keen sense of promise; she was creating herself anew. As she told Olive Higgins Prouty, she spent the first term trying out different possibilities of living from which she could select the most successful or promising aspects; those facets that did not work in her favour she could then simply confine to the refuse pile of past experience.

She quickly set herself the task of making a home of her room, an attic space that overlooked rooftops, chimneypots, gardens and sycamore trees on which gathered a parliament of enormous rooks, birds which eyed people with a strange intensity and which, she joked, surely had the capacity to eat small children after dark.[5] The room was equipped with a gas fireplace – which demanded a regular feeding of shillings in order to warm up the freezing air that Sylvia said blew off the Russian steppes – and a gas ring that she could use to heat water for tea or coffee. After a little experimentation, Sylvia discovered that she could actually serve a whole dinner using her limited cooking facilities – sherry and hors d'oeuvres, salad and steak, followed by fruit compote, wine, cheese and crackers. She did not have a refrigerator but that hardly mattered – for most of the year, the room was so cold she could keep butter and milk in it without spoiling. And, although the room was a little bare and impersonal at first, after Sylvia had bought a few choice items – a black-and-white earthenware tea service from Holland, three woven rush mats, a vase (not Lucie Rie, but a cheaper imitation), a scattering of postcards she had picked up from various galleries and a mass of art books, which she could now afford with her generous book allowance – it soon seemed a little more like home.

Each day, wearing the obligatory black gown, she would cycle to and from college. Fellow Whitstead resident Jane Baltzell Kopp remembers the distinctive way Sylvia rode her bicycle – 'She was "goal oriented", to say the least, and would pedal vehemently, head and shoulders straining forward, as though pure will power rather than her legs propelled her. She rode, say, like a passionate little girl.'[6]

Her programme of lectures and tutorials included the history of tragedy, practical criticism (she felt on shaky ground when trying to date poems to a specific period of English literature), the English Moralists, the history of literary criticism (with F. R. Leavis, whom she described as looking like a 'bandy-legged leprechaun',[7] and French. One of her lecturers, Dorothea Krook, in an essay she wrote in 1974, recalled seeing Plath for the first time. It was at the beginning of that Michaelmas term of 1955 and Krook had just walked into the Mill Lane lecture room. Standing at the front of the room, Krook assessed the students; as she looked around she met the gaze of one girl who stood out from the rest. 'I was struck by the concentrated intensity of her scrutiny, which gave her face an ugly, almost coarse, expression, accentuated by the extreme redness of her heavily painted mouth and its downward curve at the corners,' said Krook, who would later become Plath's supervisor. 'I distinctly remember wondering whether she was Jewish. This was a thought that could not have occurred to me more than half a dozen times in all my thirteen years at Cambridge; one somehow never wondered whether people were or were not Jewish, unless presumably the Jewish marks were especially prominent . . . I have remembered it often since, with the strangest emotions, as more and more has come to be known about her passionate feelings for Jews and her sense of belonging with them.'[8]

A number of Plath's 'doubles', friends such as Ann Davidow, Janet Salter and Elinor Friedman, were Jewish and, in her imagination, she identified with the group. 'Everybody today seems so rootless,' Plath had told Friedman. 'I know I do. Only the Jews seem to be part of something, to belong to something definite and rooted. I'd like to have that feeling. Maybe I'll marry one someday and give birth at a plow in Israel.'[9] Janet Salter remembers that 'if we were ever in a situation where we didn't want people to know we were referring to ourselves we would use biblical names – I would call myself Ruth, and Sylvia liked to use Esther': the Jewish queen who saved her people from annihilation and the name she would give to the heroine of *The Bell Jar*.[10]

Plath's imaginative empathy with Jews can be traced back to her adolescence, when, in her history class at Wellesley High, she was shown a series of graphic images from the German concentration camps. According to the recollections of one classmate, their history teacher Raymond Chapman had wanted to shock his students out of what he regarded as a complacent sensibility and so he 'had photographic blow-ups made of the inmates of Bergen-Belsen and Buchenwald, Dachau and Auschwitz. These tragic, skeletal inmates looking out from their packed bunk beds in their ragged striped pyjamas stared down upon our crisply shampooed heads, giving us the shudders.'[11] This identification found expression in 'The Perfect Set Up', published in *Seventeen* in October 1952 and described by Aurelia as a story about 'religious discrimination (WASP withdrawal from a Jewish neighbor)'.[12] At the end of 1955, Plath wrote to her mother, 'I am close to the Jewish beliefs in many ways,'[13] and later, in poems such as 'Daddy' and 'Lady Lazarus', Plath would use the imagery of the Holocaust to articulate her sense of alienation, abjection and victimhood, an artistic decision that many critics have seen as a metaphoric step too far. The dilemma that still faces many readers of her poetry was outlined by George Steiner. While claiming that 'Daddy' was 'the 'Guernica' of modern poetry', he said that Plath's use of the Holocaust left him feeling decidedly uneasy. 'Does any writer, does any human being other than an actual survivor, have the right to put on this death-rig?' he asked.[14] In a reading prepared for BBC radio, Plath said that 'Daddy' was about a girl with an Electra complex. The girl's father – like Otto Plath – had died at a time when she considered him to be something of a God. Yet the father figure had also been a Nazi and her mother had come from a Jewish family. The couple's daughter has to somehow deal with these two paradoxical aspects of her parents' personalities.[15]

While Plath wrestled with personal allegories and psychological exorcisms of her own, Dorothea Krook noted that for the most part, Sylvia presented herself as an archetypal all-American girl. Krook, whom Plath would later call a 'genius saint',[16] remembered that while at Cambridge, Sylvia was immaculate, her clothes were 'girlish' and her hair always held back in place by a bandeau on the crown of her head. 'This charming American neatness and freshness is what I chiefly recall about her physical person, even more than her beauty [. . .]' she said. 'Eager, and mobile, tranquil and serene, all at once: I never saw her face express anything else in the many long supervision hours we spent together. I did not think of her as one of my most "brilliant" pupils [. . .] I thought of her rather as one of the most deeply, moving, responsive pupils I had ever had. I felt the things I said, we said, her authors said, mattered to her in an intimate way, answering to intense personal needs, reaching to depths of her spirit to which I had no direct access.'[17]

During Sylvia's two-year's in Cambridge, Krook never again saw that look of concentrated intensity cross her pupil's face. It was only much later, in February 1963, when Krook opened the pages of the *Observer* and saw the photograph that accompanied a report of Plath's death, that she caught a glimpse of that strange expression, 'in the wildly, feverishly staring eyes of that dreadful unfamiliar face, the desperate-defiant look in the eye intensified by the distaff of unkempt hair hanging about her shoulders.'[18]

Only a few days after the start of the new term, Sylvia came down with one of her dreaded sinus infections. She checked herself into the Newnham 'hospital' – in effect a sick bay with three beds – and was astonished by the treatment she received. Instead of the cocaine sprays, penicillin and sleeping pills that she was used to in America, she was given an aspirin; when she asked for Kleenex the nurse said she could tear up an old sheet for her. When she was served an unappetising mass of white fish paste and lukewarm mashed potato followed by a dollop of custard, she decided she'd had enough and checked herself out, preferring to cycle through the streets of Cambridge to audition for the Amateur Dramatic Club (ADC). She chose one of Rosalind's speeches from *As You Like It* and a section from Tennessee William's *Camino Real* and, to her surprise and delight, was accepted. Almost immediately she was cast as a 'mad poetess'[19] in *Three Hours after Marriage*, an eighteenth-century comedy written by Gay, Pope and Arbuthnot, which was staged as one of three one-act 'nursery' productions highlighting the society's new talent in mid-October. Plath loved performing in front of an audience – Sylvia described her character, of Phoebe Clinkett, as a loquacious woman with ridiculous aspirations to write poetry and plays.[20] The next month she auditioned for a part in Ben Jonson's *Bartholomew Fair* – which starred Daniel Massey – but she was turned down for a major role. Although the rejection bruised her ego, logically she knew it was for the best as she would now have time to concentrate on her writing. 'I would rather be a mediocre writer than a bad actress,' she said.[21] At the last minute she was given the role of Dame Alice – 'a rather screaming bawdy woman who gets into a fight' and who has only five lines in the whole play.[22] Although she had enjoyed her time with the ADC, she had to admit that she was no Sara Bernhardt.

There were, however, some occasions when people felt like laughing at, rather than with, Sylvia. 'I remember one evening, when we were looking for a restaurant in Cambridge, Sylvia went up to a policemen and asked him, in her Massachusetts accent, if he knew anywhere "really picturesque and collegiate" where we could eat,' remembers Jane Baltzell. 'My first impression of her was that she was instantly recognizable as an American, as indeed I was. But, whereas some of us were somewhat circumspect about advertising ourselves as American, she was completely uninhibited. I was, I must admit, a little embarrassed about her sometimes. She was totally unaware of how her American behaviour and talk seemed rather comic to the British.'[23] Jane can still picture the full set of white and gold Samsonite luggage that accompanied Plath whenever she travelled down to London. 'On weekends when she would be glimpsed surrounded by all of this on Cambridge or London station platforms (its creamy whiteness made all the more conspicuous by the sooty backdrops of British Railways), she was the inspiration of much amazement, incredulity, and humor among the British,' she later wrote.[24] On another occasion, one breakfast time at Whitstead, a fellow student, a high-born South African who looked like Virginia Woolf, turned to Plath and said, '*Must* you cut up your eggs like that?' All the other girls looked at Sylvia's plate and saw a complex array of fried eggs cut up into rhomboids, squares and trapezoids; they realised that Plath had been using both her knife and fork to slice into them, making a great deal of noise as she did so. Sylvia remained calm and cool as she turned to the South African girl and replied, 'Yes, I'm afraid I really must. What do you do with your eggs? SWALLOW THEM WHOLE?'[25]

During that first term at Cambridge Sylvia had to prove to herself – and to the world – that she was attractive and she did everything in her power to notch up as many potential suitors as possible. It wasn't difficult as the ratio of men to women was ten to one. But, as was often Sylvia's style, once she knew that she had secured the attentions of a man she felt she had no choice but to let him go; once the chase was over, she often felt bored. One of her closest companions at this time was nineteen-year-old Mallory Wober, a tall, dark-haired Jewish boy who was reading natural sciences at King's College. She had met him at a Labour Party dance in October 1955; after that initial meeting, Wober had written her a note inviting her to take tea in his rooms. Within days, the two were inseparable. 'There was something in the fibre of her personality that told me she was a genius,' he says. 'And other people could feel it too. I remember one day, towards the end of October, I invited her to a concert in the dining hall of King's College organized by the musical society. We were late and crept in – we were careful to be silent – but at the moment when Sylvia walked into the room everyone turned around to look at her. I was astonished and I'm convinced it was because people could sense the strength of her personality.'[26]

When Plath came down with flu in December Mallory wheeled a harmonium on a trolley from Magdalene Bridge to Whitstead on the Barton Road and carried it up to her room, where he proceeded to play a selection of pieces by Beethoven, Bach and Scarlatti. 'On another occasion I got something like ticker-tape and wrote a series of messages for her. I carefully cut open some walnuts, took out the nuts, inserted the messages and glued the nuts together again,' he says. Sylvia appreciated Mallory's kind and thoughtful gestures, and in letters to her friend Elinor Friedman she described him as a character she had constructed herself – a cross between Hercules and Dmitri Karamazov. Compared to some of her other boyfriends he was, she said, a real man; she loved the fact that while he was as strong as a lion he possessed a soft, gentle nature. For his part, it was obvious he adored her. 'I was only in my second year so I had a lot to look up to and be in awe of – she was a genius and I was just an ordinary guy,' he says. 'She was all out to conquer Cambridge and she did in short order. She was like a bloody meteor going off on its own course.'[27]

Other men she socialised with included David Buck, an English student at Christ's College who had a large part in the ADC production of *Bartholomew Fair*; John Lythgoe, who was studying natural sciences at Trinity College; and Nat LaMar, who had known Warren at Exeter and who was on a Henry fellowship and studying at Pembroke College. In a letter to her mother, Sylvia described LaMar as an extroverted, artistic character, a young black man who was, in terms of personality, remarkably similar to herself, being ebullient, highly expressive but perhaps a little too trusting.[28] Plath admired the fact that he was already a published author – his story 'Creole Love Song' had appeared in the *Atlantic Monthly* in June 1955 – and she regarded him as a kind of psychic brother, a view endorsed by LaMar. 'Our relationship was purely platonic – we genuinely liked each other and we had quite a lot in common as we had both travelled down parallel paths,' he says. 'She had studied under Kazin at Smith, while I had had Archibald MacLeish at Harvard. She did discuss her past difficulties quite openly, but she talked about the subject with a certain distance, as if she were removed from it. I remember one day at tea she told me about what had happened in the past, and she talked about the events with a certain kind of allure. She said it was something that she felt she had to do, something she felt she had to go through. I remember her as like a hummingbird going from person to person – she felt compelled to get to know as many people as she could, and her neck was on a kind of swivel all the time. It was as if, "Who is the next person coming into this room – I must talk to them in case they are worth knowing."'[29]

In the first term, Sylvia also saw something of Dick Wertz, Richard Sassoon's former roommate at Yale who was reading theology at Westminster College, Cambridge. As they talked about Sassoon, who had won a place at the Sorbonne, Sylvia realised just how much she missed him. The boys at Cambridge, although equal in age, just could not measure up to Richard and in November she started writing long, elaborate letters to him, some of which she did not send. Through these letters, Plath was able to give Sassoon an insight into her life as seen through the prism of her poetic imagination. Without naming Mallory she described him as a 'rugged jewish hercules hewn fresh from the himalayas' ready to be shaped by the influence of a female pygmalion.[30] Plath alluded to Wober as a product of her own making, a character that she had created from the rich gloop of her imagination. In contrast, as she writes in the same letter, 'In the beginning was the word and the word was sassoon [. . .]'[31]

On 4 December – a day that Plath marked with a star in her 1955 Heffers diary – Sassoon himself materialised in the flesh when, on a visit over to England, he stopped by to see her and Dick Wertz in Cambridge. In many respects, Plath preferred the platonic ideal – the idea of something or someone – to the less-than-perfect reality, a view that prompted her to write a letter to Elinor Friedman in which she compared him to Gregor Samsa's metamorphosis into an insect in Kafka's famous tale.

Yet so contradictory were her impulses that, a week later, Sylvia wrote another letter, in which she pleaded for his support to help guide her through a psychological crisis. She outlined how she carried with her an enormous sorrow, 'with as many facets as a fly's eye, and I must give birth to this monstrosity before I am light again.' She wrote that she must stop herself from identifying too closely with the seasons, 'because this English winter will be the death of me.' Why couldn't she enjoy the present moment, she asked herself, without destroying it through over analysis? What did she want? Everything or nothing? She felt, she said, as though she were in the process of constructing an extremely fragile bridge across a number of gravestones while a giant slept below her. Would he, she asked, help her build this beautiful bridge?[32]

Sylvia explained her problems to Olive Higgins Prouty in more straightforward terms in a letter she wrote on 13 December. Her biggest problem, she told Prouty, whom she viewed as a kind of second mother, was the realisation that she could not be perfect. Now that she occupied an arena that did not monitor success by the endowment of various prizes she felt unsure of her own abilities. The challenge of being an adult, she wrote, was to try and accept the possibility, indeed the inevitability, of tragedy and loss. It was a mistake to try and flee pain by taking refuge in fantasy and self-delusion. Facing difficult situations took courage, she said, something she suspected she did not possess.[33]

After term ended, Plath planned to catch up on her reading and get back into some sort of writing routine. She hoped to be able to set aside a couple of hours each day and treat it as a kind of discipline, like doing scales on the piano. Some of her peers had been accepted by the Cambridge literary magazine *Chequer*, which had been accepted, but she was pessimistic about her general prospects. Yet she still enjoyed the physicality of poetry, especially the act of reading it aloud, which she often did with Mallory. She realised that she would never be happy as an academic, spending time doing research on some obscure aspect of English literature in order to gain a doctorate. She realised that, fundamentally, she would always be more interested in people rather than books.[34]

On 12 December, Plath experienced one of those intense moments that would stay branded on her consciousness for years. She had made a date with Dick Wertz to go riding in Cambridge. Since this was her first time, the horse selected for her, Sam, had a reputation for being gentle, and for the first few minutes he proved to be so. However, when the horse approached a busy crossroads he bolted and galloped to the other side of the road. At the same moment, Sylvia's foot slipped out of the right stirrup and she had to hold on to the horse's neck to keep her from being thrown to the ground. As the horse ran, cars came to a swift halt and pedestrians had to duck out of the way for fear of being injured. The experience was so intense, so thrilling, it reminded her of the time when she had hurtled down the ski slope at Mount Pisgah at top speed and had broken her fibula.[35] The horse-riding incident would inspire her 1958 poem 'Whiteness I Remember' – 'Whiteness being what I remember/About Sam: whiteness and the great run/He gave me.'[36] It was, she said, a 'hard' subject for her as horses were alien to her, 'yet the daredevil change in Sam and my hanging on God knows how is a kind of revelation: it worked well.'[37] The nerve-wracking experience would also inform her October 1962 poem 'Ariel', which also details another horseride: 'And I/Am the arrow,/The dew that flies/Suicidal [. . .]'[38]

On 17 December she went with her friend John Lythgoe to a family wedding in a fourteenth-century church in Grantchester. From there, John and Sylvia took the train down to London; during her three-day visit Plath saw the musical *Salad Days* at the Vaudeville, and visited Mallory at his family home in Golders Green. On 20 December she set off on what was supposed to be a perfect vacation – a trip to Paris to see Sassoon. Plath had paid $25 for the round trip by air, but when she arrived at the air terminal she learned that bad weather had grounded all planes. After a three-hour wait she was told that the company would bus the passengers to the coast, where there would be a ferry waiting for them. Luckily, amid all the chaos, Plath found a friendly face to talk to – Jane Baltzell, who was travelling to Italy via Paris. The Channel crossing was so rough that the deck, where the two young women huddled together under a Burberry raincoat, was awash with vomit. By the time they arrived in Paris it was almost eleven at night – nearly twelve hours later than expected – and as Jane had nowhere to stay it was natural for Sylvia to offer to share her room. After checking in at the Hôtel des Deux Continents on rue Jacob, Sylvia felt so excited to be in Paris – and within walking distance of Richard Sassoon's apartment – that she wanted to explore the city. Jane was so exhausted that she fell into bed, agreeing to let Sylvia in when she knocked on the door. Unfortunately, Jane was so tired from the journey that she did not hear Sylvia – who had enjoyed a late meal with Richard – return. Despite banging on the door, and enlisting the help of the hotel manager, it was no use – Jane was not only dead to the world but had also left the key in the lock, preventing anyone from opening it from the outside. Plath had no choice but to share a bed with two 'vivacious' girls from Switzerland. In the morning, Sylvia was in one of her rages. 'Jane, how could you?' she shouted when she confronted her the next morning.

'Rarely have I felt more hopelessly embarrassed,' wrote

Jane. 'My fault was the more grievous, of course, in that she had been doing me a kindness. At the same time, I found the peculiar intensity of her anger inappropriate. I had not, after all, locked her out on purpose; but she was angry just as though I had. She somehow conveyed as much, alluding to her doppelganger theory [. . .] I felt certain nightmare sensations that I had not felt since childhood.'[39] The two young women tried to patch things up, and Jane agreed she would go and look for another hotel; she would return later, she said, to collect her bags. 'When I returned to the hotel, I opened the door to find Sylvia and Richard in bed,' she says. 'I remember him as being small and dark, a man who could have been French. I must say I did think it was odd that Sylvia seemed so impressed by him. I think Sylvia must have been imagining most of what she saw in him.'[40] Although the couple were not in the middle of making love, Jane felt struck by embarrassment – 'my timing seemed [. . .] to compound my offense of the night before,' she said. 'With minimal farewells I collected my belongings and fled.'[41]

Sylvia and Richard enjoyed an idyllic time in Paris. He was, Sylvia told her mother, a godsend. He not only showed her the tourist sights of the city – including the Louvre (where they saw the works of El Greco, *The Winged Victory of Samothrace*, and da Vinci's *Virgin of the Rocks*), the gardens of the Tuileries, the Champs Élysées, the Arc de Triomphe, Sainte-Chapelle and Montmartre – but also its hidden underbelly: she relished the sight of the prostitutes who clustered around the Place Pigalle. Evenings were taken up with theatre – they saw a French translation of Emlyn Williams' play *Le Monsieur qui attend*, and *Jeanne d'Arc* by Charles Péguy at the Comédie Française – eating delicious food and drinking wine. She noticed that the city seemed populated by stylish young people, in contrast to those she had seen in London who, to her eyes, seemed rather dowdy. On Christmas morning Richard took her to Notre Dame, where they sat in the darkened interior facing the altar to the Virgin and Child, ablaze with flowers, and listened to the organ fill the vast space, a sound that Plath likened to the voice of God.

On New Year's Eve the couple boarded the night train to Nice. Plath was a self-confessed sun worshipper and could not wait to see the bright skies of the south of France and the glistening Mediterranean. In her journal she described the joy she felt after leaving Cambridge and London behind. She wouldn't miss England's saturated ground, biting winds, leaden skies and frost-bitten mornings.[42] As the train tore south Sylvia stared out into the night and listened to the sound of the wheels, a sound which she compared to a nihilistic nursery rhyme which continually repeated the line, 'god is dead, god is dead.'[43] Finally, by the time the train reached the Côte d'Azur, she saw what she had been waiting for: 'the red sun rising like the eye of God out of a screaming blue sea.'[44] The couple took breakfast in the dining car as Sylvia became increasingly entranced by the scenes that flashed by: pastel-coloured villas, palm trees, curved inlets, green hills and the forever-present Mediterranean. In Nice they rented a cheap room with a balcony that looked out towards the Alpes-Maritimes, which they could see in the distance, mountains that Sylvia compared to the breasts of Aphrodite. They rented a Lambretta which they used to explore Beaulieu, Villefranche, Menton, Cap Ferrat and Monaco, where Sylvia lost the equivalent of $3 in the casino. From there, they travelled on to the Matisse Chapel, which Sylvia had wanted to visit for years. When they arrived at the church – which Sylvia described in a letter home as being a small white building with a blue roof that glinted in the sunlight[45] – they discovered that it was closed (it was, they learned, open to the public only two days a week). A local informed Sylvia that each day a number of wealthy people turned up; despite offering substantial amounts money they too were often refused admission.[46] Sylvia's spirits suddenly plummeted and she felt, she said, 'like Alice outside the garden'.[47] In a letter to her mother she described walking around the outside of the building, staring through the barred gate and, as she returned to the front she started to cry. With tears running down her cheeks, she heard a voice that said, '*Ne pleurez plus, entrez*,' and the mother superior gestured for her to enter. For Sylvia, the experience – the sight of the three sets of stained-glass windows (yellow for the sun, green for the land, blue for the sea) took on near-mystical proportions and, on her return to Cambridge in January 1956, she wrote a twenty-five-page story, 'The Matisse Chapel', which she sent off to the *New Yorker*. In the story she does not bother to change Richard's name, while she casts herself as Sally – a girl who has grown up in New England and is travelling in Europe for the first time, courtesy of a Fulbright Fellowship. If she ever felt in the grip of a black mood, Sally – who had been a student in Smith – would open her art book and dream about visiting the Matisse Chapel. The visit results in a conflict between the two lovers, and Sally withdraws her hand from Richard's arm.

Six years later, Richard Sassoon published a companion piece to 'The Matisse Chapel' titled 'In the year of Love and unto Death, the fourth – an Elegy on the Muse'. Talking about Plath for the first time, he told me, 'You will find therein a story by me that does obviously reflect on my relationship with Sylvia. Although the story is fictional and more of a self-contemplation than a realistic tale, your reading of it may offer some clues of use to you. As I read it the account of the visit to the Matisse chapel may be pretty biographical.'[48] In another email he writes that the story, 'really did record, much more than anything present now in my brain or feeling, some actual facts and my memory and imagination of our relationship as they arose for me when I was writing it.'[49] The story, which runs to twenty-one pages, opens with the line, 'So that no matter what happens, I shall always, very simply, love you,' words taken from a letter written to him from a girlfriend. She is never named, but it is obvious that it is Sylvia: 'She stands, her weight a little more on one foot than the other, by habit perhaps, being just barely taller than I, her head thrown slightly back so that her throat is swollen out like a pigeon breast, vulnerable. The sun golds her as a chosen object, its midday brilliance gloating on the straw-blond luxuriance of her hair, its warmth and light burnishing what is bare of her shoulders in the wide-necked, loose-clinging dress.'[50] In the story he writes tenderly of their train journey down from Paris to Nice and relates a conversation they had in their shared third-class compartment.

> 'Do you pursue me,' she asked. 'Or do I pursue you?'
>
> 'We pursue each other [. . .] we always shall.'
>
> 'Is it,' she teased, ruffling gently my hair, 'a vicious circle?'
>
> 'Somewhere beyond the blessed confines of laboring humanity, a god who observes panoramically might think, and that might be just his thought. A god could endure it.'
>
> 'Sometimes [. . .] do you not think that you also could? Oh my darling, my very darling . . .'
>
> Desperately, feverishly, she closed her arms about me, and in a fanatical rashness, an inspired temper, of womanhood she drew back a hand and tore open her blouse before pressing her lips hard against mine.'[51]

Sassoon writes in detail of the source of the argument that ensued after Plath had discovered that the Matisse Chapel was closed. Sylvia had stormed off, leaving Richard outside, at which point the mother superior had invited him inside. When he had finished the tour, he came out into the sunlight to meet a very angry Sylvia. 'Very simply, I won't ever forgive you – completely – for this,' she told him. Richard tried to explain himself – that she wasn't around, that there was no point waiting for her, that he thought she had disappeared – but Sylvia would not listen.

> 'I asked you to wait for me.' [she says]
>
> 'You said nothing. You were quite silent [. . .] You were angry because it was closed to visitors and you got angry at me and you were . . .'
>
> 'You should have understood.'
>
> 'I did. I left you there, and I waited here and would have waited for . . .'
>
> 'You went in without me!'
>
> 'Listen, I . . .'
>
> 'Afterward, you were breathless to tell me!'
>
> 'Should I have hidden the fact?'
>
> 'Maybe!'
>
> 'Let's go now.'
>
> 'I won't go! I won't go until I've been inside. I'll stand here and starve until they open to me.'
>
> 'Oh, the hell . . .'
>
> 'Hell! Why do you say that? Why do you say hell?' Her eyes flashed and she brought clenched fists abruptly to her chest in a motion of terrifying violence; she seemed possibly about to cry. 'Why do you say hell? Because it's I that will go there, not you!!!'[52]

In Sassoon's eyes, Sylvia was 'as various as the sea'.[53] He remembered one occasion when he left their hotel to go and buy a packet of cigarettes and returned to their room to find her standing naked at the window. She told him that she had pretended to herself that the hotel was full of 'false wooers, all after me and swearing that you were dead, and only I knew that you were alive, and I prayed and prayed that you would come back in time [. . .] if only you would come back in time!' At this point, she threw herself 'in a bliss of anger' into his arms.[54] He also recalls the hours they spent together on the beach, which was almost empty despite the mild weather, and how the 'soporific and muting sound of the surf permitted the exploitation of language to its limits and beyond, words and phrases that in silence or amid the static noises of cities would have foundered and wrecked on the impasses of the nonsequential and the ridiculous.'[55]

Before leaving France, Sassoon told her that it would be best if they didn't see each other for a while. He said that after his spell at the Sorbonne he would have to return to America to serve in the army for two years and then he wanted to be able to set himself up in business so that he would be financially independent. He would always love her, he told her, but until they met again it was only right, he said, that she should be free to have affairs with other men. Sassoon was, Sylvia told her mother, 'the only boy I have ever loved so far.' He was, she said, not only the most intuitive person she had ever met but also the cleverest. Unfortunately, he also suffered from bouts of depression and fragile and unpredictable health. 'But he is the most honest, holy person I know.'[56] From Cambridge, Plath wrote him an impassioned letter telling him she would be faithful – most probably the same letter that contained the sentence, 'So that no matter what happens, I shall always, very simply, love you,' which Sassoon used as the opening line of his story 'In the year of Love and unto Death, the fourth – an Elegy on the Muse'.

Sylvia severed contact with the gaggle of boys she had met in her first term at Cambridge, apart from Mallory Wober. She was determined to live a more pared-down existence, devoting herself to reading and writing. As she told her mother, 'Muteness is sickness'; the state of non-writing resulted in acute anxiety and fear.[57] For her the act of writing enhanced her life, which in turn fed back into her writing. She did her best work, she said, when she was at her happiest, as her sense of humour prevented her from being trapped within the confines of melancholy solipsism.[58]

Ironically, as Plath tried to relive one of her most rewarding, spiritually uplifting experiences – her visit with Sassoon to the Matisse Chapel, which she used as the basis of a story that she hoped to sell to the *New Yorker* or *Ladies' Home Journal* – so she began to feel more and more depressed. Cambridge had been gripped by more extreme winter than usual. Sylvia went to bed dressed in flannel pyjamas, a ski sweater and ski socks and even though she had a hot water bottle she felt desperately cold. In the mornings she would have to use a knife to scrape the ice away from the window in order to see outside. The gas fire, which cost the equivalent of $3 in shillings a week to use, seemed to be effective only on one side, leaving the rest of the room feeling as cold as 'the other half of the moon'.[59] During the first months of 1956 she came down with one cold after another. One night at the end of January she woke up racked by pain and after vomiting rather violently, she fainted. A doctor was called, who admitted her to hospital thinking that she might be suffering from appendicitis. There she spent a miserable night in a ward full of thirty women, all groaning in pain, but doctors could find no traces of appendicitis and after diagnosing her with colic, a condition that she said meant nothing to her, she was discharged. She was also discouraged to learn that the two poems that had appeared in *Chequer* had received bad reviews and saddened to hear that her dear grandmother would have to undergo an operation for stomach cancer, a disease that would ultimately claim her a few months later in April 1956.

Despite her black mood, she knew that at least now she had the ability to put things in perspective. Looking back at her breakdown and suicide attempt in 1953, she told her mother that she was pleased that she had had that experience. Now, she didn't have to be afraid of feeling a little bit down or low. She had, after all, faced what she called 'The Worst' and she had managed to pull herself through that black hole and to the other side. Surely now she could enjoy life for its joys and challenges – she may suffer from the occasional bout of depression, but she said she would never feel so 'desperate' again.[60]

On 18 February, Sylvia was walking over one of Cambridge's many bridges when a group of young boys started to throw snowballs at her. Although none of them hit her, she found the experience quite unsettling as it served as a reflection of her own vulnerable psychological state. She knew there was no rational reason why she felt gripped by such a deep sense of fear, she wrote in her journal. But the snowball throwing incident had sparked off a series of inner associations and emotions, namely 'inner doubt' and insecurity.[61] She made an appointment to see Dr Brian Davy, a psychiatrist at Cambridge University's Student Health Service. The week before her visit she wrote in her journal of her desperate need for a father or mother figure, somebody older who could guide her. She felt, she said, like Lazarus. 'Being dead, I rose up again, and even resort to the mere sensation value of being suicidal'.[62]

Each night, after dark, she would walk into Newnham College gardens to see a copy of del Verrocchio's sculpture *Boy with Dolphin* that, in her mind, she associated with Richard. Alone, in the light of the moon, Plath felt she could be herself, stripped of the masks of normality. It was obvious that her love for Sassoon was beginning to unbalance her as she could not tolerate the role he had imposed on her of the silent woman. On 20 February, Plath wrote in her journal of the empathy she felt with fictional characters who 'commit suicide, adultery, or get murdered'.[63] In the same entry, she recorded that she had written a poem, 'Winter Landscape, With Rooks', in which she compares the sun to the eye of a Cyclops (an image she had first noted in her journal during her trip to the south of France with Sassoon), a work she said described the terrain of her mind. The next day she heard back from the *New Yorker*: although Plath had had high hopes for 'The Matisse Chapel' – she told Elinor Friedman that she was sure the story would immortalise her – the magazine returned it with a standard rejection slip. She wrote of how she stashed it under a heap of papers as if it were a bastard child that had died before birth.[64]

On Friday 24 February, Plath went to bed suffering from yet another bad cold. She spent a night tossing and turning; the fever was accompanied by period cramps and she woke up feeling exhausted. Somehow, on Saturday morning, she managed to drag herself to see Dr Davy and confessed to him the details of her recent split with Sassoon. She felt she could talk to the psychiatrist, she said, as she related to him as a father figure. In her journal she wrote of how she wanted to sob on his shoulder and ask him to calm her down.[65] The problem, as she saw it, was that not only were there not enough older figures at Cambridge whom she could talk with and confide in – she missed her Smith professors Alfred Young Fisher, Alfred Kazin and George Gibian – but there was no one at Newnham whom she could regard as a role model. The women tutors were, for the most part, 'bluestocking grotesques' who learned about life only from books. Cambridge had a definite lack of colourful, strong woman, she wrote to her mother. In fact, in many respects it seemed as though the university town was still trapped in Victorian times.[66] In the same letter she told her mother that later she planned to go to a party to celebrate the publication of a new literary journal.

That morning, Plath had bought a copy of *St Botolph's Review* from Bert Wyatt-Brown, a boyfriend of Jane Baltzell's, and what she had read impressed her. She admired the work of Lucas Myers, particularly his grasp of technique and his disciplined form,[67] while Hughes' poems were 'strong and blasting like a high wind in steel girders'.[68] When Sylvia met Ted at the *St Botolph's Review* party on 25 February she found his physical presence just as overwhelming. Within minutes of meeting, Ted kissed Sylvia hard on the mouth and ripped the hair band from her head; in turn, Plath bit Hughes on the cheek, drawing blood.

Soon after the party, which she compared to an 'orgy',[69] she realised that Hughes was the 'one man since I've lived who could blast Richard',[70] yet after the encounter she feared she would never meet Hughes again; after all, Ted had the reputation of being the biggest seducer in Cambridge. That night she left Falcon's Yard with her date, Hamish Stewart, and, still drunk, accompanied him back to his college, Queens'. The entrance had been locked and, while climbing over the gates, Sylvia slipped, a spike spearing her skirt and hands, but she was too numb from alcohol to feel anything. Back at Hamish's rooms, Sylvia started to castigate herself – she called herself a slut and a whore – but her friend tried to reassure her that actually she was just a silly girl. Later, in her journal, she wrote how she enjoyed the physical sensation of him lying on top of her and the feel of his mouth on hers.[71] At 2:30, after making love, he smuggled her out of the building and walked her home to Whitstead.

Two days later she was still feeling the after effects of the party, and while enveloped in this state she wrote 'Pursuit', a Blakean poem about the 'dark forces of lust' and her encounter with Ted

Hughes.[72] The quotation at the beginning of the poem was taken from Racine's *Phèdre*, '*Dans le fond des forets votre image me suit*' ('In the depths of the forest your image follows me'), a line that Plath said summarised the relationship between passion and death. She wrote to her mother to tell her that the quote symbolised the allure of death as well as the contradiction, 'the more intensely one lives, the more one burns and consumes oneself.'[73] The words could easily apply to Plath's own brief life.

After St Botolph's, she felt slothful and tired, and guilty that she had neglected her French studies. She noted that she had a rather 'puritanical conscience' that pricked her whenever she felt she had fallen short of her ideals.[74] At the beginning of March she came down with another sinus infection – she was amazed that so much green slime could build up in her nose – and confessed to her mother that she was suffering from another period of black melancholy.[75] She asked Aurelia to send her some more thyroid pills, a medication that she had been taking for some time and that she believed gave her more energy.

Despite the temporary passion she felt for Ted Hughes, Plath was still in love with Richard Sassoon. She knew that in many ways the relationship was an impossible one – he had, after all, told her that they couldn't see one another for a couple of years – but it was this impossibility that she found all the more alluring. It was also, at times, almost unbearably painful. On 1 March, five days after meeting Hughes, she wrote to Sassoon begging him to free herself from him. The letter reads like an epistle from Ariel to Prospero, a desperate plea for liberation. If he could just write one harsh sentence – an admission that he had a mistress, for instance – that would effectively kill his image and somehow free herself from the confines of her feelings for him. 'For I must get my soul back from you; I am killing my flesh without it.'[76] On 6 March she wrote in her journal of how that afternoon she had received a letter from Richard that had been agony to read. 'I love that damn boy with all I've ever had in me and that's a hell of a lot,' she said.[77] She wrote to him to tell him that she wanted to visit him in Paris over the Easter holiday, and that she didn't understand his resistance to the trip. She told him that she felt like he had taken on the role of Signor Rappaccini, the father in Hawthorne's short story who had bred his daughter to eat only poisonous food and who emitted a toxic aura that would kill any potential suitor. Not surprisingly, this letter left him feeling 'disillusioned' and the same day he sent her a postcard with a drawing of himself posing as a kind of intellectual gargoyle perched on Notre-Dame. Finally, Plath realised that she would not be free of him unless she saw him. She couldn't bear the agony any longer, she said, as it made her feel 'schizophrenic'. Although her physical reality was centred around her student life in Cambridge, mentally and spiritually she felt like she was living in a community of angels with Sassoon.[78] In her journal she copied out the last two lines of Joyce's poem 'I Hear an Army', 'My heart, have you no wisdom thus to despair?/My love, my love, my love, why have you left me alone?' She said these words expressed the extremes of torment she was feeling.

It was while Plath was still trapped in this purgatorial state that she lent some books to Jane Baltzell. Noting that Sylvia had underlined key points in the texts in heavy black ink, Jane followed suit, using only pencil. Although she had every intention of erasing her marks, Jane forgot and soon after she had returned the volumes, she heard a knock at the door. 'Sylvia was incandescent with rage,' Jane says. Sylvia's first words were the familiar, 'Jane, how could you?' Jane backed away, at which point Sylvia shouted at her about the pencil marks. 'I have never seen rage like it,' she says.[79] 'It was such an extreme reaction, and for some reason, those pencil marks triggered something pathological in Sylvia.'[80] Plath noted in her journal, 'I was furious, feeling my children had been raped, or beaten, by an alien.'[81] The argument, which Plath described as cathartic, ranged across various points of tension that had been building up between the two young women over the last couple of months: Jane had felt at a loose end in France because Sylvia was too preoccupied with Richard; Plath believed she behaved in a slow-witted manner in her housemate's company, while Jane said she thought she became remarkably clumsy around Sylvia; and, at least in Plath's mind, Baltzell was her double. When the two were together there was a battle for domination, Plath wrote in her journal.[82] Sylvia had cast Jane as yet another 'doppelgänger' figure and projected on to her feelings, thoughts and perceptions that had no basis in reality. 'As time went on, it seems that Sylvia began to see me as competition,' says Jane. 'I don't know why, as we did not compete in the same arenas at all. We only shared one class together – tragedy – and we didn't really mix in the same friendship circles. At the time it made no sense to me – it only made sense later when I read her journals (where she calls me "the blonde one") and I saw that it was some kind of pattern that she felt she had to repeat.'[83]

In many respects Plath was psychologically blind to the needs of others, a lack of perception that took a literal form when on 17 March she had to be admitted to Addenbrooke's Hospital for the removal of a splinter of glass from her eye. Gary Haupt, a friend whom she had known in America and who was studying English at Pembroke, took her to the casualty ward where a doctor, after giving her local anaesthetic drops, operated on the eye. And while Plath was well aware of the literary allusions – throughout the procedure she chatted away about Gloucester in *King Lear* and Sophocles' Oedipus and how the two characters achieved a new sense of clarity after losing their vision[84] while the doctor quoted Housman back at her, 'If it chance your eye offend you/Pluck it out [. . .] and be sound' – she could not always see her own flaws.

'I didn't witness her temper, but I knew she felt a certain amount of resentment towards some people, and she felt jealous of people when often there was no need,' says Nat LaMar. 'I know she felt she could talk openly to me, and what she said was often not very complimentary. I also got the sense that she was moving at a rapid clip to a place or destination she didn't know. It was almost as though she was like a train rushing towards something or someone unknown.'[85]

Her immediate destination was Paris, her quarry, Sassoon. Before she left Cambridge, however, she continued her flirtation with Ted Hughes, who one night, with his friend Lucas Myers, threw stones at what they thought was her window. On 23 March, Sylvia and Ted spent the night together in Rugby Street, central London, at a flat owned by the father of Daniel Huws. The next day, bruised and sore from the sexual encounter – and still smarting from the fact that Ted had awoken at five in the morning and called her Shirley, the name of one of his girlfriends – Sylvia set off for France with Emmet Larkin, a Fulbright student from the LSE, and another girl. She arrived in the French capital in the early evening of 24 March, and, despite feeling exhausted from the 'sleepless holocaust night with Ted', she planned to make her way from her hotel on the rue de Lille to Richard's room on the rue Duvivier.[86] As she walked down into the lobby she realised that she had left her map of Paris in Larkin's car and so when a handsome man in a telephone booth smiled at her she returned the gesture. Within minutes the two got talking – she confessed that she was in a foreign city without a map and he introduced himself as Giovanni Perego, the Paris correspondent of the Italian newspaper *Paese Sera*. That night, after he took her to a little brasserie where they enjoyed steak tartare, wine and meringues, Plath went back to the hotel alone, determined to seek out Sassoon the next day. On Sunday morning, still feeling worn out from her night with Hughes, Sylvia walked down the rue du Bac, past Les Invalides to the rue Duvivier. She had prepared a speech to win over Richard and she was in a good mood, but when the concierge emerged and told her that Sassoon was not at home – he was in Spain and would not return until after Easter – her spirits plummeted. 'I had been ready to bear a day or two alone, but this news shook me to the roots,' she said.[87] The concierge let Sylvia sit in a chair in the sitting room, where she wrote a letter to Richard; as she scribbled away the 'tears fell scalding and wet' on to the paper and the radio blared out the popular song 'Smile'. Plath had to face the prospect that she had been rejected, something she was not used to – 'never before had a man gone off to leave me to cry after,' she wrote in her journal.[88]

Although Richard has never spoken publicly and in any depth about his relationship with Plath – and he told me that he never will – an insight into his frame of mind at this time can be found in the story 'The Diagram'. In it, Sassoon, knowing that a girlfriend was about to descend on him in Paris, left France to travel through Spain. 'I was trying to make up my mind about a girl I most genuinely loved who was coming to Paris to see me, where I wouldn't be because of having gone away to try to make up my mind,' he writes.[89] One of the reasons Sassoon decided not to meet Plath in Paris – at least suggested by this autobiographical story – was that she had sent him a series of letters designed to make him jealous of her burgeoning relationship with Ted Hughes. The emotional blackmail obviously did not work with him. From these letters Richard 'understood [that she] was going to start having an affair with a certain fellow so as to make me jealous and give me a mind to marry her, which I was unwilling to do just because of this imminent unfaithfulness.'[90] Plath's feelings for Sassoon were so intense that, had Richard decided to stay in Paris, it's highly probable that she would never have returned to England to marry Hughes. It was his rejection that catapulted Sylvia into Ted's arms – 'if he would come today I would stay here with him,' she wrote of Richard at this time.[91]

While waiting in vain for Sassoon to return to Paris, Sylvia made an effort to enjoy herself. She continued to socialize with Perego and his friends; met up with Tony Gray, a new friend who was studying in Oxford, and his sister, Sally; spent hours sketching scenes in the Tuileries and the bridges over the Seine; and went to see a production of Anouilh's *Ornifle*. After the play – which she didn't particularly enjoy, as the sight of dozens of couples sitting side by side in the stalls made her feel even more alone – she walked back to her hotel feeling desolate. In her room, she cursed Sassoon for deserting her. 'I cried in black velvet on the yellow bedspread and wondered at my not having one to love,' she wrote in her journal.[92] On 30 March, after a day spent walking through Montmartre to Sacré-Coeur with Tony Gray, followed by lunch at the Auberge du Coucou, the couple returned to Plath's hotel, undressed and kissed on the bed. Sylvia nipped into the bathroom for a moment but on her return Tony had changed his mind about making love. In her journal, Plath wrote that she was disappointed as his body had looked so 'lovely and strong and golden.'[93]

Plath had already arranged to spend the latter part of her vacation with Gordon Lameyer – who had thirty days' leave from the navy and was flying in from an air-force base in New Jersey in order to research a university place in Germany. But as the moment of their reunion neared she began to have doubts about her decision. She knew how she behaved with Gordon. Could she stop herself from lashing out for just a week? How could she prevent herself from giving him acid looks or sharp comments? Lameyer too felt anxious about the journey, as he later recalled. 'I remember looking out the window of her fourth-floor walk-up at all the rooftops of Paris with their flat, Cezannesque, cubistic surfaces and feeling very depressed,' he said. 'We both sensed that it would be a mistake to travel together after we had broken up a year before. There was no longer a romantic attachment on either side, and I had thought of going right on to Germany alone to look for a university when Sylvia urged me to let her at least accompany me to Munich and spend a few days in Italy.'[94] As they were leaving the Gare d'Orléans on a train bound for Munich, they started to discuss the death of Dylan Thomas: Gordon had given Sylvia a copy of John Malcolm Brinnin's *Dylan Thomas in America*, in which the author described the poet drinking himself to death while in the United States. Plath vehemently disagreed with the statement and blamed Brinnin for not stepping into help Thomas when he needed it most. Lameyer argued that one could not hold Brinnin to account as it was obvious that the poet had a strong death wish. 'Sylvia was outraged,' said Lameyer, because 'she identified strongly with Thomas.' By the time the train had arrived in Munich, a blizzard had set in, and the couple decided to take a pair of rooms at the Bahnhof Hotel. Before dinner, while Gordon was preparing to shave, he cut his thumb on a razor blade. Sylvia, who heard his cry, came into his room and sucked his bleeding finger before wrapping it in a towel. 'We then sat on the bed while we waited for it to stop bleeding,' he said, 'her head leaned against my shoulder as we sat in silence, our backs against the wall, but our hearts, miles apart.'[95] Plath's experience in Munich with Gordon inspired part of her lost novel *Falcon Yard*. A segment of one of the surviving chapters, titled 'Venus in the Seventh', details the deteriorating relationship between Jess and Winthrop, whom

Plath modelled on herself and Gordon. After the couple arrive by train in Munich on a snowy day just before Easter, Winthrop leads the way to an expensive hotel near the railway station, but Jess can't help feeling resentful of everything: the inclement weather, Winthrop's increasingly dogged behaviour, the hotel manager's snooty disposition, and the overpriced rooms. At least, as Plath writes in the novel, travelling with a man you despised always had its compensations.[96]

From Munich, they continued on their toxic grand tour to Venice. There, in the 'cradle of a black, coffin-like gondola' Gordon took some photographs of them using a time-exposure device on his camera.[97] Sylvia, dressed in a thick baby-blue polo-neck sweater, beige mackintosh, black scarf, a red polka-dot headscarf, looks directly into the camera with a knowing gaze, the smile on her face rather artificial and fixed. 'How ridiculous!' she said at the time. 'To others it must look as if we were lovers.' After two days in Venice they travelled on to Rome, where they stayed in a pensione near the Piazza di Spagna, and where they decided to go their separate ways. One day Sylvia bumped into Don Cheney, whom she had known since sixth grade and who was studying in the city on a Fulbright. 'Like a northern barnacle, Sylvia attached herself to Don,' said Gordon, 'who promised to show her the Etruscan art treasures found in the caves north of the city.'[98] Sylvia adored the fact that Cheney could speak fluent Italian and she wrote to her mother about sitting in the sun eating dates in the Forum, the spectacle of the Coliseum, and the splendours of the Eternal City.

On their last day in the Italian capital Sylvia and Gordon met by chance under the nave of St Peter's. 'I remember in the frigid semi-darkness of the Basilica the supplicants, kissing and wiping the toes of the statue of St Peter, seemed to represent the absurd plight to which our journey together had led,' wrote Lameyer later. 'However, we both wanted to see the Sistine

Chapel with the Michelangelo paintings on the ceiling and the front wall, the ones of Adam and Eve and God. Soon we separated again. Later in the afternoon, as I was walking through the crowded galleries of the Vatican museum, Sylvia approached me and, in what seemed to me a belated play for sympathy, told me how she had almost fainted earlier in the day, getting off a bus. What came to mind and what I said were Rhett Butler's words to Scarlett O'Hara in *Gone with the Wind*: "Frankly, my dear, I don't give a damn." I felt it was poetic justice, but Sylvia was livid.'[99]

The next day, on Friday 13 April, her father's birthday, Gordon took Sylvia to the airport and bought her a ticket to London. As Lameyer watched the plane take off and disappear he felt a great sense of relief; he never wanted to see her again. Yet, a year or so later, he wrote her a letter in which he confessed that, during their European tour, he had felt overburdened by jealousies and resentments of his own. 'I know at the time we felt each other intolerable burdens, heavier than all luggage,' he told her.[100] In his unpublished memoir of Plath, Lameyer recalled how, on their last day together in Rome, the couple had been breakfasting together in a café. At one point, Sylvia 'had gotten up brusquely and had tried to walk out, crashing into a transparent glass door [. . .] Alice could no longer pass through her magic mirror.'[101]

Sylvia knew that she was nearing what she called a 'historic moment'.[102] The day before she had left France for Munich, Sylvia had talked to Giovanni Perego of the three fatal choices facing her: should she devote herself to Richard, Gordon or Ted? If Sassoon returned from Spain she would, she said, fall into his arms; Gordon was, she knew, no longer an option for her, as she could hardly hide her dislike for him. That meant that there was, in her mind, only one man for her: Ted Hughes.

AFTERWORD

Soon after returning to England, Plath sent a letter to Richard Sassoon asking him never to write to her again – she was engaged to Ted Hughes. The couple married on 16 June 1956, four months after that first meeting and she thought it would be better if she and Richard severed all contact. Initially, Sassoon went along with Sylvia's wishes, but then – after what he described as an 'exceptionally strange night', at the end of which he read through all of his former lover's letters – he felt compelled to write to her.

'There is really no reason for me not to believe that you are happier now than you ever were or could have been with me [. . .]' he said. 'Except that your letter to me was not the letter of a happy woman.' He acknowledged that it would take many years for him to come to terms with the breakdown of their relationship – he felt, he said, like 'a carcass from whom the interior has been taken' – but stated that there was little point in conducting a post-mortem about what had happened between them. 'Long before I was your bien-amie, I was something else to you, and I think always I was somewhat more than a paramour, always [. . .] You tell me I am to know that you are doing what is best for you; it is so if you believe it, Sylvia, and if it is so, then it is.'[1] Using the Wallace Stevens poem 'The Well Dressed Man With a Beard' to illustrate his point, Richard realised that Sylvia's decisions at this moment in her life would have far-reaching consequences: 'I read somewhere that "after the final no, there comes along a yes/And on that yes the future world depends," which strikes me as very profound.'[2]

On 11 February 1963, Plath – who had separated from Ted after discovering his affair with Assia Wevill – made final arrangements to end her life at her flat on Fitzroy Road, Primrose Hill, London. She made sure that her two children from her marriage to Hughes – Frieda, almost three years old, and Nicholas, just one – were safe in high-sided cots in their bedroom on the top floor. She brought two cups of milk and a plate of bread and butter up to them, opened the window and then sealed the door frame with tape and pushed tea towels into the gaps. She walked back downstairs to the kitchen, again sealed the door with tape and towels, put a little folded cloth in the oven and knelt down. She placed her head on the cloth in the oven, turned on the gas, slowly lapsed into unconsciousness and died. She was thirty years old. Only a few days before, Plath had written the poem 'Edge', which opens with these words:

> 'The woman is perfected
> Her dead
> Body wears the smile of accomplishment'.[3]

ACKNOWLEDGEMENTS

This book could not have been written without those close to Sylvia Plath. I must thank Warren Plath, Sylvia's brother, and Susan Plath Winston, her niece, who gave me permission to quote at length from the published and unpublished correspondence of Aurelia Plath. I am also grateful for the extraordinary curatorial zeal of Aurelia Plath, who preserved every scrap of her daughter's writing from an early age.

The two large Plath archives, held at Smith College, Northampton, Massachusetts and the Lilly Library, Bloomington, Indiana have continued Aurelia's passion for preservation with the highest degree of professionalism. At Smith I must single out Karen Kukil, whose edition of Plath's journals is considered something of a Bible among Plath scholars, for her endless help, support and friendliness. She made my stay in Northampton both creatively stimulating and highly enjoyable. Also at Smith I must thank Susan Barker, Barbara Blumenthal, Nanci Young, and all the other curators who helped me with my research. At the Lilly Library, I would like to thank Cherry Dunham Williams, David Frasier, Zach Downey and all the other staff and librarians who guided me through the enormous archive.

No work of biography can be written in isolation and I must thank Plath scholar Peter K. Steinberg, who has helped me source a wide range of archival material. His expertise is second to none and I owe him a great deal.

I would also like to thank those who lent me letters from private archives, particularly Blair Cruickshank, who was sitting on a valuable collection of letters that once belonged to Aurelia Plath (and which has since been returned to Frieda Plath). I'll never forget that winter's day at her home outside Boston when she passed a fat batch of papers across her kitchen table and told me that I could take them away to read. I'd only just arrived in Boston – I think it was my second day of research – and I was astounded by the material, a biographer's dream.

For access to previously unpublished material I would also like to thank Tom Derr, Jane Mills and Mary Derr Knox; Constantine Sidamon-Eristoff (who died in December 2011); Jane Anderson (who died in February 2010); Mallory Wober, whose letters from Plath are now held by King's College, Cambridge University; Jim McNeely (for his unpublished diary entries) and the late Gordon Lameyer (and his widow Betty Lameyer Gilmore) who gave me permission to publish extracts from the unpublished memoir Dear Sylvia (held at the Lilly Library). I must thank Alex Beam, whose recorded interview with Ruth Beuscher, Plath's therapist, is full of insights and also Debbie Matsumoto and her family for permission to quote from Eddie Cohen's compelling letters to Plath. Thank you also to the individuals who have written directly to me: Olwyn Hughes, Igor Karmiloff, Janet Rafferty, Bob Riedeman, Richard Sassoon, the late Marcia Stern, Betsy Wallingford, and Professor Melvin Woody.

During the course of the book I have interviewed many of those who knew Plath. Each of the following played an important role in bringing the young Sylvia to life: Peter Aldrich (who also gave me a driving tour of Wellesley), Jane Baltzell Kopp,

Ann Burnside Love, Ann Hayes, Mary Derr Knox, Tom Derr, Frank Irish, Elinor Friedman Klein, Ruth Geissler, Louise Giesey White, Nat LaMar, Frederic Mayo, Philip McCurdy, Jim McNeely, William Moore, Perry Norton, Janet Rosenberg, Sylvia Scully, Constantine Sidamon-Eristoff, Betsy Wallingford, Guy Wilbor, Mallory Wober, Professor Melvin Woody, Laurie Woolschlager and Ray Wunderlich.

Many others have either helped me with leads, comments or information. Thank you to Terry Bragg (McLean Hospital), Reid Buckley, Ellen Cormier, Despine Coulis, Blair Cruickshank, Francis Edmonds, Patricia Elliott Riedeman, Mandy Ferrara, Sally Fisher, Sarah Funke Butler, Anita Helle, George Gebauer, Annette Karmiloff-Smith, Kyra Karmiloff, Elizabeth Kaspar, Paul Keegan, Richard Larschan, Karen Maroda, Clement Moore Henry, Dick Norton, Patricia Pratson, Carl Shedd, Katy Swartz, Frances Wilson, Molly Woehrlin, David Wunderlich, and Alexia Ziemba.

For the use of photographs I would like to acknowledge Elizabeth Lameyer Gilmore (for use of the images taken by her late husband); Elinor Friedman Klein; the Lilly Library; Susan Plath Winston for the use of copyright images in the Helle Collection (Smith College), Debbie Matsumoto, Karin and Gary Wellington (Eddie Cohen), Janet Rosenberg; Betsy Wallingford and Ruth Geissler; Molly Woehrlin (Jane Anderson), and Nanci Young (Smith College archivist for the use of Nancy Hunter photo).

At Simon & Schuster in London I would like to say a big thank you to Mike Jones, who commissioned the book, editor Briony Gowlett, Nick Venables (who designed the jacket), director of publicity Hannah Corbett, rights director Sarah Birdsey, copy editor Monica Hope, and all the team in London, while at Scribner in New York I would like to thank Carolyn Reidy, Nan Graham, Kelsey Smith, Elisa Rivlin, and Kate Lloyd.

I would also like to thank Clare Alexander, my inspirational agent and friend, Sally Riley and Cassie Metcalf-Slovo and everyone who works at Aitken Alexander in London.

Finally, I would like to thank my family and friends, particularly Christopher Fletcher, who was partly responsible for the genesis of the book, and Marcus Field, who has shared me with Sylvia Plath while I was researching and writing this biography.

NOTES

Abbreviations used throughout:

AP: Aurelia Schober Plath
AW: Andrew Wilson
BJ: *The Bell Jar*, Sylvia Plath, Faber & Faber, London, first published 1963, edition used 1966
CP: *Collected Poems*, Sylvia Plath, ed. Ted Hughes, Faber & Faber, London, 1981
DS: *Dear Sylvia*, Gordon Lameyer, unpublished memoir, Lilly Library
EB: Edward Butscher
JA: Jane Anderson
JP: *Johnny Panic and the Bible of Dreams*, Sylvia Plath, Harper Perennial Modern Classics, New York, 2008
JSP: *The Journals of Sylvia Plath* 1950-1962, ed. Karen V. Kukil, Faber & Faber, London, 2000
LH: *Letters Home*, ed. Aurelia S. Plath, Harper Perennial, New York, first published 1975, edition used 1992
LL: The Lilly Library, Indiana University, Bloomington, Indiana
OHP: Olive Higgins Prouty
SC: Mortimer Rare Book Room, Neilson Library, Smith College, Northampton, Massachusetts
SP: Sylvia Plath
TH: Ted Hughes

INTRODUCTION

1 *JSP*, p. 210.
2 *Ibid.*

3 Daniel Huws, *Broadsheet*, quoted in Keith Sagar, *The Laughter of Foxes: A Study of Ted Hughes*, Liverpool University Press, Liverpool, 2000, revised ed. 2006, pp. 48–9.
4 Daniel Huws, *Memories of Ted Hughes 1952–1963*, Richard Hollis, imprint Five Leaves Publications, Nottingham, 2010, p. 34.
5 *JSP*, p. 211.
6 Huws, *Memories of Ted Hughes*, *op. cit.*, p. 34.
7 *JSP*, p. 211.
8 *Ibid.*
9 *Ibid.*
10 TH, 'Law in the Country of the Cats', *Collected Poems*, ed. Paul Keegan, Faber & Faber, London, 2003, 2005, p. 41.
11 SP, 'Pursuit', *CP*, p. 22.
12 *JSP*, p. 211.
13 TH, 'Law in the Country of the Cats', *op. cit.*, p. 41.
14 *JSP*, pp. 211–212.
15 TH, 'St Botolph's', *Collected Poems*, *op. cit.*, p. 1052.
16 TH, 'Sylvia Plath and Her Journals', *Ariel Ascending: Writings About Sylvia Plath*, ed. Paul Alexander, Harper & Row, New York, 1985, p. 152.
17 TH, Foreword, *The Journals of Sylvia Plath*, ed. Fran McCullough, Ballantine Books, New York, 1982, p. xiii.
18 TH, 'Sylvia Plath and Her Journals', *op. cit.*, p. 153.
19 Robert Lowell, Introduction, *Ariel*, Harper & Row, New York, 1966, pp. ix–x.
20 TH, Foreword, *The Journals of Sylvia Plath*, *op. cit.*, p. xiv.
21 TH, Introduction, *CP*, p. 16.
22 *Ibid.*
23 The full poem is available on various websites, such as: www.neuroticpoets.com/plath/poem/madgirl/
24 *JSP*, p. 233.
25 TH, 'Sylvia Plath and Her Journals', *op. cit.*, p. 152.
26 SP, 'Adolescence', 1949, LL.
27 SP, unpublished letter to Ann Davidow, January 1952, SC.
28 *JSP*, p. 98.
29 *JSP*, p. 20.
30 SP, unpublished letter to Warren Plath, around 12 May 1953, LL.
31 *JSP*, p. 36.
32 Letter from Peter Davison to EB, 17 September 1973, SC.
33 Letter from Clarissa Roche to EB, 22 May 1973, Olwyn Hughes folder, EB Collection, SC., reprinted as 'Sylvia Plath: Vignettes from England' by Clarissa Roche, in *Sylvia Plath: The Woman and the Work*, ed. Edward Butscher, Dodd, Mead & Company, New York, 1977, p. 84.
34 *DS.*
35 *Ibid.*

36 SP, 'Lady Lazarus', *CP*, p. 245.
37 *BJ*, p. 65.
38 SP, 'Two Views of a Cadaver Room', *CP*, p. 114.
39 *BJ*, p. 65.
40 *JSP*, p. 523.
41 Craig Raine, 'The double exposures of Ted Hughes', *TLS*, 22 November 2006.
42 Letter from TH to AP, 15 March 1963, LL, reproduced in *Letters of Ted Hughes*, ed. Christopher Reid, Farrar, Straus & Giroux, New York, p. 215.
43 *JSP*, pp. 320–321.
44 *JSP*, pp. 32–33.
45 Letter from TH to AP, 13 July 1966, LL, reprinted in *Letters of TH*, *op. cit.*, p. 260.
46 SP, 'Neither Moonlight nor Starlight', LL.

CHAPTER ONE

1 *JSP*, p. 401.
2 *Ibid.*
3 Mark Twain, 'A Tramp Abroad', *The Works of Mark Twain*, Wildside Press, Holicong, PA, p. 123.
4 *JSP*, p. 168.
5 SP, 'The Ghost's Leavetaking', *CP*, p. 90.
6 Letter from AP to Frieda Hughes, 29 September 1973, Cruickshank Archive.
7 SP, *BJ*, p. 34.
8 Letter from AP to Nicholas Hughes, 29 September 1973, Cruickshank Archive.
9 *LH*, p. 9.
10 Max Gaebler, 'Sylvia Plath Remembered', *Wisconsin Academy Review*, Spring 2000.
11 *LH*, p. 9.
12 *Ibid.*
13 *LH*, p. 10.
14 SP, *BJ*, p. 175.
15 Letter from AP to Frieda Hughes, 24 March 1978, Cruickshank Archive.
15a FBI files on Otto Plath, courtesy of Peter K. Steinberg.
16 *LH*, p. 8.
17 Otto Plath, *Bumblebees and Their Ways*, Macmillan Company, New York, 1934, p. 1.
18 *LH*, p. 13.
19 Otto Plath, *op. cit.*, p. 7.
20 Linda Heller, 'Aurelia Plath: a lasting commitment', *Bostonia*, Spring 1976, Aurelia's edited copy at SC.

21 *LH*, p. 4.
22 *JSP*, p. 64.
23 *LH*, p. 5.
24 *Ibid.*
25 Letter from AP to Frieda Hughes, September 1974, Cruickshank Archive.
26 Letter from AP to Frieda Hughes, 21 April 1978, Cruickshank Archive.
27 *LH*, p. 12.
28 *LH*, p. 13.
29 Anita Helle, 'Family Matters: An Afterword on the Biography of Sylvia Plath', *Northwest Review*, 26:2, 1988.
30 AP note on SP's hair, LL.
31 AP, SP's baby book, LL.
32 AP, notes in SP's baby book, LL.
33 *Ibid.*
34 *LH*, p. 12.
35 *LH*, p. 16.
36 *Ibid.*
37 SP, 'Ocean 1212-W', *JP*, p. 24.
38 Letter from AP to Ellen Moers, 25 July 1976, SC.
39 AP, SP's baby book, LL.
40 *LH*, p. 16.
41 Heller, *op. cit.*
42 *BJ*, p. 57.
43 SP, 'Ocean 1212-W', *JP*, p. 22.
44 SP, poem, *Boston Sunday Herald*, 10 August 1941.
45 *Voices and Visions* TV documentary, New York Center for Visual History, 1988.
46 *Ibid.*
47 *LH*, p. 18.
48 *Ibid.*
49 *JSP*, pp. 429–30.
50 Interview with Ruth Geissler, 12 February 2011.
51 *JSP*, p. 35.
52 *JSP*, p. 366.
53 *LH*, p. 19.
54 *Ibid.*
55 *JSP*, p. 154.
56 Letter from Susan Plath Winston to AW, 14 October 2011.
57 *JSP*, p. 519.
58 Sigmund Freud, *The Basic Writings of Sigmund Freud*, translated and edited with an Introduction by Dr A. A. Brill, The Modern Library, New York, 1938, pp. 298–300; SC holds SP's copy.
59 *JSP*, p. 52.
60 *JSP*, p. 399.
61 SP, 'Full Fathom Five', *CP*, p. 93.

62 SP, 'Among the Bumblebees', *JP*, p. 320.
63 AP, 'Thunder Song', 11 August 1937, personal papers, SC.
64 SP, 'Among the Bumblebees', *JP*, p. 324.
65 SP, 'Among the Bumblebees', *JP*, p. 327.
66 *LH*, p. 22.
67 *Ibid.*
68 *LH*, p. 23.
69 *Ibid.*
70 *Ibid.*
71 *LH*, p. 24.
72 *LH*, p. 25.
73 *Voices and Visions*, *op. cit.*
74 Interview with Ruth Geissler, 12 February 2011.
75 *JSP*, p. 431.
76 *JSP*, p. 430.
77 *Ibid.*
78 C. G. Jung, *The Collected Works, Volume 17: Development of Personality*, edited and translated by Gerhard Adler and R. F. C. Hull, Routledge, London, first published 1954, this edition 1991, pp. 170–1.

CHAPTER TWO

1 *LH*, p. 28.
2 Beth Hinchliffe, 'A Brief History of Wellesley', www.wellesleyma.gov/pages/wellesleyma_webdocs/about
3 *Ibid.*
4 *DS.*
5 *LH*, p. 29.
6 Interview with Betsy Wallingford, 12 February 2011.
7 Hinchliffe, *op. cit.*
8 Letter from Philip McCurdy to his mother, 18 June 1966, SC.
9 Letter from Philip McCurdy to AW, 13 March 2011.
10 'Two of a Kind: Poets in Partnership', radio interview with Sylvia Plath and Ted Hughes, 18 January 1961, BBC.
11 *LH*, p. 30.
12 Interview with Betsy Wallingford, 12 February 2011.
13 'Two of a Kind', *op. cit.*
14 Letter from AP to Elizabeth Sigmund, 28 April 1963, SC.
15 Letter from AP to Frieda Plath Hughes, 29 September 1973, Cruickshank Archive.
16 AP's comment to Ted Hughes, related in his deposition during *The Bell Jar* libel case, 26 March 1986, Box 3, Jane Anderson papers, SC.

17 SP, memorandum notebook, 1944, SC.
18 SP, diary, 10 August 1944, LL.
19 SP, memorandum notebook, 1944, SC.
20 Letter from Betsy Wallingford to AW, 28 June 2011.
21 Letter from Dorothy H. Humphrey to EB, 4 January 1973, SC.
22 *Girl Scout Handbook, Intermediate Program*, Girls Scouts of the United States of America, 1947, pp. 449–50.
23 SP, thought patterns on paper, 17 September 1946, LL.
24 Interview with Betsy Wallingford, 12 February 2011.
25 Interview with Ruth Geissler, 12 February 2011.
26 *Ibid.*
27 School report, 14 November 1944, transcribed by SP in her 1944 diary, LL.
28 SP, 'The Disquieting Muses', *CP*, p. 75.
29 AP's annotations to 'The Disquieting Muses', SC.
30 AP, Authors' Series Talk, Wellesley College Club, 16 March 1976, SC.
31 Interview with Louise Giesey White, 23 March 2011.
32 SP, birthday greeting to mother, SC.
33 AP's notes on playbill of *The Tempest*, 20 January 1945, personal papers, SC.
34 Interview with Frank Irish, 10 February 2011.
35 *The Phillipian*, April 1945, SC.
36 Commendation cards, June 1945, Alice L. Phillips Junior High School, LL.
37 AP to SP, 27 October 1945, transcribed in 1944 diary, LL.
38 SP, riddle, 1947, SC.
39 *JSP*, p. 130.
40 Letter from Philip McCurdy to AW, 14 March 2011.
41 Letter from Philip McCurdy to AW, 13 March 2011.
42 SP, 'Ocean 1212-W', *JP*, p. 25.
43 Interview with Ruth Geissler, 12 February 2011.
44 Interview with Perry Norton, 25 February 2011.
45 SP, 'The Shadow', *JP*, p. 151.
46 Gaebler, *op. cit.*
47 Sara Teasdale, 'The Falling Star'.
48 SP, diary, 20 February 1947, LL.
49 SP, 'Fireside Reveries', *The Phillipian*, February 1947.
50 Interview with Betsy Wallingford, 12 February 2011.
51 SP, diary, 22 January 1947, LL.
52 AP, *LH*, p. 33.
53 SP, 'I Thought That I Could Not Be Hurt', *LH*, p. 34.

CHAPTER THREE

1 Harold H. Kolb, 'Mr. Crockett', *Virginia Quarterly Review*, Spring 2002.
2 *Ibid.*
3 Letter from SP to AP, 8 September 1947, LL.
4 Kolb, *op. cit.*
5 *Ibid.*
6 Wilbury Crockett, quoted in SP's 1947 diary, 10 September 1947, LL.
7 SP, *The Snake Pit*, film review, LL.
8 Interview with Philip McCurdy, 9 February 2011.
9 *Ibid.*
10 *Ibid.*
11 SP, 'America! America!', *JP*, p. 55.
12 SP, 'America! America!', *JP*, p. 56.
13 AP, note on letter of 6 October 1952, *LH*, p. 95.
14 SP, 'Initiation', *JP*, p. 299.
15 SP, 'Initiation', *JP*, p. 300.
16 SP, 'America! America!', *JP*, p. 56.
17 Interview with Perry Norton, 25 February 2011.
18 *Ibid.*
19 Interview with Philip McCurdy, 9 February 2011.
20 SP, diary, 14 February 1948, LL.
21 Letter from SP to AP, 24 July 1948, LL.
22 *Ibid.*
23 Letter from SP to AP, 20 July 1948, LL.
24 Letter from SP to Hans Joachim Neupert, 13 April 1947, SC.
25 Letter from SP to Hans Joachim Neupert, 24 September 1948, SC.
26 SP, 'Family Reunion', *CP*, p. 301.
27 SP, 'Sunday at the Mintons'', *JP*, p. 318.
28 SP, 'Among the Shadow Throngs', 1949, LL.
29 AP, *LH*, p. 35.
30 *Writer's Year Book*, 1952, p. 27.
31 '50 Girls and One Man', *Time*, 16 May 1949.
32 SP, 'And Summer Will Not Come Again', *Seventeen*, August 1950.
33 *Ibid.*
34 AP, *LH*, p. 36.
35 SP, 'And Summer Will Not Come Again', *op. cit.*
36 *Ibid.*
37 *JSP*, p. 124.
38 SP, diary, 22 July 1949, LL.
39 *Ibid.*
40 SP, summer diary, 30 August 1949, LL.
41 SP, diary, 13 November 1949, LL.

42 SP, diary, 27 November 1949, LL
43 Letter from Bob Riedeman to AW, 3 August 2011.
44 SP, diary, 13 November 1949, LL, extract published in *LH*, p. 40.
45 Letter from Ruth W. Crawford to AP, 5 October 1949, SC.
46 *Ibid.*
47 SP, 'America! America!', *JP*, p. 55.
48 *Ibid.*
49 'Bradford Announces Incoming Editors', *The Bradford*, 7 June 1949, SC.
50 SP, 'America! America', *JP*, p. 54.
51 *Ibid.*
52 Notes on Scholarship and Co-operative Houses, 1950, SC.
53 Letter from Mary E. Mensel to AP and SP, 21 February 1950, SC.
54 Letter from Samuel M. Graves to Smith Admissions, 27 February 1950, Vocational Office, SC.
55 Letter from Wilbury Crockett to SC, SC.
56 Letter from Elizabeth Cannon Aldrich to Mary E. Mensel, 3 February 1950, SC.
57 SP, 'America! America!', *JP*, p. 55.
58 Nietzsche, *Thus Spake Zarathustra*, translated by Thomas Common, George Allen and Unwin, London, 1932, p.72.
59 SP, *LH*, p. 40.
60 *Ibid.*
61 Nietzsche, *Thus Spake Zarathustra*, *op. cit.*, p.71.
62 Letter from SP to Eddie Cohen, 11 August 1950, LL.
63 Nietzsche, *Thus Spake Zarathustra*, *op. cit.*, p. 96.
64 SP, 'Kindness', *CP*, p. 270.
65 Nietzsche, *Thus Spake Zarathustra*, *op. cit.*, p. 70.
66 Nietzsche, *Thus Spake Zarathustra*, *op. cit.*, p. 154.
67 Nietzsche, *Thus Spake Zarathustra*, *op. cit.*, p. 167.
68 Nietzsche, *Thus Spake Zarathustra*, *op. cit.*, p. 179.
69 Nietzsche, *Thus Spake Zarathustra*, *op. cit.*, p. 125.
70 Nietzsche, *Thus Spake Zarathustra*, *op. cit.*, pp. 125–6.
71 Nietzsche, *Thus Spake Zarathustra*, *op. cit.*, p. 164.
72 SP, 'Lady Lazarus', *CP*, p. 244
73 Nietzsche, *Thus Spake Zarathustra*, *op. cit.*, p. 177.
74 Letter from SP to Hans Joachim Neupert, 2 January 1950, SC.
75 *Ibid.*
76 SP and Perry Norton, 'Youth's Plea for World Peace', *Christian Science Monitor*, 16 March 1950.
77 *Ibid.*
78 *Ibid.*
79 Interview with Perry Norton, 25 February 2011.
80 Letter from SP to Hans Joachim Neupert, 12 August 1950, SC.
81 Thomas Hardy, 'The Man He Killed', http://allpoetry.com/poem/8442929-The_Man_He_Killed-by-Thomas_Hardy.

82 Thomas Mann, 'The Making of the Magic Mountain', *Atlantic Monthly*, Vol. 191, No. 1, January 1953.
83 Mann, *Buddenbrooks*, Vintage, London, 1999, pp. 526–7.
84 SP, 'The Invalid', LL.
85 SP, 'The Ghost's Leavetaking', *CP*, p. 90.
86 SP, 'Midnight Snow', LL.
87 Letter from SP to OHP, 29 November 1950, Faculty File, SC., reproduced in *LH*, p. 61.
88 SP's High School Year Book entry, SC.
89 SP, 'Class Song', 1950, published in Wellesley School Year Book 1950, SC.

CHAPTER FOUR

1 SP, 'The English Bike', LL.
2 *JSP*, p. 8.
3 *JSP*, p. 174.
4 *JSP*, p. 8.
5 *JSP*, p. 11.
6 *Ibid.*
7 *JSP*, p. 10.
8 Notes on SP story 'The Estonian', 30 October 1951, LL.
9 Notes on SP story 'The Latvian', 29 February 1952, LL.
10 Helle, *op. cit.*
11 Letter from Eddie Cohen to SP, 3 August 1950, LL.
12 SP biography, *Seventeen*, August 1950.
13 Letter from Eddie Cohen to SP, 3 August 1950, LL.
14 Letter from SP to Eddie Cohen, 6 August 1950, LL.
15 *Ibid.*
16 Letter from Eddie Cohen to SP, 8 August 1950, LL.
17 *Ibid.*
18 *Ibid.*
19 *Ibid.*
20 Letter from SP to Eddie Cohen, 11 August 1950, LL.
21 *JSP*, p. 22.
21 Letter from Eddie Cohen to SP, 17 August 1950, LL.
22 Letter from Eddie Cohen to SP, 19 August 1950, LL.
23 *Ibid.*
24 Letter from Eddie Cohen to SP, 25 August 1950, LL.
26 Letter from Eddie Cohen to SP, 17 August 1950, LL.
27 Letter from Eddie Cohen to SP, 2 September 1950, LL.
28 Letter from Eddie Cohen to SP, 15 September 1950, LL.
29 Letter from Eddie Cohen to SP, 17 December 1950, LL.

30 *JSP*, p. 14.
31 *JSP*, p. 13.
32 *JSP*, p. 14.
33 *JSP*, pp. 14–15.
34 *JSP*, p. 18.
35 *JSP*, p. 19.
36 SP, 'Den of Lions', *Seventeen*, May 1951.
37 Letter from Eddie Cohen to SP, September 1950, LL.
38 *JSP*, p. 20.
39 John M. Greene, An Address at the Centennial of the Birth of Sophia Smith, 27 May 1896.
40 Mary Ellen Chase, 'Smith College – A Definition', *Smith Review*, Fall 1952.
41 *Ibid.*
42 Letter from SP to AP, 26 September 1950, LL.
43 Letter from SP to OHP, 29 November 1950, Faculty File, SC., reprinted in *LH*, p. 61.
44 *Ibid.*
45 *LH*, p. 45.
46 *LH*, p. 46.
47 *Ibid.*
48 *LH* p. 48.
49 Interview with Ann Hayes, 13 March 2011.
50 *LH*, p. 49.
51 Interview with Ann Hayes, 13 March 2011.
52 *JSP*, p. 37.
53 *LH*, p. 50.
54 *Ibid.*
55 *LH*, p. 53.
56 Letter from Eddie Cohen to SP, 12 October 1950, LL.
57 Letter from Bob Riedeman to AW, 3 August 2011.
58 *JSP*, p. 23.
59 Interview with Ann Hayes, 13 March 2011.
60 *JSP*, p. 28.
61 Interview with Guy Wilbor, 21 February 2011.
62 *JSP*, p. 29.
63 *LH* p. 57.
64 SP, 'Tea with Olive Higgins Prouty', SC.
65 *Ibid.*
66 *Mademoiselle*, August 1955.
67 *LH*, p. 61.
68 *LH*, p. 59.
69 *LH*, pp. 57–8.
70 *LH*, p. 61.
71 *LH*, pp. 61–2.

72 OHP, *Now, Voyager*, originally published 1941, First Feminist Press, New York, 2004, p. 12.
73 OHP, *Now, Voyager*, p. 43.
74 *JSP*, pp. 26–7.
75 *JSP*, p. 29.
76 *JSP*, p. 30.
77 *JSP*, p. 31.
78 Letter from OHP to SP, 6 December 1950, LL.
79 SP, 'Tea with Olive Higgins Prouty', SC.
80 *Ibid.*
81 *Ibid.*
82 *LH*, p. 60.
83 *LH*, p. 65.
84 Letter from SP to AP, 5 March 1951, LL.
85 *LH*, p. 67.
86 *Ibid.*
87 Letter from Eddie Cohen to SP, 5 November 1950, LL.
88 *Ibid.*
89 Letter from Eddie Cohen to SP, 8 December 1950, LL.
90 Letter from Eddie Cohen to SP, 13 December 1950, LL.

CHAPTER FIVE

1 Letter from AP to Elizabeth Sigmund, 18 May 1976, SC.
2 *JSP*, p. 35.
3 *JSP*, p. 34.
4 *LH*, p. 82.
5 Letter from Eddie Cohen to SP, 28 December 1951, LL.
6 *LH*, p. 64.
7 Interview with Ann Hayes, 13 March 2011.
8 *JSP*, p. 33.
9 Letter from SP to Ann Davidow, dated 14 September 1951 but more likely written early 1951, SC.
10 *Ibid.*
11 Letter from Eddie Cohen to SP, 4 January 1951, LL.
12 *JSP*, p. 32.
13 *JSP*, p. 46.
14 *JSP*, p. 32.
15 *JSP*, p. 33.
16 *JSP*, p. 43.
17 *Ibid.*
18 *JSP*, p. 44.

19 Letter from Marcia Stern to AW, 28 August 2011.
20 *Ibid.*
21 Marcia Brown Stern, Panel Interview, 75th Year Symposium, Smith College, 26 April 2008.
22 *Ibid.*
23 Letter from SP to Ann Davidow, 14 February 1951, SC.
24 Letter from Dick Norton to SP, 7 February 1951, LL.
25 Letter from William B. Norton to EB, 15 December 1973, Butscher Collection, SC.
26 *LH*, p. 66.
27 *Ibid.*
28 SP, undated letter to AP, LL.
29 *JSP*, p. 48.
30 *JSP*, p. 49.
31 Letter from Eddie Cohen to SP, 6 March 1951, LL.
32 Letter from SP to Ann Davidow, 17 March 1951, SC.
33 *BJ*, p. 61
34 Eleanor Blau, '"Bell Jar" Jury Is Told of Suffering', *New York Times*, 29 January 1987.
35 Testimony of Jane Anderson, 4 June 1985, JA, SC.
36 Deposition of Jane Anderson, Volume 3, 7 March 1986, JA, SC.
37 Deposition of Jane Anderson, Volume 2, 7 March 1986, JA, SC.
38 *Ibid.*
39 Letter from Dick Norton to Jane Anderson, 4 January 1950, JA, SC.
40 Letter from Dick Norton to Jane Anderson, 25 April 1950, JA, SC.
41 'End of Derby Day', *Time*, 26 March 1951.
42 *Ibid.*
43 Deposition of Jane Anderson, Volume 2, *op. cit.*
44 *Ibid.*
45 *Ibid.*
46 *Ibid.*
47 *Ibid.*
48 *Ibid.*
49 *Ibid.*
50 *Ibid.*
51 Letter from SP to Marcia Brown, 25 June 1951, SC.
52 Letter from Eddie Cohen to SP, 19 March 1951, LL.
53 *Ibid.*
54 Letter from Eddie Cohen to SP, 11 April 1951, LL.
55 Letter from SP to AP, 15 April 1951, LL.
56 Deposition of Jane Anderson, Volume 2, *op. cit.*
57 SP, 'April 18', *CP*, p. 301.
58 *JSP*, p. 57.
59 SP, 'April 18', *CP*, p. 301.

60 Letter from Eddie Cohen to SP, 1 May 1951, LL.
61 Letter from Eddie Cohen to SP, 3 May 1951, LL.
62 Letter from Eddie Cohen to SP, 6 May 1951, LL.
63 *LH*, p. 69.
64 *Ibid.*
65 Letter from SP to Ann Davidow, May or June 1951, SC.
66 *Ibid.*
67 SP, diary, March 1951, LL.
68 *JSP*, p. 63.
69 *JSP*, p. 64.
70 Letter from SP to Marcia Brown, 6 June 1951, SC.
71 *Ibid.*
72 *Ibid.*
73 Letter from SP to Marcia Brown, June 1951, SC.
74 Letter from Eddie Cohen to SP, 19 May 1951, LL.
75 *JSP*, p. 63.
76 *JSP*, p. 64.
77 *JSP*, p. 58.
78 *JSP*, pp. 64–5.
79 *JSP*, p. 79.
80 Interview with Frederic Mayo, 15 February 2011.
81 *LH*, p. 70.
82 *LH*, p. 72.
83 Letter from SP to AP, 6 July 1951, LL.
84 *JSP*, p. 68.
85 SP, 'The Babysitters', *CP*, p. 174.
86 *Ibid.*
87 Interview with Frederic Mayo, 15 February 2011.
88 Letter from Mrs Frederic Mayo to Smith Vocational Office, 25 March 1952, SC.
89 Interview with Frederic Mayo, 15 February 2011.
90 *Ibid.*
91 *JSP*, p. 71.
92 *Ibid.*
93 Marcia Brown, diary excerpt, 24 July 1951, EB, SC.
94 Letter from SP to Marcia Brown, 3 July 1951, SC.
95 *JSP*, p. 76.
96 *Ibid.*
97 Letter from Dick Norton to SP, 18 July 1951, LL.
98 *Ibid.*
99 *JSP*, p. 77.
100 Letter from SP to Ann Davidow, 12 September 1951, SC.
101 Letter from Eddie Cohen to SP, 15 September 1951, LL.
102 *Ibid.*

103 *Ibid.*
104 Letter from Dick Norton to SP, 26 September 1951, LL.
105 Letter from Eddie Cohen to SP, 26 October 1951, LL.
106 *BJ*, p. 1.
107 *BJ*, p. 71.
108 Letter from Eddie Cohen to SP, 28 December 1951, LL.
109 *Ibid.*
110 Letter from SP to Ann Davidow, January 1952, SC.

CHAPTER SIX

1 Letter from SP to Marcia Stern, 10 September 1951, SC.
2 Faculty Card File on Maureen Buckley, SC.
3 *LH*, p. 75.
4 *Ibid.*
5 *LH*, p. 76.
6 *LH*, p. 77.
7 *Ibid.*
8 Interview with Constantine Sidamon-Eristoff, 3 March 2011. He died in December 2011.
9 *Ibid.*
10 *LH*, p. 78.
11 *Ibid.*
12 *LH*, p. 79.
13 *JSP*, p. 533.
14 *JSP*, p. 534.
15 *JSP*, p. 533.
16 Note by AP on letter from SP to AP, 9 December 1951, LL.
17 Letter from SP to AP, 29 October 1951, LL.
18 Letter from Eddie Cohen to SP, 16 October 1951, LL.
19 *JSP*, p. 534.
20 *LH*, p. 81.
21 Interview with Constantine Sidamon-Eristoff, 3 March 2011.
22 *Ibid.*
23 SP, 'Sonnet: To Eva', *CP*, pp. 304–5.
24 *Ibid.*
25 *LH*, p. 82.
26 T. S. Eliot, quoted in Plath's notes on a lecture given by Elizabeth Drew, 'Twentieth-Century Literature', SC.
27 Letter from SP to AP, 14 November 1951, LL.
28 Evelyn Page, notes on SP's story 'Mary Ventura', 14 December 1951, LL.
29 Letter from Dick Norton to SP, 4 January 1952, LL.

30 Letter from Eddie Cohen to SP, 13 February 1952, LL.
31 *Ibid.*
32 Letter from SP to AP, 4 March 1952
33 'True Confessions' entry, *Writer's Year Book*, 1952, copy annotated by SP, SC.
34 Letter from Eddie Cohen to SP, 27 February 1952, LL.
35 Sarah-Elizabeth Rodger, 'A Corner of Your Own', *Writer's Year Book*, 1952, SP's copy, SC.
36 *LH*, p. 83.
37 Letter from SP to Ann Davidow, January 1952, SC.
38 Letter from Eddie Cohen to SP, 26 March 1952, LL.
39 Letter from Eddie Cohen to SP, 11 May 1952, LL.
40 *Ibid.*
41 *JSP*, p. 104.
42 *JSP*, p. 105.
43 *JSP*, p. 107.
44 *Ibid.*
45 *Ibid.*
46 *LH*, p. 84.
47 SP's professor's comment on the story 'Sunday at the Mintons'', LL.
48 *LH*, p. 87.
49 *LH*, p. 86.
50 *LH*, p. 87.
51 Letter from SP to AP, 14–15 June 1952, LL.
52 *Ibid.*
53 Jon Wilson, 'Memories of Sylvia', *Neighborhood Times*, 30 November 2003.
54 Interviews with Ray Wunderlich, 13 March 2011, 26 June 2011.
55 Letter from SP to Marcia Brown, 8 July 1952.
56 *Ibid.*
57 Letter from Harold Strauss to SP, 26 June 1952, LL.
58 *JSP*, pp. 117–118.
59 *JSP*, p. 118.
60 *Ibid.*
61 Letter from SP to Marcia Brown, 25 July 1952, SC.
62 *Ibid.*
63 *LH*, p. 91.
64 *LH*, p. 92.
65 *Ibid.*
66 *JSP*, p. 132.
67 *JSP*, p. 142.
68 *JSP*, p. 134.
69 *JSP*, p. 136.
70 *JSP*, p. 142.
71 Jim McNeely, diary, 17 July 1952, courtesy of Jim McNeely.
72 *JSP*, p. 137.

73 Interview with Eddie Cohen, quoted in *Rough Magic: A Biography of Sylvia Plath*, Paul Alexander, Penguin edition, New York, 1992, p. 90.
74 *Ibid.*
75 Letter from Eddie Cohen to SP, 15 December 1952, LL.
76 Letter from Eddie Cohen to SP, 24 September 1952, LL.
77 *Ibid.*
78 Letter from Eddie Cohen to SP, 25 November 1952, LL.
79 *Ibid.*
80 Letter from Eddie Cohen to SP, 15 December 1952, LL.

CHAPTER SEVEN

1 Letter from SP to AP, 25 September 1952, LL.
2 Interview with Janet Rosenberg, 6 February 2011.
3 *Ibid.*
4 *LH*, p. 95.
5 Interview with Janet Rosenberg, 6 February 2011.
6 *Ibid.*
7 *JSP*, p. 144.
8 *Ibid.*
9 Letter from Dick Norton to SP, 23 October 1952, LL.
10 *JSP*, p. 149
11 *Ibid.*
12 *JSP*, p. 150.
13 *JSP*, p. 151.
14 Interview with Janet Rosenberg, 6 February 2011.
15 Anne Stevenson, 'Writing as a Woman', *Women Writing and Writing About Women*, ed. Mary Jacobus, Croom Helm, London, 1979, p. 160.
16 *JSP*, p. 151.
17 *Ibid.*
18 Letter from Dick Norton to SP, 14 November 1952, LL.
19 *LH*, p. 97.
20 Letter from Dick Norton to SP, 14 November 1952, LL.
21 *JSP*, p. 152.
22 *Ibid.*
23 *LH*, p. 100.
24 *Ibid.*
25 *LH*, p. 101.
26 *BJ*, p. 101.
27 *BJ*, p. 102.
28 *JSP*, p. 154.
29 *JSP*, p. 155.

30 *LH*, p. 102.
31 *JSP*, p. 159.
32 Letter from SP to AP, 16 January 1953.
33 *JSP*, p. 159.
34 *JSP*, p. 160.
35 *JSP*, p. 161.
36 *JSP*, p. 162.
37 *Ibid.*
38 *JSP*, p. 163.
39 SP, 'Dialogue', 19 January 1953, LL.
40 *Ibid.*
41 *Ibid.*
42 Robert Gorham Davis, critique of SP's 'Dialogue', January 1953.
43 Letter from Eddie Cohen to SP, 26 January 1953, LL.
44 *Ibid.*
45 Dick Norton, 'Individualism and Sylvia Plath: An Analysis and Synthesis', SC.
46 *Ibid.*
47 *Ibid.*
48 Virginia Woolf, 'Final Section (III)', *To the Lighthouse*, Grafton Books, London, 1977, p. 140.
49 Letter from SP to AP, 28 February 1953, LL.
50 *LH*, p. 104.
51 Letter from SP to AP, 30 April–1 May 1953, LL.
52 Freud, *op. cit.*, p. 25, SC.
53 Freud, *op. cit.*, p. 298.
54 SP, annotation in her copy of W. H. Auden's *The Collected Poetry*, Random House, New York, 1945, SP's copy, SC.
55 SP, annotation, Auden, *op. cit.*
56 *DS.*
57 Interview with Janet Rosenberg, 6 February 2011.
58 Auden, 'The Composer', *Collected Shorter Poems 1927–1957*, Faber & Faber, London, 1969, p. 125.
59 *DS.*
60 Letter from SP to AP, 10 February 1953, LL.
61 *DS.*
62 *JSP*, p. 175.
63 *JSP*, p. 176.
64 Letter from SP to AP, 23 February 1953.
65 SP, 'Mad Girl's Love Song'.
66 Letter from OHP to SP, 29 May 1953, LL.
67 Letter from the *New Yorker* to SP, quoted in *LH*, p. 106.
68 Letter from Russell Lynes to SP, quoted in a letter from SP to AP, 25 April 1953, LL.

69 *Ibid.*
70 'A Short, Short History of *Mademoiselle*', LL.
71 *Ibid.*
72 SP, critique of *Mademoiselle*, August 1952, LL.
73 Paul Woodring, 'So You're a Brain', *Mademoiselle*, August 1952.
74 William H. Young, Nancy K. Young, *The 1950s: American Popular Culture Through History*, Greenwood Press, Westport, CT, 2004, pp. 11–12.
75 Jane Davison, *The Fall of a Doll's House: Three Generations of American Women and the Houses They Lived In*, Holt, Rinehart and Winston, NY, 1980, p. 161.
76 Davison, *op. cit*, pp. 164–165.
77 J. D. McCarthy, ed. *Ogden Nash, Dorothy Parker, and Phyllis McGinley*, Random House, New York, 2003, p. 43.
78 *LH*, p. 157.
79 Alex Witchel, 'After "The Bell Jar", Life Went On', *New York Times*, 22 June 2003.
80 Letter from Marybeth Little to SP, 5 May 1953, LL.
81 Letter from *Mademoiselle* to SP, 28 May 1953, LL.
82 SP, 'I Lied for Love', LL.
83 *Ibid.*
84 *LH*, p. 112.
85 *Ibid.*
86 *LH*, p. 114.
87 *LH*, p. 113.

CHAPTER EIGHT

1 Interview with Laurie Woolschlager, 14 March 2011.
2 Letter from SP to AP, 4 June 1953, LL.
3 Witchel, *op. cit.*
4 Michael Callahan, 'Sorority on E. 63rd St.', *Vanity Fair*, April 2010.
5 Letter from SP to AP, 8 June 1953, LL.
6 *BJ*, p. 4.
7 Letter from *Mademoiselle* to SP, 28 May 1953, LL.
8 Betsy Blackwell, 'Former Magazine Editor Dies', *Los Angeles Times*, 18 February 1985.
9 *Ibid.*
10 Madelyn Mathers, 'Guest Editor-in-Chief Letter', *Mademoiselle*, August 1953.
11 Interview with Laurie Woolschlager, 14 March 2011.
12 Letter from Mademoiselle to SP, 28 May 1953, LL.
13 *BJ*, pp. 105–106.
14 *LH*, p. 116.
15 Analysis of SP's handwriting by Herry O. Teltscher for *Mademoiselle*, 3 June 1953, LL.

16 Cyrilly Abels, *Mademoiselle*, September 1971.
17 Letter from Janet Rafferty to AW, 20 April 2011.
18 *LH*, p. 116.
19 *BJ*, p. 6.
20 Letter from Janet Rafferty to AW, 20 April 2011.
21 Interview with Ann Burnside Love, 13 March 2011.
22 *BJ*, p. 28.
23 Ann Burnside Love, 'The Legend of Plath, The Scent of Roses', *Washington Post*, 29 April 1979.
24 SP, 'Mlle's Last Word on College, '53', *Mademoiselle*, August 1953.
25 *BJ*, p. 2.
26 *BJ*, p. 3.
27 Burnside Love, 'The Legend of Plath, The Scent of Roses', *op. cit.*
28 Interview with Ann Burnside Love, 13 March 2011.
29 Interview with Professor Melvin Woody, 18 April 2011.
30 *LH*, p. 120, quoting D. H. Lawrence, *Women in Love*.
31 *LH*, p. 117.
32 Letter from Janet Rafferty to AW, 20 April 2011.
33 *JSP*, p. 542.
34 *BJ*, p. 1.
35 *LH*, p. 120.
36 *BJ*, p. 77.
37 *BJ*, p. 86.
38 Letter from Igor Karmiloff to AW, 14 February 2011.
39 *JSP*, p. 187.
40 *LH*, p. 120.
41 *JSP*, p. 187.
42 *BJ*, p. 111.
43 *BJ*, p. 113.
44 Interview with Ann Burnside Love, 13 March 2011.
45 Burnside Love, 'The Legend of Plath, The Scent of Roses', *op. cit.*
46 Interview with Ray Wunderlich, 23 April 2011.
47 Wilbury Crockett, *Voices and Visions*, *op. cit.*
48 Letter from Mary Ellen Chase to SP, 25 July 1953, LL.
49 *LH*, p. 123.
50 *Ibid.*
51 *Ibid.*
52 Letter from AP to Marcia Brown, 23 July 1953, SC.
53 Interview with Peter Aldrich, 31 January 2011.
54 *JSP*, p. 543.
55 *JSP*, p. 545.
56 *DS*.
57 *JSP*, p. 186.
58 SP, 'Tongues of Stone', *JP*, p. 277.

59 Letter from SP to Gordon Lameyer, 18 August 1953, *DS*, LL.
60 *LH*, pp. 123–4.
61 *LH*, p. 124.
62 *Ibid.*
63 *Ibid.*
64 Silvia B. Sutton, *Crossroads in Psychiatry: A History of the McLean Hospital*, American Psychiatric Press, Washington DC, 1986, p. 246.
65 Letter from SP to Gordon Lameyer, 23 July 1953, LL.
66 *DS.*
67 *Ibid.*
68 *Ibid.*
69 Interview with Peter Aldrich, 31 January 2011.
70 *DS.*
71 Letter from AP to Leonard Sanazaro, 4 May 1982, Cruickshank Collection.
72 AP, notes on Elizabeth Hardwick, undated, SC.
73 Letter from AP to OHP, 29 August 1953, LL.
74 SP, 1953 calendar, LL.
75 Letter from AP to OHP, 29 August 1953, LL.
76 *LH*, p. 133.
77 Interview with Professor Melvin Woody, 18 April 2011.
78 Letter from Professor Woody to AW, 8 May 2012.
79 *BJ*, p. 164.
80 *DS.*
81 Interview with Professor Melvin Woody, 18 April 2011.
82 *JSP*, p. 269.
83 *BJ*, p. 179.
84 *LH*, p. 125.
85 *Ibid.*
86 'Police, Boy Scouts Hunt Missing Student', *Boston Evening Globe*, 25 August 1953.
87 Interview with Peter Aldrich, 31 January 2011.
88 'Day-Long Search Fails to Find Smith Student', *Boston Daily Globe*, 26 August 1953.
89 *LH*, p. 125.
90 *Ibid.*
91 Interview with Elinor Friedman Klein, 19 February 2011.
92 Interview with Richard Larschan, 16 February 2011.
93 *LH*, p. 125.
94 *DS.*
95 Letter from AP to OHP, 29 August 1953, LL.
96 Letter from Gordon Lameyer to SP, 30 August 1953, LL.
97 Erich Lindemann, 'Symptomatology and Management of Acute Grief', *American Journal of Psychiatry*, 1944.
98 SP, 'Daddy', *CP*, p. 224.

99 Margin notes, letter from AP to OHP, 29 August 1953, LL.
100 Letter from AP to OHP, 29 August 1953, LL.
101 *Ibid.*
102 *Ibid.*
103 Letter from OHP to AP, 2 September 1953, LL.
104 Sutton, p. 251.
105 *Ibid.*
106 Taped interview with Ruth Tiffany Barnhouse Beuscher by Alex Beam, 9 August 1997, SC.
107 Sutton, p. 251.
108 Sutton, p. 256.
109 Sutton, p. 257
110 Franklin Wood quoted in Alex Beam, Public Affairs, *Gracefully Insane: The Rise and Fall of America's Premier Mental Hospital*, Perseus Books Group, Cambridge, MA, 2001, p. 120.
111 Taped interview with Ruth Tiffany Barnhouse Beuscher by Alex Beam, *op. cit.*
112 Testimony of Jane Anderson, Vol. 2, JA Papers, SC.
113 *BJ*, p. 197.
114 Karen Maroda, 'Sylvia and Ruth', *Salon*, 29 November 2004.
115 *Ibid.*
116 *BJ*, p. 203.
117 *BJ*, p. 204.
118 Nancy Hunter Steiner, *A Closer Look at Ariel: A Memory of Sylvia Plath*, Faber & Faber, London, 1974, p. 21.
119 Letter from OHP to Ruth Beuscher, 11 October 1953, LL.
120 Letter from OHP to Dr William Terhune, undated, LL.
121 Letter from AP to Judith Kroll, 1 December 1978, SC.
122 *Ibid.*
123 Letter from OHP to Dr William Terhune, undated, LL.
124 Letter from OHP to AP, November 18 1953, LL.
125 *JSP*, p. 429.
126 Maroda, *op. cit.*
127 Pencil note from OHP to AP, added to a copy of a letter to Erich Lindemann, 21 November 1953, LL.
128 Letter from OHP to AP, 27 November 1953, LL.
129 *Ibid.*
130 Letter from OHP to SP, 10 December 1954, LL.
131 Letter from OHP to Erich Lindemann, 21 November 1953, LL.
132 Taped interview with Ruth Tiffany Barnhouse Beuscher by Alex Beam, *op. cit.*
133 *BJ*, p. 226.
134 *BJ*, p. 227.
135 Taped interview with Ruth Tiffany Barnhouse Beuscher by Alex Beam, *op. cit.*

136 Jane Anderson Testimony, Volume 2, JA Papers, SC.
137 *Ibid.*
138 Deposition of Francis de Marneffe, 2 April 1986, JA Papers, Box 3, SC.
139 *Ibid.*
140 *BJ*, p. 211.
141 Testimony of Jane Anderson, JA Papers, Box 2, SC.
142 *Ibid.*
143 Testimony of Jane Anderson, JA Papers, Vol. 1, SC.
144 *Ibid.*
145 *Ibid.*
146 *BJ*, p. 252.
147 Deposition of Francis de Marneffe, 2 April 1986, JA Papers, Box 3, SC.
148 Taped interview with Ruth Tiffany Barnhouse Beuscher by Alex Beam, *op. cit.*
149 Letter from Franklin Wood to OHP, 25 November 1953, quoted in *Rough Magic*, Paul Alexander, p. 133.
150 Letter from SP to Gordon Lameyer, 25 December 1953, LL.
151 *Ibid.*
152 Faculty Meeting Notices, 27 January 1954, Vocational Office, SC.
153 Deposition of Francis de Marneffe, 2 April 1986, JA Papers, Box 3, SC.
154 Interview with Philip McCurdy, 9 February 2011.
155 Letter from Philip McCurdy to EB, 26 February 1973, EB Collection, SC.
156 Interview with Philip McCurdy, 9 February 2011.
157 Letter from Philip McCurdy to EB, 11 February 1975, EB Collection, SC.
158 Taped interview with Ruth Tiffany Barnhouse Beuscher by Alex Beam, *op. cit.*

CHAPTER NINE

1 Letter from SP to Phil McCurdy, 4 February 1954, SC.
2 Estella Kelsey, 'I remember Sylvia Plath', courtesy of Alma Kelsey Rhodes, SC.
3 Letter from OHP to SP, 9 February 1954, LL.
4 *Ibid.*
5 *Ibid.*
6 Nancy Hunter Steiner, *op. cit.*, p. 15.
7 Nancy Hunter Steiner, *op. cit.*, pp. 15–16.
8 Nancy Hunter Steiner, p. 16.
9 *DS.*
10 Nancy Hunter Steiner, *op. cit.*, p. 17.
11 *Ibid.*
12 *Ibid.*

13 Nancy Hunter Steiner, *op. cit.*, p. 31.
14 Nancy Hunter Steiner, p. 18.
15 Helle, *op. cit.*
16 Nancy Hunter Steiner, *op. cit.*, p. 49.
17 Nancy Hunter Steiner, *op. cit.*, pp. 50–1.
18 Nancy Hunter Steiner, *op. cit.*, p. 13.
19 Nancy Hunter Steiner, *op. cit.*, p. 17.
20 AP, notes on Sylvia's scholarship grants, undated, SC.
21 Letter from George Gibian to EB, 20 October 1972, EB Collection, SC.
22 Letter from SP to Jane Anderson, 25 February 1954, JA Collection, SC.
23 *Ibid.*
24 Interview with Elinor Friedman Klein, 19 February 2011.
25 Nancy Hunter Steiner, *op. cit.*, p. 21.
26 SP, 'The Devil's Advocate', 24 March 1954, LL.
27 Fyodor Dostoevsky, *The Brothers Karamazov*, translated by Constance Garrett, J. M. Dent, London, 1957, Vol. 2, p. 296.
28 Letter from Gordon Lameyer to SP, 4 March 1954, *DS*, LL.
29 Letter from SP to Gordon Lameyer, 6 February 1954, *DS*, LL.
30 SP, 'A Sorcerer Bids Farewell to Seem', *CP*, p. 324.
31 Nancy Hunter Steiner, *op. cit.*, pp. 19–20.
32 Interview with Elinor Friedman Klein, 19 February 2011.
33 Letter from SP to AP, 5 March 1954, LL.
34 Letter from SP to Jane Anderson, 25 February 1954, JA Collection, SC.
35 Interview with Mary Derr Knox, 5 February 2011.
36 Interview with Tom Derr, 4 February 2011.
37 Letter from Tom Derr to Mary Derr, 15 April 1954, courtesy of Mary Derr Knox and Tom Derr.
38 Interview with Janet Rosenberg, 6 February 2011.
39 *Ibid.*
40 *Ibid.*
41 Interview with Professor Melvin Woody, 18 April 2011.
42 *LH*, p. 137.
43 Letter from Eddie Cohen to SP, 28 April 1954, LL.
44 *Ibid.*
45 Letter from Eddie Cohen to the *New York Times*, in response to a review of 'Bitter Fame', October 8 1989.
46 Letter from SP to Gordon Lameyer, 6 April 1954, *DS*, LL.
47 *Ibid.*
48 Letter from SP to Philip McCurdy, 26 April 1954, SC.
49 Letter from Richard Sassoon to SP, 20 April 1954, LL.
50 Interview with Professor Melvin Woody, 18 April 2011.
51 Letter from Richard Sassoon to SP, undated, but April/May 1954, LL.
52 *Ibid.*
53 *Ibid.*

54 *Ibid.*
55 Letter from Richard Sassoon to SP, 3 May 1954, LL.
56 Letter from Richard Sassoon to SP, undated, but April/May 1954, LL.
57 Estella Kelsey, *op. cit.*
58 Letter from SP to Philip McCurdy, 28 April 1954, SC.
59 *Ibid.*
60 Interview with Professor Melvin Woody, 18 April 2011.
61 Letter from Richard Sassoon to SP, 28 April 1954, LL.
62 Letter from SP to Gordon Lameyer, 3 May 1954, LL.
63 *LH*, p. 137.
64 Letter from Richard Sassoon to SP, undated, but April/May 1954, LL.
65 Letter from Richard Sassoon to SP, 11 May 1954, LL.
66 *LH*, p. 138.
67 Letter from Mary Mensel to OHP, 29 April 1954, LL.
68 Letter from SP to AP, 18 May 1954, LL.
69 *Ibid.*
70 Letter from SP to Gordon Lameyer, undated, but written early June 1954, LL.
71 *Ibid.*
72 *DS.*
73 *JSP*, p. 513.
74 *LH*, p. 138.
75 *DS.*
76 Letter from SP to Philip McCurdy, 15 April 1954, SC.
77 *DS.*
78 Nancy Hunter Steiner, *op. cit.*, p. 33.
79 Nancy Hunter Steiner, *op. cit.*, p. 34.
80 *Ibid.*
81 *BJ*, p. 237.
82 Nancy Hunter Steiner, *op. cit.*, p. 36.
83 Nancy Hunter Steiner, *op. cit.*, p. 37.
84 Nancy Hunter Steiner, *op. cit.*, p. 39.
85 Nancy Hunter Steiner, *op. cit.*, p. 42.
86 Nancy Hunter Steiner, *op. cit.*, p. 43.
87 *DS.*
88 *BJ*, p. 240.
89 *DS.*
90 *Ibid.*
91 SP, 'Lady Lazarus', *CP*, p. 246.
92 *JSP*, p. 447.
93 Letter from Olwyn Hughes to AW, postmarked 29 March 2011.
94 SP, 'Berck-Plage', *CP*, p. 197.
95 SP, 'Little Fugue', *CP*, p. 188.
96 SP, 'Electra on Azalea Path', *CP*, p. 116.
97 SP, 'Electra on Azalea Path', *CP*, p. 117.

98 SP, 'The Colossus', *CP*, p. 129.
99 *JSP*, p. 163.
100 *JSP*, p. 182.
101 SP, 'Platinum Summer', LL.
102 *Ibid.*
103 Letter from SP to Gordon Lameyer, undated, but written in the summer of 1954, LL.
104 *DS.*
105 Nancy Hunter Steiner, *op. cit.*, p. 48.
106 Nancy Hunter Steiner, *op. cit.*, p. 49.
107 Nancy Hunter Steiner, *op. cit.*, p. 51.
108 *DS.*

CHAPTER TEN

1 SP, '20th Century', Miss Drew lecture notes, English 211, SC.
2 *LH*, p. 148.
3 *JSP*, p. 103.
4 *JSP*, p. 166.
5 *JSP*, p. 147.
6 Mary Ellen Chase, reference for SP, 15 December 1954, Vocational Office, SC.
7 Elizabeth Drew, reference for SP, 14 December 1954, Vocational Office, SC.
8 George Gibian, reference for SP, 6 January 1955, Vocational Office, SC.
9 Newton Arvin, reference for SP, 14 December 1954, Vocational Office, SC.
10 Estella Kelsey, reference for SP, 18 January 1955, Vocational Office, SC.
11 Ruth Beuscher, reference for SP, undated, but written late 1954 or early 1955, Vocational Office, SC.
12 Maroda, *op. cit.*
13 *LH*, p. 141.
14 *LH*, p. 148.
15 Letter from SP to Gordon Lameyer, undated, but written end of September 1954, LL.
16 *LH*, p. 144.
17 *LH*, p. 147.
18 SP, 'The Neilson Professor', *Smith Alumnae Quarterly*, Vol. XLVI, Fall 1954, No. 1, SC.
19 Interview with Elinor Friedman Klein, 19 February 2011.
20 Letter from Alfred Kazin to EB, 13 October 1972, SC.
21 *LH*, p. 147.
22 *Ibid.*
23 Kazin's notes on SP story 'The Day Mr. Prescott Died', 6 January 1955, LL.
24 Alfred Kazin, reference for SP, 6 January 1955, Vocational Office, SC.

25 Interview with Elinor Friedman Klein, 19 February 2011.
26 Elinor Klein, 'A Friend Recalls Sylvia Plath', *Glamour*, November 1966.
27 *Ibid.*
28 Interview with Elinor Friedman Klein, 19 February 2011.
29 Klein, *op. cit.*
30 Interview with Elinor Friedman Klein, 19 February 2011.
31 Dostoevsky, 'The Double', translated by Constance Garrett, in *The Eternal Husband and Other Stories*, William Heinemann, London, 1917, p. 37.
32 Dostoevsky, 'The Double', *op. cit.*, p. 33.
33 Dostoevsky, 'The Double', *op. cit.*, p. 37.
34 Janko Lavrin, *Dostoevsky: A Study*, quoted by SP in her thesis 'The Magic Mirror', LL.
35 Dostoevsky, 'The Double', *op. cit.*, p. 87.
36 Dostoevsky, 'The Double', *op. cit.*, p. 130.
37 *JSP*, p. 155.
38 Dostoevsky, 'The Double', *op. cit.*, p. 121.
39 Dostoevsky, 'The Double', *op. cit.*, p. 135.
40 Marc Slonim, Introduction to *The Brothers Karamazov*, The Modern Library, New York, 1950, p. vii.
41 Dostoevsky, *The Brothers Karamazov*, Vol. 2, *op. cit.* p. 296.
42 Dostoevsky, *The Brothers Karamazov*, Vol. 1, *op. cit.* p. 10.
43 Dostoevsky, *The Brothers Karamazov*, Vol. 2, *op. cit.* p. 266.
44 SP, notes in margin of her copy of *The Brothers Karamazov*, SC.
45 Dostoevsky, *The Brothers Karamazov*, Vol. 2, *op. cit.* p. 347.
46 Nancy Hunter Steiner, *op. cit.*, p. 21.
47 Letter from SP to Gordon Lameyer, undated but written late 1954, early 1955, LL.
48 Letter from OHP to SP, 10 December 1954, LL.
49 *LH*, p. 146.
50 Alfred Kazin, Introduction to *A Raw Youth* by Dostoevsky, quoted in SP, 'The Magic Mirror', LL.
51 Letter from Richard Sassoon to SP, undated, but likely to be mid-October 1954, LL.
52 Letter from Gordon Lameyer to SP, undated, but written late 1954, LL.
53 Letter from Richard Sassoon to SP, undated, but written late 1954, LL.
54 *Ibid.*
55 *DS.*
56 Letter from Richard Sassoon to SP, undated, but late 1954, LL.
57 Letter from Richard Sassoon to SP, 18 December 1954, LL.
58 Letter from Gordon Lameyer to SP, 31 January 1955, LL.
59 Letter from SP to Jon Rosenthal, 13 December 1954, SC.
60 Letter from AP to SP, 13 November 1954, SC.
61 Letter from SP to AP, 10 February 1955, excised from the letter dated 11 February 1955 in *LH*, pp. 161–3.

62 Letter from Woodrow Wilson Fellowship to SP, 26 January 1955, SC.
63 *LH*, p. 152.
64 *Ibid.*
65 *Ibid.*
66 *LH*, p. 154.
67 *LH*, p. 163.
68 Letter from OHP to SP, 16 October 1954, LL.
69 SP notes, 'The Novelist and the Unknown', March 1955, SC.
70 *DS.*
71 SP, 'Spinster', *CP*, p. 49.
72 Interview with Elinor Friedman Klein, 19 February 2011.
73 *DS.*
74 *LH*, p. 169.
75 *LH*, p. 168.
76 Marianne Moore, inscribed in SP's copy of her *Collected Poems*, 16 April 1955, SC.
77 Letter from Edward Weeks to SP, April 1955, LL.
78 *LH*, p. 171.
79 *Ibid.*
80 *LH*, p. 176.
81 *LH*, p. 172.
82 *LH*, p. 175.
83 *Ibid.*
84 Letter from Alfred Kazin to SP, 22 May 1955, LL.
85 Letter from Richard Sassoon to SP, 23 May 1955, LL.
86 *Ibid.*
87 Clarissa Roche, 'Sylvia Plath: Vignettes from England', *Sylvia Plath: The Woman and the Work*, ed. Edward Butscher, Dodd, Mead & Company, New York, 1977, p. 88.
88 Nancy Hunter Steiner, *op. cit.*, p. 53.
89 Nancy Hunter Steiner, *op. cit.*, p. 54.
90 Nancy Hunter Steiner, *op. cit.*, p. 55.
91 Interview with Sylvia Scully, 10 February 2012.
92 Letter from SP to Lynne Lawner, 8 June 1955, SC.
93 Nancy Hunter Steiner, *op. cit.*, p. 57.
94 *LH*, p. 176.
95 Letter from OHP, 4 May 1955, LL.
96 Letter from Gordon Lameyer to SP, 3 June 1955, LL.
97 Letter from SP to Warren Plath, 6 July 1955, LL.
98 Letter from Richard Sassoon to SP, 25 June 1955, LL.
99 Letter from Richard Sassoon to SP, 9 August 1955, LL.
100 *LH*, pp. 176–7.
101 Letter from Richard Sassoon to SP, 1 August 1955, LL.
102 Peter Davison, *Half Remembered: A Personal History*, Story Line Press, 1991, p. 170.

103 Letter from Richard Sassoon to AW, 13 June 2011.
104 Letter from Richard Sassoon to SP, 8 August 1955, LL.
105 Letter from Richard Sassoon to SP, 9 August 1955, LL.
106 *Ibid.*
107 Davison, *op. cit*, p. 170.
108 Davison, p. 171.
109 Davison, *One of the Dangerous Trades: Essays on the Work and Workings of Poetry*, University of Michigan Press, Ann Arbor, 1991, p. 207.
110 Davison, *The Heroine*, 1970–72, EB, SC.
111 Postcard from SP to AP, 30 August 1955, LL.
112 Letter from SP to Gordon Lameyer, 25 August 1955, LL.
113 Letter from OHP to SP, 12 September 1955, LL.

CHAPTER ELEVEN

1 *LH*, p. 182.
2 *Ibid.*
3 *LH*, pp. 182–3.
4 SP, 'Leaves from a Cambridge Notebook', *Christian Science Monitor*, 5 March 1956.
5 Letter from SP to Marcia Brown, December 1955, SC.
6 Jane Baltzell Kopp, '"Gone, Very Gone Youth": Sylvia Plath at Cambridge', 1955–1957, *Sylvia Plath: The Woman and the Work*, *op. cit.*, p. 59.
7 *LH*, p. 186.
8 Dorothea Krook, 'Recollections of Sylvia Plath', July 1974, published in *Sylvia Plath: The Woman and the Work*, *op. cit.*, p. 47.
9 Klein, *op. cit.*
10 Interview with Janet Rosenberg, 6 February 2011.
11 Al Strangeways, '"The Boot in the Face": The Problem of the Holocaust in the Poetry of Sylvia Plath', *Contemporary Literature*, Vol. XXXVII, No. 3, Fall 1996.
12 *LH*, p. 36.
13 *LH*, p. 201.
14 George Steiner, cited by Strangeways, *op. cit.*
15 Reading prepared for BBC radio, cited in notes, *CP*, p. 293.
16 *LH*, p. 317.
17 Krook, p. 48.
18 Krook, p. 47.
19 *LH*, p. 190.
20 *LH*, p. 189.
21 *LH*, p. 194.
22 *LH*, p. 196.
23 Interview with Jane Baltzell Kopp, 5 February 2011.

24 Baltzell Kopp, *op. cit.*, p. 60.
25 Baltzell Kopp, *op. cit.*, p. 61
26 Interview with Mallory Wober, 5 April 2011.
27 *Ibid.*
28 *LH*, p. 194.
29 Interview with Nat LaMar, 18 February 2011.
30 *JSP*, p. 191.
31 *JSP*, p. 193.
32 *JSP*, p. 194.
33 *LH*, p. 202.
34 *LH*, p. 195.
35 Letter from SP to Gordon Lameyer, undated but written end of 1955, LL.
36 SP, 'Whiteness I Remember', *CP*, p. 102.
37 *JSP*, p. 403.
38 SP, 'Ariel', *CP*, pp. 239–40.
39 Baltzell Kopp, *op. cit.*, pp. 66–7.
40 Interview with Jane Baltzell Kopp, 5 February 2011.
41 Baltzell Kopp, *op. cit.*, p. 67.
42 *JSP*, pp. 547–8.
43 *JSP*, p. 548.
44 *JSP*, p. 549.
45 *LH*, p. 203.
46 *LH*, pp. 203–205.
47 *LH*, p. 205.
48 Email from Richard Sassoon to AW, 12 March 2011.
49 Email from Richard Sassoon to AW, 13 June 2011.
50 Richard Sassoon, 'In the year of Love and unto Death, the fourth – an Elegy on the Muse', *Northwest Review*, 5:1 (1962: Winter) p. 104.
51 Sassoon, 'In the year of Love and unto Death . . .', *op. cit.*, p. 113.
52 Sassoon, 'In the year of Love and unto Death . . .', *op. cit.*, p. 108.
53 Sassoon, 'In the year of Love and unto Death . . .', *op. cit.*, p. 117.
54 *Ibid.*
55 *Ibid.*
56 *LH*, p. 211.
57 *LH*, p. 207.
58 *LH*, p. 208.
59 *LH*, p. 217.
60 *LH*, p. 215.
61 *JSP*, p. 196.
62 *JSP*, p. 199.
63 *JSP*, p. 204.
64 *JSP*, p. 205.
65 *JSP*, p. 209.
66 *LH*, p. 219.

67 *JSP*, p. 207.
68 *JSP*, p. 212.
69 *JSP*, p. 210.
70 *JSP*, p. 212.
71 *JSP*, p. 214.
72 *Ibid.*
73 *LH*, p. 222.
74 *JSP*, p. 215.
75 Letter from SP to AP, 5 March 1956, LL.
76 *JSP*, p. 217.
77 *Ibid.*
78 Letter from SP to Elinor Friedman, 9 March 1956, SC.
79 Baltzell Kopp, 'Gone, Very Gone Youth', *op. cit.*, p. 68.
80 Interview with Jane Baltzell Kopp, 5 February 2011.
81 *JSP*, p. 226.
82 *JSP*, p. 227.
83 Interview with Jane Baltzell Kopp, 5 February 2011.
84 *LH*, p. 229.
85 Interview with Nat LaMar, 18 February 2011.
86 *JSP*, p. 552.
87 *JSP*, p. 553.
88 *Ibid.*
89 Sassoon, 'The Diagram', *Chicago Review*, 17:4, 1965, p. 111.
90 *Ibid.*
91 *JSP*, p. 567.
92 *JSP*, p. 559.
93 *JSP*, p. 562.
94 *DS.*
95 *Ibid.*
96 SP, 'Venus in the Seventh', Falcon Yard, SC.
97 *DS.*
98 *Ibid.*
99 *Ibid.*
100 Letter from Gordon Lameyer to SP, 1 May 1957, LL.
101 *DS.*
102 *JSP*, p. 568.

AFTERWORD

1 Letter from Richard Sassoon to SP, undated, 1956, LL.
2 *Ibid.*
3 SP, 'Edge', *CP*, p. 272.

PICTURE CREDITS

The author and publishers would like to thank the following copyright-holders for permission to reproduce images in this book:

Estate of Aurelia Schober Plath, Mortimer Rare Book Room, Smith College: 1, 2, 3, 4, 5, 7, 8, 10
Courtesy of Betsy Wallingford and Ruth Geissler: 6
Courtesy of Betsy Wallingford: 9
Mortimer Rare Book Room, Smith College: 11, 12
Courtesy of Lilly Library, Indiana: 13, 15, 16, 24
Courtesy of Debbie Matsumoto: 14
Courtesy of Elizabeth Lameyer Gilmore, Lilly Library: 17, 23, 25
Estate of Warren Plath, Lilly Library: 24
Courtesy of Molly Woehrlin: 19
Courtesy of Janet Rosenberg: 20
Courtesy of Elinor Friedman Klein: 21
Copyright the Smith College Archives: 22

The author and publishers have made all reasonable efforts to contact copyright-holders for permission, and apologise for any omissions or errors in the form of credits given. Corrections may be made to future printings.

INDEX

(the initials SP in subentries refer to Sylvia Plath)

The Reading Guide

Reading Group Questions

The book takes its title from a poem Plath wrote in 1953. How are the themes of this poem reflected in the book?

The book opens with the famous meeting of Sylvia Plath and Ted Hughes in Cambridge in February 1956. How would you describe this encounter? What does it tell us about both Plath and Hughes?

In June 1956, four months after that meeting, Plath and Hughes were married in London. Yet Ted Hughes is largely absent from this biography. How does his absence inform the book? How is our perception of Plath changed by the non-presence of Ted Hughes?

Sylvia Plath felt the urge to write from a very early age. Why do you think she felt compelled to express herself in writing? What did writing give her? How did she define herself through her writing? How did she feel when she could not write?

Plath's father, Otto, died when she was only eight years old. How did his death affect Plath's life? How did she represent him in her poetry?

Plath had a complex relationship with her mother, Aurelia, and she observed that the umbilical cord between daughter and mother had never been cut properly. Do you think Aurelia had her daughter's best interests at heart? How was Sylvia shaped by her mother? How do you think Aurelia felt when she learnt of her portrayal in poems like *The Disquieting Muses*?

How was Plath shaped by her social and economic circumstances? Why do you think money – or the lack of it – played such a central role in her life? Do you think she would have been a different (better or worse) writer if she had been born into a family of greater means?

To what extent do you see Plath as an angry young woman? How did sex and its repression feed into her sense of injustice and anger?

Why do you think Plath sought out young women whom she cast as doubles? Why did the concept of the double fascinate her so much?

In what way is Plath similar to and different from the character of Esther Greenwood in her novel *The Bell Jar*?

According to Jane Anderson – whom Plath cast as Joan Gilling in *The Bell Jar* – Plath would have benefited from a longer course of psychotherapy. Do you agree? Do you think therapy might have helped her deal with some of her internal tensions and confusions? How do you think therapy might have affected her writing?

At the end of the book Plath is faced with a choice: should she settle down with Gordon Lameyer, Richard Sassoon or Ted Hughes. Do you think she made the right decision? How do you think her life would have been different had she chosen not to marry Ted Hughes?

How did *Mad Girl's Love Song* change your view of Sylvia Plath?

About the Book

Mad Girl's Love Song is the first biography of Sylvia Plath that concentrates on the poet's life before her marriage to fellow poet Ted Hughes. It draws on a number of unpublished archives as well as interviews with friends and lovers who have spoken about Plath for the first time.

About the Author

Andrew Wilson was born in Lancashire and now splits his time between a flat in Bloomsbury and a house near the sea in south Devon, where he lives with his partner and two cats.

After taking an English degree at King's College, London, he worked as a journalist for a wide range of publications including the *Mail on Sunday*, the *Daily Mail*, the *Independent on Sunday*, the *Observer*, the *Sunday Times* and the *Daily Telegraph*.

He is the author of *Beautiful Shadow: A Life of Patricia Highsmith*, which was shortlisted for the Whitbread Biography Prize, and the winner of an Edgar Allan Poe award for best biography. His other books include a psychological thriller, *The Lying Tongue*; *Harold Robbins: The Man Who Invented Sex*, about the world's first playboy author; and *Shadow of the Titanic: The Extraordinary Stories of Those Who Survived*.

that one poem was missing from the list: *Mad Girl's Love Song*, a poem written in 1953 and one I had never read before. When I read the haunting first line, 'I close my eyes and all the world drops dead', I immediately knew that I had found the title for the book.

The 'mad girl' I write about is an angry young woman driven to desperation by the constrictions and conventions of America in the 1940s and 1950s. It's important to remember, for instance, that while there was an explosion in the female labour market (between 1950 and 1960 the number of women in work in the US grew from 18 to 23 million) most of these positions were in clerical, secretarial or nursing jobs. Only one third of women who entered college during the 1950s actually graduated. At Plath's graduation from Smith College in 1955, Adlai Stevenson, who was the governor of Illinois and a Democrat, stood up and said that a woman's 'highest vocation' was a 'creative marriage' and it was the duty of these young women to use their education to help their husbands make wise, rational decisions. One of Plath's own creative writing teachers – a man – hoped that none of his pupils harboured a wish to become published authors as, in his experience, female writers always lived terribly unhappy lives. Not surprisingly, Plath was infuriated by his comments.

During the course of the research at the two big Plath archives (Smith College, Northampton, Massachusetts and the Lilly Library, Bloomington, Indiana), I was astounded to discover there an enormous amount of unpublished material – Plath's early diaries, hundreds of letters she had written to friends and lovers, and 200 or so poems. I came across an extraordinary cache of colour photographs taken by Gordon Lameyer, one of Plath's boyfriends. These images, most of which had never been published before, were so vibrant and full of life they literally took my breath away. The photographs really show Plath in Technicolor.

I also interviewed dozens of friends and lovers who had never spoken about Plath before. I think many of them were reaching an age when they could either talk to a biographer or take their secrets to the grave. Luckily for me, they felt they could entrust me with their memories. I use the interviews throughout the book and their voices really enrich the narrative.

I hope you enjoy reading *Mad Girl's Love Song* as much as I did researching and writing it.

To find out more about Andrew, visit his website www.andrewwilsonauthor.co.uk or follow him on Twitter @andrewwilsonaw.

Author Article: The story behind *Mad Girl's Love Song*

I started reading Sylvia Plath's poetry when I was a teenager and I immediately felt a connection with her. I loved the intensity of poems such as *Lady Lazarus* and her distinctive, disturbing imagery. At the same time I read *The Bell Jar* and immediately became intrigued by the character of Esther Greenwood, who experiences a breakdown while working as a guest editor on a magazine in New York in the 1950s. The story of Plath's life, and her death (she committed suicide at the age of 30 in London in 1963) always fascinated me, but I never dreamt that one day I would write her biography. I had assumed there was nothing left to say, as Plath is one of the most written about subjects in twentieth-century literary history.

Over the years, I followed the controversy surrounding biographies of Plath, particularly the heated debate on the publication of Anne Stevenson's 'authorised' biography published in 1989. (For reference, Stevenson only devotes 89 pages to Plath's life before Hughes.)

I also knew that Plath was a 'dangerous' subject for a biographer, especially after reading Janet Malcolm's brilliant book *The Silent Woman* (1994), which uses Plath as an example of the problems of writing biography. It was while I was reading Malcolm's book that I came across a description of Richard Sassoon as 'the most elusive and, in many ways, the most beguiling' of Sylvia's lovers. The habit of longing for him has passed from Plath to the community of her biographers. Not one of them has been able to find him; he has disappeared without a trace.'

Of course, as soon as I read that I immediately wondered whether it was possible to track him down. Would he talk to me? What would he say? If Sassoon was alive perhaps there were other boyfriends and friends who had never talked before? What was Sylvia like before she met Ted Hughes? I knew from Hughes' introduction to Plath's *Collected Poems* that Sylvia had written a great deal of poetry before she had met him in 1956, poetry that Hughes dismissed as 'juvenilia'. But what was the poetry really like?

One day, while studying the so-called 'complete list of poems composed before 1956' at the back of Plath's *Collected Poems* I noticed